Westchester

Westchester

History of an Iconic Suburb

ROBERT MARCHANT

McFarland & Company, Inc., Publishers
Jefferson, North Carolina

LIBRARY OF CONGRESS CATALOGUING-IN-PUBLICATION DATA

Names: Marchant, Robert, author.
Title: Westchester : history of an iconic suburb / Robert Marchant.
Description: Jefferson, North Carolina : McFarland & Company, Inc.,
Publishers, 2019 | Includes bibliographical references and index.
Identifiers: LCCN 2018049375 | ISBN 9781476673240 (softcover :
acid free paper) ∞
Subjects: LCSH: Westchester County (N.Y.)—History.
Classification: LCC F127.W5 M24 2019 | DDC 974.7/277—dc23
LC record available at https://lccn.loc.gov/2018049375

BRITISH LIBRARY CATALOGUING DATA ARE AVAILABLE

ISBN (print) 978-1-4766-7324-0
ISBN (ebook) 978-1-4766-3390-9

Front cover image: a postcard of Playland, Rye Beach,
Westchester County, New York, date issued 1927
(New York Public Library)

Printed in the United States of America

*McFarland & Company, Inc., Publishers
Box 611, Jefferson, North Carolina 28640
www.mcfarlandpub.com*

For Beth and Julianna

Acknowledgments

This book would not exist without the concerted efforts of the staffs and volunteers at the many historical societies, archives and libraries I visited across the county in the course of my research. Many thanks to those who helped me track down sources and images, especially Ben Himmelfarb and the staff at the White Plains Public Library; Alex Vastola and Karen Smith of the Briarcliff Manor-Scarborough Historical Society; Patrick Raftery, Katherine Hite and the Westchester County Historical Society; Jackie Graziano and the staff at the Westchester County Archives; Natalie Barry and the Hastings Historical Society; Elaine Massena and the White Plains City Archives; Graciela Heyman and the Westchester Hispanic Coalition; Sara Mascia and the Historical Society of Sleepy Hollow and Tarrytown; the Croton Free Library; the Yonkers Public Library; the Field Library of Peekskill; the Rockefeller Archive Center; the Schomburg Center for Research in Black Culture; Ellen Belcher and the John Jay School of Criminal Justice; Tom Tryinski; the Greenwich Public Library; the Greenburgh Public Library; the New Rochelle Public Library; and the Loft.

Special thanks to James Collymore, A'Lelia Bundles, Marc Cheshire, Ned Thanhouser and Nancy Crampton for providing photographs and illustrations from their fine personal collections and family archives, and to Tyler Sizemore for his new photographs.

I am very grateful to my friends, neighbors, and family who listened to my ideas, read early drafts and offered advice and encouragement along the way, in particular Michael Steger, Cornelia Cotton, Rob Ryser, John Alcott, Sharen Conway, Jean Leslie, Sofia Marchant and Giovanna Marchant. Many thanks to my in-laws, David and Evelyn Stevenson, for their ongoing generosity.

My wife, Beth, who has long shared my passion for the history of the Hudson Valley, deserves my deepest and heartfelt thanks for her editorial insights and the support she gave me at every step.

Table of Contents

Introduction

Consider the suburb: Not city, not country, but something in between, the suburb emerged as a boundary between the two older forms of human habitation. As the name implies, it is a place that falls outside the city, derived from the Latin "suburbium," or under the city. The term first appeared in the 14th century, but its modern usage was popularized during the 1800s when writers like Charles Dickens began describing the expanding residential areas of the London metropolis.

The suburb has often been defined for what it is not: less dangerous, dense and noisy than the urban neighbor with which it is intrinsically linked, but also devoid of its high culture, intensity and dynamism. In the popular imagination, the big city appears on the skyline like a glittering mountain among the dimmer suburban foothills.

Westchester County, like other suburbs around the world, has long fallen under the shadow of an adjacent, magnetic metropolitan center. But New York City, the great leviathan of American urban experience and one of the world's largest cities, is no ordinary neighbor. As a result, Westchester has often been relegated to the footnotes of New York's story; a tangent—or worse, an afterthought—in the chronicles of our country's collective narrative.

In fact, the county's history is perhaps more representative of American society as a whole than New York City's, and it has its own particular story to tell, one that reveals the polarities of American life: inclusion and exclusion, labor and capital, prudery and wanton excess, simplicity and luxury, subjugation and liberty.

Westchester continues to thrive on these contrasts. It's long been a destination for ambitious strivers and newcomers of all kinds who have left their marks on the county, some for the better and some for worse. It can also be many things at once: parochial and restrictive, a desirable haven for those seeking privacy, as well as a safe, nurturing place to raise a family and educate generations to come. Rolling hills and skyscrapers can appear in a single view. It is an evolving global crossroads yet remains insular at the same time.

Although the long, rich story of Westchester has been unified by a common purpose—to define and build a sense of shared space—duality is part of the county's DNA: back and forth between modern and traditional, the bucolic and the man-made, the rich and the poor. This fuller, deeper history has often been overlooked or entirely forgotten, but there are remarkable stories to be told.

Beneath Westchester's well-planned suburban and natural façade lies a place where civic and moral values clashed and evolved, where battles were fought and lost, bayonets and cannon fire determined the fate of empires, and where murder and violent death made themselves right at home. The county's history teems with jailbreaks, riots, heinous

1

crimes, manmade disasters and epic feats of daring that captivated the attention of an entire nation. Bootleggers, bare-knuckled brawlers, race-car drivers, exotic dancers, executioners, elephant herders and fearless aviators all plied their trade. Here, as elsewhere in the nation, slavery's chains left their mark on human flesh. Along with arrivals who came through the slave trade, merchants, entrepreneurs, laborers and strivers from every corner of the world streamed through the county, and the story of Westchester bears a diverse international imprint.

That history, however, can be hard to glimpse. On its surface, Westchester County looks like any other modern suburban region: sprawling residential neighborhoods ribboned with highways and punctuated by bustling towns, glass-and-steel office parks and pockets of green. To a visitor, its uniformity speaks of a landscape shaped by the efforts of traffic engineers, real-estate developers and civil servants to maximize profit, tax revenue and efficiency.

But an attentive observer can trace the still visible shape of history written across its landscape. Within a short drive or a long hike, one can see stone walls where farmers marked their land, weathered tombstones in colonial cemeteries that mark the passing of ages and red-brick factories that powered a growing nation. Beyond that, great dams and waterworks hewn from granite—the visible symbols of a country advancing through industry, technology and immense ambition—come into view. At its edges, waves lap against the rocky outcroppings along the Long Island Sound, and further upcountry, horses roam through grassy paddocks. A bald eagle, returning in increasing numbers year after year, takes flight over the Hudson River. The natural history of Westchester is still very much a part of its present and a reminder of its pastoral roots.

Far more than a bedroom for the big city, Westchester has made common cause with the natural world. Its rhythms have always been more in sync with country life, and the primacy of hearth and home has played an undeniable, outsized role in the landscape of a county that continues to bring a restful escape from the demands of a city that never sleeps. In this way, Westchester has long been attuned to a pared-down, localized approach to family life, community and the surrounding planned and natural environments.

As with any old place, stories and ancestral memories are layered on top of one another in a shifting landscape, making Westchester as much a location as it is a continuing narrative with unusual twists and turns. The county still holds secrets and revenants of ghoulish experiments on the dead, a notorious grave robbery, madcap get-rich-quick schemes and a menagerie built to the specifications of an eccentric millionaire. No matter where you stand in Westchester, you sense the memories of distant generations—their anxieties and their ambitions, their struggles and their pleasures—subtly conveyed into the present.

The county has also long been a test lab for American democracy, a place where our nation's social architecture was designed and built, neighborhood by neighborhood, brick by brick. Whether the rollout of the auto as the indispensable feature of modern life, or domesticity re-imagined as a house with a patch of green out front, or African Americans, newer immigrants and women fighting for equal rights to gain that patch of suburbia—it all happened in Westchester.

Opposite: **Westchester became a national leader in the construction of parkways and parks, aiming to create a suburban utopia for the middle class (image from 1929).**

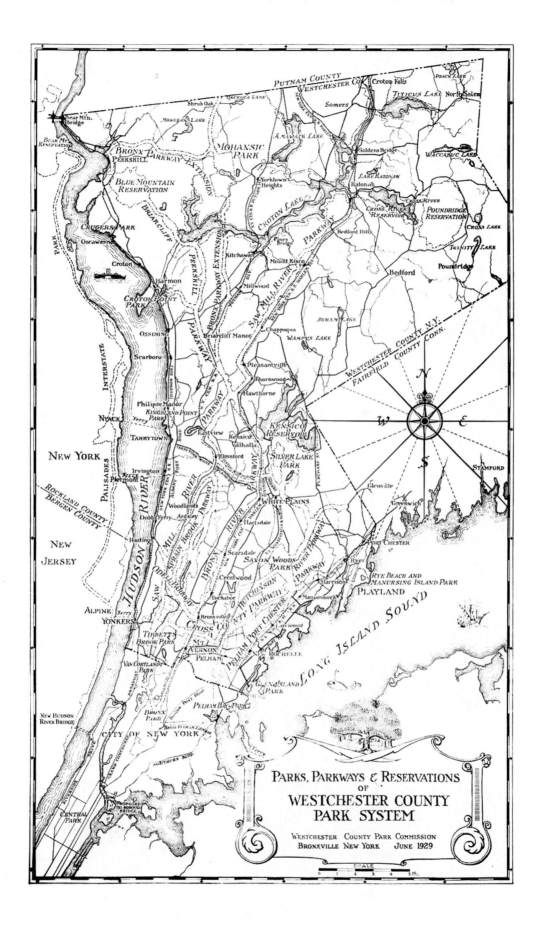

PARKS, PARKWAYS & RESERVATIONS
OF
WESTCHESTER COUNTY
PARK SYSTEM

WESTCHESTER COUNTY PARK COMMISSION
BRONXVILLE NEW YORK   JUNE 1929

Through the years, this rich tapestry of interwoven tales has become both a birthright and a guide to the future, a through line from the past that can signal the way forward. The struggles and successes of Westchester's people, from the earliest Native American inhabitants, settlers and slaves to the rich assemblage of vivid characters, innovators, entrepreneurs and extraordinary everyday citizens, are part of a much larger American story that needs to be told in its entirety. This book, while not intended to be encyclopedic, aims to present those stories within the context of their time across a single narrative history of the county up to the present day.

As the urban historian Lewis Mumford observed, "once one begins to find the threads of local history … one finds they lead in every direction."[1]

1

Uneasy Neighbors
The Lenapes, the New Dutch
and the Fight for Survival

On September 13, 1609, a Dutch ship captained by an Englishman looking for a northern passage to Asia anchored in the waters off Yonkers. It was 85 feet long and held a crew of 16, and it set the course for another arrival in the northern reaches of the New World yet to come: colonists from Europe.

Henry Hudson, a driven and headstrong mariner, knew he had found something amazing on the banks of the river that would later carry his name, even if it did not reveal a new route to China, a quest for which he eventually gave his life. "The land is the finest for cultivation that I have ever in my life set foot upon," he wrote in his log.[1]

For the Lenape Indians who greeted him and the crew of the *Half Moon* on the shore, it would prove to be a turning point. There was a mixture of curiosity, awe and dread among the native inhabitants when they first saw the ship's sails fluttering on the waves. According to an oral tradition preserved and recorded in 1800 by missionary John Heckwelder, the Indians first called it "a house of various colors" floating on the water. They went on to describe a meeting on shore with a man in "a red coat all glittering in gold lace."[2]

Hudson's trip up the river was met by each local village of the loosely related Lenape tribes with a similar mix of awe, curiosity and fear, resulting in friendly overtures at some points but deadly encounters at others. According to a journal kept by Robert Juet, a mate on the *Half Moon*, trouble followed in the wake of the compact little ship. Suspecting the potential hostility of the Lenape, the crew took two of them hostage during an encounter on land. The Indians later escaped.

On the vessel's trip back from Albany, near Peekskill, some Indians came on board after trailing alongside the ship by canoe. Leaping from their narrow boat up onto the deck one took "a pillow and two shirts and two bandoliers" from a stern cabin, Juet wrote. When the crew discovered the apparent theft, a mate "shot at him and struck him on the breast and killed him."[3] Startled, the other Indians jumped in the river, and a boat was lowered to recover the stolen items, leading to further bloodshed. More Lenape deaths followed in Juet's detailed account. A conflict broke out when an Indian in a canoe tried to stop the ship and come aboard before Hudson's cook "seized a sword and cut off one of his hands and he was drowned." An even larger battle took place the next day after the Indians, insulted by Hudson's attempts to take hostages, attacked in several canoes. Nine or ten among the convoy were killed.[4]

It would become a familiar pattern through the years between the Indians and the successive rounds of newcomers to the colonies. In 1621, based on the information Hudson had collected on his voyage, the Dutch West India Company formed; two years later trading stations were established at New Amsterdam (now New York City) and Fort Orange (now Albany). Through the early period of Dutch settlement, Indian land was sold to the new inhabitants, who developed a profitable cycle of trade spun on beaver pelts and the colonists' goods.

This arrangement was fraught with misunderstandings and peril for everyone involved.

The Indians had lived in the hills and hollows of the region for centuries, if not thousands of years, in shifting settlements built largely around long, narrow communal row houses and small fields of corn. According to one of the most thorough accounts of the Indian settlements, written by prominent Dutch scholar and landowner Adriaen van der Donck, the tribes used the bark of ash, elm or chestnut to build their lodgings. "When building a house, large or small—for sometimes they make them as long as a hundred feet, but never more than twenty feet wide—they stick long, peeled hickory saplings in the ground," observed van der Donck, who created perhaps the earliest farmstead in Yonkers. "The sapling poles are then bent over and fastened one to another, so that the frame looks like a wagon or an arbor as are put in gardens.... Next, strips like split laths are laid across the uprights from one end to the other.... This is then covered all over with very tough bark.... In sum, they arrange it so their houses repel rain and wind and are also fairly warm."[5]

A replica of the *Half Moon* took to the waters of the Hudson River in 1909. The original ship carried a Dutch crew under the command of an Englishman, Captain Henry Hudson. The crew clashed with native inhabitants on its journey up and down the river (Library of Congress).

The longhouses were communal dwellings, home to multiple families who lived alongside one another in close proximity. "From one end of the house to the other along the center they kindle fires, and the space left open, which is also in the middle, serves as a chimney to release the smoke," he explained in the book he published in Holland. "There may be sixteen to eighteen families in a house, more or less according to the side of the house. The fire is in the middle and the people on either side. Everyone knows his space and how far it extends. If they have room for a pot and a kettle and whatever else they have, and a place to sleep, they desire no more."[6]

The Lenapes, particularly the men, were seen as vigorous, fit and strong people averse to menial labor of any kind. "In figure, build and shape of the body, both men and women are equal to the average and well-proportioned sort here in the Netherlands," van der Donck wrote. "In height, and as well as between height or weight and girth, they vary as elsewhere, the one less, the other more, and seldom deviate from the average. Their limbs are nimble and supple, and they can run strenuously with striking stamina, carrying big and heavy packs with them. They are very good at all voluntary physical exercise when so inclined but quite averse—chiefly the menfolk—to heavy sustained labor of a slavish type. They arrange all their tasks and affairs accordingly, so they will not need to do or work so much."[7]

Despite these recorded observations, the Dutch initially knew little about the larger nations or specific tribal groups of native inhabitants that preceded them. Several regional tribes along the Hudson River were living in close proximity, including the Wiechquaeskeck at Dobbs Ferry, the Alipkonck at Tarrytown, the Sintsinck at Ossining, the Kitchawan at Croton-on-Hudson, and the Kestaubniuck near Peekskill.[8] Artifacts found at the mouth of the Croton River in the late 1970s suggest to some archeologists that the earliest ancestors of these people arrived some 6,000 to 10,000 years ago. The Dutch, however, collectively called the Indians "wilden," or the wild people. Conflicts inevitably ensued as European settlers slowly began to hack down tall trees, plant crops and raise livestock on land where these tribes had lived for millennia.

Van der Donck himself witnessed the progression and took part in it. He came to the New World in 1641 and was given a vast land grant by the Dutch West India Company—a wide area encompassing Yonkers down to the Harlem River—as a reward for forging a peace deal with the Indians after a period of hostilities.

He built one of the first saw mills in the region and a dam at the old Nepperhan River, near present-day Larkin Plaza. He was referred to as the "Young Gentleman," or "Jonker" or "Yonkheer," as was his farm, giving the current city its name. He died in 1655 on his property, most likely the victim of an attack by the Indians who were conducting raids across the region that year during another round of warfare.[9]

As the Dutch colonists expanded up the river, so did their farms and pastures; grazing cattle often trampled Indian corn fields as a result. In response, the Indians would kill Dutch cattle and horses, mounting tensions as more Dutch continued to arrive from Europe.

The Lenape had a very different set of beliefs regarding land ownership. Rather than viewing the new Dutch occupation as an outright transfer of property, as the Dutch did, the Indians understood the payments from white settlers in tools, clothing, liquor and jewelry as a form of rent combined with a military alliance. This fundamental divide led the Dutch into their largest organized conflict with the native people, resulting in unimaginable acts of cruelty and slaughter.

It was called Kieft's War, after the Dutch West India Company's Director General of New Amsterdam, William Kieft, a strong-willed authoritarian who left a trail of failed business ventures and dubious ethics behind him before taking on his new duties in the Dutch outpost. While the warriors on both sides fought with flintlock muskets, sabres, arrows and hatchets, everyone was in some sense on the battlefield. This kind of warfare encompassed every dark category of ethnic conflict and butchery—mass slaughter of women and children, reprisals, torture, mutilation and unspeakable acts of brutality. The largest and most strikingly inhumane massacre of the whole bloody affair happened near the present-day village of Bedford: the burning deaths, in 1664, of some 500 Indians.[10] It was a very dirty war.

A well-connected yet inflexible man who had been driven out of France and the Ottoman Empire after business trouble,[11] Kieft was given total control over the colony, with disastrous results. In addition to clashes between whites and the Indians, there was also fighting between Indian tribes over old grievances. Kieft wanted Indians who were seeking refuge from attacks by the northern tribes—eager to gain control over the abundant natural riches of the lower Hudson Valley—to pay for "protection," essentially a demand for tribute that caused great bitterness and unrest.

Based on reports of a theft of hogs from Staten Island, evidently carried out by whites, Kieft ordered a raid on a band of Lenapes called Raritans that ended in the deaths of several Indians. The Raritans responded by killing four farm hands working for a prominent landowner, David DeVries, on Staten Island. Kieft then issued a bounty to encourage the killing of Raritan tribe members, convinced the Indians were "daily exhibiting more and more hostility." He offered "ten fathoms of sewan [decorative beads] for each head."[12] Only one head was collected by an Indian enemy of the Raritans, but this gruesome demand dramatically escalated tensions—and reprisals.

In August 1641 Turtle Bay in Manhattan, Claes Swits, a popular old innkeeper and wheelwright, was attacked and beheaded. The axe was held by an Indian whose uncle, simply looking to trade furs, had been killed by Europeans in Tarrytown in 1626. The young nephew, 12 at the time, vowed to take revenge, and when he became an adult he took it on an aged public citizen known by locals and travelers alike. That spark swiftly turned into a wildfire.

Kieft called a war council of 12, many of whom were reluctant to go to battle; he nevertheless ordered troops under his command to go on the attack. In his account of the war published in a journal years later, DeVries, the Staten Island farmer, said the Dutch director told him he had "a mind to wipe the mouths of the savages."[13]

But DeVries was wary of the potential consequences and told Kieft it was a dangerous business. "You will also murder our own nation," he said, "for there are none of the settlers in open country who are aware of it."[14] His words proved prophetic. Following Kieft's orders, Dutch soldiers carried out raids in lower Manhattan and Pavonia (now Jersey City) against Indians who had come south to avoid the fierce attacks of the warring Mohawks and sought protection from the Dutch. Eighty Indians were killed in the Pavonia Massacre, some in the most brutal fashion imaginable; even small children were killed in front of their parents.

Indians retaliated with ferocity, and though rarely seen, with a unified force. Tribes rose up en masse in 1642 and 1643 to stage attacks on poorly protected farmsteads in Manhattan, Long Island, New Jersey and Westchester. The outspoken former Puritan Roger Williams, who was in New Amsterdam to travel to England at the time, recorded the sense of dread and doom: "Mine eyes saw the flames of their town, the frights and hurries of men, women and children, and the present removal of all who could to Holland."[15] Tomahawks, fire brands and scalping knives were the tools of war employed by Indian raiders, and they aroused a special kind of panic among white settlers.

Some, however, were blind to the rising threat, consumed by their own convictions in a new land. Anne Hutchinson, a woman with strong ideas about God, religion and redemption, wanted to do away with the concept of mortal sin, one among a number of several other dissenting beliefs that put her in severe opposition to the Puritan hierarchy. On the run from Puritans in Massachusetts, she had decamped to Rhode Island with her followers, becoming, with Roger Williams, one of that colony's founders. When it appeared Rhode Island was to fall under the sway of the Puritan leaders of the Bay Colony, she and her family again took to the road. Seeking a more accommodating residence where she could practice her beliefs, she turned to the Dutch, who allowed Christian dissidents to settle in New Amsterdam.

Governor Kieft let Hutchinson and her extended family stay in an area that became present-day Pelham—a dangerous place to be, as it turned out, since it occupied a kind of no-man's land between the Indians and the Europeans. She had enjoyed good relations with Indians in New England and appears to have been unconcerned about hostilities with tribes in the Hudson Valley. It was a fatal mistake. Less than a year after settling, she was massacred with six of her children and nine other settlers. The only survivor, her granddaughter, was taken hostage by the Indians and remained in captivity for a long time. As a subsequent account put it, "From swamps and thicket the mysterious enemy made his sudden onset. The farmer was murdered in the open field. Women and children, granted their lives, were taken into long captivity. Houses and boweries, haystacks and grain, cattle and crops were all destroyed."[16]

In desperation, the Dutch sent out a call for volunteers and mercenaries to cleanse the countryside of Indian settlements, hoping to destroy their will to fight. A man just right for the brutal job came forward. Captain John Underhill, according to contemporary accounts, was a quarrelsome and difficult person. He had already made a name for himself as an Indian fighter after the massacre of the Pequot people in Connecticut in 1637. He had even clashed with Puritan leaders and had been declared *persona non grata* in the same religious dispute that sent Hutchinson into exile. He was more than willing to avenge her death.

After gaining information about a large Lenape settlement from an Indian source, Underhill and 130 Dutch and English militiamen set out by boat for Greenwich in late February 1644. From shore they marched through fresh snow to their destination under a full moon, surrounding three long row houses in the early morning hours, then struck. The Lenape fought back with arrows and hatchets, killing one and wounding a dozen other militiamen, but they were no match against the muskets deployed against them, and the blood of nearly 200 Indian warriors was staining the deep snow under the glaring moon. It became clear their position was hopeless.

They retreated into their longhouses and continued to shoot arrows. The Dutch and English, on Underhill's command, then set fire to the structures, a replay of the same tactic he had used in the massacre of the Pequots years before. Those inside resigned themselves to death, and an eerie silence blanketed the scene, a chilling echo of van der Donck's observation that the Indians made it a point of pride "to scorn pain and suffering."

As the houses burned, they became funeral pyres for the hundreds of Indians trapped within, including a large number of women and children. Archaeologists have yet to pinpoint the site of the massacre, and historians have only been able to guess at its approximate location. An oral tradition repeated in Bedford in the early 1800s suggested there was a large mound marking a significant Indian burial site near present day Bedford Village,[17] although other sites have also been proposed in Pound Ridge and southern Connecticut near Cos Cob.

Wherever the exact location may lie, one fact stood out above all others in the historical accounts of the massacre—the complete silence with which the doomed Lenape lost their lives. It was a final communal gesture, made more powerful by the size of the group, that seemed to damn the attackers from the grave.

An account discovered in Holland written by a first or second-hand witness, as yet unnamed, described the scene: "They returned back to the flames, preferring to perish by the fire than to die by our hands. What was most wonderful is, that among this vast collection of men, women and children, not one was heard to cry or to scream."[18] Underhill's force later marched for two days to reach Stamford. "A thanksgiving was proclaimed on their arrival," wrote a chronicler of the massacre.[19]

Hundreds of Indians died during the war across Long Island and the Hudson Valley, as well as dozens of colonists. The Europeans barely gained the upper hand after it was all over, and the Dutch settlement of the New World was dealt a significant setback, substantially weakening its fortunes. But it was a victory of sorts for the settlers, and the deaths of the 500 Lenapes at the hands of Captain Underhill and his comrades was credited with forcing the original inhabitants to give up their united opposition, the capstone to the brutal wars. A peace treaty was eventually concluded in 1645.

Richly rewarded by the Dutch for his role in the Lenape massacre, Underhill was granted a large plot of land in lower Manhattan where Trinity Church now stands. He continued a prominent and prosperous life after his bloody career in the Indian wars, appointed surveyor of customs, sheriff and high constable on Long Island. Among his peers, he died a paragon of respectability in old age. Far less is known of the anonymous men, women and children who died in flames inside a burning building, their world and lives coming to an end, and silently bound themselves together in death.

Director General Kieft, however, came to a bad end. Recalled to Holland to answer complaints against him and explain the course of action he had taken against the native population, and the resulting dangerous predicament into which the Dutch settlement had lapsed, he never arrived to answer for his alleged crimes. Kieft died in a shipwreck off the coast of Wales on September 28, 1647. The *Princess Amelia*'s captain mistook the much narrower and rocky Bristol Channel for the English Channel, killing some 80 other passengers when the boat sank. Among them was one of Kieft's most vociferous critics, clergyman Everardus Bogardus, whose sermons frequently denounced Kieft's administration.

Weakened by the Indian wars, the Dutch colony's defenses had eroded through neglect and sustained conflict. The English, long eying the great harbor in New Amsterdam with envy, seized the opportunity in 1664 and re-christened the city New York in a bloodless invasion. While a new flag flew over the region, the English retained many of the Dutch ruling traditions, including an open-door policy that set New Amsterdam apart from colonial settlements in North America. The Dutch had proclaimed in 1638 that any settler, regardless of religious beliefs, could join the colony, and the proclamation helped make it a magnet for religious dissenters of all stripes, including Quakers, who had been persecuted in England, and non–Christians. New Amsterdam was known for permitting Jews to settle and worship in their own spaces.

French Protestants, who had suffered savage treatment during the religious wars of the period, were eager to find a new homeland where they would not be hunted down and wiped out for their beliefs. With that imperative in mind, Jacob Leisler—the son of a Calvinist French minister who had prospered in the New World—made available a larger portion of land to French colonists in what was to become known as New Rochelle. Leisler brokered the deal for 6,000 acres with John Pell, the lord of Pelham Manor, and the stipulation included a proviso that Leisler's descendants would have to provide a "fatted calf" to Pell's descendants on demand in perpetuity, a deal that was honored more in jest than as a legal formality for generations. With the ascension of the Dutch-born William and his English cousin Mary to her father's throne in 1688, a bloodless coup known as the "Glorious Revolution," a power vacuum arose in the leadership of the New York colony. Leisler stepped forward to fill it. His move to take control of the colony during a time of uncertainty, and his initial refusal to cede control to a royal delegation, led to his eventual execution in May 1691.[20]

Now under British rule, six manors were established in an area encompassing most of northern Westchester; the largest were Philipsborough (also known as Philipse and later, Philipsburg), granted in 1693, and Cortlandt, in 1697. The manor system established a form of tenant farming whereby individual landholders paid rent to the lord of the manor. Westchester County came into being in 1683, created by an act of the New York General Assembly. The northern borders of the county with Connecticut were also redrawn, putting Rye and Bedford inside Westchester County and New York. The new borders settled a longtime conflict but miffed residents of those towns who had long associated themselves with Connecticut.[21]

This period in the region and across the colonies was known for self-sufficiency and rustic living. Every home had its own loom to make linen from sheep wool. Transportation was difficult. Food was simple and typically consumed with wooden utensils.

With the Indian wars on the wane, a measure of stability was also restored to the region. But unrest and fear of another kind still percolated among the settlers here, resulting in Westchester's very own witch hunt. A Calvinist interpretation of the Bible led the earliest colonists to take the demons of hell and eternal damnation quite literally, and these beliefs posed dangers to those who aroused suspicions.

Witch hunting was at its most ardent where the Puritan flame burned brightest, especially in Salem, Massachusetts, where, in 1692, 19 people were hanged and one man pressed to death after being tried for witchcraft. But even in other parts of the New World where Puritans lived alongside those with a variety of religious and superstitious folk beliefs, sorcery and the dark arts were taken seriously and feared.

In Connecticut, nine people were executed on witchcraft charges. A wealthy widower named Katherine Harrison was almost on that list. While she escaped death in the Connecticut colony, she was tried for a second time when she moved to Westchester. She had been accused once again by her neighbors of practicing sorcery.

The trial of Katherine Harrison was a small footnote in a wider campaign of terror and hysteria that began in late medieval Europe. Witch hunting became an institution embedded in law and enshrined in popular myth that sent tens of thousands of victims, almost all of them women, to gruesome deaths from Sweden to Spain to Salem.

Economic feuds and religious strife set the stage for witch trials, though the real issue was often little more than spiteful envy and hatred toward those who appeared different from the norm. Victims in many cases were women who, in one sense or another, defied prevailing customs of the day.

Harrison was in many senses typical of the kind of women who were burned, hanged, crushed, drowned or garroted across the world throughout the great witch hunt. Born in England in modest circumstances, she worked as a servant in Hartford for a prominent merchant. She went on, however, to marry John Harrison, who gained wealth in the Connecticut colony and left her a sizable estate and three daughters when he died in 1666. Beside regularly quarreling with her neighbors over property disputes, she was seen as someone who had risen far above her true station in life—an affront to community norms. She also never remarried after her husband's death, another oddity that set her apart.

Perhaps most significantly, it was also believed she was "a cunning woman," a kind of prescient being who could offer advice and insight to neighbors on life's problems—an intermediary between this world and the spiritual realm whose unique qualities had enjoyed semi-official status in farming communities for generations. But "cunning folk," as they were called, were likely to fall under suspicion for engaging in more disturbing behavior than creating herbal remedies and dabbling in divination.[22]

It was within this heady brew of superstition and contempt that Harrison found herself in danger of death. The accusation lodged against her in Wethersfield, Connecticut, said bluntly she was a menace to the God-fearing farming community: "Katherine Harrison, thou standest here, indicted by ye name … as being guilty of witchcraft for that thou, not having the fear of God before thine eyes, hast had familiarity with Satan, the grand enemy of God and mankind, and by his help has acted out things beyond and beside the ordinary course of nature."[23]

Testimony against Harrison included a report that a dog with her face on it had visited a local woman and tormented her. A 20-year-old woman named Mary Hale told the court that the dog, whose form she believed Harrison had taken, spoke to her directly. "I will make you afraid before I have done with you," she claims the animal said, before it then bodily "crushed" and "oppressed" her.[24]

Witnesses also recounted Harrison's facility with folk remedies, astrology and fortune-telling. During the lengthy trial that dragged on intermittently for months, neighbors told of Harrison's habit of forcing herself into situations where she was not wanted, and of the bad outcomes that followed. She was also called perpetually deceitful.[25]

The trial continued with more testimony against Harrison, concluding in October 1669 with a guilty verdict,[26] and the implication that a death sentence would follow. But magistrates in a special session in Hartford overturned the court's finding that she was guilty of witchcraft, ordering her to leave the colony. Connecticut Governor John Winthrop, Jr.—a known skeptic of witchcraft trials and the lurid testimony they relied on—took part in the decision, a stroke of good fortune for Harrison.

Harrison took refuge, as others fleeing Puritan persecution had before her, in Westchester. She was taken in and given shelter in the south of the county by Captain Richard Panton, a prominent landowner and military and civic leader in the early colony who helped formulate the town boundaries between Eastchester and Pelham.

Harrison's reputation, however, followed her, and it was only a matter of months before she was again accused of consorting in the dark arts. In a petition lodged against

A painting by John Ward Dunsmore depicts Jonas Bronck signing a treaty with Native Americans in 1642. The painting was made in 1908 (Westchester County Historical Society).

her in 1670, her Westchester neighbors alleged she was "reputed to be a person lyeing under the Supposicion of Witchcraft [and] hath given some cause of apprehension to the Inhabitants there." For her second trial, Harrison was able to enlist a number of supporters, in addition to Panton, who testified to her good character and innocence. When the case against her in New York was dismissed, it was ordered that she "hath Liberty to remaine in the Towne of Westchester where shee now resides, or any where else in the Governmt during her pleasure," according to the document signed by Governor Francis Lovelace.[27]

The trial had nonetheless shaken Harrison, and she left Westchester soon after. She was litigated by her new neighbors yet again, legal records show, although her fate is not known for certain. She turned up again in New York City in the 1670s,[28] but little about her has emerged in the historical record. It is clear she escaped the hangman's noose.

The good people of Salem were not so lucky. As the age of enlightenment slowly cast its light across Western civilization, witch hunting became a thing of the past. Stable and orderly rule took hold, and the small colony on the edge of the New World began to prosper. A pioneering Dutchman (and a native of Sweden) named Jonas Bronck in 1639 became the first European to set up a farm stand north of the Harlem River,[29] initiating a long line of farmers drawn to cultivate the soil in Westchester. As the demand for labor grew, so did the arrival of slave labor, with men and women brought to the region in shackles from as far away as Madagascar and forced to work. Woodland gave way to farms and pastures, all of it toiled by the back-breaking work of slaves and indentured farmhands from around the world.

Under British rule in the early 1700s, the county was on its way to becoming a productive agricultural region, and one of the most prosperous. To those early settlers, the thought that their new home would be laid to waste and made desolate by nearly a decade of war, must have seemed far-fetched. But the storm clouds were already on the horizon.

2

Slavery's Legacy and Westchester at War

The issue of liberty, both personal and collective, was to be a burning topic in the American Colonies in the 1700s. The struggle for personal liberty from institutionalized slavery, and national independence from colonial power, also profoundly shaped Westchester County and its people. America's complicated history with slavery, so often linked to the cruelties of the cotton and sugar economy in the south, has led to a kind of collective amnesia about the extent and severity of the slave trade in the northern colonies. Yet for more than a century and a half, Westchester was a place where slavery flourished. The county was the state's second largest slaveholding district outside New York City, itself the largest concentration of slave labor outside the south in the 18th century.

Amid a growing tide of abolitionist sentiment in the north during and after the War of Independence, New York State passed a law in 1799 for the gradual abolition of slavery that nevertheless perpetuated its legacy well into successive generations: the children of slaves born after 1799 were free but were required to work as indentured servants for most of their young adult lives. Large segments of Westchester landowners, in fact, held onto slaves in the years leading up to and following the Revolution and continued to buy and sell them as property well into the early 1800s. Slavery was the first global economy in the modern age, a market of enormous wealth and human misery that stretched from Africa to Liverpool to Jamaica to Manhattan Harbor to the dairy fields of Sleepy Hollow. It is estimated that ten to 15 million Africans were transported to the New World by 1800. Thousands ended up in the fields and farms of colonial Westchester.

The first cargo of African slaves arrived in New York City's harbor in 1626 when 11 of them disembarked from the ship under the direction of the Dutch West India Company. Efforts to enslave Indians had shown few signs of success, as European settlers saw it, and indentured servitude from Europe did not meet the insatiable demand for labor in the New World. In the search for able-bodied men, women and children, the slave trade turned its attentions to Africa.

The trans-Atlantic market in human bondage swiftly accelerated in the 1700s: from 1732 to 1754, more than a third of all immigrants officially passing through New York harbor were slaves. By mid-century, about a quarter of the population making up New York City, Westchester and adjoining counties were black slaves.[1]

In the same year the first slaves set foot on New York soil, a man was born in Holland who would become Westchester's biggest slave trader. Frederick Philipse was a carpenter for the Dutch West India Company who came to New York in the 1650s. He married well, taking the hand of Margaret Handerbroek de Vries, the widow of a prosperous merchant. With his sights set on big business, and pledging allegiance to the new British authorities, he acquired Philipsburg Manor, a vast tract of land stretching between the Hudson and Bronx rivers from the Croton River to Spuyten Duyvil Creek, under the land system adopted by the new colonial administrators. Philipse began slave trading in 1680 and his business prospered.

According to letters he wrote to his associates, Philipse wanted as many slaves as he could get, believing them to be the source of great potential profit.[2] He was intensely disappointed when his partner, a ship's captain named Adam Baldridge, obtained only 34 slaves from the island of Sainte Marie off the coast of Madagascar. He had wanted 200 adult slaves. "For negroes in these times," he wrote, "will fetch 30 pound and upwards the head, unless they bee children or superannuated. It is by negroes that I finde my chiefest profit, all the other trade I look upon as by the by.... Besides, of the 34 negroes that you putt aboard, there were 15 of them children, three years sucking."[3]

Philipse professed to be both an honest and ethical businessman who played by the rules. "I was never known to bee sharp or severe with any man," he continued in his letter to the underperforming ship's captain. "I would be as faire to all the world as they deserve they should be to me."[4] Despite his self-serving declarations, the manner in which his slaves were coerced into servitude was anything but fair. In 1695 Philipse commissioned the construction of a ship, named *The Margaret*, after his wife, specifically for the slave trade. His aim was to bring rum, salt and clothing to the African island of Sainte Marie to sell to pirates as part of the arrangement to procure slaves. The ship, according to his instructions, also carried brass neck collars and "arm rings" to shackle his human cargo. Philipse died in 1702. At the time he listed 40 slaves in his possession. His son, Adolph, continued in the slave trade and was eventually embroiled in litigation that he was sponsoring piracy through his extensive involvement in the African business network.[5]

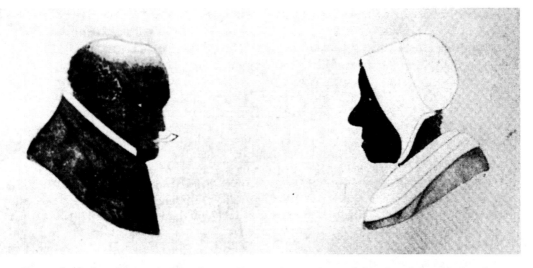

Slavery had a long history in Westchester. Domestic servants and farmhands kept in bondage, like Billy and Jinny, were an integral part of everyday life well into the 1800s. A series of gradual emancipation laws eventually ended slavery in New York State in 1827 (Westchester County Historical Society).

Most slaves in the area worked on small farms planting and sowing crops, milling grains and tending animals. Many also carried out domestic duties, living in the kitchens or attics of the families they served, or in nearby sheds. The close-knit nature of northern slavery was said to foster a greater sense of humanity between the servants and the served, but the documented record of runaways, public whippings and families broken apart by the whims of an owner's business interests tell another story.

Towns in Westchester were required to hire "public whippers" to discipline slaves, and punishment of up to 40 lashes were often meted out in village squares near churches and other public buildings.[6] Runaway slaves were common, and posted notices and advertisements from colonial newspapers around the region showed that slaves often sought to escape, particularly to avoid the breakup of families. An 1811 advertisement in the *Westchester Gazette and Peekskill Advertiser* promises $10 to anyone who could help find "a Negro man about 21 years old … well made, active and is named 'York,' but sometime calls himself John Cook or James Cook." The notice included a description of his clothing when last seen—a sailor's coat, muslin shirt and a cravat.[7]

Defiance of any kind often met the cruelest punishment. Three slaves in Rye were executed for unspecified "crimes and misdemeanors," one in 1714, and the other two in 1719. The name of the slave executed in 1714 was Primus, but nothing about his alleged misdeeds, or those of the other condemned men, have emerged from the historical record.[8] All that was recorded is how their owners were repaid. Under the custom of the day, the state compensated slave owners for execution of their "property."

New Rochelle under the Huguenots had a substantially higher proportion of slaves than other communities. Around 1700, there was one slave for every 2.3 adult Huguenots in New Rochelle.[9] The Huguenots also showed a reluctance to free their slaves, as was gradually being done elsewhere. In 1766, in New Rochelle, a male slave owned by an English settler was accused of murdering a French Huguenot woman, one Madame De Blez, with an axe blow to the head. The unnamed slave was later executed in a public burning.[10]

At slavery's height, deep-rooted ideas about racial inequality bred an atmosphere of destructive insecurity. The fear of insurrection and revolt by slaves was a constant source of dread around the region. Westchester militiamen were called down to Manhattan in 1741 when a series of fires was blamed on a conspiracy of slaves and several white accomplices. Thirty black men and four whites were hanged and burned in one of the grimmest spectacles that the city has ever witnessed.

Perhaps the most infamous of all Northern slaves in the early post-colonial period was a Westchester native. Although Rose Butler was born on a farm in Mount Pleasant in 1799 to an enslaved mother, under the terms of gradual emancipation passed that year, she was still required to perform 25 years of service to the Straing family. The Straings nevertheless sold her when she was ten, and she eventually ended up in lower Manhattan working for the Morris family.[11] Butler clashed with the family and was accused of arson after a fire in the kitchen damaged the Morris home; it later burned to the ground while Butler was imprisoned. Accused of pilfering from the household, taking cash and silver, she faced a death sentence in a trial that attracted widespread attention by both proponents and enemies of the institution of slavery, even in a so-called free state. Found guilty of arson, she was hanged in July 1819, after a long procession through city streets that was viewed by thousands. It was the last public hanging in one of the city's original potter's fields, now Washington Square Park.[12]

Few remnants of Northern slavery, such as old shacks in Port Chester, lasted into the contemporary era. One can travel for miles over country roads and main thorough-fares in Westchester, where slaves worked the land, herded cows and tended to rich men's households for generations, without finding a single trace of their existence. But the men and women whose labor was co-opted and personal liberty stripped from them were also considered highly valuable property. As such a commodity, the law of the time was scrupulous in how they were purchased and sold.

Looking through old records of slave transactions, written with archaic cursive pen-manship in faded ink, one can glean brief glimpses of that world. Slaves and the children of slaves were often sold when they were very young, as was the case for Rose Butler. One such document concerned the life of Prince, a six-year-old boy without a surname, in 1781. He was to be given by Peter Van Tassel of Philipse Borough (the original name used for the Philipsburg Manor area in Sleepy Hollow) to Gould Bouton of South Salem[13] and serve 12 years with his new master, "at which time the slave will be about the age of 18 years." The transaction declared "said negro boy … shall well and faithfully serve his lawful commander gladly and shall not absent himself from his master's service." The contract required that Bouton "provide for the negro boy meat and drink and apparel fit and sufficient for a servant, [who] will be taught to do farming." It concludes with a small legacy provision: "in consideration of his services, at the end of his service, the negro boy, he shall be given unto him his waring [sic] apparel."[14]

Some documents also record when a slave was given freedom. One case involved Jack, a man just under the age of 50, who was discharged from the ownership of Hakaliah Purdy of Rye. Purdy bought the man and made an agreement to manumit, or free him, after five years. "Five years having finished this day, and he having served me faithfully, honestly and soberly and industriously the said Jack is free, agreeable to our bargain," reads the document, approved by the town clerk in Mamaroneck.[15] Another sale document outlines the purchase of a young boy in 1784 for "seventy pounds [of] lawful money by Elijah Purdy of White Plains." The sale deed, in an echo of the traditional wedding vow, gives Purdy "one certain Negro Boy named Harrey to have and to hold said Negro boy."[16]

The legacy of slavery was to have immense consequences for the young nation. These documents, and the stories of slave life preserved at historic sites and museums, may be all that is left of Westchester's slaveholding past that bears direct witness to a merciless institution enslaving generations of men, women and children. Questions of mastery, submission, liberty and freedom were to resound in other ways as the 1700s moved onward to a cataclysmic struggle between the new world and the old.

The so-called Zenger trial, in which a bedrock principle of the freedom of the press was established in the American colonies, had a strong Westchester connection. Gou-verneur Morris, an architect of the U.S. Constitution who was raised in Westchester, later said, "the trial of Zenger in 1735 was the germ of American freedom, the morning star of liberty."[17]

John Peter Zenger, a publisher who opposed royal governor William Cosby, carried an account of voter fraud in 1733 on the Eastchester village green in which an opponent of Cosby's was seeking elected office. Zenger's publication, the *New York Weekly Journal*, printed an account describing the efforts by Cosby's supporters to prevent the governor's opponents from voting, and the printer was charged with libel. A trial in 1735 in lower Manhattan acquitted Zenger, establishing truth as defense in libel cases and creating a precedent for a free press as a defense against authoritarian rule.[18]

Although the region was to play a significant strategic role during the War of Independence, the fires of revolutionary fervor never burned as brightly in Westchester as they did in other parts of the northeast, namely in neighboring Connecticut and Boston. Like New York City, the prosperous farm country that Westchester had become nestled comfortably in the embrace of the British Empire. In fact, some of the most ardent voices against the coming war for independence came from Westchester's prominent citizens. Most argued that it would be a crime and a folly to break away from British rule, and that disagreements over trade policy and taxation could be remedied without resorting to armed conflict.[19] The debate over freedom from British rule was to play out in local church pulpits and taverns as the calls for self-rule grew more passionate.

A war of words preceded the actual war, with Alexander Hamilton dueling in ideas and ink against a leading Westchester intellectual. The Rev. Samuel Seabury was fiercely loyal to the Crown. When talk arose about a plan to shut down trade with England as a protest, Seabury would have none of it. Though his authorship of a Tory pamphlet was never authenticated with absolute certainty, historians have long believed that Seabury's pen was behind a series of articles attacking the cause for independence. A vigorous clergyman with outspoken convictions, he was rector of St. Peter's Church in the town of Westchester, which spread from Eastchester south to the Harlem River.

In November 1774, as calls for a boycott with England intensified, a pamphlet signed by "a Westchester Farmer" was printed in New York City by Loyalist John Rivington. "We shall have no trade at all and consequently no vent for the produce of our farms, such part of our wheat, flaxseed, corn, beef, pork, butter, cheese as was not consumed in the province, must be left to rot and stink on our hands.... Let me entreat you, my Friends, to have nothing to do with these men, or any of the same stamp. Peace and quietness suit you best. Confusion, Discord, and Violence, and War are sure destruction to the farmer."[20] His essays compared the independence leaders to a "venomous brood of scorpions." The pamphlet appeared in Westchester shortly after it was printed.

The rival factions both came to White Plains to show support for their cause. In April 1775, a conference of county leaders in favor of independence met at the courthouse in White Plains to select delegates to the Continental Congress scheduled for Philadelphia later in the year. Colonel Lewis Morris of the large land-owning family in the south end of the county was elected Chairman. Meanwhile, Reverend Seabury and about 300 Loyalists came out to oppose New York's participation in the Second Continental Congress. Reverend Seabury and his like-minded supporters met at a tavern in White Plains to proclaim their allegiance to the crown and issue their own declaration denouncing the congress.[21] That same year, Seabury and "the Westchester Farmer" found a response from another anonymous writer, later credited to a young scholar named Alexander Hamilton, who supported the argument for the establishment of a Continental Congress. "The sacred rights of mankind are not to be rummaged for among old parchments or musty records," Hamilton declared. "They are written, as with a sunbeam, in the whole volume of human nature by the hand of divinity itself and can never be erased or obscured by mortal power."[22]

But the boldest response to the Westchester Farmer's arguments came in the form of a band of marauders wielding weapons, not printer's ink, who went after Seabury with a vengeance. Isaac Sears was a founder of the Sons of Liberty in New York and a staunch advocate for the cause of independence. He and some 100 or more raiders in November 1775 decided to make Loyalists pay for their outspoken allegiance to Great Britain. Setting out from New Haven, Sears rode into Westchester hell-bent on causing destruction. The raiding party under Sears' direction pillaged homes in Rye and burned a boat in Mamaroneck that was said to be owned by a supporter of the crown.

One detachment of riders ransacked the printing press and newspaper run by Rivington in lower Manhattan, the *Gazetteer*; the other went after the Rev. Seabury at his home in southern Westchester. The raiders thrust a bayonet at Seabury's wife, rampaged through his home and eventually took him captive. Under armed escort, he was locked up in New Haven for six weeks before he was eventually freed. He refused to say whether he had written the Westchester Farmer articles; he later told British authorities, however, that he was indeed the author.[23]

Hamilton, his antagonist in print, was appalled by the whole affair and decried the use of mob violence to suppress dissent. During the Revolutionary War, Rev. Seabury took shelter with British and Loyalist forces on Long Island. After the war, he remained in New York and pledged his allegiance to the new government. Isaac Sears, however, became a pariah when it was revealed he was buying up promissory notes to veterans at a pittance, and speculating on land seized from Loyalists. He left the country in disgrace and died in China.

As the controversy in White Plains and nearby towns in April 1775 demonstrated, there was little unity on the question of independence. Both factions showed fervent support for their cause, anticipating the deadly conflict that would turn colonies into a battleground and a civil war fought between Americans on opposing sides. It was a conflict that pitted neighbor against neighbor.

The price of liberty ran high in Westchester. The war brought freedom from colonial rule but devastated the region, spilling the blood of both soldiers and non-combatants along the county's rocky outcroppings.

The county was of major strategic importance. British control of the Hudson River would have allowed its military to strike a wedge between the northern Colonies, isolate the revolutionary movement in New England and execute a classic divide-and-conquer strategy. In addition, the productive farms, pastures and orchards in the region were an important source of supplies for both sides of the fight, leading to massive plundering and devastation.

Westchester and the lower Hudson Valley made up the longest running battlefield of the Revolution and provided the martial stage for a remarkable cast of characters. The Patriot cause was led by many of the nation's founders, who squared off against an enemy that included ruthless British opponents—including the most renowned traitor in U.S. history—and brutal Loyalist death squads. Ambushes, reprisals, espionage, pillage and assassination marked the long struggle. It was here that General George Washington and his lieutenants learned to become masters of disengagement and guile, using stealth and deception to fool a much larger force.

Facing an enemy that outmatched them in numbers and equipment, Washington and his troops broke the rules, relied on cleverness and played a game of chance with their lives. When it was all over, Westchester emerged in ruins, its prosperity wrecked by war, losing two thirds of its pre-war population.

Events moved quickly as the 13 colonies prepared to declare independence. In New York City, a Provincial Congress had been meeting to lay the groundwork for establishing self-rule. When fighting began between British troops and Patriot militias at Lexington, Concord and Bunker Hill, the time had come to make a choice. The Declaration of Independence followed in July.

The Fourth Provincial Congress adjourned to White Plains on July 9, as British warships were already in sight in lower Manhattan's New York Harbor. It was correctly assumed the British would invade the city. After decamping from New York under threat, the congress ratified the Declaration of Independence as its first order of business, and on July 11, on the steps of the White Plains Courthouse, the Declaration was read aloud to the beat of a drum as copies of the document were distributed. The State of New York also came into being on those courthouse steps, no longer a province of Great Britain. John Jay, the even-tempered jurist from Rye and Bedford who would one day serve as the first Chief Justice of the Supreme Court, was then appointed to draft the state constitution. Gouverneur Morris, the high-living scion of a prominent Westchester family credited with writing the final draft of the U.S. Constitution, was also in attendance at the reading of the Declaration in White Plains.[24]

The time for celebration was short. A massive British fleet was unfurling its sails in lower Manhattan in the summer of 1776, disembarking forces on Long Island intent on destroying the fledgling Continental Army and its new leader, General Washington, as quickly as possible. The British marched up the Hudson Valley and nearly succeeded in wiping out the new republic in its infancy in major battles in Westchester. But the Patriot army was saved by quick decision-making and determined resistance that allowed it to regroup and fight another day.

New York State officially came into existence when the Declaration of Independence was read aloud on the steps of the White Plains courthouse. "The Birth of the State of New York," a painting by George Albert Harker in 1915 depicts John Thomas of Rye reading the document (White Plains City Archives).

The battles Washington fought in Westchester were a kind of warfare using cunning plans and quick escapes that he perfected during the long fight ahead. In the early days, it looked as if the conflict would be over quickly. The British Army chased the rebels out of Long Island and New York City, giving Washington's fighters a thrashing at the Battle of Brooklyn on August 27. With the success of the recent campaign, the British generals prepared for a final knock-out blow and supposed that this war would be a short one crowned with knighthoods and other tokens of the King's appreciation for subduing a troublesome colonial revolt.

But during a lull in the fighting—a tendency toward inaction that Washington was able to exploit later—the crafty commander of the Continental Army was granted a respite to consider his options. Though he had only sketchy knowledge of Westchester, Washington had received reports that stores and provisions would be made available to his army at White Plains, which also afforded a strong defensive posture. And he moved, followed shortly by the British. Looking to encircle Washington's army, the British landed at Pell's Point near the present day section of the northern Bronx on October 18 with a force of 4,000 British and Hessian troops to cut off the Patriot forces moving north from Manhattan.[25]

Only about 750 Americans in lower Westchester under the direction of Colonel John Glover stood between encirclement of the main Patriot force. Glover immediately recognized the danger when he spotted with his spyglass dozens of flat boats filled with British and Hessian troops in Long Island Sound. He also realized he was on his own. As he later wrote to a friend in New Hampshire, "Oh! The anxiety I was then in for the fate of the day.... My country, my honor, my own life and everything that was dear, appeared at that critical moment to be at stake. I would have given a thousand worlds to have had … some other experienced officer present, to direct, or at least approve, of what I had done."[26]

But there was no indecision on his part as he sought to delay the British with every means at his disposal, which turned out to be bravery, a cool head and the stone walls that lined the roads leading from the point to the mainland through Pelham and New Rochelle.

Glover placed his men, many of them Massachusetts fishermen, behind rows of stone walls and directed them to fire when the British approached, then retreat to another wall further along the line of march. The process was then repeated. The relay tactic was improvised but decidedly effective, and the Hessians in the front of the attacking columns paid a heavy toll in casualties. Estimates on the number of killed and wounded vary significantly, though losses for British and Hessian troops were creditably inferred at several hundred. Glover's forces escaped with far fewer casualties; as few as a dozen men were killed.[27]

Exhausted from battle, Glover and his men marched to Dobbs Ferry without supplies for the cold night ahead. Devoid of food or drink as the sun set, they carried little else but their weapons with them. "The heavens over us and the earth under us … was all we had, having left our baggage at the old encampment we left in the morning," Glover later wrote.[28]

The Massachusetts colonel delayed enemy action long enough for Washington's army to escape the trap and march to White Plains, site of the next great clash of arms. While the Continental Army took stock of its new location in the little village known for its morning fog—reaching it just ahead of their enemies—the British began preparing what they hoped would be their final assault. While headquartered about ten miles away in New Rochelle, the British army took reinforcements—8,000 additional Hessian soldiers by way of Long Island Sound—then launched their offensive on White Plains on October 28 under the command of General William Howe. Hoping to take the Continental Army by surprise, they attacked early in the morning.

It was a bloody battle, a full day of pitched combat between armies of equal size, about 13,000 each. The heaviest fighting took place around the Bronx River and Chatterton Hill in the lower end of White Plains, which the British eventually seized. One Patriot soldier attached to General Henry Knox's artillery, Ebenezer Withington of Dorchester, Massachusetts, recalled a day of gunpowder and death. "A very heavy cannonading all day," he wrote. "A smart engagement ensued, the enemy got masters of the hill, the loss was great on both sides. The action began in the morning and lasted until evening, terrible slaughter around the field, how the mighty are fallen."[29]

The battle amounted to a draw, though it was generally credited as a British win since Washington's army was forced to retreat. It was also a notable day for a young Alexander Hamilton, the future treasury secretary, who discovered on the slopes of White Plains that he had a proficiency for warfare as well as for words and numbers. He was praised by superiors for acquitting himself well in command of a canon battery, harassing an enemy advance and drawing his guns off the battlefield after his position became untenable.[30]

While Howe was preparing for another assault, Washington and his army slipped away under cover of heavy rainfall and moved to North Castle. Each side suffered about two or three hundred casualties, though estimates are inconclusive. Washington and his army then crossed the Hudson and encamped in New Jersey for the next phase of the war.

Alexander Hamilton, the future treasury secretary, earned distinction at the Battle of White Plains while commanding an artillery battery. His wartime exploits in Westchester were captured in a 1926 painting by painter E.L. Ward for a postage stamp (White Plains City Archives).

While the big battles were done on its soil, Westchester was hardly done with the war. It was called the "neutral ground," but that term barely describes the irregular warfare and frequent raids that marked the fighting from one end of the county to another. These skirmishes persisted up until the end of the war, and torture, looting, rape and other atrocities against civilians were common aspects of the conflict. The Patriot side was known as "Skinners," while those associated with the Loyalist cause were called "Cowboys" for their propensity for cattle rustling. Cows had to be hidden in the woods or even in basements to keep them safe from theft. Men and women were on their own. There were spies everywhere—later the subject of a novel of wartime espionage by James Fenimore Cooper, who wrote *The Spy* in 1820 while living in Scarsdale on Mamaroneck Road when memories of the conflict were still fresh.[31]

Among the most hated Loyalist leaders during the conflict was James DeLancey, the former sheriff of Westchester, who raised a troop of some 500 irregular fighters. They knew the local landscape intimately. Known as the Westchester Refugees, they and their British allies garrisoned in large bases around Yonkers and Morrisania, mounted attacks on Patriot strongholds with devastating effect.

DeLancey was responsible for some of the most "unspeakable miseries and Distress this County has suffered," Abraham Leggett, a Westchester leader, wrote to Governor George Clinton on December 6, 1777. He accused DeLancey of "acting with the Greatest Venom Imaginable against the Good People of this county" and pleaded for a military response to end DeLancey's reign of terror.[32] The plea was never fulfilled. A Patriot strike on Morrisania proved unsuccessful in capturing DeLancey, who ended his days among the sandy banks of Nova Scotia, Canada.

The Continental Army had established a line of defenses along the Croton River, as well as fortifying strongholds along the Hudson to keep the British fleet from advancing. A raid on a Patriot supply depot at Peekskill in March 1777 demonstrated the British desire to take the offensive on the shores of the Hudson. But those plans never came to pass. An ingenious engineering feat that stretched from Cold Spring to West Point (about ten miles north of Westchester), which employed massive, 35-ton iron links set atop wooden pontoons—the so-called "Chain Across the Hudson"—was built in 1780 to deter ships from sailing north.[33] British forces campaigned on the western shore of the Hudson but could not achieve the strategic breakthrough they sought. While unable to pierce the defenses and forts established in northern Westchester and the lower Hudson Valley, British and Loyalist forces remained on the lookout for weak points and targets of opportunity. They found more than a few.

One of the most devastating raids on Westchester soil was led by a British officer with an equally infamous reputation. July 2, 1779, was an especially bad day for the cause of American independence when a cavalryman from Liverpool named Banastre Tarleton led the charge. The son of a wealthy merchant, he gambled away a family fortune before finding better luck with a cavalry sabre. He was detested by Patriots for his apparent ruthlessness in engagements across the colonies, becoming a British military hero in the process.

Tarleton rode up from Yonkers with about 300 horsemen under his command, all of them wearing the lime-green tunics associated with Loyalist forces. His unit was called the British Legion, and it was bent on wiping out Patriot strongholds in Pound Ridge and Bedford with fire and the sword. His immediate goal was to capture a rebel leader and destroy a detachment of cavalry operating from an outpost along the Connecticut and New York border. While not successful in that regard, their bloody work that day was mostly a victory: Pound Ridge lay destroyed and a Patriot home in Bedford was put to the torch. It was a humiliating blow. In a final demoralizing touch, the battle flag of the Second Continental Dragoons was snatched by "Bloody Ban" and his raiders, plucked from a farmhouse in Pound Ridge that served as the regional headquarters of the independence cause.[34]

The Dragoons' battle flag was stitched together with French silk, a red-and-white-striped emblem depicting a winged cloudburst with golden thunderbolts at its center. Before the day when the Stars and Stripes were created, individual battle flags were the primary symbols behind which fighting men rallied—and died for. The Dragoons, or mounted infantry, fighting with Colonel Elisha Sheldon, carried their Latin motto in abbreviated form on their flag: "Speeding thunderbolts for my country," or more poetically in schoolboy Latin, "Our country calls, and we answer with thunder." The captured flag was later sold at auction by Tarleton's descendants for $12.3 million.[35]

Tarleton, then a lieutenant colonel at the age of 24, wrote in an after-action memorandum to his commander, Henry Clinton, that his use of the torch was a military necessity. "Firing from houses and out-houses obliged us to burn some of their meeting and some of their dwelling houses, with stores," he wrote. "They persisted in firing until the torch stopped their progress, after which not a shot was fired."[36]

The cavalry commander achieved even greater infamy in the southern campaign of the Revolutionary War. In May 1780, Tarleton's Legion overran a Patriot detachment in Waxhaws, South Carolina. They raised a white flag of surrender before Tarleton and his men massacred over 100 of them.

Even in the depths of winter, with snow lying thickly on the ground, the fighting continued. A foray was mounted in February 1780 against the Young House, a Patriot stronghold in Thornwood. About 550 Loyalists, Hessians and British attacked the home of property owner, Joseph Young, where 400 soldiers fighting for the cause of independence were billeted. The attackers surrounded and overwhelmed the defenders, inflicting heavy losses and carrying off more than 70 prisoners. One witness to the aftermath, Hannah Miller, recalled the carnage in vivid detail. "Capt. Scott [a wounded American officer] was brought to our house in a litter and died the next morning," she wrote. "At Young's house, the fire [met] the snow, and the wounded when they cried for water, had their thirst quenched with water mixed with their own blood. A number of wounded lay around the house."[37]

While the shooting war continued, a less visible fight played out, the game of espionage. In one the most notorious cases of a double-cross in American history, Benedict Arnold and a high-ranking British officer played their parts as traitor and spymaster in the picturesque hills of the lower Hudson Valley.

Arnold was a proud and intense man with a taste for the good life. Spurred by an acute sense that he had been badly snubbed and deprived of recognition for his skill on the battlefield, and losing faith in the Revolutionary cause, he decided to switch sides and profit handsomely. In August 1780 Arnold persuaded Washington to post him to West Point, a crucial fortification that blocked British ships from advancing up the Hudson. He was preparing to deliberately weaken the defenses around the fort, unhook the chain across the Hudson just north of Westchester and then surrender West Point to the British when they advanced on it. While serving as its commander, Arnold amassed documents that showed where the ordinance was stored, the size of the garrison and all of its strengths and weaknesses, which he planned to pass on to the British. His price: 20,000 British pounds sterling, a vast sum at the time.

Arnold made contact with the British about his plans to turn over the fort, and Major John André was dispatched to finalize the arrangements. André, charming and proficient with languages, had recently been named spymaster for the British army. Although he had distinguished himself as a staff officer, he was inexperienced in the ways of spycraft, as subsequent events would soon demonstrate.

After meeting with Arnold in West Haverstraw, the major was set to return to New York City on the *Vulture*, a British sloop. Before the *Vulture* reached him, as it rounded Croton Point, two militiamen affiliated with Washington's army were out making cider at a farm on Teller's Point. John Jacob Peterson, an African American volunteer for the Patriot cause who was said to be a crack shot, had only recently escaped from British custody. He and another local man, Moses Sherwood, scrambled for their weapons when they spotted the *Vulture*. They began firing at the ship and a small boat alongside it with muskets; their shots brought other militiamen with a small cannon.[38] The *Vulture* was forced to retreat downriver without André, forcing him to make an overland journey to British lines. Wearing civilian clothes, he took with him six pages of documents that Arnold had provided him. The military officer in disguise had been expressly warned not to carry incriminating documents, and instead encode them in some harmless looking documents or commit them to memory.[39] André crossed over the river to Verplanck and began a journey down through northern Westchester that ended at the bottom of a noose.

André ran into three men in military garb in Tarrytown, where he gave away his allegiance to the Crown on the mistaken impression, from their clothing and demeanor, that they held Loyalist sympathies. It turned out the three men, John Paulding, Isaac Van Wart and David Williams, were not allies but enemies. In short order he was searched and the documents were found. He offered to bribe them but was swiftly rebuffed.

The major was held in Lower Salem, then transported to West Point, where a court martial returned a guilty verdict and a death sentence. The trial and subsequent execution on October 2, 1780, was witnessed by an army surgeon, James Thacher, who wrote one of the best known memoirs of the conflict. "During the trial of this unfortunate officer, he conducted with unexampled magnanimity and dignity of character," Thacher observed. "So firm and dignified was he in his manners, and so honorable in all his proceedings on this most trying occasion, that he excited the universal interest in his favor. He requested only to die the death of a soldier, and not upon the gibbet [gallows]." The request to die by firing squad was denied by Washington himself, and André was hanged at Tappan not far from West Point. "However abhorrent in the view of humanity, the laws and usages of war must be obeyed, and in all armies it is decreed that the gallows be the fate of spies from the enemy," Thacher continued. "Not a murmur or sigh ever escaped him, and the civilities and attentions bestowed on him were politely acknowledged."[40] Arnold, wily to the end, did escape on the Vulture down river. He later took a commission with the British Army and moved to London.

As a war that turned even ardent Patriots like Arnold into traitors dragged on, it had a demoralizing effect on the citizens in its wake. The county's entire population, even those who were loyal to the cause, were exhausted and discouraged by the durability and ruthlessness of the Crown's forces. "The People of Westchester County think themselves given up to ruin, are discouraged, and worn out, and believe they shall receive no further help," Philip Pell, a member of the New York State Assembly and an army officer, wrote in a letter to a colleague, Robert Benson, in December 1780. "I believe that unless something is done, Westchester County, in less than a month, will be totally in the Enemy's power."[41] Citing the destruction of northern towns and the ease in which DeLancey and the Refugees attacked new targets, Pell, of the aristocratic family that gave Pelham its name, painted a gloomy picture. The county, he believed, was "open to the ravages of DeLancey's thieves," and the fortunes of war meant that "those who were once good men [would] become corrupt by trading with the Enemy."[42] The fighting would endure with ferocity.

Pines Bridge on the Croton River in lower Yorktown was a strategic conduit that the Continental Army knew needed reinforcing. The men of the First Rhode Island Regiment were given the duty of defending the bridge and the army's southern flank. The regiment, under the command of Colonel Christopher Greene, was made up of black soldiers and was distinguished by the white uniforms and headgear adorned with the shape of a ship's anchor they wore. Many were former slaves who signed up for service with the promise of freedom at the end of war, giving it the name "the black regiment." A dozen Wampanoag Indians as well as a number of freed blacks also joined the regiment. While the British had offered freedom to slaves who served under the Crown, the Continental Army was much more ambivalent to the question of admitting black soldiers, though enlistments for Washington's army by African Americans continued through the war.

Earning praise from commanders in engagements in New England and New Jersey, the regiment saw its worst ordeal in the spring of 1781 when Greene and the regiment were stationed at Pine's Bridge. The colonel had selected the nearby Davenport House as his headquarters with a few dozen of his men. It was an unfortunate choice. On May 14, taking advantage of an intelligence report about the shift in sentries in the area, a Loyalist force of 60 horsemen and 200 infantry under the command of DeLancey himself attacked at sunrise.[43] The defenders were caught completely unaware. Greene was cut down as he drew his sword and lunged at an assailant. His second in command, Ebenezer Flagg, had already been shot dead at a window, pistol in hand.[44]

Greene, badly wounded, was thrown over a horse as the attackers sped south toward their base at Morrisania, but drew his last breath after a mile or two. In a final, insulting gesture, the raiders threw his body off the horse onto the side of the road. DeLancey's unit suffered negligible casualties. More than 40 Patriots were wounded and 14 died. DeLancey also captured 30 of the Rhode Island volunteers, who were chained and marched to New York City, where DeLancey had them sold to slave traders. Shipped to the sugar plantations of the West Indies, they were never heard from again in their former country.[45]

Disastrous as the day had proved for the Continental Army, the battle of Pines Bridge became a source of pride in black history, and abolitionist scholars later cited the engagement as an example of bravery in the face of doom. "Colonel Greene, the commander of the regiment, was cut down and mortally wounded," wrote William Nell, a black historian and abolitionist in an 1855 account of the battle. "But the sabres of the enemy only reached him through the bodies of his faithful guard of blacks, who hovered over him, and every one of whom was killed."[46]

Dark days for the cause of independence were numerous, but a change in fortune arrived under the fleur-de-lis banner of the king of France. In early July 1781, the French army under General Jean-Baptiste, Comte de Rochambeau, arrived in the North Castle area around Mount Kisco after marching from Rhode Island. Their resplendent blue uniforms and abundant supplies buoyed hopes for victory. The French made camp with their American allies in a long line stretching from Dobbs Ferry to White Plains. On July 15 a shipping raid against Tarrytown and Patriot sloops anchored there brought a clash of arms between French and British fighters for the first time in the war. The boat raid was repelled with minimal losses to Patriot stores.[47]

The fighting continued in the region, but Rochambeau and Washington were not distracted from their larger mission of chasing the British out of the independent states of America. As they dined together and conferred in central Westchester, drinking copious quantities of Madeira wine that Washington favored, the commanders of the two armies eventually settled on the strategy that would bring victory: feigning an assault on New York City, while taking the real fight to the British Army in the tidewaters of Virginia with the French Navy in support.[48] It was a successful effort, culminating in a British Army forced to surrender at Yorktown, Virginia, the crowning conclusion to a daring strategy worked out in Westchester. Ships flying the Union Jack were eventually seen departing New York Harbor for passage home. The final removal of British troops from the region took place on November 25, 1783.

While distant battles were waged in the south, small-scale fighting and foraging raids persisted in the county right up to the end of the war. The seven years of conflict had left a landscape scarred by destruction and ruin in its wake. The Rev. Timothy Dwight, who served as a chaplain in Washington's army and would later become president of Yale University, recalled the utter devastation he encountered as he rode through Westchester. The populace, he noticed, seemed apathetic, their housing conditions deplorable, stunned into a kind of passive trance ruled by fear of reprisals. "Their houses were … in great measure scenes of desolation," he wrote. "Their furniture was extensively plundered or broken into pieces. The walls, floors and windows were injured both by violence and decay; and they were not repaired because they had not the means of repairing them, and because they were exposed to the repetition of the same injuries. Their cattle were gone. Their enclosures were burnt … their fields covered with a rank growth of weeds and wild grass. Amid all this appearance of desolation, nothing struck my own eye more forcefully than this great road—the passage from New York to Boston. Where I had heretofore seen a continual succession of horses and carriages, and life and bustle lent a sprightliness to all environing objects, not a single solitary traveller was visible from week to week, month to month. The world was motionless and silent."[49]

3

Old Weird America, the Suburban Ideal and the Civil War

As Westchester recovered from the devastation of the Revolutionary period, it had many natural advantages that primed it for its next chapter: abundant land for farms, orchards and pastures; bountiful fisheries; a good supply of fresh water; and easy access by boat to the largest consumer market in the Northeast.

The natural ingredients were close at hand. But while the county eased into agrarian prosperity, a land of regular habit and honest labor, there was much of the "old, weird America," as cultural critic Greil Marcus phrased it, that often ruptured the respectability of the county's quiet hamlets.

The 1800s were a time of charlatans and itinerant preachers, bare-knuckled fights and public executions. A citizen from that era might have heard about, or even witnessed, a notorious grave robbery and ghoulish experiments on the dead. It was a period when popular entertainment consisted of flickering torch lights underneath a canvas tent, showcasing exotic animals and galloping trick-riders. Mysterious figures moved across the landscape, like a solitary tramp in a handmade leather suit making his curious rounds, perhaps as a form of penance for some long-ago crime.

This era of extremes saw savage violence and retribution, cruel forms of entertainment and blood sport for the masses. It was the kind of world Edgar Allan Poe (who lived in a cottage at Fordham when it belonged to the county) both inhabited and envisioned. Intensely physical, it was hand-hewn and candle-lit. Cold stone granite, iron rails, whips, chains, hatchets, canvas and steam engines were the material that girded this burgeoning society, one in which hermits, showmen, hucksters, tattooed seamen, bigamists and executioners all played their part. While it was outwardly a law-abiding place, a sense of lawlessness and recklessness was never far below the surface. Destiny had a capricious aspect to it, and an outlaw could get away with murder—or face the hangman—depending on the seeming whims of fate. Outsized ambitions and man-made disasters tended to be the norm, not the exception. The sinister and the ridiculous coexisted, vying for dominance. And the circus held it all under one large canvas tent.

The expertise that county farmers gained on their pastures and paddocks with big animals meant they were well-poised to harness a new kind of entertainment that made its way across the American cultural landscape in the early 1800s. The dairymen of northern Westchester and neighboring Putnam County, adept at herding cattle, oxen, horses, sheep and other big critters, were the perfect kind of shepherds for a new form of animal wrangling with spectacle its primary motive.

The traveling circus was started by Yankee entrepreneurs and cattle drovers in Somers and other towns in northern Westchester in the early 1800s. They knew how to handle big animals, and later learned how to make a dollar through ingenuity and a showman's flair (Westchester County Historical Society).

The story of the elephant who came to America to astonish the crowds is a murky one. But this much is definite: Hachaliah Bailey, born in Somers in 1774, purchased an elephant which became the biggest traveling circus act of the era, giving Somers its designation as the "cradle of the American circus." Bailey was a drover who was a regular customer at the Bull's Head Tavern in lower Manhattan, a favorite haunt of ship captains and mercantile traders. He was always looking for new opportunities. Sometime around 1805, seized by some kind of inspiration, Bailey paid $1,000 (accounts differ on the sum) for an elephant who had landed on the docks shortly before. It was likely the second elephant to have reached America, the first one having arrived in 1796.[1]

He took the animal, naming it Old Bet in honor of his young daughter, Betsy, and shipped it up the Hudson to Ossining. The beast slowly made its way on a walk to Somers. Bailey may have thought the beast would prove useful as a draft animal in farm country, but it is more likely he sensed that country folk would pay money to see such an exotic creature. His suspicion was entirely correct, and off he went all over the Northeast to exhibit the big beast to paying customers. Bailey took Bet on the road at night, perhaps so that farm folks couldn't get a good look at her without paying for it, then sought out a barnyard for the big show; sometimes he built his own wooden ring, which became "the sawdust arena."[2] Bet was soon joined by a tiger, a bear and performing dogs (though accounts differ here as well). On the labors of such four-legged creatures, Bailey and other entrepreneurs set themselves up as maestros of a grand menagerie beginning in the 1820s. Their achievements clearly shaped the circus that modern audiences know today.

Before long, an entire industry had built itself on the crack of the whip, growling tigers and the wrinkled frame of a giant pachyderm. The circus industry provided plenty of job opportunities for farm hands of northern Westchester and Putnam County, long accustomed to herding and tending animals after generations in the dairy business.

The sight of these exotic animals stirred great interest. "Money being scarce, the men pawned their jackknives, and women brought stockings, to look at the strange beast," recalled one observer.[3] Farmers would pawn their tools and all manner of farm fare—apples, oats and rum—were bartered for admission to the spectacle. Old Bet met her end in 1816. A Maine farmer with an Old Testament perspective found the display of an exotic creature for money sinful, even blasphemous. He shot her dead and was punished by a two-day jail sentence.[4] Bailey would procure two more pachyderms for his growing menagerie. He became a wealthy man, a major landowner in the region, and later served two terms in the New York State Legislature. He built the Elephant Hotel in Somers in 1823 and adorned it with a distinctive statue of an elephant out front, a final testimonial to his gifts as an entrepreneur and showman.

Other circus men soon joined in the budding venture. Joshua Purdy Brown of Somers, who died in 1834, was credited with the creation of a circular canvas tent, the big top. He also came up with several other long-lasting ideas, including using advertisements to promote the show, wagon trains to carry the animals from town to town, and a big parade into each village to announce their arrival. All of it allowed him to cover more ground and entice bigger crowds. The field had so many imitators and new entrants the circus men met at Somers in early 1835 to form the Zoological Institute. Its ostensible purpose was to "more generally diffuse and promote the knowledge of natural history and gratify rational curiosity," but the true motivation was to create a cartel that would bar newcomers to the circus trade.[5]

The circus trade was very much a family enterprise from the start, and members of Hack Bailey's extended family worked in the big show as clowns or stunt riders. His descendants passed along the DNA of Yankee determination and enterprise on which the circus trade thrived for generations. George Bailey of North Salem, a nephew, became one of the great impresarios of the early circus and gained fame by acquiring a hippo and touring the Midwest with it in the 1850s; he had a vast fortune of a half-million dollars when he died at the age of 85 in 1903.[6] James A. Bailey, who was befriended by Hack Bailey's nephew, Frederick, and eventually took the Bailey surname as his own, was described as the "King of the Circus Men." He lived at a grand estate called the Knolls in Mount Vernon.

Hachaliah Bailey's influence loomed large in the early circus world, in particular his sharp business acumen. P.T. Barnum, the master showman, wrote of his great admiration for Bailey, whom he met as a young man. His death held a strange kind of irony for a man accustomed to domineering big animals. He was kicked in the head by a horse in 1845, and suffering a fatal blow, was buried under a headstone in a Somers cemetery that reads "Enterprise, Perseverance, Integrity."[7]

As the early circus men knew, the region was well suited to raising livestock. Pastureland was a plentiful and valuable commodity. Plots in the county were sold or given to Patriots in the early 1800s, enabling many veterans to earn a reward for their services. Thomas Paine, the fiery author and revolutionary who used his pen to give valuable moral and intellectual support in the fight for independence, was a recipient of such a grant. The writer and free-thinker had chronic financial difficulties, and after making his hardship known to influential friends in 1784, the New York State Legislature granted Paine 277 acres of farmland and a home in New Rochelle confiscated from a Tory landowner, Frederick Devoe.[8] Paine made his living from a pen, not the plow, and never spent much time in New Rochelle, renting the land there for income. It was clearly not the best fit for him, an irreligious man, to live in a community of steady church-goers.[9] His troubled residency in New Rochelle gave way to an even more troubled passage in death.

A disgruntled handyman angry over a payment dispute fired a pistol at Paine while he was in his New Rochelle cottage on Christmas Eve 1805, nearly hitting him.[10] The following year, Paine (a native of Great Britain) had the indignity of being turned down to vote in a Congressional election when the registrar informed him he was "not American." When he died in 1809 at the age of 72, poor and forgotten, he was refused burial in a city cemetery owned by Quakers, the faith of his father, due to his opposition to organized religion. So a small group of his friends took him from lower Manhattan to New Rochelle in a mahogany coffin for burial at the farm. Six people attended his funeral, two of them black men. He was entombed under a walnut tree near North Avenue.[11]

A peculiar fate awaited Paine's remains. In one of the strangest cases of grave robbery ever recorded, Paine was removed from his New Rochelle burial plot ten years after he was interred. Parts of his body have been turning up ever since, a grotesque but perhaps fitting journey for a man who once said, "The world is my country."

Paine's body was dug up by an admirer of his who believed that America had not done enough to honor the author and pamphleteer who gave his life to the overthrow of the ruling hierarchy. He may have been right—Paine's headstone in New Rochelle was repeatedly vandalized and damaged. The man who exhumed him, William Cobbett, was a radical writer himself who envisioned a grand monument to Paine in England, and so in 1819, with several confederates under cover of darkness just before dawn, he exhumed the coffin and spirited it away. A county sheriff was hastily summoned to go after the grave robbers, but the sheriff did not show much persistence in the chase. Cobbett was able to escape with his prize: the body of Tom Paine.[12] He took Paine with him on a ship to England—and soon discovered that the author of "The Rights of Man" was rather unpopular in the country of his birth. It also became evident the English public was not very keen on the idea of grave robbery. The concept of a grand memorial faded, and Paine's corpse languished in Cobbett's attic. Cobbett died in 1835, and here the mystery began: what happened to the body? Cobbett's son, J.P., had money troubles, and handed the body down to a laborer and a furniture maker before both became lost to history. A few souvenirs may have been taken as the coffin exchanged hands on its path to oblivion. A Unitarian minister in England claimed in the 1850s that he had Paine's skull and hand, and other purported parts of Paine's body have turned up as far away as Australia. The Paine House in New Rochelle, which was turned into a museum, also lays claim to two small portions of Paine—a small section of his brain, evidently taken by an associate of Cobbett's, and a lock of hair. The brain section was returned to New Rochelle and interred there in 1905 by a Paine biographer and admirer, Moncure Conway. The location of the rest of Paine's remains has never been definitively determined.[13]

A morbid story of disinterment was Paine's unfortunate fate after he was buried in Westchester soil, pulled from the grave and condemned to an uncertain journey in death. For the men sent to Westchester against their will, a different kind of justice awaited them inside a stony mortuary, often for the remainder of their lives.

The origin of Sing Sing Prison began with an unusual sight in 1825. Beneath a bluff overlooking the Hudson River, 100 convicts marched to a spot near the village of Sing Sing, whose Indian name meant rock upon rock, and began quarrying rock for a new building. Measuring 476 feet in length, and 32 feet in height, it was to be filled with little granite cubicles. They were building their own stone tomb, as it turned out, and they were also creating what would become the most famous prison in America. As a symbol of what happens to men and women who defy the laws of a free society, it became an icon of American history. The terminology that entered the language from Sing Sing— "being sent up the river," "breaking rocks," "The Big House"—makes clear what a powerful place it occupied in the country's imagination. Alexis de Tocqueville, the noted French commentator who traveled across America, wrote in 1831 that it was impossible to contemplate the granite prison walls "without being struck by astonishment and fear."[14]

The building wasn't the only thing striking fear into inmates and visitors alike. Elam Lynds, a former army officer charged with erecting a new prison to accommodate the state's growing population, ran Sing Sing with an iron grip. While the stated goal of the institution was to turn criminals away from their past behavior through hard work, discipline and an orderly life by virtue of the design of the structure, there was little but punishment and privation behind its walls.

Lynds told Tocqueville that he didn't put much stock in theories about reform and re-education initiatives. "I do not think you can control a large prison without the use of a whip, whatever those may think who only know human nature from books," he said.[15] Beatings and whippings were common, and prisoners who broke the rules were locked into pillories or suffocated in a cold-water shower bath. A march across the grounds was held every morning with the prisoners trooping in lockstep, leg to leg and arm to arm, a practice that continued until the early 1900s. And that was just at the beginning of the day. Inside the prison, rations of pain and brutality were served all day long, with little food to go with it.

An insight into the cruel conditions behind the walls was penned by a former inmate, Levi Burr, outraged at what he experienced at Sing Sing. A former army officer who had served in the War of 1812, Burr was a lawyer who was convicted of perjury over a convoluted business dealing—a legal trick used by unscrupulous landowners at the time, and leading to a conviction Burr vehemently denied. Once released after a three-year sentence at Sing Sing, he wrote a scathing indictment of prison conditions that he sent to state officials.[16]

New prisoners coming to the prison had their hair cut short, but it was mostly a cruel introduction into a world of misery. "His head is so much disfigured by clips and gashes in his head that he would hardly be known by an acquaintance," Burr wrote about a fellow inductee. New prisoners were also told to remain silent and not to speak to other prisoners for days, or weeks, after their arrival. Any violations were quickly met with whips and clubs, and often there were no violations at all to begin a beating. "A man was flogged for breaking his arm—another for smiling; and for mere trifles, those miserable hirelings put the unhappy subjects to the greatest torture," Burr recounted. One guard who didn't beat prisoners was dismissed in a few weeks.[17]

Burr recalled watching one whipping where 133 strikes were landed from "the cat," a weapon made of six strands of hard cord wound tight at one end, fastened to a stick. "While the afflicted subject was begging upon his knees and crying and writhing under the laceration that tore his skin in pieces from his back the deputy keeper approached and gave him a blow across his mouth with his cane that caused the blood to flow profusely," he wrote.[18]

The other tool of the trade Burr witnessed at Sing Sing was the cudgel, "a stick or cane of various sizes," and it was used liberally by the jail keepers. "The enumeration of times that I have seen this applied is wholly impossible.... I have seen it applied daily and almost every hour."[19] After the morning lockstep march, which Burr called a march "imitating or rather mocking a military drill," followed a day of heavy labor on the quarry. Intense hunger was a constant companion. "When there is a daily deficiency in food and the stomach not once satisfied for weeks together, the subject is in continual distress; and that such has been the case, I am a suffering witness. The cry of hunger was general."[20]

The morning began with a pint of "rye coffee," and the midday meal was a small piece of bread, about a quarter of a loaf, meat the size of a "hen's egg," and three or four small potatoes. The meal was usually pork, or beef less commonly, and sometimes cod and rice were served instead. At night, the meal was mush "which is made of Indian meal," or corn meal. Burr confessed that he ate the roots of shrubs and trees where he could find them. Prisoners worked in the quarry, loading granite blocks onto carts, with "the frequent application of the accustomed Cat and Cudgel." There was also a blacksmith's shop, a shoe shop and a locksmith's shop. Burr was struck by the mortality rate at the prison. "Many men have died in their cells in the night from various causes," he recounted, "and others, who have sought death by their own hands to end their miseries."[21]

In conclusion, the ex-convict said the institution did little to make a better future for prisoners. "The severity with which men are treated, certainly cannot benefit the state," he wrote. "Those who survive one or two years' service are afterwards little able to obtain a livelihood by manual labor. They are broken down in spirit and constitution, and are fitter subjects for the almshouse, than for any other employment. I know of many men who are broken down by hard service and by beating." Burr insisted above all that state leaders know what conditions were like behind prison walls: "It is only necessary that the people should be rightfully informed of the existence of an evil, that a remedy may be applied." His righteous exposé, however, did little to change conditions at the prison, and Sing Sing continued to be run with brutal applications of whips and clubs for decades.[22]

Sing Sing was famous for its varying forms of punishment, including the ultimate punishment, when it later became the home of the electric chair, a device that sent 614 convicts to their deaths. But before the electric chair, there was another form of law enforcement that dispensed justice with a very firm hand—at the end of a noose fastened around the neck. In the 18th and 19th century, the hangman was a literal, not a figurative job description.

The County Jail in White Plains, first built in the 1750s and then re-located in 1856, functioned as a death house for condemned prisoners. Eight men were known to have been executed at the jail between 1793 and 1884[23] and many other law-breakers were publicly whipped at the jail during the 1700s and 1800s.

Crowds of townspeople came from all over Westchester to watch the men die, and entrepreneurs sold space near the jailhouse walls for prime viewing spots. It was a strange mixture of carnival culture and gruesome spectacle. Local hotels and saloons did big business, and picnics were often spread out before the jailhouse. The death march to the gallows had its own set of traditions, and in their own way, the customs that sprung up under the noose and the 20-foot-high stone walls at the old prison were as illustrative of an earlier notion of criminal justice as the electric chair was for a later time.

The earliest execution on record took place in 1793. Thomas Ryer, a Loyalist in the Revolution who was connected with the ruling families of the county, shot a deputy sheriff in a barroom fight in Fordham (now in the Bronx, then in Westchester). He went to Canada but was extradited back to face punishment. He wrote one of the most literary farewell letters ever penned on death row to his wife. He referred to his upcoming execution by noting he was "soon to experience a separation between body and soul." Calling on his wife to lead a virtuous life after he was gone, Ryer wrote in the hours before his death, "I am now called upon to pay a debt.... I must therefore bid you adieu; wishing you not to mourn for me."[24]

One of the more macabre deaths combined an execution with the early form of medical experimentation. In 1837, Thomas Harland, 24, an Irishman by birth, attempted to rob a prominent Yonkers merchant. The robbery thwarted, he attacked with a meat cleaver a clerk who had pursued him. The clerk, William Wood, later died, and Harland was sentenced to death in January 1838. Several hundred people came out to watch the execution, and the state militia was called out to ensure order. Harland was duly hanged by the neck—but the state wasn't finished with him yet. His corpse was turned over to a team of physicians who ran primitive electrical currents through various appendages. These "galvanic" experiments, powered by a small battery, were conducted to determine whether muscular contractions could be created with electrical stimuli. During one phase of the experiment, which might have impressed Dr. Victor Frankenstein, it was reported that "muscular contractions of the arms ensued, at times raising up the hand and repulsing the hand of the assistant."[25]

An execution that drew enormous popular attention was that of George Wilson, a drifter who signed on to work as a cook and deckhand on the Eudora. The small schooner ran coal from New York to Connecticut, and one night while they slept in their bunks, Wilson murdered the captain, William Palmer, and a mate, Gilbert Pratt, with a hatchet, stole their belongings and lowered a boat to escape near City Island. He threw the bodies overboard and weighed them down, then scuttled the ship. Palmer's body was later identified by its tattoos; Pratt's was never found. Wilson was taken into custody and found in possession of the dead men's belongings, and he made a number of incriminating statements. After a lengthy legal proceeding over where he would be tried for a crime committed on the Long Island Sound, Wilson was put to trial in White Plains and issued a death sentence. Several thousand people came from all over the region to watch his death, and as a black man convicted in the killing of two white men, rumors abounded that the jail would be stormed and Wilson would never make it to the gallows erected by prison authorities. Militiamen were called out from across the state in a heavy show of force, fixing their bayonets as a throng of people jostled to watch the hanging on July 25, 1856, the first execution at the new county jail yard on Martine Avenue. "The place outside the prison was like a fair," reported the *New York Times*. "Booths were erected for the sale of beer, cider, oysters, clams, cakes, pies and cigars. One would have thought a great jubilee was to take place, and not that a man was to be hanged."[26] The hatchet used to cut the rope, dispatching Wilson, was the murder weapon used on his shipmates.

The newspapers of the era covered executions with enormous relish, and jailhouse interviews with the soon-to-be executed prisoners were staples of the popular press. Authorities were only too happy to oblige. The *New York World* under Joseph Pulitzer ran a two-day series on Angelo Cornetti as he awaited hanging in 1883. The grotesque behavior of his final hours, the pathetic howls as he was dragged to the platform where he would die, were all minutely detailed under a front-page headline in the *World*.[27]

The last to die by hanging was Thomas Hoffman, a 22-year-old drifter from Port Chester convicted of robbing and killing a local peddler with an axe in 1883. He was made to carry his own noose to the gallows, another old custom reserved for the condemned. In 1889, the state legislature ruled that executions would be carried out by electrocution.[28]

The hangings at the old county jail, which was shut down in 1938, were not done with the professional exactitude that a good hangman would approve. The executed apparently all died of asphyxiation, not by broken necks as intended. The structure on Martine Avenue was demolished in 1957 to make way for a parking lot. After the jail was shut down, visitors were allowed in for a final look. Old movie posters of silent-film stars, tattered and faded, were still plastered on walls. The most significant artifact still on site was the upright beam of the old gallows, carved with the initials of the men it had sent to the grave, the sole remaining artifact of an ancient punishment that dealt justice at the end of a rope.[29]

As the executions demonstrated, the public had a taste for violent spectacle. The pugilistic tradition, dating back to the days of the gladiators in ancient Rome, held a fascination in the world of 19th-century entertainment. Men who fought with their fists could become major celebrities and draw vast throngs of spectators, despite the sport's poor reputation with more refined society. Proximity to New York and the ease of river traffic also made Westchester a convenient location for Gotham's underworld to indulge its pleasures.

A bloody contest that evoked the fight-to-the-death ethos of the Roman Coliseum took place on a picturesque stretch of ground at Hastings-on-Hudson in 1842. Since boxing matches at the time were viewed as little more than criminal conventions accompanied by heavy drinking and rowdy behavior that often led to street brawls and rioting, city cops took a very dim view of the business, forcing fight promoters to look for out-of-the-way places to stage their shows. A pasture in Hastings near the Hudson was the designated spot. But what promised to be a demonstration of "the manly arts" turned into something else, a grisly death match. It was described in the contemporary press as the first fatal prize fight in the United States, and it darkened the sport's reputation for decades.

For two men who were paid to use their bodies and bare hands as weapons, they were rather small. Christopher Lilly weighed 135 pounds and was 23 at the time of the fight, while Tom McCoy, just past 21 years of age, was even lighter. He stood at five foot, two inches tall. Lilly was of English descent, while McCoy, who worked as a "boatman," traced his ancestry to the Emerald Isle. The two held a previous grudge of some sort and were eager to fight.

The promoter of the contest was James "Yankee" Sullivan, a bare-knuckle fighter himself who knew what life was like on the wrong side of the law. Born in Ireland, he came of age in London before being transported to Australia on a criminal conviction. He became a brawler who put his talents to work in the ring and the rough-and-tumble world of politics in New York City as a saloon owner and enforcer. Sullivan arranged the match between Lilly and McCoy and chartered boats to bring spectators to the site in Hastings for the big show. On a bright, clear Tuesday morning, twelve vessels steamed up from the city: The *Saratoga* carried McCoy, and the *Indiana* served as Lilly's ship. About 2,000 to 3,000 people showed up for the fight by coach or steamship from the city, while a small contingent of locals also assembled. About 20 to 30 women were drawn to the spectacle, but the crowd was almost entirely men.

The boxing game that Lilly and McCoy engaged in followed a code from the London Prize Ring Rules that forbade eye-gouging, hair-pulling and other dirty tricks. But it would be decades before this country adopted the new standards of the fight game, the Marquis of Queensbury rules which established timed rounds and prohibited the most punishing blows and "ungentlemanly" tactics. Too late for Lilly and McCoy. In their day, fights could go on for hours. A single round lasted until a fighter went down to the ground, usually by some kind of wrestling move. At that point a 30-second break was called before the fighters had to return to a center line in the canvas, called "coming to scratch." No matter how badly beaten a fighter was, no one stopped the fight. And since fighters had a break and time to recover between knockdowns, knockouts were almost impossible. The only way for a fight to end was for a boxer to surrender, or fail to "make scratch." Both Lilly and McCoy had been involved in small-time fights before in the New York area, but nothing prepared them for the gladiator-like conflict that awaited them on the banks of the Hudson on September 13, 1842.

It was an ideal spot for the purpose. "The position of the ground was excellent, being on a flat, lying between the Croton Aqueduct and the Hudson, slightly declining, thus giving an amphitheatrical view from the ropes to the top of the reservoir," recorded Enoch Camp, a reporter for the *New York Herald* who gave the fullest account of the battle and later provided a deposition in the criminal inquiry.[30] The two fighters stripped down to their britches and, as per tradition, Lilly tossed his hat in the ring, and McCoy did likewise, meaning they had accepted a challenge to fight. They would do battle for a prize of $200. But before they could begin trading blows, a curious visitor entered the ring.

Jasper Golden, a schoolmaster from Dobbs Ferry and justice of the peace, tried to stop the fight. He had walked two miles to Yonkers to gather a posse of citizens to intervene, and unsuccessful in his attempts to find anyone to accompany him, returned to the sporting grounds by himself. Given the go-ahead by Yankee Sullivan to address the crowd, the schoolmaster entered the ring and asked "in the name of the law, to desist." He was met with stony silence and a few jeers, then left. Golden stayed on to watch the fight so he could give testimony, he later explained, on what he viewed as a criminal enterprise. "I had no officer with me, and as the parties were so numerous, I did not proceed any further in the attempt," he later said.[31]

The fight was on just before one o'clock. McCoy fought in the traditional style, relying mostly on body shots to fell an opponent. Lilly was a practitioner of a new form of boxing that concentrated blows to the head and neck, and it was a technique—blow after blow to the head—that was likely to inflict extensive damage to an opponent. McCoy punched hard in the first rounds and gave the impression that he would make a fight of it, but his blows did not make much of an impact on Lilly. The reverse was the case, as Lilly landed blows on McCoy, and after the first 30 minutes had elapsed, it was clear who held the upper hand. As each successive blow landed on McCoy's face, the fight turned into a lopsided contest about an hour in, prompting one spectator to shout: "Ain't Chris [Lilly] a portrait painter?"[32]

As the *Herald* reported in its description of every round of the fight, McCoy was taking big shots to the head: "Round 20—Lilly put in another potato-trap smasher, and threw his man in the clinch…. Round 25—Lilly gave him one on the old spot, the dice box, and at the clinch they both went down…. Round 62—McCoy's breeches were wet through with perspiration which flowed off his back in streams. Lilly was comparatively dry and his face was free from scratch except the slight cut on his nose…. Round 78— McCoy came up bleeding at mouth and nose, and appeared as though he could not catch his breath free, from the clotted blood in his throat."[33]

By the 86th round, both McCoy's eyes shut, while Lilly scarcely showed a mark. McCoy was clearly losing, but he refused to yield. Before the encounter, he had tied a black bandana in his corner of the ring, an indication that he was prepared to fight to the death. As the *Herald*'s sportswriter noted, "McCoy never expressed a desire to leave the ring, but appeared determined to win, or die in the effort."[34]

McCoy still came on well after the two-hour mark. Barely recognizable behind a mask of blood and swollen flesh, both eyes lanced to allow him some vision, the fighter struggled again and again to make scratch. His final words, heard by his cornermen, were ones of astonishing bravado: "Nurse me, nurse me, and I'll beat him yet."[35] Cries of "Take him away, shame, shame" were heard from the crowd, but still it continued. By the 119th round, "it was evident now that he was as near gone as a man could be," the *Herald* reported. McCoy was finally unable to stand for the 120th round, two hours and 42 minutes after the fight had started.[36]

As Enoch Camp reported, Lilly was declared the victor, and "he bounded over the ropes, amid the cheers and huzzahs of a large proportion of the assemblage." Inside the ring, his opponent lay dying. "In an instant, we heard the cry of 'Stand back, give the man air,' and on rushing to the centre of the ring, discovered McCoy lying upon the ground in the last struggles of death. He breathed loudly for several aspirations, and then ceased," the *Herald* sports reporter wrote.[37]

McCoy's body was loaded upon a wooden board and placed aboard the *Saratoga* for the trip back to New York City, and the spectators, now sullen and gloomy, quickly dispersed. News of the pugilist's death caused an outrage in New York and Westchester. Crowds thronged to McCoy's brother's house in Manhattan where the body was taken. A coroner's inquest found that McCoy had died from "strangulation from blood proceeding from his mouth and nose." The autopsy also revealed that his nose was "flattened upon the face and the bones broken."[38] The doomed bare-fisted boxer was denied a Catholic-cemetery burial and laid to rest at Potters Field, the eternal home of the indigent and the truly unfortunate. An untimely death, and an anonymous grave: it may be one of the saddest American sporting stories of them all, and one of the oldest. A grand jury quickly convened and issued arrest warrants for the principal organizers of the fight. Lilly shipped out to Canada and then England to avoid prosecution.

A trial was held at White Plains, attracting a major sensation. The inns of White Plains were booked as prosecutors laid out their case against Sullivan and two organizers, John McClusky, Lilly's second, and George Kensett, the assistant to McCoy. Gaudily dressed gamblers up from the city to watch the case contrasted sharply with the village folks of White Plains and a jury composed of farmers and tradesmen. Guilty verdicts eventually came back for the three ringleaders of the fight. Sullivan was sentenced to a two-year term but spent only a few weeks at Sing Sing, using his political connections to gain a governor's pardon. McClusky was sentenced to eight months in the county jail; Kensett got four months.[39]

They might have gotten off lightly, but the violence of the boxing world followed the prize fight winner and the promoter. Sullivan later committed suicide in a San Francisco jail cell in 1856, cutting himself and severing an artery in his arm, though an alternate theory contends he was murdered there. Lilly died in a military adventure in 1857 in Nicaragua where he signed on as a hired gun.

The sport of boxing was tarnished by the "Battle of Hastings" for years afterwards. The *Westchester Herald* fulminated "that if this class of bullies ever again pollute our soil, the power of the country, in the shape of bayonets and musket balls, if needed, will teach them they deserve to be treated as outlaws of society."[40] Commentators saw grave dangers in the lawless gangsters and ruffians, often recent immigrants, threatening the orderly status quo. As the *New York Tribune* articulated, the fight game was in its view just one appendage of a larger, more insidious enterprise: "How shall we speak of the getters up and encouragers of this fight?—the gamblers, the brothel-masters, and keepers of flesh-groggeries, who were ever the chief patrons of 'the ring,' and who were the choice spirits of this festival of fiends? They were in rapture as the well-aimed, deadly blows descended heavily upon the face and neck of the doomed victim … they yelled with delight as the combatants went down … with a force that made the earth tremble around them."[41] Many commentators hoped the deadly battle of Hastings would put an end to boxing in New York forever. They were overly confident in their predictions, and many others joined Tom McCoy on his trip to the coroner's slab.

The scene the boxing spectators saw on their journey up the Hudson was one of bucolic and agricultural splendor. Fruit tree orchards, wheat fields, pastures and barns mottled the hills overlooking the river. It was a vast breadbox for the growing city below it. Much of the land holdings that once belonged to the Loyalists, including the huge estate of Philipsburg Manor, was turned over to farmers who would otherwise have remained tenants on the land. It developed a culture of thrift and self-sufficiency.

What the area needed was stability and a determined work force, and in the 1800s, those ingredients came together to form a powerful new dynamic of commerce, transportation, infrastructure and agriculture.

The farming life was difficult, and hard work was an absolute necessity. But the farming life was softened by community and a shared sense of purpose. The recollection of the county's agricultural heritage by Jacob Read, a soldier who fought in the Revolution, paints a picture of a landscape enriched with orchards, fields and gardens, of homes lit by candles and open hearths. Cattle drives were a familiar sight.

"Through the 1820s and 1830s and up to the 1840s, the principal crops were oats, rye, wheat, corn, hay, potatoes and pickles," recalled Read, who lived in Yonkers. "The fruits were apples"—including "Pound Sweets," "Catheads" and "Fall Pippins"—as well as "peaches, pears and cherries…. We used to call tomatoes 'love apples' but nobody ate them," he went on. "I never ate tomatoes until 1847. We had good walnuts and chestnuts. The garden truck the farmers raised was for their own use only. Tables in those days were supplied with plenty of fresh meat. I remember that Mr. David Horton, with whom I lived, would kill a sheep in summer, or a lamb or a pig in the fall, so as to have fresh meat, and would send a quarter over to [neighboring farmers] and when they killed, they returned the favor. The poultry in the farm-yards also supplied the tables. Barrels of salted meats and hogsheads of cider, as also butter, lard, turnips and potatoes stocked the cellar. Blacksmiths, wheelwrights and carpenters made many agricultural instruments which they are not expected to make to-day."[42]

Livestock was a big production. "Beef and ham were smoked in the farmers' smoke-houses," Read wrote. "Up to 1845 sheep were kept. The lambs were sold in New York. Pork and poultry were also sent to New York. Large droves of cattle and sheep from the north passed through Yonkers down the Albany post-road. Perhaps as many as two hundred or two hundred and fifty cows and from three hundred to five hundred sheep would be in a single drove. Two or three men or two men and a boy could manage a drove." Each season had its varying demands. January and February was the time to cut enough wood to last through the summer, and teams of oxen would pull heavy sleds packed with timber. March was the month to repair stone walls and fences, to cut back brush. The construction of new stone walls and the preparation of fields consumed April. Corn and potatoes were planted in May. In June, the cucumbers were sown—every farmer had a pickle patch to satisfy New York's insatiable demand for the briny snacks—and sheep were sheared and cherries picked. The great harvest of corn, hay and vegetables fell in July. August was framed by apples sent to market and pickling cucumbers that were plucked. September was another market month, bringing the farm's bounty to the wider world, and October the month for husking corn. November was the time to dig potatoes, slaughter hogs and poultry, make cider. December was a quiet month on the farm.[43]

While luxury was rare for most, simple pleasures and attractions of the natural world were abundant. "The bay was alive with people of all ages, sexes and conditions," wrote artist Benson Lossing one wintry day in the 1850s on the banks of the Hudson. "It was the first day since a late snow-storm that the river had offered good sport for skaters and the navigators of ice boats. It was a gay scene. Wrapped in furs and shawls, over-coats and cloaks, men and women, boys and girls, were enjoying the rare exercise with the greatest pleasure. Fun, pure fun, ruled the hour. The air was vocal with shouts and laughter; and when the swift ice boat, with sails set, gay pennons streaming, and freighted with a dozen boys and girls, came sweeping gracefully toward the crowd…. There was a sudden shout, and scattering and merry laughter."[44]

Lossing also saw ice fisherman attending to their duties. "I encountered other groups of people, who appeared in positive contrast with the merry skaters on Peek's Kill Bay," he wrote. "They were sober, thoughtful, winter fishermen, thickly scattered across over the surface, and drawing their long nest from the narrow fissures which they had cut in the ice." Striped bass, perch and sturgeon pulled from the water "instantly congealed in the keen wintry air."[45]

This world of rustic pleasures and handmade tools was not without oddities and mystery. The Leatherman was a strange visitor who beguiled the populace in Westchester and southern Connecticut with his unusual appearance and perplexing routine. He wore a leather suit of his own design, stitched together with patches recovered from old boots and horse harnesses. His hat was similarly made of leather and he wore this bespoke crazy quilt in all kinds of weather. If his appearance was unkempt, his travels across the countryside were almost as regular as clockwork. He walked a 365-mile circuit between Connecticut and New York on a regular schedule, stopping in the same locations every time with eerie precision. The route ran from the Connecticut River and the Hudson River, with stops in South Salem, Mount Kisco, Croton Falls, Bedford, Yorktown, Mount Pleasant and Briarcliff. He slept in caves, impromptu tents and lived off the charity of well-wishers who fed him along his solitary path.[46]

From the mid–1850s on until his death at the George Dell farm in Mount Pleasant, the Leatherman remained shrouded in mystery, despite the best efforts of newspaper reporters, scholars and friendly inquisitors to pierce the leathery veil of obscurity that cloaked him on his strange journey.

One account held that he was Jules Bourglay, from Lyon in France, and that he had been bankrupted and heart-broken through some bad dealings with a wealthy leather merchant, and his journeys represented a form of penance.[47] But this version was simply the creation of a fanciful newspaper writer. Other observers believed he was French Canadian. The Leatherman would occasionally converse in short phrases in accented English or French with visitors, but more often grunted and remained silent.

The Leatherman was a hermit who lived in plain sight. He wore a leather suit of his own design and roamed Westchester and southern Connecticut with near-clocklike regularity. A profound mystery to those who observed him on his route, his strange journey ended in a grave at the Sparta Cemetery in Ossining in 1889 (Westchester County Historical Society).

Despite his fearsome getup, he was harmless. Perhaps he was autistic, as some latter-day observers have suggested.

Other vagabonds were not as easily tolerated. The 1870s saw a major economic downturn, and tramps were everywhere, and likely to be locked up, but the odd leather-encased traveller was permitted to carry out his wanderings without incident. The laws were never applied to the Leatherman.

He appeared to travel with a French prayer book and a grip-sack containing a small hatchet and other utensils. He had gray eyes, a weather-beaten face and used a wooden staff as he walked. Occasionally he would sit for a photographer to take his picture. His portrait reveals a peculiar, almost enchanted enigma, a childhood fairy tale come to life.

In the final years of his life, the old tramp developed a cancerous lesion on his face after a longtime habit of tobacco consumption. Medical authorities in Connecticut tried to intervene and at one point took him to Hartford Hospital, but he escaped and resumed his journey. Even the massive Blizzard of 1888 only slowed him down by a few days from making his appointed rounds. The cancer spread, and made the Leatherman an even more pitiable sight. He could only eat bread soaked in coffee during those last months.

His journey of some 100,000 miles came to an end in March 1889. He was found dead in a cave, and the coroner ruled he had died of blood poisoning associated with cancer. A pauper's grave in the Sparta Cemetery was his final resting place. The original grave site was next to the highway. As his fame grew in the 20th century and a memorial was erected in his honor, regular visitors were posing a safety threat. In 2011 his grave was relocated to a more central place in the cemetery. It was hoped that some DNA samples or other artifacts could shed light on the mystery of the Old Leatherman. But nothing remained except for a few coffin nails.[48]

Chauncey Hotchkiss was one of the Leatherman's supporters who often visited with him when his journey took him to a cave in Bristol, Connecticut. Hotchkiss told the *Hartford Globe* in 1885, "The more one knows concerning him, the more enigmatical he appears. I have arrived at this conclusion, that no mortal will ever know the real 'story of the Leatherman.'"[49] That description, more than 100 years later, has proven remarkably apt.

The agricultural plentitude that could sustain wanderers like the Leatherman also sustained the vast city to the south. New York City received the bounty of Westchester's farms and orchards by ship from the waterways of the Hudson River and Long Island Sound. The "sloop," as it was known, from the old Dutch word "*sloep*," was the small single-masted maritime workhorse that cruised the waters laden with fresh produce, grain, flour and lumber. Easy to maneuver, fitted with a retractable keel, the sloop was well designed to sail the Hudson and its shoals. The docks at Ossining and Port Chester (then known as Sawpits) were maritime hubs for the transport of produce destined for the city. On any given day a traveler on the Hudson River could take in the sight of dozens of boats plying the winds against the backdrop of the Palisades. On Long Island Sound, boats skimmed the waves and harvested the abundant beds of shellfish. Boat-building was a major enterprise all over the region, and the men who sailed the sloops were held in high regard.

Moses Collyer, a captain whose father, Thomas, was a boat builder from Ossining, recalled the various skills that the Hudson River sloop captains needed to run their operation. "These North River sloop boatmen, as they were called in those days, were prominent men, and were the businessmen of the Hudson Valley. They not only had to know how to sail and manage their sloops in all kinds of weather, but also to know the depth of water all along the Hudson…. Their captains also had to know good harbors and anchorages, and where the winds from different quarters would be dangerous. Their captains, also, had to be good businessmen."[50] Steamboats began to make an appearance on the river alongside the wind-driven sloops after Robert Fulton's Clermont made its first Hudson trip in 1807.

The easy access to the river and Long Island Sound offered great potential to the growing metropolitan region. The river and the Sound were both majestic sights and valuable conduits for transportation. The water in those bodies were not, however, drinkable, and this posed a great challenge for the growth of the region.

Great cities are built with bricks, mortar and steel, but perhaps more than anything else, they are built on water. Since ancient times, when the aqueducts of Rome became symbols of its power, cities have risen based on their ability to deliver water. The power to bend nature to its will is the first requirement of urban life, of a city on the move. New York City was no different. The construction of the aqueduct, the great engineering marvel that surged its way through Westchester with dynamite and stone, brought clean Westchester water to New York City in 1842 and finally eliminated the major geographical impediment that stood in the way of Gotham's rise to greatness. It also transformed Westchester, literally changing the landscape of the region as well as the people who lived in it.

The city was troubled from its earliest days by a lack of potable water, due to its position at the mouth of two salt-water rivers. Several freshwater springs in lower Manhattan became fouled as industry and residences grew up around them, and the inaccessibility of a good water supply became one of the city's best-known shortcomings. "It is a pity that so rich and luxurious a city which lavishes countless thousands upon curious wines, cannot afford itself wholesome water," the writer Washington Irving commented to a friend in 1832.[51]

It was no laughing matter. A terrifying cholera epidemic in 1832 killed 3,500 citizens, and while medical authorities did not yet connect the disease with the deadly pathogen contaminating the water supply, as scientists would later ascertain, they correctly surmised that bad water was at the root of the problem. Vast fires that destroyed whole neighborhoods also made the implementation of a large new water source an urgent priority.

And so city engineers set their sights on Westchester. The Bronx River and the Saw Mill River were quickly dismissed as too small, but when engineers surveyed the Croton River, they saw in its watery abundance the solution to the city's water shortage. One problem was quickly apparent: it was a long, long way from the city. But there appeared to be no other feasible alternative, and the plan was approved to bring water to the city, an enormous undertaking of 41 miles of tunnels, bridges and embankments, plus the dam work itself, running down the western spine of Westchester and then into the Bronx and Manhattan—most of it hard, rocky terrain. It required all of the brawn and brilliance that an ambitious city could muster.

John Jervis, an engineering genius whose previous work on the Erie Canal gained him favor for the aqueduct project, created the final plans for the water tunnel and oversaw its construction, and in 1837 thousands of workers were put into service of one of the great engineering marvels of its age.

It was dangerous work blasting hundreds of tons of rock and ferrying huge quantities of stone. Scores were killed and injured in Westchester before it was to be completed. Delving deep underground, the brick-lined tunnel used gravity and a gradual incline to send water downstream to the city, dropping 13 inches a mile.

The dam construction was not complete without a major disaster at the dam site itself, beside the routine accidents that claimed the lives of workmen along the way. It was called "the Great Freshet" of 1841, and it was a night of terror for dozens of local families and workers who lived near the construction site of the Croton Dam. The result of an unusual weather pattern—a hard, snowy winter followed by an unusual thaw at the start of January—the floodwaters began to rise after 18 inches of melting snowpack were mixed with three days of heavy rain. On January 8, rivers and streams were at their bursting point. The still incomplete dam was at the center of a raging surge of water, and in the early morning hours, the flood smashed through the barrier. Huge chunks of ice and the remains of houses and bridges upriver came crashing down the river valley at 3 a.m. One worker, Patrick Burke, was quickly swept away after the initial burst and later found three miles away, dead, "much bruised and his clothing nearly all torn off," according to a news account following the disaster.[52]

Screams, shouts and horns awakened the nearby inhabitants of the river valley, who were soon a in foot race for their lives. Wearing bedclothes, dozens of local villagers ran for higher ground or scampered up trees to avoid the frigid, raging water. Two workers, John Evans and Robert Smith, had the misfortune of picking a short cedar tree that

Water from the Croton River allowed New York City to grow into a giant metropolis. The Old Croton Dam, completed in 1842 and depicted in a painting by Robert Havell, eliminated the scourge of cholera that had plagued the city for generations (Marc Cheshire/crotonhistory.org).

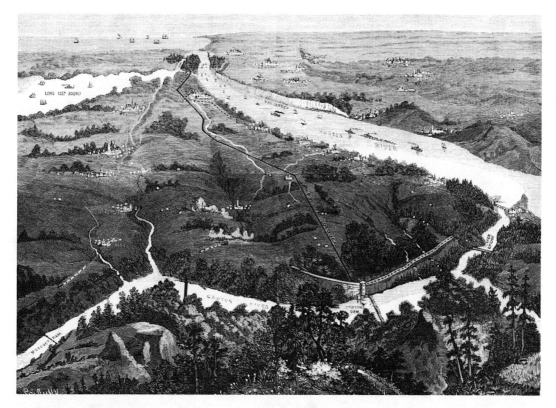

The Croton Dam and the Croton Aqueduct that brought drinking water to New York City was an engineering marvel. In this 1887 cover illustration for the *Scientific American,* a black line shows the path of the waterway as it runs south to New York City (Marc Cheshire/crotonhistory.org).

buckled under the current, and their screams rose above the roar of the water as they went under. "They were carried away amid their unavailing cry for assistance," according to the account of the disaster in the *Hudson River Chronicle.*[53] Rescuers were soon out using makeshift rafts made from barn doors plucking survivors from the trees. The last to be rescued was a mother and her infant five hours later. Observers later noted that it was remarkable that only three fatalities were caused by the flood.

The dam was badly damaged, but Jervis conceived of a new and better barrier employing an S-shape that became a standard design feature put in use at dams across the country.

The construction of the aqueduct was deeply unpopular in the county where it originated. There were fights over land rights and challenges to the old farming character of the county. It brought the city's influence where many felt it did not belong. It brought noise and disruption. And to the dismay of the many old inhabitants of Dutch and English descent, it also brought the Irish. But the work carried on. Anti-Irish sentiment, the dam burst and dismay over the corrupting influence of the city notwithstanding, the work was finished in 1842, and the tap was turned on. It was a huge celebration. The aqueduct represented the city's triumph over the twin scourges of disease and fire, and the great metropolis was finally liberated from dirty wells and a corrupt water company that supplied a thin trickle of foul-smelling liquid. The 8½-foot-high, 7½-foot-wide tunnel pumped the life blood of a city through its stone arteries.

More dams would follow the construction of the first one at Croton, as the growing metropolis' unslakable thirst for water rose with its population. New and bigger dams and reservoirs had to be built to keep up. The second Croton Dam, which ended up submerging the older one built in 1841, was finished in 1906. In 1885, the first Kensico Dam was completed, and the larger Kensico Dam was finished in 1915. The dams changed the landscape of the entire region in perpetuity. Hundreds of acres of farmland were taken for the work, and whole villages such as Katonah were uprooted and moved to new locations to accommodate the reservoirs destined for New York City faucets.

Westchester was transformed in the process. The massive dams were majestic achievements in their own rights, powerful symbols of a nation's determination to build on a colossal scale. The county and the great city to its south were also to be irrevocably bound by the underground torrent of water. The oversight and management of the water supply would remain a complicated and often controversial arrangement between the two neighbors for generations to come, but it tied the city to Westchester, for better or worse.

The waterworks were just the beginning of a new kind of union between city and suburb. The railroad was the next step, when the age of sail would soon be eclipsed by a revolutionary new device: the steam engine. The New York and Harlem line began in 1838, and it laid tracks north over the preceding years. It reached White Plains in 1844.

The work to build the new Croton Dam, completed in 1906, employed thousands of laborers. A strike by laborers mobilized the National Guard in 1900 and led to the shooting death of a guardsman from Mount Vernon by an unknown assailant (Marc Cheshire/crotonhistory.org).

Yonkers was made accessible by rail in 1847. The Hudson River Railroad came to Peekskill in 1849—and 830 passengers a day were being carried the first month of operation. Along the Sound Shore, the railroad laid tracks and opened depots in late 1848.[54] The construction of the railroad led to new opportunities and growth wherever the tracks were laid.

The new transportation system connected Gotham with its northern neighbors in ways that would have profound impacts on the region, the way people lived, worked and connected with the land. Planned communities began to emerge from the Westchester countryside, and opportunities for new housing followed as the ease of transportation made country homes an attractive option for the wealthy.

In 1842, a landscape designer with impeccable taste wrote a book, *Victorian Cottage Residences*, that changed the way homes were built. Andrew Jackson Downing saw the home and the family as the twin pillars of a successful and virtuous society, and he set out to make the open spaces outside the city into something exceptional. As architectural historian Adolf Placzek summarized, "He was the propagator and pioneer of the small inexpensive detached house—the cottage—in a non-urban setting. This type of dwelling in all its variations … created the American suburb and, as has been said, made over the face of the land."[55]

Downing was the first great tastemaker of the American suburb. While he worked explicitly for the very wealthy, his ideas carried over into every strata of society. Above all he believed that virtue was best enclosed by a one-family home with some greenery around it. "A good house (and by this I mean a fitting, tasteful and significant dwelling) is a powerful means of civilization," he wrote. "When smiling lawns and tasteful cottages begin to embellish a country, we know that order and culture are established."[56]

Working in collaboration with architect Alexander Jackson Davis, he developed plans for cottages, farmhouses and villas, and in their proper construction, for the ideal American way of life. A popularizer and advocate, channeling the ideas of high-end architects, his opinions on color of homes, furnishings, landscape were spread far and wide. He was a great believer in the front porch, which became a characteristically American addition to a home.

Though his clients were extremely wealthy, Downing was put off by ostentatious displays of wealth and criticized homes which he believed to be too large for their own good. "These attempts at great establishments are always and inevitably, failures in America. And why? Plainly, because they are contrary to the spirit of republican institutions; because the feelings on which they are based can never take root; except in a government of hereditary right; because they are wholly in contradiction to the spirit of our time and people," he wrote.[57]

The home of Washington Irvington just north of Tarrytown was held up as a model of country living and a strong link to the natural world by Downing and Davis. Downing, a resident of Newburgh, designed an estate in Bedford off Croton Lake Road known as the Woodpile. His colleague, Davis, was the architect of Lyndhurst in Tarrytown and Wildcliff in New Rochelle.

Downing's life came to an end in 1852 in a spectacular disaster. The growing transportation network along the Hudson that allowed for commuters and travelers to get to and from Westchester was not without its share of perils, and Downing was one of those who paid the price as progress rumbled recklessly ahead.

The explosive nature of the steamships were a persistent and deadly feature of the era, "the nineteenth century's first confrontation with industrialized mayhem," in the words of historian Walter Johnson.[58] The disaster on the Hudson was the result of two steamships embarking on a customary practice on the river at the time: a race.

The *Henry Clay* was a side-wheeled steamer of the latest design and technology that likely made her the fastest ship on the river. The 300 or so travelers who paid a half-dollar to board her on that day in late July in Albany (with stops at Hudson, Catskill, Poughkeepsie and Newburgh) looked for a speedy, comfortable and pleasant ride to lower Manhattan. But the prospect of a scenic trip down the river vanished when it became clear the ship was engaged in a race with the nearby *Armenia* to test each other's speed and skill—a reckless habit that steamship crews carried out despite earlier disasters. As they sped down the Hudson, the two ships maneuvered and jousted with each other, even bumping once along the way. The passengers yelled at the crew to stop the antics, but the race continued, and at Sing Sing, trouble took hold in the *Henry Clay*'s overheated boilers as strange noise emanated from the ship's bowels. The *Armenia* was far behind, unable to keep pace.[59]

By the time the ship reached Yonkers, the first wisps of smoke could be seen drifting up from a hatchway amidships, and they soon turned into a thick plume of black smoke and fire. Now fully aflame, the pilot, Edward Hubbard, turned the bow into shore at Riverdale and rammed the ship onto land. "Down the stream with fearful rapidity came what seemed a mass of living fire," wrote Russell Smith, a state Assemblyman on whose property the ship crashed. "Beneath her rolled the waters of the Hudson; above and around her forked flames of fire darted forth; while at the same moment a hundred human voices rent the air with their shrieks."[60]

Boats and steamships were a major form of 19th century transportation. *The Mary Powell*, framed here against the Hudson Highlands, plied the river from 1861 to 1917 (Hastings Historical Society).

The ship ran 25 feet up the river bank, and the tremendous impact knocked loose the ship's timbers and gave new breath to the flames. About 80 people died in the disaster, the Hudson's worst. The inquest was held in Yonkers, where bodies were stored in pine coffins for identification. Downing was one of the victims. A capable swimmer, he stayed on board and assisted other passengers. He was later found to have drowned. His wife, Caroline, survived the wreck.

"The last scenes of the day were singularly impressive and solemn," Westchester County coroner William Lawrence wrote in his diary that night. "The night was remarkably clear, the full moon dimly lighting up the river and the hills ... the bow still slowly burning; half revealed in its lurid light lay bodies of two men.... The surface of the stream, placid and silent as the grave, was broken only by the oars of a few men who were still dredging for bodies." Lawrence was forced to draw his pistol at one point in the night to chase off a boatload of looters who descended on the crash site.[61]

Five victims, three women and two men, were never identified or claimed, and more than a week after the wreck, the time came to lay them to rest. "The bodies were placed on a cart, and the melancholy procession moved slowly up the hill of Yonkers.... The solemn tones of the village bell rung out for those so untimely and fearfully hurried into strange and unhonored graves," the *New York Times* reported before internment at the St. John's Cemetery.[62]

The inquest and subsequent criminal charges led to a trial a year after the wreck in which the defendants, the officers associated with the misconduct aboard the doomed ship, were acquitted. State legislators, meanwhile, passed rigid new laws that put an end to steamboat races.

New York and its northern suburbs had long benefited from maritime trade that the *Henry Clay* embodied. Merchants in the city, along with insurance brokers, financiers and associated business interests, thrived on trade—and not just any kind of trade, but trade that made its profits from slavery. The cotton, sugar and tobacco that flowed from the south made businessmen in New York very rich, and slavery was an inextricable part of that market. While New York had banned all slavery from its soil in 1827, following the gradual act of emancipation that began in 1799, the institution had flourished in the south, and the division between free and slave was impossible to ignore.

The Underground Railroad, as it was known, was set up by abolitionists to help runaway slaves escape their bondage. It took the fugitives who had escaped their slave masters and transported them to Canada or abolitionist strongholds in the United States, like Upstate New York, where they would be safe. The Fugitive Slave Law of 1850 established penalties for those who sheltered runaway slaves, and it gave bounty hunters the license to capture fugitives anywhere in the United States. It pushed the conflict over slavery into new directions, and it also brought out renewed resolve on the part of those who opposed slavery to help those in need.

While there were a number of other more well-traveled routes to freedom, a portion of the Underground Railroad ran through Westchester. Specifics are hard to come by. The secretive nature of the work, the dangers it entailed and the unpopularity of the assistance to slaves even after the institution of slavery had passed all militated against the preservation of records or testimony.

Much of the local impetus to shelter runaway slaves in Westchester came from the substantial Quaker population in the county. The Society of Friends, as the Quakers are known, have a long history in Westchester. Persecution by Puritans, and a particular hostility from the Dutch toward the movement, drove large numbers of Friends to the region. Mamaroneck was where Quakers first congregated in 1680s, and they then spread to an adjoining area, where Friend John Harrison bought a large tract in 1695 from Indians that came to bear his name. Settlement of Harrison by Quakers took place in the early 1700s, and later in Scarsdale, whose population was about one-third Quakers by the middle of the 1700s.[63]

Guided by a belief that an "inner light" connected a person with God and pointed the way to a meaningful life, Quakers were distinctive for their plain clothing, simplicity, unadorned churches and services with no ministers. They believed strongly in the improvement of the larger world around them, a devout sense of equality, education and total honesty. It was a faith that gave women a much more equitable role in society than other religious traditions, and women were allowed to speak and "preach" at Quaker meetings when such practices were unheard of in other faiths. It was common for townsfolk to send their children to Quaker markets to buy goods and food, knowing the youngsters would not be cheated. Many of the Quakers were prosperous farmers and tradesmen. They refused to take an oath of allegiance using the words "in the name of God," believing it implied they were otherwise untruthful. Their belief in pacifism became legendary.

While Quakers in the early days of the colonies had owned slaves, it eventually became anathema to their beliefs, and the Society of Friends became a major force in the anti-slavery cause. When Congress passed the Fugitive Slave Law in 1850 requiring runaway slaves to be returned to their masters—and making it a crime to assist or shield a runaway slave in the north—these abolitionists put their faith to the test, even if it ended in a jail cell.

Besides the Quakers, Westchester had an abolitionist leader with an illustrious family name who championed the fight against slavery at the national level. William Jay, the son of Chief Justice John Jay, who resided at the family estate in Bedford and served as a Westchester county judge, was one the movement's most ardent advocates. A founder of the New York Anti-Slavery Society, he lost his seat as a local judge serving on the county bench due to his outspoken abolitionist sentiment. Jay once handed out anti-slavery tracts in Arabic on a visit to Egypt. The historical record is somewhat unclear on where or how he hid fugitives himself, but his correspondence indicated he was an active participant. "I have a fugitive who wishes to go to Boston, via Albany. Do give me via return mail the names of one or more in each place to whom a consignment can be safely made," he wrote in an 1854 letter to an Underground Railroad organizer, Sydney Howard Gay, that was later uncovered.[64] His son, John Jay II, was also an abolitionist.

The Quakers believed in living their principles, and in 1840, a Friend, Joseph Carpenter, started a black cemetery in New Rochelle, on Weaver Street near Stratton Road (aka Quaker Ridge), where he and his wife were eventually buried themselves. In a stunning photo of Joseph Carpenter from the era, he poses with a young black girl about five years old.[65] His son-in-law, Moses Pierce, became a leading figure in the Westchester branch of the Underground Railroad. Born in 1816, he owned a farm in Thornwood and later moved with his wife, Esther, to Pleasantville.[66]

At his Quaker eulogy at the Chappaqua meeting house a year after his death in 1886, it was recorded: "Early interested in the abolition of slavery, he did all he was able to accomplish that end; and it was his privilege to aid many fugitive slaves, in their escape from bondage."[67]

Pierce collaborated with William Jay, and a letter from Jay in Bedford to Pierce, published in abolitionist newspapers in Pennsylvania and Boston, spelled out their cause and their tactics: "As we fear God and hope for his favor at the last day, let us harbor, succor, secrete and aid with food, clothing, money and advice, every fugitive who seeks our protection, regardless of the statutes which make such acts of mercy penal offences [sic]; and then let us unresistingly enter the dungeons to which sinful laws may consign us."[68]

Jonathan Pierce, Moses's son, described the operations of the Underground Railroad in 1939, as the story was handed down to him by family members. He referenced Joseph Carpenter in New Rochelle, the place where his mother was raised, as the point of origin for runaways heading out from New York City. "My mother's home, Joseph Carpenter, New Rochelle, was the first Station out of New York City; my father's home…. Pleasantville, was the second Station; Judge John Jay, Bedford, was the third station. The aunt's home, David Irish, Quaker Hill (Pawling), was the fourth Station. At that place, 60 miles from N.Y., the fugitives

Joseph Carpenter, a Quaker and farmer from New Rochelle, sheltered runaway slaves on the Underground Railroad heading north from New York City. He started a cemetery for African Americans and was buried among them (Aaron Powell, *Personal Reminiscences of the Anti-Slavery and Other Reforms and Reformers,* Caulon Press, 1899).

were far enough on the way to Canada to find their way safely." The runaways were typically hidden in wagons concealed with produce.[69]

While the Underground Railroad put a small number of slaves on the road to freedom, about a thousand a year, the institution of slavery was not only enduring but expanding into new territories. The question of slavery was the national dilemma, and Westchester was divided. The county tended to follow New York's political and commercial inclinations, and that meant a proclivity toward the cause of slavery. Slavery was good business for the mercantile sector of New York, so what was good for slavery was good for the banks, shipping companies and insurers of the North that profited from "the peculiar institution," as it came to be known.

Westchester was solidly in the ranks of the Democratic Party, which was ill at ease with the cause of abolition and sought accommodation with the Southern states. When the presidential election of 1860 was held, the Republican candidate, Abraham Lincoln, got 39 percent of the county's vote, 6,771 to 8,100 for candidates on the other slate.[70] His vote totals were higher the further north of New York City one went.

Before he was even seated in the White House, the Southern states had seceded from the Union. As Lincoln made his way to Washington to take the oath of office, he made many stops along the way during a 12-day sojourn to promote his legitimacy after the contentious election and prove his bona fides as a strong national leader. He had no initial plans to stop in Westchester on his way to New York City, but as a favor to a former congressional ally and friend from Peekskill, William Nelson, he agreed to make a stop on the shores of the Hudson.

The *Highland Democrat* of Peekskill reported that the president-elect looked "jaded, fatigued and as if just aroused from a nap, but when he commenced speaking, his whole countenance lighted up."[71] According to a reprint of the speech in the *New York Herald*, he acknowledged "the difficulties that lie before me and our beloved country." He concluded his short remarks by asking for help, from the kind of citizens who had come to hear him speak. "Without your sustaining hands I am sure that neither I nor any other man can hope to surmount these difficulties," he said. "I trust that in the course I shall pursue, I shall be sustained not only by the party that elected me, but by the patriotic people of the whole country." His five-minute speech at 2 p.m. was met with applause, cheers and waving of handkerchiefs. Among the crowd were the resplendently attired cadets from the Peekskill Military Academy and the local militia, presaging the military entanglements that were soon to come. "As the speech was finished the crowd gradually disappeared," attendee Henry Free (1842–1930) later recalled, "the locomotive was attached to the train and it continued on its way. As I watched it going, I wondered how hard that man would hit the shackles that held a race in bondage." Free himself later saw action in the war as a sailor.[72] As the presidential train trundled down the Hudson tracks, prisoners at Sing Sing saluted, crowds cheered along the way and cannons were fired at Yonkers.

The roar of cannons would be heard that same year across the land after the opening shots were fired at Fort Sumter, South Carolina. The Southern states proved to be a brutal killing ground for the men of the North and the volunteers from Westchester with them.

The soldiers called it "seeing the elephant," an expression to describe the act of combat. It was a rather whimsical phrase for sudden death by exploding shells or concentrated rifle fire. Many never returned after seeing the beast.

Servicemen from Westchester were heavily represented in the Sixth New York Heavy Artillery Regiment, mustered in Yonkers, the Fourth New York Heavy Artillery Regiment, and the Fourth New York Cavalry. Under Captain Elijah Taft of

Admiral David Farragut, a Southerner who lived in Hastings-on-Hudson in the 1860s, was a naval commander who reputedly called on his sailors to "damn the torpedoes, full speed ahead," as they raced to capture the rebel port of Mobile, Alabama, during the Civil War (Hastings Historical Society).

Mamaroneck, the Fifth New York Battery recruited dozens of Westchester men who fought at Gettysburg and other major battles.[73] Many local volunteers also served in the navy, including Admiral John Worden, a Scarborough native who commanded the famed Union ironclad *Monitor*.[74]

Admiral David Farragut, who led the Union navy at the Battle of Mobile Bay that led to the capture of an important shipping center, lived in Hastings-on-Hudson with his family for a short period during the Civil War, visiting when his schedule permitted.[75] Westchester women also served as nurses.

Many of the local contingent saw hard fighting with the Army of the Potomac, taking part in the battles of Cold Spring and Petersburg in 1864. On one disastrous day during the Virginia campaign in August 1864, the Fourth Artillery was caught off guard by a Rebel attack at Ream's Station, losing 375 men in one day, dead and wounded. Casualties were nearly 30 percent in one company of the Fourth Artillery, where many men from northern Westchester were serving. A mournful day was felt when the casualty lists were printed in the local papers a few days after the engagement, and dozens of local names appeared on it. Thirty-two men from the towns of Somers and North Salem alone died in the fighting in the war.[76]

Sometimes the presence of a large concentration of men from the same town in a unit produced poignant final encounters. When Charles Harting of Tarrytown was mortally shot in the chest at the Battle of Gaines Mill in Virginia in 1862, his hometown friend Frank Taxter dragged him to safety, under a shade tree. Harting, 21, passed along his silver watch and asked his friend from Tarrytown to tell his mother how he died.[77]

What the war looked like to a young soldier can be found in the letter of James Muller, a farmer from Bedford who enlisted at the age of 17 and a half in June 1861. Serving with the 38th New York Regiment, he saw action at the First and Second Battles of Bull Run, Chancellorsville and Fredericksburg. He was five feet, six inches tall and had spent time in the county poorhouse.

After the First Bull Run, he wrote to Arnell Frost Dickinson, who had taken him in as a farm hand and acted as a father figure, that he had taken part in the eight-hour battle after a 60-mile forced march. "It is a horrible thing to see our comrades shot down so," he wrote. "We was too engaged to carry off the wounded."[78]

He wrote of the privation he was experiencing in November 1862. "I am in need of clothing verry [sic] much but I can stand it as long as the rest of the boys. We are willing to do anything to bring the war to an end." Muller often complained about cowardly officers and meddling politicians, and he noted the poor performance up to that point of the war of the Union's commanders, in particular the hapless Ambrose Burnside. Writing in 1863, Muller noted the bad outcome of the Fredericksburg debacle: "On Monday we had a grand review by Major General Burnside. The general was received very coolly. Did not receive a single cheer. The Gen. tried to look cheerful but the loss of fifteen thousand of our brave comrades must have rested heavily on his head." In his final letter to Bedford during the war, Muller projected an air of despondency. "Am sorry to say it, but the country is full of stragglers and deserters," he wrote. "The men are completely discouraged and say there is no use of fighting any longer." Muller survived the war but died of tuberculosis at the age of 29.[79]

Despite the lukewarm support for Lincoln and the Republican Party's aggressive approach to the breakaway of the Southern states, Westchester saw a good turnout for enlistments during the opening days of the war. But it would not be an easy fight, and naysayers expressed their doubts about Lincoln's leadership and the goals of the war promulgated in Washington. In August 1861, a grand jury cited the Democratic newspapers of Westchester County for sedition, claiming "they might prevent enlistments and retard the successful prosecution of the war." The grand jury asked the District Attorney to investigate editors of the Democratic papers, if after being warned "they should persist in giving aid and comfort to the enemies of the government." No prosecutions were ever mounted, and the grand jury action had little effect on the newspapers, the *Yonkers Herald*, the *Highland Democrat* (Peekskill) and the *Eastern State Journal* (White Plains), which continued stinging criticism of Lincoln and his policies. The *Eastern State Journal* published the same paragraph in every edition for over a year beginning in 1861: "Mr. Lincoln is not the United States government. This government is OURS, and we owe allegiance to it. Mr. Lincoln is not ours, and we do not owe allegiance to him."[80]

The hostility to the war in some quarters did not have much impact on the military structures in place in the north. But Southerners were transported to Westchester during the course of the fighting. Davids Island off New Rochelle had been used for training purposes, and a medical facility was established there. DeCamp General Hospital was used to care for Union soldiers, but after the battle of Gettysburg in 1863, southern prisoners were brought there. The hospital was used throughout the war to treat wounded Confederate soldiers. It was designed to serve no more than 1,800 patients, but frequently exceeded that number, and hundreds of Southerners were treated there throughout the war. Local aid groups, typically organized by the women of Westchester, ran soup kitchens and other support operations to help the soldiers.[81] Some 500 Confederates who died on Davids Island, which did not have burial facilities, were interred in Brooklyn.

As the war ground on, disillusion with the fighting and the costs it entailed led to more and more hostility in the North, as Democratic newspaper editors were quick to point out. The Union cause was deeply unpopular in the hardscrabble industrial precincts of Westchester and the rough-and-tumble neighborhoods of Manhattan. Many of the Irish immigrants of those places were grinding out a meager existence in factories and shipping docks, and resentments ran deep against blacks who appeared to threaten their hard-won economic gains. When the federal government renewed a push for more manpower culminated in a draft, tensions mounted. In July 1863, the draft agency began to select names of conscripts who could not pay their way out of service with a $300 waiver, and New York City erupted in violence.

The Draft Riots brought the slaughter of the Civil War's front lines to the home front, a civil war within a civil war. Symbols of the war effort and Republican leadership that supported it were attacked and burned, and mobs attacked blacks anywhere they were encountered.

The disturbances in Westchester never approached the ferocity of the mob violence in Manhattan, but it was inevitable that the flames of the Draft Riots would scatter some sparks in the normally tranquil countryside north of the city. In the southern section of the county (now part of the Bronx), rails were torn up in Morrisania and draft documents put to the torch. A mob marched from the quarries at Tuckahoe into Mount Vernon, where a noisy demonstration and stone throwing resulted.[82] The Chappaqua home of *New York Tribune* editor Horace Greeley, an abolitionist and ardent supporter of the Union cause, was the scene of another unruly gathering by a local mob. He was not in Chappaqua at the time, but Greeley's wife, Molly, and daughters Ida and Gabrielle were at home. The children were sent to a nearby Quaker neighbor by the farm manager, and

Greeley's wife laid a circle of gunpowder around the house, as well as inside the home, as a deterrent to intruders.[83]

Several black families in Tarrytown left the village and camped out in nearby hills around Pocantico in fear of violence directed at them. Westchester County's enrolling officer, Thomas Byrnes of White Plains, was fired at by an unknown assailant as he arrived home from his office. A mob later came to his house after dark while he was away on business, burning his paperwork and ransacking the home. Byrne's wife and two children ran for their lives but were unharmed.[84]

The response by authorities was determined. A home guard was set up in Yonkers, deploying round-the-clock security to an arsenal there. Home guard units also deployed in Tarrytown, where a cannon was positioned on lower Main Street. Union gunboats on the river were put on high alert, and one armed vessel made a show of force in the waters off Tarrytown.[85] It was an ugly episode in Westchester, while the spectacle of full-scale urban warfare on the streets of New York would haunt the city for generations to come like a nightmare recalled in the light of day. Perhaps the best judgment of the whole awful affair came from the diary of William Templeton Strong, a keen observer of his time, who wrote of that bloody July: "How this infernal slavery system has corrupted our blood!"[86]

There were, of course, solidly pro-war sentiments in the county, with many ardent believers in the fight against the Southern breakaway, as well as the fight to abolish slavery. Of the latter, there was no stronger bastion of abolitionism than in the Hills section of Harrison, where the cause of freedom had a distinctly personal nature. African Americans there took up arms to break the chains of slavery, enlisting as soon as they were able to join the ranks of the Union army.

The Hills ran along Stony Hill Road in Harrison and spilled over into North Castle and White Plains. The origin of the community is not well-documented—it may have started when slaves freed by Quakers were sent there—but however it was founded it became the largest such settlement in the county. The census of 1855 listed 1,928 blacks and mulattoes out of a total population of 80,678.[87]

In 1860, as the war between the states was about to commence, several hundred blacks lived in the Hills and other sections of Harrison, mainly working as laborers, domestic workers and farmers. When war came at least 36 black men associated with the Hills signed up, largely with New England regiments that were the first to allow black enlistments.[88] They were enthusiastic volunteers, and they made a difference in the conflict.

About 180,000 black soldiers and sailors served under the Stars and Stripes during the war, giving the Union an important edge in manpower. Early doubts about their fighting abilities were soon dispelled. And not only did they often have to contend with negative treatment from their Northern comrades in arms, black soldiers were often treated brutally by Confederate captors, with dozens massacred during fighting at Fort Pillow in Tennessee in 1864.

One such volunteer in what was called "The Black Phalanx" was Simeon Anderson Tierce. He was married with a stepdaughter. His letters from the South to his wife in the Hills speak in language redolent of the Old Testament. In one letter to his wife, Sarah Jane, in February 1864, after witnessing the rise of black aspirations in New Orleans, he wrote, "God is about to do the work that has been prayed years and years before we thought about praying, for God has seen and answered prayer. He is about to pluck our root and branch in the south.... In that city of New Orleans ... God had been to work there and had moved the old slaveholders out and colored people were keeping stores themselves and I saw that they were men and women capable of doing it.... All the colored people down here welcome us here with glad hands."[89]

Tierce, who listed his occupation as a carpenter and shoemaker, signed up at the age of 32 with the 14th Regiment, Rhode Island Colored Heavy Artillery. He was promoted to sergeant in his unit, stationed near New Orleans. His letters speak of his homesickness and love of family. "I believe I send you my best respects and my love, one oxcart load and one barrel, one hogshead, two wheelbarrow loads, and a wagon body full of kisses," he wrote in the spring of 1864.[90]

He also witnessed the appalling loses to disease that a 19th century army endured. "There is more or less a death in one of the companies every day," he wrote again in March 1864, expressing his apprehensions. "They die off like rotten sheep, for [a] time there is one buried, there is another waiting to be buried. The doctor says it is not a cold but inflammation of the lungs.... I want you to have that place fixed so that if me or you should die, it will always be a good home for Sis [his stepdaughter] as long as she lives. The reason I say so I don't know how soon it may be my turn for some are taken in the morning and die before night."[91]

In one letter home in 1864, he spoke of his own bouts with fever and "ague," recalling, "I was so weak that I could scarcely walk across the floor." He died July 8, 1864, at Plaquemine, Louisiana.[92] The cause of death was listed as "intermittent fever," caused by typhoid fever, in military records.

His brother, Solomon Tierce, serving with the Connecticut 29th Infantry, was injured on his abdomen when a cannon shell blew off a tree limb that hit him while charging a rebel position at Deep Bottom, Virginia, in October 1864. Solomon Tierce died in 1891 and is buried at Sleepy Hollow Cemetery.[93]

Four men from the Hills with the Connecticut 29th were injured in October 1864 near Richmond, and one killed named John Brown.[94] That regiment had the great honor of leading the way into the fallen rebel capital of Richmond, the first Union regiment into the city, to the soul-bursting cheers of liberated slaves. Though the Northern soldiers were often afflicted by poor field commanders and bad leadership, they stitched the nation back together through terrible sacrifice. It was with their blood that the republic withstood its greatest challenge and eradicated the institution of slavery, and many from Westchester gave "the last full measure of devotion," in the words of President Lincoln.

4

Immigration, Industry and the Great War

With the war over, the nation returned to a path of growth and prosperity. The dynamism of the industrial era uprooted the old agrarian way of life and introduced a maelstrom of activity. Nearly insatiable in its demands for labor to construct big capital projects like bridges and dams, the new economy built and moved product on a previously unimaginable scale, and as the country grew, so did the range of people who contributed to it.

Expansive capital projects, like the railroad and aqueduct, depended on immigrant labor. The first to arrive in large numbers were the Irish. The landscape of Ireland, to borrow a few phrases from James Joyce, is marked by treeless hills and crooked crosses and headstones, while in the cities, the lights burn redly and hospitably in the cold night. That doesn't resemble the terrain of Westchester at all, but there came to be plenty of Ireland in the Hudson Valley, with the local landscape sculpted by waves of Irish immigrants.

The Irish constituted a small segment of the population from the 1700s. Dominated by Dutch and English Protestants, the Hudson Valley region did not prove especially hospitable to Irish Catholic immigration. But Irish surnames are evident on the muster rolls of the Westchester militia in the 1750s.[1] Immigration to the county hit high levels in the 1840s when a catastrophic potato blight, combined with a cruelly indifferent response by British authorities, devastated the island and sent its sons and daughters across the Atlantic in vast numbers through New York City. Many of those journeys ended in Westchester.

The few Irish in the country before the 1840s were mainly working in farming, domestic service or as laborers. Once they began arriving en masse, they did the heavy lifting on the railroads, on dams and on civic infrastructure projects. Irish work crews punched their way through the hard-rock hills along the Hudson to build the aqueduct and lay the track for the rail system that connected the city with the suburb.

As one New York newspaper observed in the 1860s, "There are several sorts of power working at the fabric of this Republic—water power, steam power and Irish power. This last works the hardest of all."[2] The Irish laborer often endured dangerous and backbreaking work, leading to a common refrain at the time: "You never see a gray-haired Irishman."

In 1850, according to the census, Yonkers had an Irish population of 352 females and 424 males. In that city the county's first permanent Irish Catholic Church was erected,

St. Raymond's, in 1845. The parish had started in a barn in 1843. Another large Irish enclave was in Verplanck, where the second Catholic Church was built, St. Patrick's, dedicated in 1844. According to the census, Cortlandt had the largest Irish population: 382 women and 850 men, mainly at work in the brick trade; 153 of the women worked as domestic servants. Ossining was home to 690 Irish natives.[3]

The Irish were never received with open arms. Washington Irving, who built his estate in what would become the village of Irvington, was an Anglophile whose views mirrored the landed gentry of Westchester, and in an 1840 letter to a New York newspaper editor he mocked the aqueduct workers he encountered near his home as "paddies," scoffing at their "shanties" and "whiskey-shops."[4]

Italians also came in large numbers to work on the dams as masons and laborers. Many of the new arrivals were from Sicily and Calabria. They were often met with scorn and derision in their new home, and living conditions were difficult. An Italian doctor who served the community found extensive hardship in the homes he visited in 1913. "Some of them come from good families, but when they land here they find themselves without much money," the doctor reported. "Not being able to work at their trade, if they have one, they go and dig a ditch for $1.50 a day." He found many immigrants suffering from malaria, pneumonia and rheumatism, and often horrendous housing conditions.[5] The doctor's findings appeared in a report, authored by a YMCA organizer, that went on to characterize Italians as "naturally inclined to be untidy,"[6] with residences that reeked of garlic. One section insisted, in capital letters, "THAT THEY BE AMERICANIZED."

Despite the hardships and suspicions fostered about them, life in an Italian immigrant community was not all drudgery and deprivation. Close family ties, strong community support and fine home cooking softened the days of hard labor in the quarry or on the dam. An account of her childhood by an Italian immigrant, Lena Pettinato, in 1974, described a lively place full of ordinary delights. "Larkintown [the labor camp near Croton] was a peaceful colony. People worked and were content with their little gardens and families," she recalled. Pizza, fresh bread and pastries were baked every day, plump tomatoes grew from well-tended gardens, and an abundance of wild berries made for summer delight. "We had no refrigerators, so our meat was brought fresh and eaten the same day." There were difficulties in the new country, even for a child. Two of Pettinato's classmates refused to speak to her, she recalled, and moved their seats across the room. "I could not see why the girls did this. I was always well dressed and the leader of the class. I guess they didn't like Italians."[7]

The tide of immigration also brought a Jewish community to Westchester. Moses Levy was the first demonstrably identifiable Jew who came to Westchester as a New York City merchant; he bought land at Manursing Island in 1716 in Rye.[8] He was a prominent trader associated with the Van Cortlandt family who died in 1725. There was a small number of Jews in the mid–1700s, and in the 1800s Jewish peddlers were active in Westchester. A large influx began around 1900, as immigrants from Eastern Europe came to work in factories and set up small businesses.

In 1906, the number of Jewish residents of Yonkers passed the 3,000 mark, and in 1919 totaled 5,000. About a dozen men founded Congregation Sons of Israel in 1891 in Ossining. Mount Kisco Hebrew Congregation opened in 1910.[9]

Germans, too, came in significant numbers. They built breweries that gradually supplanted the American taste for cider with beer, and they brought a musical tradition that led to the formation of orchestras and choral groups in many of the communities where

The number of Jewish residents in Westchester grew in the late 1800s and early 1900s, as pogroms and forced enlistments in the tsar's army in Russia created a wave of refugees headed to the United States. Others came for opportunity and a chance at a better life. Among them were Mendel Micklin and family members, who set up a tailor's shop in Mount Vernon in 1907 (Westchester County Historical Society).

they settled. It was a German physician from White Plains, Dr. Ernst Schmid, known for home visits and for keeping a tireless schedule when emergencies arose, who spelled out the immigrant's case for inclusion in the American fabric. In a speech he delivered in 1908, Dr. Schmid recalled an insult he once received about his foreign birth. "Let me tell the gentleman that I am an American from choice, while he is one from necessity," he said. "If there is any difference between us, it is that I came to this country with my trousers on, while he came into it naked."[10]

The immigration wave is often presented as a demographic shift, a story of numbers and statistics. But there was, of course, a human story behind every immigrant. And while only scant personal information is listed on the hundreds of naturalization forms that turned immigrants into Americans, the records kept by Westchester County during the period reveal the entire spectrum of the immigrant saga in a thousand different variations.

There was Luigi Schiavone of Monte Falcione, Italy, a student who came here to complete his education for the priesthood, and Nathan Belzer, standing just over five feet tall, a tailor from Kiev, Ukraine, with his wife, Esther. There was blue-eyed William Langtry of Glasgow, Scotland, a gardener, and Paul Sowada, an organ builder, from Freiburg, Germany, who was missing the end of his right thumb. Haroutine Gulenkian, a merchant, moved from Constantinople to Pelham. Others came from Londonderry, Palermo and Nova Scotia, from small towns and big cities in the Austro-Hungarian

Empire. Many of them listed their occupation as laborer, domestic servant and machine operator, but also butler, furrier, driver, stone mason, painter, grocer, milliner, tailor, hod carrier, bank clerk, tinsmith, brass caster, chauffeur, fireman, shoemaker and nurse. They all were required to swear allegiance to their new land and proclaim their hostility to both polygamists and extreme political philosophies by signing this declaration of intent: "I am not an anarchist; I am not a polygamist nor a believer in the practice of polygamy; and it is my intention in good faith to become a citizen of the United States of America."[11]

They also had to completely reject any and all connection to the old country: "It is my bona fide intention to renounce forever all allegiance and fidelity to any foreign, prince, potentate, state or sovereignty," each had to declare, then more specifically, for example, "and particularly to Charles Emperor of Austria Apostolic King of Hungary, of whom I am now a subject."[12]

The process toward acculturating to a new American identity was often a gradual one. It typically pushed children toward their new-found American identity, while older arrivals often struggled to leave their homeland habits behind. The story of a Hungarian family in Hastings is an example of the way assimilation worked over time.

Katherine Rapoli Brown, born in 1907, grew up speaking Hungarian. Her father worked for the American Brass Mill, her mother was a domestic. While her own education did not progress beyond the eighth grade, her sisters went through high school, and English gradually replaced Hungarian as the language spoken in the household. As she described it in an oral history project, her father was a hard-working man, tending to the big boilers at the plant for 30 years. "He worked 12 hours a day—at that time they didn't have vacations or anything," she said. "He worked five and a half days a week. There were a lot of countrymen who came from the same town. And they did the very same thing, they brought over their people."[13]

Job satisfaction had nothing to do with it. "You didn't go and work because you liked your job," she observed. "It was a necessity, you had to work…. Today the children and the people have the advantage of picking what they want. But in those days, you worked. And whatever the conditions were, it was a living. This is what they endured. Times were hard, many times. The money wasn't that great but they had to work to survive."

Eventually her father changed his attitude toward education. "I didn't go to high school," recalled Brown, who started working as a seamstress at 16 and later opened her own shop. "My father didn't believe in girls being educated. My sisters went through. In my time girls didn't need an education; all they needed was to cook and sew. I went through the eighth grade." Food was a serious business in the Rapoli household. "My mother, in the fall, would buy a bag of onions, and a bag of flour, and that would be it," she remembered. "She'd create a lot of noodle dishes. We only had meat once a week on the weekend…. A lot of cabbage, beans, that's what we lived on." There was always enough food, she said, but "there wasn't any junk food." Brown's mother gave her extensive duties in the kitchen to help prepare the meals from scratch. "My mother had to have soup every day—potato soup, stringbean soup, in the summer, fresh tomato soup. My father had to have soup every single day. My mother made mashed potatoes, no butter or milk, just mashed potatoes. She would sauté a big pan of onions and pork fat, because we used to butcher our own pigs (purchased from a nearby farm). She'd spread the potatoes onto a big plate and pour it on. And that's what we ate, soup, that, and a piece of rye bread."[14]

The work in the mills and factories brought laborers like Brown's father from across Europe, and there was plenty of work to be done. The vastness and the scale of the operations often awed those who viewed them for the first time. Truly colossal and machine-driven, they required armies of workers to keep the gears moving and the pistons pumping.

John Masefield, who would go on to become the poet laureate of England, came to the United States as a young man looking for work, unencumbered by the class strictures of his native land. A wanderer and romantic, he held down odd jobs in New York City before being steered to the carpet mill in Yonkers for factory work. He recorded his observations about his first day at the Alexander Smith factory, where he worked for two years in the 1890s. The work floor held 100 power looms. The day began early with a flood of workers entering the gates. "I saw ahead of me on the right of the road a great red brick building, three storeys high and of immense length and breadth," he wrote. "Other buildings stretched away behind it, with smoking chimneys. The road was black with crowds going in at the gates. There trolley cars were in their rush-hour service, bringing people to work: the morning flood was running…. The great seven o'clock whistle blew, and an elderly Scots engineer shut the gate on those who were late."[15] The mill's inhuman scale awed those in its wake. "It loomed up above the road, like a gigantic ship taking in passengers at a dockside," he recalled. "As I drew nearer, I heard the enormous murmur of its engines, and saw a general quickening in the steps of those entering."

Inside, a cacophony of machine clamor filled the thick air. "The shuttles were stabbing and clacking, the belts were humming, the swords were coming back with a bang, and the appalling ceiling of advancing spools shook and jerked overhead," wrote Masefield. "The noise was like nothing I had ever heard. The air was already filled with wool dust, and sweepers were moving along the gangway with their great brooms to sweep away the colored dust." The work was hard and took focus and determination, but steady wages were the reward. "We were all made to feel that if we wished to work we should get on," he concluded. "We knew we were getting a square deal; in return we gave our best…. We pitted ourselves against the task and beat it."[16]

Factory work could also be extremely dangerous. Injuries were common in an era when there was little or no concern for worker safety. If disaster struck, the sheer size of the factories and warehouses only compounded the damage. Such was the case of the great Fleischmann's fire catastrophe that broke out along the Hudson River in Peekskill. The Fleischmann factory distilled cases of whiskey and gin that it poured down the throat of a thirsty nation. Opening in 1900 in Peekskill, it was also a major producer of vinegar, and for a time the largest producer of yeast in the Unites States. About 850 to 1,100 people worked there at any given moment, and it held large stores of grain for its distilling operation.

On the last night of July in 1918, a worker and volunteer fireman named Walter Cole was finishing his shift at 11:35 p.m. when he saw a thin wisp of smoke coming from a warehouse. The curling smoke was just a small hint of the major inferno cooking within the building's walls as the fire swept through the 30,000 bags of grain stored there for whiskey distillation.[17] The fire raged into the night before it was extinguished around 4 a.m. on August 1, or so it seemed. Flames broke through a window, and the men working the fire all night did what they had to do to finish the job: bring a 45-foot ladder up to the window and let a hose take care of the embers. When the ladder hit, the percussive tap of metal rippled through the masonry and brought down the 65-foot wall, and with

Smoke-stack industry dominated the Hudson River landscape in the late 19th and early 20th centuries. The Anaconda Wire and Cable Co. in Hastings, depicted while the plant was running at capacity in the 1930s, drew immigrant workers from around the world (Hastings Historical Society).

it, tons of water-soaked grain. The avalanche of brick and sodden grain landed on a group of unfortunate firefighters standing below. They were killed where they stood.

Among the dead were Dr. Charles Greene, the department physician, Clarence Lockwood, James Selleck, Louis Barmore, George Casseles, John Torpy and Walter Cole, the man who had first spotted the flames.[18] Each man was a highly regarded member of the community, "prominent townsmen and whose loss carried grief not only to the families bereaved but to every home in the village," according to a press account.[19]

The industrialization of the county held its share of hazards for both workers and the fire service, as the disaster at Peekskill proved. Another perpetual feature of factory work was conflict between those on the line and those who paid their wages. Labor unrest in Westchester's mills, factories and large-scale construction projects was not common, but it was not unknown.

As work on the new Croton Dam progressed in the 1890s, Italian laborers became increasingly agitated by long hours and low pay. State law required an eight-hour day at $1.50 an hour, while workers at the dam were putting in ten-hour days for $1.25 an hour, according to their representatives.[20] About 700 laborers were on the job.

On April 1, 1900, they all put down their tools. The quarrymen had brought the other workers at the dam to their cause and declared a full-scale strike. Construction work was shut down, and strikers patrolled the dam works with rifles and shotguns. They lit bonfires at night and prepared defensive positions to repel incursions. There were angry confrontations with sheriff's deputies sent to protect equipment and instances of rock throwing.

Local authorities requested the militia, as New York City newspapers stoked fears of a leftist insurrection. With the approval of Governor Theodore Roosevelt, the Seventh Regiment, New York National Guard, and local Westchester companies of the Guard—

1,500 men under the command of Major General Charles Roe—were mustered and dispatched in mid–April to the dam. They set up camp around the waterworks and kept vigil on the striking workers. It was a tense standoff that soon erupted in violence.

On the night of April 16, Sgt. Robert Douglass of Mount Vernon was shot and killed while relieving sentries near the "Little Italy" section of the dam. "Lord boys, I am shot," the 28-year-old Scottish native and married father of two was said to have uttered as he clutched his abdomen. Douglass reportedly directed the men under his command to return fire, and two of his comrades fired into a clump of bushes where the deadly shot was fired, but the assailant was never captured. Douglass was a factory worker himself and made his living at a dye company.[21]

Two days later, the militia threw a long cordon around the striking workers that extended for miles with a ring of bayonets, then swept in precisely at 8 a.m. with military precision. The reserve military forces searched strikers' homes for weapons, and about 26 strike "leaders" were arrested, though labor advocates claimed they were simply workmen. The militiamen were jeered and cursed as they went about their business. Just a few pistols were found. It appeared that many of the more militant strikers had already left the dam in advance of the raid.[22]

The energy behind the strike, coupled with the military crackdown, soon deflated. By the end of April the strike was over, the militia decamped, and work resumed on the dam. Labor protests were held in the subsequent years of work on the dam, but on a much smaller scale. During that time the hourly wage increased by a small amount, and working conditions marginally improved. Those arrested in the April 1900 raid were released on bail and did not serve long sentences. The dam was finally completed in 1907.[23]

Vast new edifices of engineering were rising from the Westchester countryside, and the large tracts of productive farmland surrounding them soon became the object of ambitious and enterprising men with a much broader scope in mind. They envisioned a new kind of year-round haven: planned, resort-like communities for families of privilege that could flourish outside the city but were within easy travel distance to it by rail or boat. William Van Duzer Lawrence, a patent-medicine and real-estate millionaire, began building Lawrence Park in Bronxville in 1889. Its layout was organic and curvilinear, designed to appeal to those with a discriminating eye. The hotel he built to anchor his new development, the Gramatan, drew fashionable New Yorkers up for the weekend who were enticed to buy homes in the new village. (Sarah Lawrence College, which was built on land the philanthropist turned over for the education of young women, was named after his wife.)[24]

Briarcliff Manor was the brainchild of Walter Law, a strong-willed and wealthy Englishman who had made a fortune from a Yonkers carpet factory. In similar fashion, Law built a world-class resort hotel at the center of his town, the Briarcliff Lodge, where Babe Ruth played golf and Tarzan actor Johnny Weissmuller challenged lifeguards to friendly swimming races, which he always won.[25]

Shaping the community in his own image, Law raised an expansive herd of dairy cows and started a greenhouse business that provided flowers—including the pink Briarcliff Rose—to the breakfast tables of the Manhattan elite. Strictly enforced rules for Briarcliff residents and workers at the Lodge were a characteristic of Law's brand of paternal despotism, however.[26] He was a man of many interests and even sponsored an early road rally that drew the top talent from the racing world to compete for the Briarcliff Trophy in 1908.

Westchester's clean country air and uncrowded spaces also proved enticing for those with more modest means. In 1850, Mount Vernon was planned and developed by the New York Industrial Home Association. Promoted by newspaper publisher Horace Greeley, who had a country home and farm in Chappaqua, the association constructed 300 homes by 1852 under the leadership of John Stevens, an advocate of home ownership for the working classes.[27] Mount Vernon, named by planners after George Washington's Virginia home, became a city in 1892 after taking in outlying districts.

Eventually, the borders of Westchester took their final shape. Morrisania, West Farms and Kingsbridge—today's Bronx west of the Bronx River—were annexed to New York City in 1874 as a result of a vote. Residents in those communities believed they would see better police and fire services, and infrastructure improvements, if they could tap into the city's bountiful resources. Westchester County lost about 20 percent of its population as a result. In 1894, another vote was held, and Mount Vernon stayed within Westchester. But all the rest of the old territories in the south end of the county, including the original town of Westchester, were annexed by the city.[28] New York City consolidated its current boundaries, after taking in Brooklyn, in 1898.

Beyond the obvious attraction to homeowners and the burgeoning middle class, the open Westchester countryside was an ideal setting for sprawling campuses of higher learning. Responding to the growing population and beckoning students with their picturesque and self-contained spaces, a number of colleges and private schools opened in the county in the late 1800s and early 1900s.

The Briarcliff Lodge exemplified the well-appointed luxury that Westchester resorts offered to those who could afford it. A party of ladies made their arrival in elongated style at the Lodge sometime in the 1920s (Sandi Schneider Collection, Briarcliff Manor-Scarborough Historical Society).

Other institutions grew up around them. Orphanages, homes for troubled youth, treatment centers and mental asylums took root in Westchester in the late 19th century, under the prevailing assumption of the time that natural settings and outdoor activity could heal the mind and body. The progressive reform movement, and the novel social science theories that came with it, shaped the way the vulnerable, mentally ill and needy were cared for. These convalescent wards became, in many ways, Westchester's laboratory for new theories of human behavior.

Among the best known was the Bloomingdale Asylum. The facility moved from upper Manhattan to a 292-acre farm formerly owned by Samuel Faile in White Plains and opened in 1894. The mental institution eschewed cruel punishments and restraints in favor of a more enlightened approach to the restoration of mental health in a verdant landscape. "In looking over the buildings and hearing of the different arrangements that are being made for the relief, care and comfort of the unfortunates," the *New York Herald* wrote after the opening, "one cannot help thinking of the contrast between this and the method in vogue in olden times, when insanity was considered a crime, and the victims thrown into some dark dungeon until death released them or nature, by a supreme effort, healed the diseased minds."[29]

The New York Juvenile Asylum, which cared for homeless and runaway children on the streets of New York, came to Westchester in 1904. Fifteen cottages were built on a 277-acre parcel in Dobbs Ferry to create a family-like model for the young people who scarcely knew anything beyond the streets and the tenements.[30] It was later renamed the Children's Village.

Westchester also became an increasingly popular destination for those who needed to "take the cure." Drug and alcohol addiction were major problems at the end of the 19th century, and opiate addiction was rampant. Some historians believe one in 200 Americans were addicted to various forms of narcotics in 1900, especially patent-medicine concoctions that contained big doses of opiates or cocaine. The products were entirely unregulated, and what promised to be a cure for fatigue or menstrual pain, taken by the spoonful from a little bottle of liquid, could lead to full-blown addiction. Powerful drug concoctions could be ordered from the Sears catalogue. Alcohol addiction was common among all classes. The Keeley Institute in White Plains, founded in the early 1890s, was one of a number of treatment centers that sprang up around the country under the auspices of a Civil War surgeon. It thrived on the desperate need for treatment of "morphine fiends" and "inebriates," as they were called. Assuming the trappings of a medical establishment, its centerpiece was a treatment that involved the injection of a mysterious compound. Promoted by Dr. Lesley Keeley, the injection was said to contain a "bi-chloride of gold," and became known as "the gold cure." The institute attracted hundreds of drunks and drug addicts from all over the region, and local hotels and inns were thronged with men and women seeking help for their insatiable desires. The gilded treatment was completely bogus, a bit of quackery for the desperate and the susceptible. While the injection may have helped some addicts—they believed they were being cured and had convinced themselves they had been—it held no actual curative properties for substance abuse. The crusading newspaper reporter, Nellie Bly, came to White Plains in 1894 to take the cure—and expose the fraud. She was born Elizabeth Cochrane, and her small frame belied one of the great outsized news personalities of the age. Nellie Bly became a household name for a heavily publicized trip around the world in 72 days in 1890, but she earned her credentials as a reporter for exposing the terrible conditions inside a mental hospital at

Blackwell's Island and the wretched plight of the poor. She had an unerring eye for fakery of any kind.

Bly exposed the deception at the heart of Keeley Institute practices that year for the readers of Joseph Pulitzer's newspaper, the *New York World*. The intrepid reporter arrived in the early summer of 1894 and asked about the facility that pledged to rehabilitate alcoholics and drug-abusers. "I learned one thing very definitely: the Keeley Institute is not a welcomed addition to the pretty little town."[31] Bly, playing the part of an alcoholic, met a number of men and women whose lives were falling apart due to their addictions. She presented brief portraits of a "very wealthy New York woman," named Mrs. B, who had become addicted to morphine, and "for six months before she came here she had not seen daylight," reposing in a dark room under the grip of the drug. A Mr. Y had fallen into alcoholism in his late 60s, and "he drank so hard his life was despaired of." Nellie Bly eventually took the cure: a hypodermic syringe administered by a doctor at the clinic. "It hurt, very decidedly," she wrote. "If a needle had run into my arm, it could not have been more painful…. For two days thereafter my arm pained and was sore." Bly also took a philosophical approach to the "treatment," intuiting that the placebo effect, a strong psychological belief that any medical cure administered by so-called experts will do some good, lay behind the moderate success the Keeley Institute enjoyed. "I would not for the world cast discredit upon anything that would turn people from drink for even four weeks," she admitted. "But it is my honest opinion the cure is no cure in itself, and that it is merely working on the imagination, making men believe they are cured, that does the real good."[32]

Bly's mother had been renting a farm in White Plains, and she took a liking to it, so she later bought a home in White Plains and spent a decade in the community.[33] She tended to an orchard, and kept five dogs, 64 chickens, a horse named Chaperone, and even a parrot and a monkey there.[34] The Keeley Institute, meanwhile, dropped the flim-flam injection methods and developed a more conventional approach to treatment based on credible research; it went on to become a respected organization in the field of addiction recovery.

Abundant in cooling breezes, lengthy shorelines, striking scenery and amiable small towns, the county was also a prime getaway for vacationers and other merry-makers, and the county developed a significant leisure industry in the 19th century. In the early days of the nation, leisure was a rarity that few could enjoy, and free time was often channeled into some form of religious activity. Camp meetings and revivals were held in every corner of the county in the early 1800s, bringing thousands to the countryside for religious instruction and fresh air. Thousands came to Ossining every year for Methodist religious awakenings in what is now known as Campwoods; it was also a rare chance for men and women to socialize in mixed company.[35]

Through most of the century, only the wealthy could afford a long absence from their daily labors. In Westchester, more affordable resorts and amusement areas opened that appealed to the middle and working classes, most of them city residents who found a trip to the county by boat or train an easy and cheap form of amusement. As the transportation network grew, Westchester's prime water views, vistas and well-situated seclusion became a magnet for the very, very rich. Clad in granite and marble, ringed by acres of oak, maple and pine, and stocked with the treasures of the Old World, these vast mansions unabashedly proclaimed American wealth, power and privilege that exceeded anything before it in the pursuit of luxury. What was once the land of the prosperous farmer and the humble craftsman became the manicured estate.

John D. Rockefeller, the founder of Standard Oil and in his day the richest man in America, built Kykuit in Pocantico Hills far up above the Hudson. It was completed in 1913 after an extensive construction process; its landscaping, designed to hide the villages of the Tarrytowns below, reveals only acres of trees and the river beyond its sloping lawns. At Lyndhurst in Tarrytown, Jay Gould, the man for whom "robber baron" seemed to have been coined, took over a Gothic masterwork nearer the river's edge designed by Alexander Jackson Davis. A horticulturist, Gould built a large greenhouse that housed the largest orchid collection in the country; he liked to spend time with flowers before a day of cut-throat business dealings. A self-taught expert on horticulture, Gould imported flower bulbs from all over the world, creating his own private Eden on the grounds of his estate.[36] In the Purchase section of Harrison, newspaper tycoon Whitelaw Reid of the *New York Tribune* in 1887 hired McKim, Mead and White to rebuild a dilapidated mansion and Frederick Law Olmsted, whose work included the design of Central Park, to restore the grounds. Beginning in 1855 Simeon Leland, a hotel mogul, built a castle in New Rochelle made of granite and punctuated by black walnut doors.

The county's accumulating assemblages of wealth and opulence would have been envied even by the crowned heads of Europe. (In many cases, it sent cash-strapped aristocrats here in search of suitably moneyed spouses.) In their excesses, quite a few of these moguls could also be considered eccentric.

Few could match the peculiarity of Russell Hopkins, one of the most unconventional millionaires ever to sit in the lap of luxury. He was a sportsman who inherited his wealth from his father, John Randolph Hopkins, an Atlanta banker who also earned millions in the field of patent medicine. Young Hopkins, a Georgia native, had been an animal lover since he was a boy, and his enthusiasm for ever-more exotic beasts grew with his years. Hopkins eventually created the largest private zoo in the country at his estate on the Irvington-Tarrytown border.

A man of strong impulses, Hopkins fell in love at 18 with Vera Siegrist, herself the daughter of a wealthy family, heirs to the Listerine fortune. Hopkins had developed a keen interest in her while she was barely a teenager, but waited until she turned 17 in 1906 before he stole away on the family yacht and eloped with his bride. They tied the knot while anchored in the Peekskill harbor, with the assistance of a Methodist minister from the Peekskill congregation. The couple settled on Fifth Avenue in Manhattan and bought a country house off Sunnyside Lane in Tarrytown, nestled among the estates of other tycoons in a section that became known as Millionaire's Row. For a time Hopkins was the most talked about of them all.[37]

He began his animal collection in 1909 at his Westchester estate, named Veruselle, an amalgam of the married couple's first names. The 88-acre parcel became a menagerie of almost Biblical proportions, and Hopkins imported creatures that came from the world's forests, jungles, swamps and deserts. An extraordinary collection of species that either flew, slithered or crawled found a place in his collection. The zoo housed elephants, lions, camels, pumas, panthers, ocelots, leopards, cougars, black bears, polar bears, moose, reindeer, alligators, giraffes and a Russian brown bear named Big Ben. There was also an ape and a blue-faced baboon, wild boars, badgers, raccoons, anteaters and foxes. An ostrich, a llama and a kangaroo lived at the estate, and an artificial lake was constructed to harbor Hopkins' collection of waterfowl. An aviary housed a rare collection of birds, while an assembly of snakes lived in a collection of glass cages. Hopkins kept only one

Pictured shortly after its completion in 1913, the Rockefeller estate named Kykuit was a hilltop repository of art, wealth and power. It is now part of the Historic Hudson Valley heritage organization and open to the public (Rockefeller Archive Center).

dog, a beloved St. Bernard he called Cleum.[38] The initial cost of the menagerie was estimated at $25,000; the cost of maintaining it ran into the tens of thousands of dollars per year. Hopkins employed fifteen zookeepers to feed and care for the animals.

He had a special fondness for zebras. The young tycoon caused a sensation in 1907 when he drove a carriage pulled by the undomesticated animals—or rather attempted to drive them—down Fifth Avenue in Manhattan. There was an unresolved debate as to whether the zebras were harnessed and acting as a team, and whether Hopkins himself was holding the reins. Regardless, they rebelled within seconds, the demonstration over before it began. In Westchester, when a group of mountain sheep escaped from their pen on his property, they took a leisurely stroll along Tarrytown's streets, tying up traffic on Broadway and stunning passersby.[39]

Hopkins had a fascination with insurance, as well as assassination, for reasons that defy easy explanation, and he took out a policy from Lloyd's of London against his death at the hands of hired killers. He also had a strong affection toward the nation of Panama and struck up a friendship with its president, Domingo Obaldia; Hopkins served as the Panamanian consul general for years.[40]

It seemed as if paranoia and whimsy wrestled in the eccentric millionaire's mind for mastery. Besides collecting animals, he was a collector of antique weapons. His vast armory in Tarrytown included a pair of French double-barreled flintlock pistols from 1750, a Moorish rifle, Malay knives, Japanese samurai swords of the Katana style, a Persian battle axe from the 1700s, Civil War cavalry sabers, a Ghurka knife, English dueling pistols from 1780 and five African spears. It was enough to outfit a small army of ghost warriors—and entertain Hopkins' inner child.[41]

Great wealth can buy many things, but a long, healthy life is not one of them. Hopkins contracted double pneumonia in 1919 after an extended illness and died at his Fifth Avenue home at the age of 35.[42] An elaborate tomb was built in Sleepy Hollow Cemetery, replete with Egyptian decorative symbols that were popular at the time. Two stone Imperial Chinese guardian-lions were erected in front of the crypt, a fitting monument to a man whose ardor for the animal kingdom was as spectacular as it was exotic.

During this age of excess, the male monied classes took materialism to new heights. Country houses and year-round estates grew to huge proportions and men of power expanded their waistlines to accommodate epicurean and gluttonous diets. The 1890s heralded the creation of the "beefsteak dinner": no women allowed, no cutlery, and the assembled group of men feasted on beef with their bare hands.[43] It was in many ways a paradise for rich men, who could follow their appetites from polite, mannered society to more sequestered quarters. Do-as-I-say class privilege and male prerogatives went unquestioned.

Secret societies flourished in the 1890s and often hosted wild spectacles that included bare-knuckled boxing matches, animal fights, risqué vaudeville routines and re-enactments of famous historical scenes—all done in private and away from the prying eyes of womenfolk. Of course, another form of entertainment could also be provided, one known at the time as "immodest dancing."

In 1896, a "skirt dancer" named Little Egypt, a roomful of society swells from the Larchmont Yacht Club and a police raid made for a perfect scandal, one that set the stage for the backlash to come. The sensational exposé of rich men behaving very badly tumbled onto the pages of almost every newspaper in America, and the Larchmont group found themselves in a stormy sea of printer's ink that revealed the less savory habits of the very rich.

The dinner was a bachelor's party for Clinton Seely, thrown by his brother, Herbert. The two men in their 20s were the grandsons of the great circus showman P.T. Barnum. Twenty-two members of the Larchmont club were invited as guests to the Louis Sherry restaurant in Manhattan on December 19, 1896. Besides the extravagant meal, lavish entertainment featuring a parade of exotic skirt dancers was promised. They included "Little Egypt," also known as Ashea Wabe; Cara Routt, "The Kentucky Thoroughbred"; and other dancers in elaborate costumes that became less and less elaborate as the night wore on. A disgruntled booking agent notified police captain George Chapman about an "immoral dance" taking place at the party. Chapman raided the restaurant with two plainclothes cops and found a half-dozen women in various states of undress and a roomful of drunk men not altogether clothed themselves.[44] The headlines in the *New York Herald* told the story in 32-point type: "Guests Fondled Dancers," "Little Egypt in Transparent Gauze," "Vulgar Toasts and Gifts."[45] It later became known as the "Awful Seeley Dinner" or the "Seeley Dinner Orgy." The scandal caused an uproar in Larchmont, and when one of the Seely dancers came to a New Rochelle Rowing Club Smoker in the aftermath of the Seeley Dinner, another outrage followed.

As was often the case in that period, wealth swiftly asserted its privileges—and accused Chapman of breaking the law. The policeman was brought up on disciplinary charges for staging an illegal search at Sherry's. The witnesses testifying in the case provided newspaper fodder for days, but New York City police commissioner Theodore Roosevelt, who later became the New York State governor and president, gave his full support to Captain Chapman, and he was acquitted on departmental charges. Three of the party organizers were charged with committing a public nuisance and faced a grand jury, but the charges were dropped.[46] The upper crust closed ranks behind the men involved in the Seeley Dinner as notoriety over the case subsided. The wedding of Clinton Seeley and his betrothed, Florence Tuttle, took place as planned. A subsequent reception for the bride and groom was held at the bride's home in Manhattan; at the second Seeley party, everyone kept their clothes on.[47]

The privileges demanded by the very wealthy sometimes took a more sinister turn. It was even possible to get away with murder—not once, but twice. The so-called "crime of the century" (although the century was quite young) was certainly a startling and salacious story. Stanford White, a renowned and socially prominent architect, was murdered in 1906 by a mentally unstable millionaire, Harry Thaw. The legal proceedings, which included sanity hearings in Westchester, captivated the entire nation.

White was the leading trendsetter and architect of the day, draping new money in stone palaces as grand as those found in Europe. His work (with his associates) in the county included the Whitelaw Reid mansion in Harrison, the sumptuous home of Elliott Shepard in Scarborough (now the Sleepy Hollow Country Club) and the *Cosmopolitan* magazine headquarters in Irvington. White's designs convey a sense of dignified elegance; his personal life was much messier. With a gargantuan appetite for every form of luxury, he barely kept ahead of his creditors; a compulsion for seducing young women and underage girls with champagne and lavish gifts barely kept him ahead of the law. One of these girls was a then 16-year-old named Evelyn Nesbit, a stunning artist's and photographer's model and budding Broadway showgirl. Thaw, the heir to a Pittsburgh railroad fortune, became equally transfixed and, after pursuing her intensely for four years, convinced Nesbit to marry him in 1905. Unfortunately, Thaw was an erratic, temperamental man who drove cars through storefront windows and tormented servants on both sides of the

Atlantic. He became enraged and obsessed over his wife's previous dalliance with White and one evening marched across the rooftop terrace of the old Madison Square Garden (White's own design) to the table where the architect was enjoying an evening of musical theater. Thaw shot him dead in front of hundreds of witnesses. A man with $40 million at his disposal, however, could bend the law to suit his own purposes.

Harry Thaw's first of two trials in New York City, featuring the defense team's fairly novel strategy of "temporary insanity," ended in deadlock. The second trial, in which his lawyers employed a more conventional insanity defense, acquitted Thaw of first-degree murder but confined him to a facility for the criminally insane in Beacon, New York, the outcome his lawyers had sought. In 1908, they hatched the second phase of their strategy and began proceedings to declare Thaw sane and release him from the mental asylum. Several sanity hearings were held in White Plains at Westchester County Supreme Court, and they tantalized the press and onlookers who packed the courtroom and gathered outside. At the first in 1909, in which Nesbit testified against her husband, a judge declared Thaw mentally unfit and he was sent back upriver to Matteawan State Hospital. The next sanity hearing, held in 1912, caused a sensation. In 1910 Evelyn had given birth to a son, which she claimed was Harry's, adding to the drama. The hearing was a long, drawn out affair, featuring lurid descriptions from Evelyn about her husband's cruel and perverted behavior.

Mary Thaw, Harry's mother and staunch defender, took up lodgings at a luxury hotel in White Plains and hired the best legal and psychological experts (known as alienists at the time) to free her son. The courtroom was filled with fashionably dressed women who strained at every word. Evelyn had grown deeply estranged from Harry, and she revealed a number of disturbing details about his personal tastes. Evelyn talked about the pleasure Harry derived from whipping her, and from drawing pornographic cartoons of women bound with ropes—five women rushed from the courtroom as she described it all in detail. She also talked about a suicide pact they shared, his taste for narcotics and an explosive temper that made him rage over the slightest inconvenience. "I want it understood that Harry Thaw hid behind my skirts through these dirty murder trials, and I won't stand for it again," she screamed from the stand.[48]

Justice Martin Keogh of New Rochelle declared that Thaw could not be released, and he was sent back once again to the asylum. Three years later, in 1915, he became a free man when he was officially declared sane; he divorced Evelyn the same year. Harry Thaw used his freedom to follow his inclinations as a sadistic bully and spent more years behind bars for whipping and beating a man unconscious in California. Evelyn Nesbit became a vaudeville sensation, arguably the first sex symbol of the modern era, before a nasty drug habit dragged her into a sordid existence of cheap rooming houses, burlesque shows during the 1920s and 30s, and eventually, anonymity.[49] During World War II she settled in Los Angeles, where she had dabbled as an actress during the early film era, and later served as a paid technical consultant for the 1955 film *The Girl on the Red Velvet Swing*, a highly fictionalized account of her life. She taught art classes and lived a quiet yet bohemian life near her son and his family.[50] The stately mansions of Stanford White still stand today, their facades projecting an air of regal indifference to the private lives of those who hid behind their walls.

The era of privilege and authority, seemingly embedded in the very order of things, was coming to an end. War was on the horizon, and while the United States seemed a safe distance across the Atlantic Ocean from the maelstrom developing in Europe, there was no immunity from submarine warfare on the high seas. In May 1915, when a German U-boat sank the *Lusitania*, the prospect of war burst into the American consciousness.

Fourteen people with ties to Westchester were killed when the *Lusitania* was torpedoed. A married couple and their daughter, the Loney family of Pelham Manor—an English family returning to their native land—went down with the ship. Among the most famous victims of the sinking was Charles Frohman, a theater impresario who had a home in Purchase. Frohman, who was 58 at the time of his death, brought *Peter Pan* to the London and Broadway stages in 1904 and 1905. Frohman was said to enjoy playing croquet at his well-appointed Purchase estate. He was on his way to London to look for new material and calmly smoked a cigar as the ship began to list. Frohman was washed off the deck of the great vessel as it went down, and his body was later recovered.[51] He was buried in a Jewish cemetery in Queens.

The *Lusitania* disaster was one of many that came to mark the conflict known as the Great War. The conflagration has since been dimmed by the military triumphs and tragedies that came after it, but World War I stands as a sharp turning point in the course of human events, a conflict that yielded chemical warfare, deliberate attacks on civilian targets, concentration camps and the first examples of 20th century genocide.

While the war never left the mark on these shores that it did in the killing fields of Europe and western Asia, it still had a great effect on Westchester. The New York suburbs served as the point of embarkation for thousands of young men and women heading "over there," hundreds of whom never returned alive. Many soldiers also served in Westchester, guarding the vital water supply from enemy sabotage or manning the military installations that ringed New York City. Scores also fell from a different, opportunistic enemy: disease.

U.S. Army Sergeant Edward W. Emerson, pictured here with his wife, Sophie, was a longtime Rye resident who was stationed at Fort Slocum in New Rochelle before shipping out overseas during World War I (collection of the author).

Most of those who mustered into the army from Westchester saw service with the 27th and the 77th Army Divisions in the closing days of the war.[52] Others from the area served in the 1st Division and the famed 369th Regiment, a segregated unit of African American soldiers called the Harlem Hellfighters. As many soldiers in the U.S. Army refused to serve alongside them, the black soldiers fought with French weaponry under French command, with small number of white American officers in their ranks.

The 27th Division, under the command of Major General John

O'Ryan, who had lived in South Salem, was dispatched to Belgium in 1918 and ordered into the fighting at Flanders, a sea of mud and blood where a disastrous British offensive had collapsed the year before. The division was later used to batter the Hindenburg Line, the final line of defense for the Germans after their own failed offensive in the spring of 1918. One regiment with many local soldiers serving in it, the 107th Regiment, lost more than half its strength in attacks on the line. "The noise of all the guns was so terrible, we could not hear ourselves think," wrote James Duffy to his parents in 1919 from the hospital bed where the young private was recovering from a gas attack. "I could see fellows dropping all around, but it was breaking dawn, and you had to look straight ahead."[53]

What Duffy saw that day as the soldiers advanced into no man's land were the sudden deaths of countless Westchester friends from exploding German shells. The 77th Division, known as the Liberty Division, took part in the fierce battles around the Argonne Forest in the closing days of the war. A history of the division described the campaign there as "14 miles of heartbreaking plunging through thickets that spat death with the rapidity of the serpent's fangs."[54]

The division suffered 3,697 casualties in two weeks and later took part in the last bloody battle of the operation in September, the Battle of the Argonne. James Drumgold, a private in the Harlem Hellfighters from White Plains and a municipal employee, died on October 7, 1918, from injuries he sustained in combat in the closing days of the war. He was 33. His wife, Clara, had died two days before him in Virginia from the influenza pandemic sweeping across the land.[55] Captain Frederick Cobb of White Plains, a white commander in the 369th—which recorded more days on the front line than any other American unit—was also killed by shellfire on September 29, 1918, in fighting around Bellevue in France.[56] A total of 467 soldiers from Westchester County perished in the war.[57]

The Home Guard in Westchester, called up during World War I to protect waterworks, utilities and bridges from potential sabotage, endured long hours in frigid weather. A local Home Guard detachment, seen here on a frozen section of the Hudson River at Hastings in the winter of 1917–1918, demonstrated the harsh conditions under which the servicemen operated (Hastings Historical Society).

One of the more poignant "letters home" came from the pen of 2nd Lieutenant Jefferson Feigl to his parents in Mount Kisco. On March 21, 1918, the young lieutenant serving in the First Infantry Division, and another officer were heading back from the front in northern France for a one-week leave. At a small hill, a shell burst landed near Feigl, a Harvard graduate, and killed him instantly. A letter he had written in the event of his death was later delivered. "Dear Parents: I suppose you all's will be feeling pretty low about the time this arrives. If my instructions have been carried out, you'll already have received a cable telling you of the death of your one and only son. Please believe me, fond parents, that I realize just what the loss means to you and what a void it is going to leave in your lives. Therefore, I won't ask you to cheer up, 'cause I know it wouldn't do any good. As far as I am concerned, however, it seems as if Dame Fortune couldn't have picked a nicer and more gentlemanly manner for me to make my exit, and if it wasn't for the grief I know I'm causing you, I would be more contented now, in leaving this life, than I ever could have been while living it. If I may have a final request, it is this: that any love you had for me you'll turn towards each other, thus filling in some part, the gap I leave behind."[58]

After the war, memorials appeared across the county to honor the local men who had fallen in the Great War. Two young women from France, Jeanne Petit and Elaine Kaess, traveled to White Plains in 1921 with soil from Chateau Thierry, where a number of the city's sons were interred. The two women helped plant trees in their honor with the French dirt they carried, "a mingling of soil from the spot where your brave comrades fought to save our country and civilization," they wrote in their dedication.[59]

5

From the Bronx River Parkway to a River of Beer
Car Culture, Ward's Plan and Prohibition Crime

The sail and the locomotive defined the course of the 19th century. In the 20th century, it was the automobile that signaled the way forward to the roar of a revving engine. A fast, self-controlled and entirely private means to escape the congested public city, the car was the primary vehicle of suburban growth.

From the late 1890s through the 1920s, the automobile became the emblem of modernity across America, and Westchester its East Coast laboratory for the way people worked, played, romanced and died behind the wheel. Everything changed in the automobile's wake—housing patterns, work routines, the features of the land, even (or especially) courting rituals among teenagers and young adults. The car re-made the county, creating an iconic, interconnected haven outside New York City that came to define the American way of life. As the country's suburbs matured, Westchester was on its way to becoming the pre-eminent enclave of its kind, an arcadia for the middle class and those who aspired to a middle-class life.

The car is a curious American paradox. While it gave individuals a new form of freedom and turned small towns and villages into prosperous destinations, it obliterated vast tracts of the natural world and an older, simpler way of life. The age of the automobile was also a time of great tumult, when Prohibition opened the door to organized crime and illegal speakeasies appeared in every town. New art forms, like film, and newly mobilized political groups and organizations created anxiety and social tensions that paved the way for even more drastic changes to come. And at a former brickyard along the Hudson in 1899, a publishing tycoon began to build a vision of America as a place on wheels.

In the country's long-running affair with the automobile, John Brisben Walker was among the first to be seduced. Walker studied at West Point, traveled in China, ran a newspaper, dabbled in national politics, made a fortune, lost it, then made another. With funds from his second fortune in agriculture and real estate, Walker in 1889 bought and transformed the family magazine *Cosmopolitan* into a leading literary publication of its time, moving its operations to Irvington.

Seven years later Walker got wind of a new racing phenomenon, the first-ever U.S. automobile road race in Chicago. In 1896, Walker sponsored the country's second race, a colossal journey of 52 miles that ran from city hall in lower Manhattan to the Ardsley Country Club, then back. Six cars competed, two finished, and a driver named Frank Duryea—who, with his brother Charles Edgar, had developed the first successful gas-powered car three years earlier—won the $3,000 prize for finishing first, and finishing at all, after a two-hour race. The rough roads and multiple breakdowns on the path to the finish line, however, were nothing compared to the New York City police sent out to patrol the fledgling auto race as it careened through the Bronx. The cops detained several racers who appeared to be speeding, at about 20 miles an hour, down the borough's streets. Another driver was halted temporarily after he knocked over a bicyclist.[1]

His obsession with the new-fangled machine growing, Walker purchased a patent in 1899 from two brother inventors from New England, Francis and Freeling Stanley, for a steam-engined "horseless carriage" he intended to manufacture for the public. Walker started his enterprise with grand plans, forming a strategic partnership with asphalt pioneer A. Lorenzo Barber, who went on to pave most of Westchester's roads. Although his deal with Barber dissolved in a matter of weeks (with Barber leaving to found a rival company in Bridgeport, Conn.), Walker opened the Mobile Company of America at Kingsland Point on the Hudson, just upriver from *Cosmopolitan*'s offices in Irvington. Architect Stanford White, who had designed the magazine's building, signed on to create a new auto plant.[2] "The Westchester," Walker's first incarnation of the Stanleys' design, rolled off the assembly line at the Mobile Company in 1900. It chugged, wheezed and occasionally exploded, jolting its driver and passengers like an earthquake across the county's largely unpaved roads.

After building some 500 steamers capable of hitting speeds of 50 miles an hour, Walker and his plant went bust in 1903 during a nationwide business depression. The plant was taken over by another company, which switched to combustion engines and also later went broke. William Durant, an entrepreneur, and Louis Chevrolet, a debonair Swiss race-car driver and engineer, took over production in 1914 before joining Detroit's General Motors corporation in 1918.[3]

The models produced along the Tarrytown shoreline sped down America's roads for generations, forming a roll call of potent brand names like the Fleetmaster, Bel Air, Impala, Nova and Lumina. Twelve million vehicles were produced at the GM plant before it closed in 1996.

Walker's early industrial innovations and the race he organized in 1896 to publicize the incipient auto industry was just a warm-up lap for another event that would mark Westchester as a place where car culture was shifting into high gear.

In 1908 entrepreneur and early auto enthusiast Walter Law, the founder of Briarcliff, organized a road rally. The first stock-car race ever held on unpaved roads, The Briarcliff Trophy drew the top talents of the racing world competing in the fastest factory models of the age. A total of 22 cars from 16 manufacturers entered the race, with models by Renault, Fiat, Benz, Stearns, Panhard, Simplex and Isotta-Frascini gunning for the trophy. A thousand state militiamen were called out for crowd control, and elaborate preparations were mounted to prepare the course and viewing stands. A 32-mile circuit, designed to test both man and machine with a series of sharp turns and long straightaways, took racers from Briarcliff to Millwood to Pines Bridge, through Mount Kisco, Armonk and Kensico, and back through Eastview to Briarcliff to begin the loop again. The total distance covered by the end of the race was 240 miles.[4]

Italian Emanuel Cedrino, the odds-on favorite to win the Briarcliff Trophy at the wheel of his 60-horsepower Fiat, finished second in the 1908 automobile race. More than 100,000 spectators came out to watch. The former royal chauffeur died a month later trying to break a speed record (National Automotive History Collection, Nathan Lazarnick Collection, Detroit Public Library).

When race day came, thousands of curious spectators took specially scheduled trains from New York City. Thousands more spent the night in the Westchester countryside in festive, boisterous encampments. More than 100,000 fans eventually watched the race.

The race did not disappoint the eager, unruly throngs. The order to start—a referee yelling "Go!" and slapping the shoulder of the lead driver—came just after 5 a.m. on the morning of April 24, and crowds roared with approval as the sleek racers and their two-man crews flashed past at unimaginably fast speeds, nerves and pistons straining with tension. In Mount Kisco, where many Italian immigrants lived, crowds erupted in cheers as drivers from the old country sped by.[5] Racers surged into straight runs for battles between cars and drivers, resulting in several accidents. A prankster had painted a road-side boulder with the inscription "Prepare to Meet Thy God," though no one was seriously injured during the race. One of the more spectacular crack-ups involved a driver named Watson who took an L-turn near Eastview around 60 miles an hour and paid the price, hitting a tree. He and the mechanic were thrown clear, but amazingly, hopped back into their vehicle visibly uninjured. They even managed to rejoin the race after making emergency repairs.[6]

The Briarcliff Trophy took racers on a 240-mile double stretch of country roads throughout the developing suburbs from Briarcliff and back through Pines Bridge, Millwood, Mount Kisco, Armonk, Kensico and Eastview (National Automotive History Collection, Nathan Lazarnick Collection, Detroit Public Library).

The Briarcliff Trophy's odds-on favorite was Italian Emanuel Cedrino, a former chauffeur to Italy's Queen Helena, driving a gray 60-horsepower Fiat. But the day belonged to a savvy American, Louis Strang, at the wheel of a bright red, custom-painted Isotta-Frascini. Strang started in fourth place but took the lead before the first circuit was completed. He never gave it up for the next five hours and his steering was hailed as a masterwork of racing. Strang came to the race well prepared: he spent five weeks in Westchester training in early morning runs in a Ford, learning the nuances of every curve and bump on the county's landscape while the other drivers slept. For his labors he won a $10,000 purse. Strang's skill didn't protect him for long. He died in 1911 in a slow-motion accident when his vehicle, traveling at walking speed, tumbled down a soft embankment that gave way and flipped over into a ditch. He was 26. Cedrino finished second in the Briarcliff race, but was determined to finish his next race first.[7] He died in a crash the following month trying to break the speed record at Pimlico in Baltimore.

The speed machines of 1908 scattered dust, oil and racing legends around the countryside, but Westchester was to develop an automotive culture at a more prosaic level: building the earliest commuter road network and a series of landscaped parkways for Sunday drivers. On a blustery fall day in early November 1925, a long caravan of politicians motored over a smooth asphalt ribbon stretching 15 miles from the Bronx Botanical Garden to Valhalla. They rode behind a motorcycle escort provided by the State Police, a gleaming convoy of power and automotive glamour speeding down the most technologically advanced thoroughfare in the country. With the Kensico Dam as their backdrop, VIPs from the city and the suburbs touted the new Bronx River Parkway as the crowning achievement of the youthful automobile age, a 40-foot-wide roadway that would provide greenery and sweet country air to the city masses—and untold economic benefits to Westchester.[8]

Despite its allure, the car created unease and fear wherever it went. In the 1918 novel by Booth Tarkington, *The Magnificent Ambersons*—both a lament and a critique of the automobile's impact on the older, more genteel ways of transport—a character exclaims, "People won't permit the automobile to be used. Really. I think they'll make laws against them. People just seem to hate them. They'll never stand it, never in the world."[9] In fact, laws regarding the automobile were passed—but they were directed against pedestrians, not motorists. Los Angeles drafted the first jaywalking laws used in a large urban municipality in the country in 1925, just ten years after the word "jaywalking" entered the vernacular in Boston.[10] Westchester was an early and eager adapter to the automobile, though there was a deep suspicion about the new machines and law enforcement was quick to respond to even the smallest infractions. Police in Peekskill arrested 14 motorists on one autumn day in 1906 alone, snaring drivers headed to and from the Princeton-West Point football game. Officers set up signal flags, and equipped with stop watches, stopped and arrested drivers reaching speeds of 30 miles an hour. The guilty motorists were put before a judge and fined between $10 and $25.[11]

The Bronx River Parkway, the nation's earliest commuter road network, was an innovative achievement of scenic, landscaped roadways in the early days of the automobile. It featured some 140,000 shrubs, median dividers and nighttime lighting (courtesy Westchester County Archives).

Deadlier incidents followed. An outrage erupted in New Rochelle in the spring of 1906 after a 73-year-old woman was struck and killed on her way to church by a hit-and-run driver, with her sister mortally wounded. Sermons from ministers denounced "the desecration of the Sabbath by motorists," but those words had little effect.[12]

By 1907, one out of every 800 Americans owned a car, an increase of 1,000 percent in just a decade. America was clearly smitten. A Mount Kisco couple made headlines for driving from Westchester to a vacation home in Florida.[13]

The infrastructure for automobiles, however, remained fairly primitive until local government, auto and asphalt manufacturers, civil engineers, and the real-estate industry saw the opportunity to turn this new form of transportation into the driving force of suburban development. And in 1916, construction started on a new kind of parkway that cemented the relationship between the car and Westchester County, setting a national and international precedent.

"The Bronx River Parkway is an example for the whole country," read a proclamation by Governor Al Smith, who was unable to attend the 1925 ceremonial opening. It was a rare instance when a politician's hyperbole accurately described the event's significance.[14]

The parkway, built at an announced cost of $16.5 million, was more than just an elegantly planned artery connecting the city with the suburbs. The Model T of highway transportation, the early parkway was also an expression of an old-fashioned American ideal combined with the latest technical innovations. The parkway was imagined as an auto-filled version of Central Park in Manhattan, and it followed in the beliefs of Frederick Law Olmsted and other practitioners of landscape design who presumed they could reconnect the splintered fragments of society through trees, stone bridges, gracious boulevards and public-spirited architecture. It expressed a democratic ideal of public spaces as conduits for Americans to come together as one, and the parkway builders saw the road as a connective and collective byway for families and people of all classes, where stops for hikes and picnics were encouraged. The modern parkway reconfigured the 19th century concept of boulevards and the public park for the auto age. As parkway official Madison Grant, a Progressive intellectual and ardent conservationist—and also a prominent white nationalist of the era—put it at the dedication, "To those who come after us, we owe both the preservation and restoration of natural beauties."[15]

The builders planted 140,000 shrubs along its course, cleared away dozens of shanties from its banks and moved two million cubic yards of rock and dirt.[16] The open sewer that the Bronx River had become through years of reckless industrial and residential development was reclaimed, and engineers added new features like median dividers and nighttime lighting. An engineering marvel orchestrated to show how the car and its natural surroundings could happily coexist, the parkway was studied by transportation experts from far beyond Westchester who came to scrutinize its features. And though the actual roadway has been reshaped many times through subsequent decades, the Bronx River Parkway's original mission can still be glimpsed—to connect the motorist to the world outside the windshield. Even in its current form, the parkway offers drivers glimpses of its past as it winds the masses to and from more ordinary destinations.

Releasing people from geographical constraints with unprecedented speed, the automobile also loosened other restrictions, particularly social constraints and some of the clothing that went with them. Thanks to Henry Ford, the availability of affordable cars gave young people a new place to explore the boundaries of their passion, away from parents and other family members. "Petting parties," which started on college and high

The parkway's mastermind William Ward saw the road as a connective and collective byway for families and people of all classes, where stops for hikes, picnics and even ice skating were encouraged (courtesy Westchester County Archives).

school campuses, became all the rage in the early 1920s and soon took cover in Mr. Ford's back seat. Authorities in Topeka, Kansas, made national headlines in 1923 when they formed a vigilance committee of volunteers to patrol local streets for parking couples.[17] A number of colleges soon banned the use of automobiles by their students. But these measures were only partially successful. America's romance with the car—and in it— continued for decades. Parents and other guardians of moral order were on guard against the dangers they saw posed by trips down the proverbial "lover's lanes," and Westchester County became a central location in the battle against petting parties in 1928.

Scores of cars driven by young lovers began turning up around rural hideaways in the county, but the major attraction for most couples was the plaza beneath the Kensico Dam, a lover's superhighway. About 150 cars, some of them specially equipped with curtains, could be found in the shadow of the mighty waterworks on weekend nights that summer.[18] Traffic on the Bronx River Parkway would crawl to a standstill with young lovers driving up from New York City and southern Westchester for a night of auto-induced romance.

Mount Pleasant police were eventually called out to quell the clandestine gatherings, leading to banner headlines.[19] Cops armed with flashlights made the rounds of the Kensico plaza in the summer of 1928, shooing away cars and arresting more than a dozen young men at a time on various charges. Women were released without criminal charges filed against them. Some of the couples were described in the press as "scantily clad." The drivers came from New York City, Yonkers, Mount Vernon, Larchmont, Harrison and Tuckahoe, attesting to the popularity of the dam as a magnet for young love. After their arrest on charges of loitering or disorderly conduct, the accused were given a stern lecture by a Mount Pleasant town justice on the dangers of acquiring "a most undesirable reputation." The judge also fined them $50. By the time the crackdown was complete that summer, the town had collected $1,110 in fines from the motorized Romeos, a sizable sum in those days.[20]

The police crackdown at the Kensico Dam forced couples to find alternate places to rendezvous. Many simply drove to the other side of the dam, prompting another round of police raids. State Troopers were called out to curtail similar activities on Route 22, and local cemeteries saw a surge of night-time visitors not there to pay their respects.

The intersection of the automobile, recreation and other forms of entertainment might have created unease among older community residents, but it was all part of a grand plan to set Westchester apart from other budding suburbs across the nation. The plan's architect, William Ward, was Westchester's master builder and the visionary, who helped push through the Bronx River Parkway system and other enhancements designed to "offer a splendid opportunity to the home seeker or speculator." It was also intended to make the county "the biggest and richest in the State within the next few years."[21] Ward, or "Boss Ward," as he was frequently referred to in the press (a nickname he intensely disliked), was a quintessential power broker with a clear vision for the future. More than any other figure in the county's long history, Ward shaped Westchester into what it would become.

A consummate insider who controlled Westchester's political landscape for generations, Ward was the mastermind behind its most famous landmarks: the parkways, the

William Ward, right, seen here with his political rival, Governor Franklin Roosevelt, at the dedication of the Bronx River Parkway Extension in 1930, was the Republican boss of Westchester for decades. Governor Roosevelt, a Democrat, said the parkway system developed in Westchester was a factor in "building better citizenship" (Westchester County Historical Society).

county park system, Playland amusement park and the Westchester County Center, all adorned in the Art Deco motifs that radiated the era's stylized elegance. When author and commentator Theodore Platt wrote in the *American Mercury* two years after Ward's death in 1935 that "Westchester exemplified, in leading fashion, the suburb as a special kind of place," it was because of Ward that it earned that description.[22]

Ward was born in Greenwich, Connecticut, in 1856, the same year as the Republican party. The heir to a vast tool-and-dye family business, and a Quaker, he grew up in the Rye-Port Chester area and lived in a massive concrete castle built by his father in Rye Brook. He was athletic, rowing and playing football at Columbia, and he organized and financed a minor-league baseball club in Port Chester, the Blue Stockings, for which he occasionally took a turn at bat and in the field. Ward stood a few inches over six feet tall and walked with one shoulder slightly tilted forward, a style that made him look "like a football player carrying the ball."[23] His father made him learn the tool business on the factory floor in Port Chester with the workers, and Ward enjoyed turning out intricate metal parts at a machinist's bench well into his senior years. He married and had four children with his wife, Madge, who died in 1914. The Ward home was always filled with fresh chrysanthemums, roses and carnations that he raised in his own greenhouses, an aristocratic pursuit for gentlemen of an earlier era. The Boss also liked thin cigars made to his own specifications and drank Champagne and expensive bottled water. He took Turkish baths regularly and maintained a steady regimen of exercise through golf and walking. Impeccably attired, he favored colorful ties, bespoke suits and shoes made in England. He ruled Westchester with an iron hand encased in the softest leather gloves.[24]

Whatever his title—technically, he was the chairman of the Westchester County Republican Party—Ward was the man who ran the county during its burgeoning and formative years. While he only served one term in 1897-98 in the House of Representatives, Ward wielded power and influence behind the scenes that molded and shaped the country far into the future. During his 37-year tenure as GOP chairman, he yanked Westchester from the sway of Tammany Hall power brokers in New York City and the Democratic orbit in which it had circled for generations. Boss Ward turned the county into a major Republican stronghold.

Journalist John Crider, who interviewed Ward and wrote about him at length in the 1930s, described him as a visionary who also knew how to play politics. "He might have played hand in hand with Tammany Hall. He could have sold out to contractors and cheap real estate developers," wrote Crider, a Pulitzer Prize-winning journalist from Mount Vernon who went on to become editor of the *Boston Herald*. "Ward's Westchester was his own production," he continued, and cited his "wise use of patronage" to accomplish larger goals. "He carried on with the old tools, but made them serve the taxpayers where they had been robbed before.... He not only strove to give Westchester a decidedly attractive character, but he worked equally hard to protect its individuality by erecting barriers against the cheapening influences of the nearby metropolis."[25]

Exclusivity was Ward's primary goal. He wanted to build up Westchester as a place where what he saw as "the right sort" of people would live—middle-class white people in single-family homes—and he regularly promoted men and women throughout the county who shared that vision. While the county had always been split up into widely disparate communities that saw little interest in one another's problems, Ward insisted on taking a regional approach to the goals he set out to achieve. Above all, he wanted to keep the influence and spread of the city at bay, curtailing industry, blocking city subways

from expanding into Westchester and promoting zoning regulations that would discourage urbanized living conditions. Under his leadership, the county would become a place
where automotive transportation, single-family homes, abundant recreational opportunities, middle-class values and the comforts of an idealized domestic realm would reign
supreme.

Ward knew how to operate every setting on the political machine and used them
all. County employees were expected to support the Republican party, and those deemed
insufficiently loyal would find themselves out of a job. Dossiers were kept on monetary
contributions and voting attendance of all party members. Anyone who wanted to run
for elected office on the Republican ballot line, anywhere in Westchester, even in the
smaller villages, needed Ward's personal approval. Patronage was part of the package,
with the proviso that crucial jobs were to be held by those proven to be competent and
capable.

He took great pride in the changes he wrought, especially in ridding the county of
widespread corruption—most of it, anyway. "When I came here, conditions were pretty
bad," Ward observed late in life. "We had officials who spent a few minutes at a meeting
and then went across the street and played poker and drank rum. And that was what the
taxpayers got for their money. It took me twenty-five years to straighten things out, and
the last time an inspector was here from the state comptroller's office, he told us we have
the cleanest county in the state, and not so far from here, there are some about as dirty
as Westchester was thirty-five years ago. Those days are all over. There is little actual
thievery now. The graft that persists is in the form of that favoritism which gives the
inside track to certain contractors. As we got hold in the county offices we weeded out
those used to the old-time method. We did not send anybody to jail. We simply got them
out. From the time I was elected chairman it took me fifteen years before we had the
county completely under our control."[26]

The boss made plenty of enemies, some within his own party, but mainly in the
Democratic camp. He and Franklin Roosevelt became rivals when Roosevelt was elected
New York's governor, and their thorny relationship later extended to FDR's tenure in the
White House. (Ward was good friends with Theodore Roosevelt, Franklin's cousin.)
When Franklin Roosevelt was elected president, he appointed a special federal commissioner, Samuel Untermeyer, a prominent Yonkers lawyer and politico, to look into county
land purchases on Martine Avenue in White Plains and elsewhere in Westchester. The
county's purchase price arranged by a Ward associate in White Plains was nearly double
that of a private appraisal, and it was further revealed that a well-connected insider had
profited from the commission on the sale. The investigation led to some embarrassing
disclosures, but no indictments, and it signaled the bad relations between the county
and Roosevelt.[27] Ward himself called the land purchase legitimate and claimed the inquest
was politically motivated.

The press was also a regular critic of Ward, who regarded publicity and newspaper
reporters with scorn. Often referred to as the "Duke of Westchester" by editorial writers
critical of his high-handed ways, Ward rarely responded to criticism and chose imperious
silence instead. It was said that he helped an associate start a newspaper in Port Chester—
on the condition that his name never appear in it. Few photos of Boss Ward exist today.

Besides the construction of the parkway system, Ward also made Westchester a
leader in the field of social welfare, part of the Progressive agenda with which the Republican party was once aligned. Along with a Scarborough publisher and philanthropist,

V. Everit Macy (also a fellow Quaker), Ward revamped the county's facilities for orphans and indigents, making it one of the most advanced in the nation. Westchester County was the first in the state to open a child welfare department in 1915, with private funds. A dynamic and far-sighted social worker, Ruth Taylor, was named as the first director. The modern county-run medical facility Grasslands Hospital opened in 1920.

Ward and his brand of Progressive policies saw Westchester turn from farmland to real estate in less than one generation. By 1914, the population had hit 325,000, and land prices began to rise dramatically in the early part of the century. As the *Westchester County Magazine* proclaimed, with a note of local boosterism, "Farm land that sold for $100 an acre ten years ago is today worth from $200 to $750 an acre, and there are points where prices double and treble these figures are asked.... The future for all Westchester County real estate, however, is most propitious as those who live in the cities become better informed concerning it, and the presence of the automobile is making this knowledge more and more general from day to day. Truly the future of this great county is in front of it."[28]

When Ward, brought low by pneumonia following an operation, succumbed to death at the age of 76 in 1933, he was surrounded by his four children. It was widely observed in the press and political circles that the end of an era had gone with him. A large tract of land he helped acquire at Pound Ridge was later named after him, one of the few obvious reminders of his remarkable reign. His name has slipped into partial obscurity, even though in many respects he turned the rocky hills of Westchester into the very model of a modern suburb. A memorial tablet at the park that bears his name "Westchester's great constructive citizen leader." Perhaps a more apt memorial would have been to paraphrase another famous tombstone inscription of a master builder, London's Christopher Wren: "If you seek his epitaph, look around you."

One thing Ward could not control was a seething, boozy kind of anarchy that seemed to be everywhere. During the 1920s, lines were blurred between the good guys and the bad on a regular basis. The prohibition of alcohol that began with the Volstead Act in 1919 created a vast underworld where gangsters plied their trade with near impunity. Corruption spread its tentacles into every corner of officialdom, and a level of mayhem threatened the stability that was the cornerstone of suburban life, disrupting everything from the raising of the flag in front of city hall to a Sunday drive to church. Tommy guns, bathtub gin and gangland shootings became commonplace, all driven by huge profits generated by the illegal liquor trade. Communities all over Westchester, including Port Chester, Greenburgh, Mamaroneck Croton, and Ossining, saw a number of embarrassing episodes involving liquor—not to mention the river of beer running inside tubes planted within the municipal sewer lines of Yonkers.

The man who kept Westchester roaring through the 20s was a bootlegger named Louis Pope. The good life came easy to Pope, a man routinely referred to in the press as "bulbous," who had a taste for jewelry, silk and fine clothing. Born in 1884, the underworld entrepreneur stood out in an era full of outsized characters who made their living on the wrong side of the law. Pope worked the liquor racket under the protection of Dutch Schultz and a group of New York gangsters, while purportedly working in the real estate business. He even maintained a proper office in White Plains.

Pope threw some of the area's biggest and most lavish parties at his stately mansion in the Gedney Park section of White Plains, where his wife and a retinue of servants kept house. His home spared no detail and was built with a special underground tunnel for speedy getaways in lavish style. He favored Cadillacs and kept a fleet of them on hand, apparently for bribing officials as well as for his own transportation.[29] Pope also owned a yacht, the "Ruth M.," complete with six cabins, four tiled baths, and a .38 caliber pistol under his mattress, which he kept docked in Port Chester.[30] It became the flagship of his rum-running business and it made Pope a fortune. But it was not without its risk. He was once kidnapped by a rival group of gangsters (evidently from a gang associated with Owney Madden, a major underworld boss, seeking out new territory) and had to pay $50,000 for his freedom after several days of harrowing captivity. And of course, there was the threat of the law.

Pope and an underworld associate from Port Chester were arrested in March 1932 when Connecticut authorities came across of massive shipment of Champagne, whiskey, brandy and gin being unloaded from a steamer ostensibly carrying masonry supplies inside Stamford harbor. Pope was spotted in a nearby car, surveying the cargo being unloaded, and he was later picked up in Greenwich.[31] He had connections and good lawyers and beat the criminal charges against him. But after Prohibition ended, so did the good life for Pope. He used the tricks he had learned from the underground liquor business to trade in black market gasoline coupons that were used to ration fuel during World War II. He was arrested again and sent to jail, returning a broken man. Reduced to selling door to door, he died of a heart attack in 1950, broke and alone on his houseboat, with two cans of beer in the fridge to slake his thirst.[32]

Crime had a way of turning things upside down. Prohibition spawned an underworld army that brought big-city crime and corruption to formerly law-abiding communities. The village of Mamaroneck was caught up in one of the most sensational scandals of the period. It was where "Westchester's biggest crap game" was being run, as well as dozens of speakeasies and "disorderly houses," aka brothels. The local press reported multiple complaints in 1928 that Mamaroneck was getting a reputation of being a "wide-open town," with some 40 illegal drinking operations in the village, along with houses for other illicit proclivities.[33]

The unprecedented criminal activity made a local newspaper reporter a busy man— too busy for those profiting from the illicit activities going on in "The Friendly Village." Peter Campbell was a young Canadian working at the *Daily Times* who gained extensive knowledge of the village's thriving speakeasy and gambling trade. One January evening in 1929, as Campbell headed to his office after making his rounds on the police beat, he was jumped by a heavy-set man. The slightly built reporter, described in press accounts as weighing 135 pounds, was knocked to the ground and kicked in the face, resulting in several loosened teeth and double black eyes. Police arrested three men in the assault and later determined that the organizer was a former town constable who had been featured prominently in one of Campbell's news columns.[34] The slender Canadian had implicated the constable, Henry Gironda, in several recent crimes and incurred his wrath. Gironda was eventually convicted of initiating the attack on Campbell, and he was sentenced to over a year in prison at Sing Sing. He became a very bitter man behind Ossining's stone walls and began recounting stories about his ex-friends in Mamaroneck. Tell me more, said the Westchester County district attorney.

The ex-constable, it turned out, had been running a speakeasy as well as a high-stakes dice game in town. Betting reached thousands of dollars and earned Gironda $300 to $700 a night. The gambling boss also ran a string of slot machines and later claimed he made regular payments of cash and jewelry to local police to keep the revelries going unimpeded. In the wake of the DA's revelations, the police chief and two detectives resigned.[35] Gironda seems to have led a dangerous life. In 1933 he was shot twice at a speakeasy, the Hollywood Inn in Mount Pleasant; before the shooting, he claimed to police he had been abducted and brutalized by racketeers.[36]

The trilogy of gunfire, booze and bribery that turned quiet towns into armed camps was hardly an isolated incident in Mamaroneck. Federal agents rarely cooperated with local police when they staged a raid in Westchester, well aware that bootleggers would be tipped off in advance.

When the Feds raided Port Chester and smashed down the doors of 27 speakeasies in 1930, local cops were the last to find out. The village police department was finally tipped off when a police sergeant saw a man, who happened to be African American, with a gun drawn chasing a white man down the street. The sergeant intervened, assuming a robbery was underway, but quickly found out he was confronting a fellow lawman. The black man with the gun flashed his badge and announced he was a federal agent chasing down and arresting the proprietor of a local speakeasy.[37] A total of 28 men were arrested for serving booze everywhere from barber shops to luxuriantly outfitted saloons.

Even when a seizure of illegal alcohol was successful, things had a way of going wrong. When local cops in Greenburgh confiscated 365 gallons from an Elmsford still in October 1929, a special police guard was placed around the recovered barrels. Federal agents arrived the next morning to remove 12 drums of alcohol for destruction, only to discover that the 180-proof moonshine had turned to water.[38]

Nowhere was a bottle of liquor safe. A police chief's office, a rich man's wine cellar—neither was invulnerable to the corrupting influence of Prohibition, and booze could be purchased just about anywhere, even in a public building in Ossining. In December 1921, a janitor at the Ossining Municipal Building, George McLeavey, was caught selling a kind of high-proof hooch called "bar whiskey" to two men inside the building. A bottle held by police chief Frank Minnerly also happened to disappear around the same time. The janitor got off with a fine.[39] In 1926, a wealthy Rye resident found out that his private stock had been raided. The theft of Champagne and five quarts of gin was discovered in November when the household staff of Philip Boardman found the cellar door at his Manursing Island estate had been broken open. The criminal mastermind behind the theft, a 19-year-old electrician's helper from Mamaroneck who was working on the property, was arrested after passing out drunk at the home of a local woman nearby.[40]

Booze could be purchased just steps from the halls of the criminal justice system itself. Across the street from the Westchester County Courthouse in White Plains, liquor was served at 75 cents a glass at the New Standard House. Two federal agents walked in and ordered a drink in August 1921 and found that a discrete horse-track betting operation also appeared to be run from the establishment.[41]

Besides the rampant spread of corruption, a recklessness born of the artificial restraint on alcohol spread its way through small towns and big cities. With the car giving criminals new mobility and freedom to wreak havoc, the forces unleashed by Prohibition reached into every corner of the county, corrupting everything they touched. The public reacted with mute outrage most of the time, but not always.

The "trolley murders" of 1925 touched a nerve as few other crimes in the county had previously, and the cruelty and senselessness behind it led to a near-lynching. It was early on a Monday morning on July 20 when six passengers settled in for what was expected to be an uneventful ride on the Westchester Street Railway Co. running between

New Rochelle and Mount Vernon at 15 miles an hour. As the trolley trundled along an isolated stretch of track that is now Sandford Boulevard, a Cadillac drew up beside it. Simultaneously, one of the trolley passengers stood up and walked toward the front. The passenger, wearing a gray suit and a straw hat, pulled out a revolver and shot the trolley operator in the back of the head. The trolley ground to a stop, and the gunman turned to a security guard entrusted with a large bag of coins he was shuttling to the company's office in Mount Vernon. The assailant shot the guard once in the chest as he tried to edge away, then once in the back before grabbing the weekend's receipts.[42] Taken aback by the sheer weight of $1,800 in nickels and dimes—about 70 pounds—the gunman hesitated, strained and lifted the coins before hopping off the trolley and joining his awaiting confederate in the Cadillac. Inside the trolley, two men lay dying. Jacob Shumacher, 62, the guard who was also a longtime employee, uttered his last words: "He didn't give me a chance." The trolley's motorman, Raglan Nicoll, 30, a World War I veteran, never came out of a coma and died the next day.

The Cadillac driver took a turn too fast a mile away from the crime scene, blowing out a rear tire. The robbers ran on foot as police sirens began to wail, but the massive bag of loose change proved too heavy; they managed to hold onto only about $200 of the loot. In addition to the money, police eventually recovered two revolvers and a hypodermic syringe that contained a residue of cocaine, an example of the way crime and drugs have long been intertwined. The Cadillac gave investigators their best lead, and a short time later the vehicle was traced to a woman from East Harlem. Her husband, John "Dopey" Marino, a petty criminal with a prison record, was soon in custody, and facing the electric chair, he quickly began to talk. Marino named David DeMaio, a New Rochelle tough-guy described as a well-known bootlegger who had been involved in a Pelham robbery attempt several years previously. DeMaio, picked up with three cases of whiskey in his car, was called the mastermind of the trolley job. Also named was Frankie Daly, the triggerman, described in the *New York Times* as "a drug addict and ex-convict" who had spent time at Sing Sing on a burglary conviction. New York City cops had been searching all the known cocaine hangouts in the city for his whereabouts before he was picked up in Westport, Connecticut.[43]

The gangsterism and drug-tinged carnage that came together in that blood-spattered trolley car, combined with sickening imagery of the merciless killing of two family men for a pile of nickels and dimes, drove the public into a fury. When the suspects were finally captured and brought to Westchester, more than 1,000 people gathered in front of the Mount Vernon police headquarters, muttering threats; there were serious concerns by the authorities in charge that the men would be pulled from their jail cells and lynched on the spot. Extra police were called out.[44] Vigilante justice was not meted out, but the wheels of justice turned quickly for Daly and DeMaio. Marino gave testimony in exchange for escaping the electric chair, which was the fate of both Daly and DeMaio roughly a year after the crime. Marino died of tuberculosis at Sing Sing a few years after the trolley murders.[45]

The violation of law and order and a desire for revenge were recurring themes in the annals of the period. Commentators wondered in print whether a new breed of criminals were on the loose—more violent, amoral and ruthless—and if the new motion picture industry was bolstering the trend. A prison chaplain at Sing Sing made headlines in the late 20s when he gave a lecture to a civic group about the latest crime wave. Headlined "Criminals Are Worse Than Ever Before," the remarks given by the Rev. Anthony Petersen,

Prisoners at Sing Sing were required to march in lockstep, as seen here in the early 1900s. The prison in Ossining was infamous for the cruel conditions it imposed on inmates in its early years (Westchester County Historical Society).

a Presbyterian minister from Scarborough who had accompanied dozens of men to the electric chair, painted a picture of young thugs who "shoot left and right, without regard for life or property."[46]

The public anxiety over lawlessness was starkly revealed in 1928 following a series of robberies aimed at delivery men in Yonkers. To combat the problem, a police detective hid himself inside a horse-drawn, wagon-load of bread. When the wagon was stopped by an armed thief shortly after setting out, the detective, catching the robber off guard, promptly shot him dead. The detective was cleared in the shooting, and grand jury members gave him "sustained applause" as he left the courthouse, the county district attorney noted with satisfaction at a later meeting with law enforcement personnel.[47] Westchester County district attorney Frank Coyne went on to cite the shooting as an excellent lesson in proactive law enforcement. Speaking before the Westchester Patrolman's Benevolent Association in 1929, Coyne said gunmen should be "shot down on sight, as a means of giving them a dose of their own medicine." The county sheriff, Thomas Underhill, respectfully differed—"An officer may shoot an innocent man very often," he said, and prudence and judgment were required from police officers.[48]

The debate over police shootings was thrown into sharp relief the following year. A gunman by the name of Patrick McDonald, described in subsequent newspaper accounts as a "drug-crazed criminal of long experiences" and also known as Patsy Carroll, came to Irvington on March 3, 1929. Near an estate on Route 9, he encountered Irvington Motorcycle Patrolman George Dugan, who had stopped his machine to stretch his legs for a few moments at a picturesque section of the village. The gunman shot the officer dead without uttering a single word, then kidnapped a chauffeur on a nearby estate. He made his escape with a stolen car, telling the chauffeur, "I've got a grudge against cops.... I'll shoot every last one I get a chance to."[49] The hunt for McDonald, who had served prison sentences in New Orleans and Boston, came to an end a few days later in Harrisburg, Pennsylvania, where McDonald tried to rob the Dauphin Hotel. A clerk gave the alarm, and McDonald was shot dead after he emptied his revolver at a squad of police.[50]

As the Irvington murder demonstrated, the automobile gave criminals new liberties in pursuing criminal activities. They were far more mobile, and as a result, illegal drinking establishments turned up in residential neighborhoods. Even a Sunday morning drive to church could end up as an encounter with the criminal class. A woman going to church in Irvington on Sunday morning had her car stolen at gunpoint by a group of drunken men with lengthy criminal records on August 18, 1928. They'd spent the night in a low-end speakeasy called the Roma Gardens on Taxter Road in East Irvington. The four gunmen were finally captured after a shoot-out with a Yonkers motorcycle cop.[51]

While the Prohibition "speakeasy" conjures popular images of icy cocktails and glamour, many were low-end dives like the Roma Gardens in East Irvington. Gunfire spilled from the bar one early morning, culminating in a running shootout with police (courtesy Westchester County Archives, District Attorney files)

The lawlessness of the period affected all levels of society and the wealthy inhabitants of the county soon found themselves easy marks. In the mid–20s, a pair of smooth-talking and well-armed criminals made unannounced house calls to some of the county's most socially prominent homeowners, demanding cash and jewelry. Arthur Barry and "Boston Billy" Williams, who became known as "the ladder burglars," were two New Englanders who turned up in Westchester because it was prime territory for their line of work: high-end robberies. The two used newspaper society columns to draw up their list of targets, which read like a page out of the Social Register. Irving Berlin's mother-in-law was robbed of her belongings by the pair in Irvington, and a Rockefeller family member was taken for $35,000 in Greenwich, Connecticut. Homes up and down the county, 22 of them in all, were hit, with about $500,000 worth of jewels and belongings from the monied elite winding up in their pockets. Known for using ladders to enter upstairs bedrooms during the early morning hours, they made small talk and pleasantries while forcing victims to open safes and turn over valuables. They let some owners keep certain jewels which held sentimental attachment, even returning some jewelry by mail.

They talked a good game but the pair were also violent and used a pearl-handled automatic to hold up their victims. Barry was linked with the killing of a Scarsdale police sergeant, John Harrison, shot to death on July 23, 1923, on Fenimore Road as he pursued a pair of thieves who fit the description of the men.[52] Barry and Williams eventually had a falling out, quarreling over the spoils of a $100,000 heist, and Barry was picked up when a tipster led police to a Long Island hideaway. The tipster was his partner; Barry, in turn, informed on Williams, sending him away for a long stretch at Dannemora Prison. Both claimed that the other had shot the Scarsdale lawman, and authorities never gained enough evidence to go to trial. After Barry was brought to Westchester, he attempted several escapes and bragged to police they would have a hard time keeping him locked up.[53]

He was true to his word, and a prison uprising at Auburn on July 28, 1929, which began when an inmate sneaked into the armory there, turned into a fiery battleground that allowed Barry and three other prisoners to escape. For a while, he was one of the most wanted fugitives in America. He was eventually captured at a quiet farm in Newton, New Jersey, in Sussex County, in part because a local newsdealer recalled a man fitting his description buying New York City newspapers. Barry had developed a taste for reading the gossip columns about the glamorous people he once robbed for a living. He had also stiffed the newsdealer out of two weeks of papers.[54]

Crime had a way of penetrating wealthy enclaves and dignified old communities. It even had a way of burrowing under the streets of a city. In perhaps the most brazen instance of illicit trade and lawlessness, the case of the "river of beer" running underneath the streets of Yonkers stands out, a stunt that even in an era jaded by the exploits of rum-runners managed to capture national attention. It was called the "Great Beer Hose Mystery," though for those in the know, the caper was hardly a mystery. The strange stream of suds running through a series of underground tubes in the Yonkers sewer system was the handiwork of one of the most notorious gangsters of the era, Dutch Schultz.

The scandal came to light when a Yonkers city worker finished repairs on a sewer line and discovered a mysterious tube running through it. The hose was found to lead to an abandoned garage, where it snaked around stored beer barrels onto another network of hoses. The underground tubing eventually converged on an illegal brewery being run out of the State Cereal Co. in a neighborhood called Chicken Island, around Edward and

Ann streets near Nepperhan Avenue. It was the center of a vast distribution operation connected by the city sewers. By the time 6,000 feet of hosing, estimated to be worth about $25,000, was hauled up from city manholes, Yonkers found itself at the center of a national scandal. The Volstead Act had unleashed an entrepreneurial wave of clever engineering and backwoods chemistry, but no one had seen an underground brewing operation like this before.[55]

An assistant U.S. attorney had a very good question to ask once the operation was discovered: "We would like to know just how more than a quarter mile of four-inch hose could be run under Columbus Avenue, Elm Street, Palisade Avenue and John Street, Yonkers, without knowledge on the part of city officials or employees."[56] It was a rather embarrassing question that Mayor John Fogarty, and his commissioners, were hard pressed to answer—especially when called to appear before a federal grand jury. The mayor himself said he was "not at all satisfied" over the entire business, but didn't offer any explanations.

Editorials in the New York papers kept up a stinging fusillade of ridicule for days. "This is the sort of brainwork that keeps us in beer," the *New York Mirror* enthused. "It deserves public applause."[57] Not so, said editorial writers at the *New York Evening Graphic*. They said the beer business hardly needed such an elaborate covert operation in such reckless times, when all that was needed was to back up a truck to a brewery in plain sight and ship the illegal content to anyone who wanted it. Whoever thought of it, the paper advised, was sorely in need of re-training, and "the bootlegger college should enroll him at once."[58]

In fact, the man behind the underground river of beer, Dutch Schultz, had a Ph.D. from bootlegger university. Born Arthur Flegenheimer to Jewish parents in Harlem in 1902—and taking his moniker from an old boxer who ran with the "Frog Hollow Gang" on the mean streets of the Bronx the century before—Schultz was a curious character. A hardened gangster who made his fortune during Prohibition, he grew up poor and began a life of crime in his teens. Favoring cheap suits at a time when gangsters were expected to dress with a modicum of style, he was once described by a chorus girl of his acquaintance as looking like Bing Crosby with his face bashed in.[59] What he lacked in style and fashion, he made up for in street smarts and ruthlessness, and every morning for much of the latter 1920s, a fleet of trucks rumbled down the cobblestone streets of New York from Yonkers and other locations to pour the Dutchman's beer down the throat of a thirsty city. With the proceeds of this beer empire, along with the revenues from other organized crime rackets, Schultz became a very wealthy man during his brief life. But according to Meyer Berger, a reporter of the era who made a study of organized crime, law-enforcement observers were always skeptical about how much a strong man the Dutchman really was. "Policemen generally agreed that he had far less animal courage than the thugs and bruisers who drove his trucks and did his killings during the fierce competition in the beer trade," Berger wrote.[60] While he never had the bravado that captivated public attention, Schultz had a keen eye for organization and great accounting skills. When police went through his possessions after he was gunned down in 1935 by rival gangsters in New Jersey, they found an itemized list of his meal expenses. He was able to beat the Internal Revenue Service not once but twice on tax-evasion charges. The .45-caliber slug from mob associates served a different kind of justice, and Schultz, who had converted to Catholicism, was laid to rest in the Gate of Heaven Cemetery in Mount Pleasant.

The embarrassment over the brewery was not over for Yonkers after the hoses were pulled from the labyrinth below the streets. Schultz's widow, Frances, who worked as a cigarette girl at one of Schultz's nightclubs, ended up filing a lawsuit over the brewery, claiming that Schultz held a controlling interest in the operation and that she deserved payment for his share as his widow. She also claimed that a major Yonkers politico, Thomas Brogan, was a co-owner, which he denied. The lawsuits dragged on for years without success, and the brewery eventually went into bankruptcy.[61] Subsequent investigations revealed that Dutch Schultz used a garage in Mount Vernon, on South Street near West First Street, to keep the millions of dollars in profits from his numbers racket in southern Westchester and New York City secured. The operation, which employed some 75 clerks, was protected by Tammany Hall.[62]

Ridiculous pranks inspired by the flow of illegal alcohol co-existed with the menace of organized crime in American communities throughout the Prohibition years. New Rochelle residents woke up on a Monday morning in June 1924 to discover that Old Glory was no longer flapping in the breeze in front of city hall. In its place was a whiskey jug and a lighted red lantern, nearly 170 feet off the ground. The ropes affixing the flag—now the jug—had been cut from below, leaving the two objects flying aloft from the grounds of the city municipal complex. The spectacle first drew some curious onlookers, then a crowd. The fire department, mayor, police department and local press soon converged, as did the national press. A traffic cop was eventually assigned to the spot to keep traffic moving in front of city call. City clerk Charles Kammermeyer acknowledged the inherent humor of the situation but called it "a slap at the city's civic pride." Mayor Harry Scott was said to have been livid.[63]

It was no easy task to bring down the jug, even with a 75-foot ladder truck and the efforts of more than a dozen city employees pulling, pushing and tugging the severed ropes. The lantern did come down, but the jug stayed triumphantly aloft. The city finally called in a team of steeplejacks from Long Island, specialists who climbed and painted flagpoles. The cost to hire the services of the six men, at $75, was another blow to the city's pride and its coffers. Three days after the jug was hoisted it was finally lowered to the ground in front of a crowd of 500 who cheered as it descended. Police chief Frank Cody was the first to inspect the one-gallon offense. As the *Standard-Star* reported, "He breathed long and hard. Men looked at him with dancing light in their eyes. Women wondered. Children giggled. All were impatient to learn the answer. Instead of the chief's face brightening with smiles, it soon turned crimson with disgust."[64] Sour beer. Very sour beer. The mayor was on hand, but he wasn't giving interviews, and he was in no mood for jokes. The rancid liquid was quickly dumped down the nearest sewer grate—after police detectives dusted it for fingerprints. It became a major priority for the local cops to find out who was behind "the little brown jug."

A short time later, Mayor Scott personally signed the criminal complaints against the two suspects who were brought in and booked for malicious mischief. One was a 27-year-old World War I veteran who lost part of a finger to shrapnel in France. The other was 21 years old. They faced a year in prison and a $500 fine—as well as the bemused gratitude of most New Rochelle residents, who regarded the incident as more of a practical joke than a criminal offense, according to a number of informal newspaper polls at the time. The two men denied any connection with the deed, but eyewitnesses identified them standing in front of the flagpole late Saturday night pulling on the halyards. After a jury deliberated for four hours, they were found guilty, and each ordered to pay a $25 fine. Justice was served and the Stars and Stripes were restored to their rightful place. The pride of the city bruised by the indignity of a beer bucket sailing from its flagstaff was soon recovered.[65]

There were plenty of opportunities for jokes and ridicule during the 1920s as extremes of human nature played out amid an ever loosening social code. Greed and get-rich schemes, while a constant in every era, made spectacularly strong showings in Westchester as the stock market and other forms of speculation made their way from Wall Street to Main Street. In Yonkers, a great gold-mine scam became a case study in the way that financial judgment can shut down when dollar signs light up.

Hundreds of gullible investors staked a claim in the "Yonkers Yukon," as it came to be known, then lost it all to some smooth-talking con artists in 1922. The Iridio-Platinum-Gold Co. was the creation of an extravagant Russian emigre and newspaper editor by the name of Vasily Cherniak, who claimed to have learned the prospecting trade in the Ural Mountains of his native land. His real expertise, it turned out, was in bilking his fellow countrymen living in lower Westchester.

The swindlers first bought up farmland on an old estate in Yonkers in the Nepera Park neighborhood, then commenced to "mine" it for precious metals. Their true quarry was the suckers who believed that gold dotted the hills of the Nepperhan Valley. Cherniak and company printed up gaudy-looking stock certificates and sold them for $1 apiece to Russian immigrants from Yonkers, Hastings-on-Hudson and the Lower East Side of Manhattan, telling them that they would turn profits hundreds of times over once the mine came in.[66] The grifters were so bold that they took out advertisements in the Yonkers *Statesman* and erected a large billboard over South Broadway in the city touting the great value of their Yonkers mining venture. Skeptical investors were given a tour of the "mine": Cherniak and his associates had built a Potemkin village on the 163 acres they'd purchased in Yonkers and Greenburgh that mimicked the appearance of an actual mining camp, salting it with a few pea-sized chunks of real gold and platinum. They would routinely astound visitors when they fished out the glittering bits from piles of dirt that came pouring out of a mechanical rock crusher. They even blasted a few sections of the farm with black powder to add another realistic touch to the imposter operation, but greed did most of the work for them at their fake mine. On one occasion, a gold collar button was even planted in the soil as part of the deception. Prospective investors were apparently too crazed by gold fever to pay much attention to distracting details.[67]

The sales prospectus detailed how Cherniak had hunted for mineral wealth all the way from Alaska and California to the Carpathian Mountains before stumbling on a massive vein of precious metals just a few miles north of New York City, worth millions in gold and silver. The sales brochure characterized Cherniak as a man "who never cared for money for its own sake"; this alone should have raised warning flags among potential investors. The mining venture was duly incorporated under the laws of Delaware (Cherniak had an admirable attention to detail), and was such a hit that the company took in somewhere between $500,000 and $1 million in investments,[68] worth more than $12 million today. Most of those swindled by Cherniak were from the Russian community in the New York area, many of whom had fled the Bolshevik revolution of 1917 and the subsequent civil war, but funds poured in from across the country. Local merchants and contractors were also taken in by the fake enterprise. City officials in Yonkers somehow turned a blind eye to the "mining" operations, but the Iridio-Platinum-Gold Co. had a New York City branch office, and when a Manhattan prosecutor finally received hundreds of complaints from disgruntled investors, the cops moved in. They uncovered only four ounces of raw gold and four ounces of raw platinum but hundreds of broken dreams. Four Russian immigrants and a physician from Yonkers who once served as a consul general in St. Petersburg, Russia, were arrested in May 1922, not long before they planned to skip the country. Cherniak was picked up in a Polish boarding house in Herkimer, New York, in the Mohawk Valley, where he had recently bought a farm with a $25 cash deposit and promised shares of a gold-mining venture he was planning to start there.

He was unrepentant when the law caught up with him, and after his arrest he continued to talk about his next big score. "I am 56 years old, and my right side has become paralyzed through my efforts to strike pay dirt," he declared in his upstate jail cell. "But I'll astound the world someday by developing the greatest gold mine in history."[69] Cherniak's story was astounding, but it was a tale of egregious gullibility, not geology. A Manhattan jury deliberated an hour before returning guilty verdicts against the con artist and his associates, and he and his fellow speculators were sent to another former mining operation known as Sing Sing state prison. Stone cold walls and a striking view of the Hudson were Cherniak's final payoffs as a prospector, the ultimate reward for a mother lode of fool's gold.[70]

6

American Pursuits
Playland, the Movies and Civil Unrest

Above all his other work during his long career, Westchester power broker William Ward had a singular affection for Playland Amusement Park in Rye. Troubled by insomnia in later life, he often took late-night walks there. It was a place he knew intimately, for he had poured his creative energies into its creation: he scrutinized every aspect of the plan as it was being designed, and even consulted on the uniforms that the staff would wear. He personally selected the kind of frankfurters that would be sold there after tasting a half-dozen samples. Playland was his playpen: a venue that owed its mixture of ambition, whimsy, family entertainment and scrupulous attention to detail to Ward's own vision of the suburban good life.[1]

Playland was a massive endeavor. Workers pumped 350,000 cubic yards of fine-grained sand from the bottom of Long Island Sound to spread along the water's edge. They built thrill rides with names like the Tumble Bug and the Whip to coax screams and laughter from the crowds. A timbered monster of a roller coaster, the Aeroplane (since torn down) bestrode the park like a colossus. A bathhouse to accommodate 10,000 people rose from the shoreline, and in the rush toward opening day in 1929, 1,000 workers poured over a million square feet of concrete in three weeks.[2] When it was finally finished, they had built the nation's first fully planned family amusement park, and one of Westchester's great showpieces.

The site along the Long Island Sound had long been a popular resort area, offering visitors endless pitchers of beer, clams, bowling lanes, cabanas and cooling breezes since the 1890s. The Rye Beach Pleasure Park provided carousel rides and a Ferris wheel, and in 1921, two entrepreneurs opened a much larger "Paradise Park" on the site that became Playland. The two amusement parks were decidedly honky-tonk affairs and a noise nuisance for the nearby residential neighborhoods in Rye. Drunks and pickpockets were some of the more unsavory attractions, and a big fire in 1926 made Paradise Park even less appealing.[3] Westchester County had long considered purchasing the site to fill in swampland and eradicate the swarms of mosquitoes that bred there, and as the two amusement parks became more and more of an affront to the community, the plan to buy out the old parks and build a brand new one went into action.[4] The 220-acre park also fit in with Ward's strategy to build a network of parkways and recreational attractions, making leisure and easy automotive transportation the selling points for Westchester.

When it was competed in 1928, Playland was the first planned amusement park for family entertainment in the country. Jutting out into Long Island Sound in Rye, its Art Deco buildings, manicured midway and pristine beaches covered 220 acres (New York Public Library, Lionel Pincus and Princess Firyal Map Division).

A trade magazine for the amusement business noted the innovations the park held, as well as the harmonious blend of landscape, architecture and artistry. "The huge park … contains many features that are a direct departure from anything that has been done before in amusement parks," the magazine's editor noted. "From first to last this park is being built with the object of pleasing higher classes of patrons as well as the usual; and it is being created with the belief that certain classes of patrons that have been lost to amusement parks in recent years will come back…. Playland is national advertising for all amusement parks."[5] Among the cited new features was the music piped over loudspeakers across the entire park. "The music will be in harmony with the high tone of Playland. It is not the desire … to appeal to the hurdy-gurdy class of patrons," the magazine stated.[6]

With this high-class ideal in sight, the venture hired a prominent architectural firm, Walker and Gillette, to clad Playland's buildings in the style known as moderne, better known today as Art Deco. The park was also specifically designed to be reached by automobile, not public transportation. Frank Darling, a leading "amusement man" who had designed recreational attractions around the world, was brought in to develop the park and scrutinize every detail. As Darling described it, "No recreation or amusement area has ever been so extensively and thoroughly planned and perfected as Playland."[7]

Vigilant Rye residents insisted that the playlist for the park's audio system, the first of its kind at an amusement park, adhere to a pre-approved loop of John Philip Sousa, Richard Wagner and Irving Berlin. Jazz was strictly banned from the park's loudspeakers. The total cost was estimated at anywhere between $6 million and $10 million—adding to concerns raised by critics of Ward that the county was spending too extravagantly.[8] It was also to become the only amusement park owned and operated by a municipal government in the country, causing trouble in the years to come when operating costs exceeded revenue and put local taxpayers on the hook.

Thrill rides, roller coasters, a skating rink, musical performances and a big pool, seen here in an undated photo, continue to draw crowds to Rye Playland (courtesy Westchester County

Playland was a place for wholesome family fun, the apex of a carefully constructed empire of leisure. The celebration of idealized family life, and the depiction of America as a repository of small-town virtues, also derived from the creative output of a number of other longtime Westchester visionaries.

Norman Rockwell was born in New York City and had a thick city accent all his life. He moved with his family to Mamaroneck as a boy, and Rockwell dropped out of Mamaroneck High School as a junior in 1911 to pursue an arts career.[9] He later lived in New Rochelle on Mount Tom Road, where he forged a friendship with two of the leading graphic illustrators of the 1920s, Joseph Leyendecker, and his brother, Frank Leyendecker. Rockwell portrayed stylized portraits of apple-cheeked youth, while Joseph Leyendecker created advertising campaigns for menswear that embodied style and sophistication. The output of the New Rochelle illustrators shaped the look of American popular culture for decades.[10]

The era was famous for another empire of fantasy and make-believe, as the burgeoning new industry of motion pictures came of age in the woods, cities, villages, sand dunes and seascapes of the Northeast. When Tinseltown had a largely New York address, Westchester was at the heart of this thriving film business.

Several factors helped make New York and New Jersey the cradle of the silent-film era. Thomas Edison invented the early film technology in the 1890s and closely guarded its use from his West Orange, New Jersey, headquarters. The Broadway stage and its pool of theatrical talent were centered in New York, and the Great White Way channeled its dramatic talents into the early film industry. The suburban film studios were easily acces-

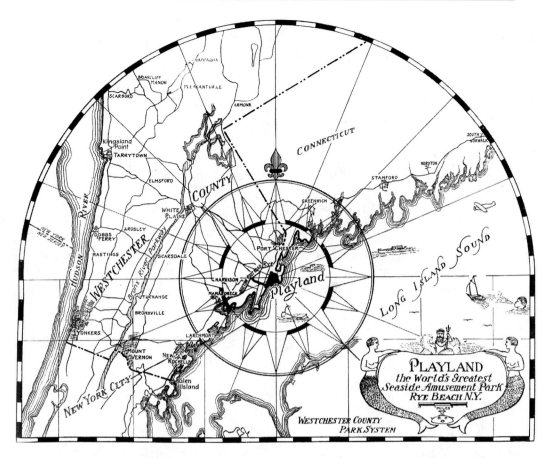

Playland was intended from the start to be both the center of Westchester leisure activity and a national advertisement for all amusement parks, as this playful early map shows (courtesy Westchester County Archives).

sible by train lines from the city, and since Westchester has abundant natural scenery, from woodlands to shorelines to folksy villages, its versatility lent itself well to filmmakers looking to create the illusions of Paul Revere's ride or Macbeth's castle.

The first Tarzan, Elmo Lincoln, thumped his chest along the banks of the Croton River in 1918, and the Battle of Concord between Minutemen and Redcoats was re-fought in front of the cameras in Somers.[11] Beginning in 1912, the Thanhouser Film Corp. in New Rochelle cranked out 1,000 melodramas and mysteries from 1910 to 1919, creating some of the first film stars of the silver screen, and the Triangle Studio in Yonkers also attracted top talent to film. The oldest complete feature film, a 1912 production of *Richard III* starring Frederick Warde, was filmed at locations around an unspecified site on Long Island Sound in Westchester and City Island in the Bronx. Warde recalled how the presence of "telegraph and telephone poles," as well as a "modern nursemaid wheeling a baby carriage" added challenges to the filming.[12]

The most ambitious of the silent-film impresarios to mount a camera in Westchester was D.W. Griffith, an undisputed master of the form credited with inventing many of the techniques used by successive generations of filmmakers. His blazing successes and long decline underscored both the light and dark sides of the business. Griffith, an aristocratic

Southerner whose shockingly crude portrayal of blacks in *Birth of a Nation* sullied his reputation for later generations, came to Mamaroneck in 1919 with big ideas. He bought the estate of an old oil baron at Orienta Point in Mamaroneck and turned it into his own cinematic domain, breaking free from the early studio system that had lost patience with his creative ways.[13]

The Mamaroneck studio drew celebrities and artists from far and wide. Jazz singer Al Jolson made an appearance there, and Abel Gance, the famed French film director, also paid a call.[14] Working on his own and unshackled from the restraints of the studios he had come to detest, the mercurial director was able to turn out some of his finest work at Orienta Point, transforming the local landscape into the Maine countryside and revolutionary Paris through the magic of set decoration, lighting and costumes. He also filmed scenes of the American Revolution in northern Westchester. Lillian Gish, Griffith's greatest star, directed the first movie to come out of the Mamaroneck studio, a comedy called *Remodeling Her Husband*, a rarity in a field dominated by men from the outset.[15] While he gave Gish the license to direct, he was himself a demanding driver of actors, and one of the most grueling film shoots took place on the set of *Way Down East*, a melodrama starring Gish as a jilted lover abandoned by a Boston playboy. A scene in which Gish drifts into an icy river in a suicide attempt was filmed during a real blizzard on Long Island Sound, and a coat of ice formed over her face during one long take. The actress later fainted from cold-induced exhaustion.[16] The picture was a smash, one of Griffith's last successes. He was forced to sell the Mamaroneck mansion in 1925 after mounting debts and the fickle nature of the movie business crushed his hopes for financial independence. He soon drifted into alcoholism and professional oblivion, dying in 1948 after collapsing in the lobby of a Los Angeles hotel where he lived alone. It was a

Enid Markey and Elmo Lincoln star in the 1918 film *Tarzan of the Apes*, filmed on location along the Croton River. Local high-school kids were used as extras (Wikimedia Commons).

D.W. Griffith began his own studio in Mamaroneck, where he filmed an epic about the French Revolution. The spit of land he purchased in 1919 on the Long Island coastline was turned into a set for *Orphans of the Storm* (Westchester County Historical Society).

grim end to a remarkable career, almost as if scripted to play as one of his earlier silent-film melodramas.[17] The downward arc of his life may have been a cautionary tale of pride and the erratic nature of the movie business, but the films themselves stand the test of time, bringing a viewer back to the creation of a new art form with lasting influence, the birth of a cinema nation.

Other legends from the world of stage and vaudeville also made cameo appearances in Westchester during the early days of film. Harry Houdini, a master magician whose name is conjured whenever someone escapes from a tight spot, made his first film in Yonkers. Houdini also gave numerous performances at Sing Sing prison, where he regularly broke out of cages and handcuffs.[18] His wife, Bess, bought a country house near Playland in Rye in 1930 and was later buried at the Gate of Heaven Cemetery in Valhalla.[19]

After years on the stage circuit, Houdini appeared in a number of short films, but he longed for cinema stardom. He came to a Yonkers studio to find it in the fall of 1918 for his first performances in feature-length motion pictures. It was a tough shoot for Houdini, who continued to carry a full load of stage bookings while he filmed *The Master Mystery*, a thriller series. The aspiring film star broke his wrist and suffered some bad bruises during an accident on the set in Yonkers, hitting a wall as he descended in a mockup of a parachute.[20] A trouper if there ever was one, he continued with his film and stage work, commuting a few miles a day from his home in upper Manhattan to the Octagon Film Corp.'s Yonkers set, a 20-minute drive. He made $1,500 a week.[21]

In the film, Houdini plays a government agent sent out to smash an evil corporation before it unleashes Madagascar Madness, a hideous disease that turns its victims into laughing imbeciles, on the public. Houdini uses his magic skills to escape numerous close calls on camera, not to mention the dangerous clutches of a beautiful villainess named De Luxe Dora. In one sequence, Houdini does battle with Automaton, a creature described in the film's publicity as a "scientific villain"; in actuality, he was a stuntman with a paint can on his head wearing lots of tin.[22] The concept was Houdini's, and it has been cited as the first time a "robot" character has appeared on film.

Houdini starred in several other films on the West Coast after *The Master Mystery*, but his movie career vanished not long after it began in Yonkers, leaving only a handful of middling reviews in *Variety* and *Billboard* to show for it. In typical Hollywood fashion, Houdini ended up suing the producers on the film for what he believed was creative accounting that cut him out of his share of the profits. The master magician was also a tough critic of his own performance on film. His intensity and outsized personality, traits that worked well in live performances, did not translate to the silent screen, and magic acts often lose their visual power when they are reproduced on camera. As Houdini later said of his film work, "No illusion is good on film."[23]

The Thanhouser Film Corp. in New Rochelle produced dozens of features, among the most popular being the *Million Dollar Mystery* series. Its leading star was an athletic beauty with emotive eyes named Florence La Badie, nicknamed "Fearless Flo" for the movie stunts, including high-speed motorcycle rides and leaps into the water, she performed for the camera. At the peak of her career came an abrupt and tragic end in August 1917. She was driving in a car with her fiancé, Daniel Carson Goodman, in Croton when the brakes failed on a hill on the Albany Post Road. She was thrown from the vehicle and badly injured. Though her condition improved, an infection evidently set in, and she died in October at the Ossining Hospital at the age of 29.[24] Her untimely death and

The Thanhouser Film Corp. in New Rochelle produced dozens of feature films in the silent era, including "The *Dashing Druggist's Dilemma*" in 1916 (Ned Thanhouser/ Thanhouser Company Film Preservation, Inc.).

A leading lady of the silent era who did her own stunts, "Fearless Flo" La Badie was injured in a car accident in Croton and died at Ossining Hospital in 1917 (Ned Thanhouser/Thanhouser Company Film Preservation, Inc.).

rumored love affairs brought out speculation and gossip, including a particularly outlandish tale of romance on a visit to President Woodrow Wilson in the White House in 1914.[25] Her death at the height of her fame launched the kind conspiracy theories that array themselves like bouquets around the casket of a deceased movie star.

The Terrytoons studio in downtown New Rochelle lasted the longest of the local studios. Begun in the 1920s, it came to New Rochelle in 1934, where it turned out cartoons for young audiences through the late 60s,[26] featuring stalwarts like Heckle and Jeckle, the two talking magpies, and Mighty Mouse.

The golden age of filmmaking in New York would fade to black not long after D.W. Griffith shot his final roll of film in Mamaroneck. Blame it on the weather: the California sun eclipsed the filmmaking enterprise in Westchester and New Jersey as the insatiable demand for new pictures quickly turned Hollywood into the kind of factory town where a veritable assembly line churned out product. As for accommodating mild temperatures, and the opportunity to film outdoors 365 days a year, Tinseltown had plenty of it. Throw in a cooperative municipal government, cheap land and labor, and film moguls were soon packing their bags to build a new fantasy empire on the opposite coast.

As Griffith showed with *Birth of a Nation*, the medium of film was a potent vehicle to deliver the extremes of political and racial attitudes to a mass audience. And the heightened anxiety and social tensions that came with it crested into the suburbs in the 1920s. White robes and burning crosses were typically associated with the South, where Jim Crow seg-regation laws unleashed a brutal form of oppression that had blacks living in fear since the 1870s. But the fires of racial and religious intolerance also burned bright during Westchester's nights.

The Ku Klux Klan surged into the Northeast in the 1920s after a long hiatus, turning a regional force into a national phenomena, in large part due to the publicity Griffith's film gave to the extremist group. About four to five million Americans once pledged an oath of loyalty to the Klan after it re-emerged as a powerful political force. The KKK had an especially large following on Long Island, and the group caused a number of distur-bances and riots in New York City. Westchester, too, provided fertile ground for the spread of the so-called "Invisible Empire." The record levels of immigration propelled the growth of the Klan in the Northeast, and much of the Klan's fiery attacks in Westch-ester were aimed at Catholics, though Jews and blacks were targeted, as well. The growing prominence of Irish-Catholic leaders like New York governor Al Smith drove the Klan to mount its own campaign against people like him—and a gathering of almost 10,000 Klansmen in New Jersey came together to block the Democratic nomination of Smith for president in 1924. With its emphasis on tradition and a deeply nostalgic version of the past, the Klan also attracted those who held an aversion to modernity in its many forms and feared what a changing society would bring.

While its numbers always remained small, the Klan remained a visible force in the northern suburbs for much of the period. Cross burnings were the preferred symbol of this hooded mob. The KKK's extensive presence in Westchester first became known in January 1923 when Yonkers cops arrested Herbert Storm on a weapons charge.[27] He was a security guard for Otis Elevator Co. by day, an "exalted cyclops" of the Ku Klux Klan by night. Under questioning, he told authorities that the Klan had thousands of members across the county and regular committees meeting in Ossining, Peekskill, New Rochelle, Mount Vernon, Port Chester and Yonkers. As part of the Klan's growing visibility, Storm chatted amiably with reporters and happily agreed to pose for photos. Storm was later convicted of carrying a blackjack, an illegal weapon, and placed on probation. The "exalted cyclops," his official Klan title, was clearly inflating the numbers of the Klansmen in Westchester, as local authorities were quick to point out, but there was no doubt the group had a strong local following—the evidence was as clear as a torch on a moonless night.[28]

The Klan torched a cross near St. John's Cemetery in Yonkers in March 1923,[29] and the property of St. Patrick's Church in Armonk, where a chapel was to be built, was illu-minated by a fiery cross standing 12 feet high in May 1924.[30] The KKK insignia was splashed in paint at a road running past the Seminary for Foreign Missionaries in Ossin-ing in 1925.[31] Cross burnings were reported in a number of other communities during the period, and while the Klan's activities were generally targeted at groups, they could also be frighteningly specific.

Twenty Klansmen surrounded a car driven by a biracial couple seeking to obtain a marriage license from a town clerk in Kent, Putnam County, in April 1926. A young woman from Peekskill, who had African American ancestry, was preparing to marry a farmer from Mahopac when a letter arrived from the Klan telling them to expect "a warm reception" at their wedding. They later came to menace her personally in the vehicle she and her fiancée were driving in.[32] As the couple's experience showed, the Klan had a par-ticularly strong hold in northern Westchester.

The Ku Klux Klan was a formidable political force in the 1920s, using ballots, violence and menace to achieve its goals. Rallies that attracted tens of thousands of Klan adherents met annually in Peekskill, including a women's auxiliary (Westchester County Historical Society).

A farm outside Peekskill on Locust Avenue in Cortlandt was the setting for large rallies through the 1920s. Speeches, a 22-piece band, amusements and food were proffered to the crowd of 6,000 to 7,000.[33] Klansmen armed with baseball bats guarded the perimeter, and 100 fully gowned Klansmen marched at a sunset parade. In 1930, it was estimated that the Klan rally outside Peekskill drew about 10,000 or so men and women from all over the northeast to the conclave, with 500 marching in Klan regalia. A giant "K" was torched on a nearby hillside, and a Klan leader, James Fayers, urged a fight "for the recognition of white supremacy."[34]

Those Klan rallies were often met with resistance from the locals, most spectacularly in the hamlet of Verplanck, part of the town of Cortlandt. When a caravan of 80 Klansmen decided to drive through Verplanck—waving signs and wearing robes—to celebrate the defeat of Al Smith in the presidential race of 1928 to Herbert Hoover, a melee broke out in the heavily Irish Catholic community that had voted for Smith by a large majority. The ill-conceived victory parade on November 7 ended in a downpour of rocks and bricks (aka Irish confetti, in the street slang of the day) and threats of violence. The conflict ended when 14 state troopers arrived to pluck the rash Klan victory paraders from what promised to be a bloody rebuke.[35]

Certainly the Klan had many enemies, as well as friends, and not just those armed with rocks. Vigilance committees sprung up when Klan activities were reported, as was the case after the Armonk cross burning, and ministers and the local press were quick to denounce their activities and take a stand against them. Timothy Walsh, editor of the *Hastings News*, penned a vitriolic piece against what he described as "the type of people who admit membership in the bedsheet order." The editor, noting that he had been apprised that a lawsuit was being considered against him for his newspaper's reporting on Klan members and activities, wrote, "I hope I will always have strength enough to fight this anti–American viper, the Ku Klux Klan. I deem it an honor to be hated by the klan."[36]

The Klan and its leaders took a new approach in the 20s as they sought new members, and the Klan's leaders talked about "Americanism" and "doing right by people." With their new strategy, they exerted a powerful influence in state houses around the nation, as well as on national politics. But their public relations campaign did nothing to change the fact that the organization was built on terrorism and the menace of hooded thugs, and those actions spoke far louder than their political slogans. Indeed, in August 1922, as the Klan sought to portray itself as stewards of "traditional" American values, a cloaked mob of 15 Klansmen wearing black robes attacked a group of black men driving home from a picnic in Morehouse Parish, La., near the Arkansas border, and hauled two of them away. Their bodies were eventually found at the bottom of a lake. A grand jury refused three times to indict the suspects, all Klansmen linked to the case, and they walked free.[37] And whatever they said about "Americanism," those who marched and set crosses alight in Westchester shared the same ill faith.

While the period saw an explosive growth in the rise of racial extremists declaring their hatred for blacks, it was also a time when black culture manifested a new sense of confidence and creative vitality. As a reaction to the oppressive forces arrayed against them, African American writers, artists, entrepreneurs and scholars, such as Langston Hughes, Zora Neale Hurston and Duke Ellington, saw intellectual and creative achievement as a way to elevate the status of African Americans as a whole. While the 1920s roared on, an outpouring of black literature, painting, music, poetry and film helped to shatter long-standing stereotypes. Known as the Harlem Renaissance, it was also a great party, and some of its most glittering soirees happened in Westchester.

Irvington's Villa Lewaro, the home of A'Lelia Walker, hosted many of these gatherings. Rising above the Hudson along the tony strip known as Millionaire's Row, the grand home soon became a destination for ambitious blacks from all walks of life, where Harlem's and Manhattan's black and white elite toasted themselves and danced until dawn to the rhythms of the Clef Club Orchestra.

Walker's mother, Madam C.J. Walker, had broken more than one barrier herself before commissioning the white neo-Palladian-style mansion among this haven for white industrialists and financiers in 1917. Born Sarah Breedlove to former slaves in Louisiana and working for many years as a washerwoman, Madam Walker was a widow, single mother and divorcee before founding the hair-care empire said to have made her the first black woman millionaire (though financial journalists at the time, and even Walker herself, said the value of her holdings was below the $1 million mark).[38] Money aside, she had a powerful desire to succeed and promote others in her community—becoming not just a prosperous entrepreneur but an early champion of civil rights and an advocate for black America. The senior Walker often recounted the story about rising above a load of washing, her body weary from the toil, and wondering how she would ever provide for herself and her daughter in her old age. Hard work, a fearless sense of purpose and a savvy plan to train thousands of black women to sell her hair conditioning cream to their peers eventually changed her path. Despite her humble beginnings, she was interested in self improvement from an early age and developed a deep love of music, elegant clothes and fine furnishings. Even her 1912 divorce from third husband Charles Joseph Walker, whose name inspired her newfound identity, was a minor distraction as she pursued her personal and business goals. A black newspaper of the period noted "she had an inordinate desire to move among the things of culture and refinement."[39]

Walker chose Vertner Tandy, the first licensed black architect in New York State, to design Villa Lewaro, a verbal play on her daughter's name at the time, Lelia Walker Robinson. (While her mother was alive, Lelia Walker Robinson used both her stepfather's name and married name. She divorced John Robinson in 1914 and changed her name to A'Lelia Walker sometime during the 1920s.)[40] Designed in a neo–Palladian style, it became the "Xanadu of Harlem's artistic and intellectual elite," as one historian described it.[41]

Painted in luminous white and decorated with European details like a frescoed dining room ceiling, and a $9,000 gold-plated organ, Madam Walker's dream home made a powerful statement about black ambition and determination, especially to her wealthy neighbors. In a cruel twist of fate for someone who broke so many barriers to achieve a mansion on Millionaire's Row, she died there just two years later in 1919 at the age of 51.

Madam C. J. Walker, credited as the first African American woman to become a millionaire, built an estate in Irvington. She entertained visiting dignitaries, black veterans of the Great War and sales associates of her hair care company (A'Lelia Bundles/Madam Walker Family Archives).

As the new mistress of Villa Lewaro at the dawn of the Jazz Age, her daughter, now calling herself A'Lelia Walker, preferred playing bridge to literary talk,[42] though she opened her doors to all and was able to converse with anyone, rich or poor.[43] She also knew how to throw a party: Immensely proud of her role as a patron of the arts, she took great pleasure in indulging her mischievous sense of humor whenever possible. At one fabled gathering, she served her black guests Champagne and caviar while segregating her white guests at tables stocked with moonshine and chitlins.[44]

Many of the leading lights of the Harlem Renaissance passed through the stately villa on the Hudson, and with growing pride, black Americans looked to the retreat for cultural guidance, closely following the social and political whirlwind that took place under its roof. Earlier, some of the founders of the early civil rights movement, including Walter White, Ida B. Wells and A. Philip Randolph, had come to the estate for conferences, part of Madam Walker's plan to use her home as a think-tank and organizational center for

Madam Walker's company trained and employed thousands of sales beauticians, all of them black women like her, across the United States. The most successful "Walker Agents" were annually honored at the Madam Walker Beauty Culturists Union Convention, shown here at Villa Lewaro in 1924 when Walker's daughter A'Lelia owned it (A'Lelia Bundles/Madam Walker Family Archives).

the black cause.[45] During A'Lelia Walker's time, the mansion became more of a social and cultural center. Alberta Hunter, the jazz singer, entertained guests among its high walls to the accompaniment of that gilded organ. Another regular visitor was Enrico Caruso, the Italian operatic tenor (it was he who suggested abbreviating the first syllables of A'Lelia Walker Robinson's name to create "Villa *Le-wa-ro*"). Black veterans of World War I were given a two-week invitation to come up with their families and enjoy the younger Walker's hospitality, and the first black physician to command a U.S. Army field hospital, Colonel Joseph Ward, was one of the house guests. The president of Liberia, C.D.B. King, made a visit in 1921 and was given a July 4 fireworks show in his honor.[46]

Not all of A'Lelia Walker's neighbors were pleased by the steady stream of guests and social activity at Villa Lewaro, just as they had questioned her mother's intentions when she first built their home. Many were shocked when they learned Madam Walker had purchased the site using secretive channels African Americans were forced to employ during the era, and cool feelings persisted.

Against the backdrop of white hostility, the burst of creative output that marked the Harlem Renaissance gave the black intelligentsia a sense of renewed confidence and optimism that a hopeful future for blacks in Westchester, and America, was not out of reach. Unfortunately, it was a belief that proved to be unfounded in their generation. Hard times and the Depression brought an end to the Renaissance, and A'Lelia Walker declared bankruptcy after years of extravagant living. In 1930 she sold off the home's belongings—almost all of it to white people—at an auction that brought a half-mile of parked cars to Irvington's North Broadway. Some of the more disrespectful buyers drove up through the villa gates and parked on the grass.[47]

An account in the *Tarrytown Daily News* referred to the "frenzy" of "the mob of buyers" at the "Negro Palace," noting that quite a few of the neighbors were unhappy with the black family who moved in there: "Many of those whose homes are near Villa Lewaro deeply resented the intrusion of the Queen of Dark Harlem and hair tonic wizard into the exclusive precincts of Irvington, and never drove past her Georgian palace without making a wry face."[48] When A'Lelia Walker's possessions, many of them inherited from her mother, were put up for auction, it was a white crowd that came forward to buy them. "Very few Negroes were present and they kept in the background and unobtrusively out of the crush and clamor. The crowd was almost solidly white," the daily newspaper reported. "They were spending money with gay abandon."[49]

The bang of the auctioneer's gavel was a jarring coda to the arias and jazz orchestrations that once resonated beneath the 18-foot ceilings in the home's main hall. A'Lelia Walker died a year later in Manhattan, and the house itself was sold.

The 1920s were a time of nonconformity and testing boundaries, whether racial, political or cultural. Extremism came in many shapes and forms during the period. Cultural and societal roles were also being re-invented by bohemians, non-conformists and radicals of nearly every stripe, and Westchester had its own outpost of the rebellion against social norms. While the widening suburb was a place born from and reared on capitalism, for some of its residents, there was another side of the story.

The women wore mauve and bold yellow colors, and the men talked of Socialist revolutions while mixing drinks on the veranda. They arrayed themselves against prevailing norms of the period and saw their duty to dig the grave of the old bourgeois and all it represented. Pioneers of new forms of freedom in the arts, sex and politics, they lived their lives in enclaves where the rules of the old order did not apply.

The most radical small-town neighborhood in America was set on a rocky knoll in Croton. Mount Airy, the community the radicals came to adopt as a kind of country seat in the highlands above the Hudson, offered an

Madam Walker's daughter, A'Lelia Walker, a devoted patron of the arts, hosted spirited parties at Villa Lewaro during the Harlem Renaissance (A'Lelia Bundles/ Madam Walker Family Archives).

ideal site to take in refreshing bucolic air and contemplate revolution. It was a place where avant-garde dance recitals were held, "free love" was openly discussed and far-left political causes promoted. The locals called the Mount Airy neighborhood "Red Hill," while its most famous resident, John Reed, referred to it as the "Mount Airy Soviet." Bohemians and rebels of almost every category came to Croton in the early part of the 1900s to dance, write, make love, argue and make war on the established order.

The Croton radicals saw themselves fighting on behalf of the oppressed, but they were also self-promoters of the highest order. Their exploits were the subject of numerous biographies, novels and Hollywood treatments, most notably 1981's *Reds*, directed by and starring Warren Beatty as John Reed. The ambitious journalist and provocateur, a former Harvard cheerleader who turned his back on his affluent Oregon background, was just one of a number of leftist luminaries to take to the heights on Red Hill. Mabel Dodge, Reed's one-time lover, ran a literary salon where subversive talk was served with tea, and anarchists dropped in to spend the night. Max Eastman and Floyd Dell, two other Croton regulars, edited a leftist magazine called *The Masses* and nearly ended up in jail for opposing the American entry into World War I. It is quite possible that Leon Trotsky, then living in New York City and corresponding regularly with his friend, Eastman, made an appearance in Croton, though it has never been formally documented.

The radicals went beyond politics into the social realm in their disdain for convention, and the Croton commune also upended traditional roles for women. Women like Mabel Dodge, a flamboyant patron of the arts, Louise Bryant (Reed's wife) and dance impresario Elizabeth Duncan (sister of modernist innovator Isadora Duncan) played prominent parts in the Croton circle. The Bohemian collective was one of the few places in America at the time where women could stake an equal claim to fame as men. Dodge, a wealthy Buffalo heiress, served as a catalyst for the radical circle that moved through the home that she rented on Mount Airy beginning in 1915. She held a famed peyote party in Greenwich Village in 1914 that introduced mind-altering hallucinogens to the counterculture.[50] Though Greenwich Village was the main base of the Bohemian set, Croton became a secondary outpost through much of the teens and twenties. Reed called his Croton home "my sanctuary," where "within its walls I meditate in a world of my own and write."[51] There were other suburban outposts of the vanguard downriver from Croton. Hutchins Hapgood and his wife, Neith Boyce, leftist writers and bohemian free spirits, lived in Hastings and Dobbs Ferry. It was in their home in Dobbs Ferry that Mabel Dodge, in a romantic rage following a breakup by John Reed during their volatile love affair, smoked incessantly and attempted to take her own life with an overdose of pills.[52] Margaret Sanger, the early feminist leader and birth-control advocate, made a home in Hastings in the early 1900s.

The Westchester bohemian set was often described as "parlor pinks," and far worse. "They were sublime egotists," wrote literary critic R.L. Duffus. "They were individualists first and reformers or revolutionaries afterward."[53] Duffus did concede they were driven by a restless energy and a keen desire to experiment and see the world in all its chaotic diversity.

In the end, the radicals did not create a new world order. They did, however, create a sensibility that far transcended their own time in history and reached far into the future. They spawned a movement that has been channeled into everything from the beatnik underground, the hippie scene, the feminist crusade and various attempts to alter consciousness from within. It was not a utopia they left behind, but a cultural critique that cuts across the ages.

The leftist intelligentsia based in Croton was the most visible form of the early 20th century counter-culture, but they were part of a much larger constellation of radical activists. The extreme political left made a place in Westchester for decades, and carved out a small red niche inside the bastion of capitalism. The leftist political tradition drew strength from the heavy industry that characterized the era, as well as the waves of immigrants who brought labor politics and Marxism from their homelands in Europe.

Though their numbers were never large, leftist political groups counted on a substantial following. Robert LaFollette, the socialist and progressive candidate for the presidency in 1924, earned 12 percent of the vote in Westchester, compared to about 16 percent nationwide. Some 20,000 county residents cast their ballot for the left-wing candidate in that election.[54]

The county's proximity to leftist circles in New York City also bolstered the movement, which had a number of local outposts. Indeed, with a sturdy pair of walking shoes, one might have journeyed across the entire realm of the far-left ideological spectrum in a daylong hike across northern Westchester in the 20s and 30s, stopping in for anarchism at Mohegan Lake, communism in Peekskill and trade-union militancy and socialism in Katonah. The only labor college in America operated at the Katonah site, where it was founded in 1921 as the Brookwood Labor College, and it offered classes on economics, labor history and sociology to hundreds of young workers and labor organizers. Just over the Westchester border, democratic socialism thrived among picnic tables and leisurely swims at the Three Arrows Cooperative in Putnam Valley ("a country home ... at a proletarian price," it once boasted).[55]

The city of Yonkers was home to not one but two Communist party leaders, Earl Browder and Gus Hall, a perennial presidential candidate who was once locked up at Leavenworth Prison for eight years for his political activities.

As the surge of political energy from the left pulsed through the early 1900s, one of the greatest political conflagrations of the era took place at Tarrytown when the great Red Menace, as it was known, reached one of the strongholds of capitalism, pitting radicals against the might of the Rockefeller family. The tranquil Hudson River towns were transformed into a stage for radical political theater—the propaganda of the deed, as the anarchists would call it—as billy clubs crashed down on rioters and shouting mobs hurled insults. On the receiving end of those police batons and insults was a tough outfit: the Industrial Workers of the World, a firebrand collection of radicals and anarchists who wanted to tear down the capitalist structure and replace it with "one big union." Fiery oratory was the group's stock in trade, but its members were known to back their rhetoric with bullets and bombs. Known as the Wobblies, they were the shock troops of the union movement in labor struggles all over the West, where cruel and dangerous conditions were the norm in factories and mines. One of those work sites, the Ludlow mine in southern Colorado, exploded in violence in April 1914 when state militiamen fired on a camp of striking mine workers during hostilities, later burning it to the ground. Eleven children and two women were killed in the attack, part of 20 deaths that day, and the Ludlow Massacre brought outrage to the doorstep of the Rockefeller family more than 2,000 miles away.

The chief owner of the mine, John D. Rockefeller, Jr., protested in written statements that he did not condone violence, but the fury over the Ludlow Massacre, and the repellent imagery of the youngsters who perished in the violence, would not be blunted by press releases. The Wobblies launched a campaign against Rockefeller personally, and Kykuit, the family estate in Pocantico Hills near Tarrytown became its primary target. The Wobblies first arrived in May 1914 to picket the estate, wearing signs and dressing in black to mourn the slain mining families. They clashed with Rockefeller's security force that guarded the property, which, for reasons known only to the Rockefellers and their representatives, were composed entirely of African American men.[56] But that was just the beginning.

A large contingent of Wobblies later arrived to do battle in Westchester, under the guidance of one of the most ardent radicals of the era, Alexander Berkman. Sasha to his friends, Berkman was an anarchist who spent 14 years in prison for an unsuccessful assassination attempt on industrialist Henry Frick, a business leader especially hated by working-class agitators for his ruthlessly anti-labor stance. Berkman and the Wobblies, who adopted the principle of free speech as a primary tool in their campaign, sought to stage a march in Tarrytown to denounce Rockefeller. Refused a permit by village authorities, the Wobblies held a large rally in defiance at a main square in Tarrytown, and saw 11 of their members locked up by local cops for blocking traffic and holding a street assembly without a permit. Trouble continued the next day, May 31, when a few dozen Wobblies got off the train in Tarrytown to press their free-speech initiative, and a riot broke out. The Wobblies were met by a large contingent of local police, and the battle was on. The Tarrytown police, backed by about 500 spectators, swung their billy clubs and chased the Wobblies over the village line into Sleepy Hollow (then called North Tarrytown), where they were rushed back over the village line after Berkman stood on a chair and made a very short speech. More clubbing ensued. The crowd of onlookers directed their own verbal barbs at the Wobblies and urged the cops "to 'soak them' and 'beat them up.'"[57] The street battle ended with 15 Wobblies under arrest. Packed tightly into cells at police headquarters, they sang protest songs and banged on the doors. Their comrades were forcibly boarded onto a train back to New York, bruised and bloodied.[58] Those arrested in the street melees were later transported to the county jail in White Plains, where more Wobblies demonstrated and shouted slogans outside the jail, disrupting the generally quiet city for days.

The Wobblies vowed to return to Tarrytown to secure their rights to free speech and a permit to stage a rally, but the village administration was unyielding in its refusal to allow the Wobblies to hold a rally. A tense standoff ensued, and when Upton Sinclair, the socialist activist and author, harangued the village board in demands to give them permission to speak at a public place in Tarrytown, he was coldly rebuffed.[59]

The Wobblies were never popular in the mainstream press or among conventional society. The *Tarrytown Press-Record*, for instance, called them "free-lovers, non-citizens, ex-convicts," as well as "grifters," "fakirs" and "self-centered, untruthful, publicity-seekers and professional agitators."[60] Many others called them far worse. The Wobblies eventually accepted an invitation by a wealthy local woman, a suffragist named Anna Gould, to speak at "the Greek theater" at her estate on June 14. (Anna Gould was not related to the family of Jay Gould in Tarrytown or his daughter, Anna.) Even that compromise ended badly, when angry local residents rushed the stage, enraged at being insulted as "vipers, snakes and cowards" by an IWW speaker.[61]

Cooler heads in the audience, and a handful of police detectives, restored order. Another Wobbly appearance on June 22 along the Croton Aqueduct ended with the labor agitators being pelted with rocks, tomatoes and eggs by a local mob.[62] The showdown eventually petered out. The seven demonstrators charged with disturbing the peace were given 60 days in the lock-up. The sentencing in the Tarrytown courtroom was heavily secured—a large delegation of cops from Yonkers had been detailed for the security job.[63]

John D. Rockefeller, Jr., maintained a stoic appearance and went about his business, paying little outward notice to the hostilities around his grand estate beyond hiring more security and skipping a few church services. Berkman was eventually deported to Russia. But while there was a certain comic-opera undertone to the Great Anarchist Riot of Tarrytown, there was no doubt a wider menace, with its accompanying violence and brutality, waiting just offstage.

On July 4 of that year an apartment on upper Lexington Avenue in Manhattan exploded with enough force to take off the top three floors of the building. Inside was Arthur Caron, or rather what was left of him after the blast. An unemployed civil engineer and the Wobbly ringleader of the Tarrytown riots, Caron possessed a powerful voice and a fierce determination. He was one of the first to be yanked off a soapbox by a cop when he tried to give a speech, and when pelted with eggs and rocks on the Croton Aqueduct, his cheek cut open, he shouted about the Indian blood that ran in his veins to taunt his aggressors. He later spent a week in jail in White Plains before he was bailed out with his comrades, who cursed the name of the Rockefellers and the Tarrytown police chief to anyone who would listen. With Caron died three other anarchists who had also made their presence known on the streets of picturesque suburban village.[64] It became clear that the intended destination of the load of dynamite before it was set off was the Rockefeller estate. An accidental discharge ended those plans with a blast of deadly force. It was a vivid reminder of the ways in which violence can follow its own strange logic, with a fuse lit in one place exploding in another.

Besides the turmoil generated by the radical movement, there were many other currents running through the social history of the era. The rise of women to positions of power and leadership, their emancipation from the limits of domestic responsibility and their acquisition of voting rights, were a fundamental change in American society.

The liberation of women and their ascent to equality as citizens, workers, scholars and leaders came out of the leadership of Westchester women. From a home in New Rochelle where a commitment to equality between the races and sexes defied tradition, to a wooded estate in North Castle where the "winning strategy" for a woman's right to vote was formulated, over to the Beechwood estate in Scarborough where organizational meetings were held, the movement that broke down the barriers that kept women subservient began on Westchester ground.

Lucretia Mott, a Quaker, as were many of the other early proponents of suffrage, or the women's right to vote, was the daughter of a whaling merchant and mariner who spent long periods at sea and a mother who ran a household as well as a business. She spent time with her husband's family in Mamaroneck as a young woman and helped start an anti-slavery organization that had a chapter in New Rochelle.[65] Susan B. Anthony, another strong-willed and independent Quaker, taught school in New Rochelle for a time as young woman, at Eunice Kenyon's Quaker boarding school in 1839.[66] She made reference in her diary to the beauty of Long Island Sound, where "all seemed calm and tranquil save the restless wash of the waves against the beach."[67]

Stanton, Anthony and Mott, whose steely-eyed portrait of determination became the face of the American women's movement, were instrumental in the birth of the modern women's rights movement at Seneca Falls, New York, in 1848. Their descendants were the ones who won the right to vote in 1920, and the great battle over the ballot box found its field marshal in a pioneering and resolute Midwesterner who settled in Westchester in 1919.

Carrie Chapman Catt was an educator, journalist and a gifted public speaker, possessed of a powerful voice. Born in Iowa, she was permitted by her father to attend Iowa State University, where she was the only woman to graduate in her class. She ran a school district for a time in Iowa, another precedent. Strong-willed and used to operating from a position of strength, she wanted other women to gain that same access. The power center of New York was the locus of societal changes, and it was natural for Catt to come east to take up the cause of suffrage. She came to Briarcliff in 1919, and made her home there until 1928 (later moving to New Rochelle, where she resided until her death in 1947).[68] Westchester was more amenable to the suffrage movement than other sections of the country, though it still faced opposition. The suburbs in general were more recep-

tive to the idea of women in positions of authority. As an editorialist wrote in the *New Rochelle Evening Standard*, "Women in many 'Old World' countries have been 'door mats.' In this country, they have always done about as they chose. Those who saw fit to cultivate their brains and independence have never been 'door-mats' at any period in this country."[69]

Catt became the president of the National American Woman Suffrage Association beginning in 1915, a post she held to 1920, when it was at the forefront of the voting-rights movement. In 1916, at a NAWSA convention in Atlantic City, she unveiled what was called by strategists as the "Winning Plan," an initiative to campaign simultaneously for suffrage on both the state and federal levels. Catt showed a willingness to compromise where necessary for partial suffrage in certain states and deftly held the often competing factions within the women's movement together.[70]

While living at Juniper Ledge, her country home on Ryder Road in the town of New Castle near Briarcliff, Catt worked out the outline for an organization to be called the League of Women Voters, which became one of the most influential advocates for good government in the nation. She toured relentlessly to speak for the ratification of the 19th Amendment. She also held conclaves at Juniper Ledge with other feminist leaders to organize their activities. Catt was an astute communicator with a commanding voice

One of a number of women's rights activists from Westchester, Carrie Chapman Catt developed what became known as the "Winning Plan" for the right to vote at her home outside Briarcliff Manor. A meticulous organizer and natural mediator, Catt coordinated the activities and messages of hundreds of suffragists across the nation (Wisconsin Historical Societym WHS-1818).

who was also deft with publicity. She was relentlessly "on message." Besides advocating for the 19th Amendment and founding the League of Women Voters, Catt was an early opponent of Hitler and supporter of Jews in Europe who faced the Nazi menace.

Catt's efforts to gain the right to vote bore fruit in 1920, when the 19th Amendment was passed. Westchester County voted to approve suffrage by a wide margin of 7,000 votes.[71] Outside her public life, Catt, who was twice widowed, enjoyed the pleasures of the garden and the company of tall trees. In her later years, she lived openly with another woman.[72] She dedicated trees on her Briarcliff property to 14 famous suffragettes who had preceded her in the struggle.

Another major organizer in the movement was Narcissa Cox Vanderlip of Scarborough. She became the first co-president of the New York State League of Women Voters.[73]

But while the right to vote had been secured, there were still many obstacles to full equality, particularly within the political mainstream. The first woman elected to a municipal office in Westchester was Belle M. Knight, who served on the White Plains Common Council from 1920 to 1923.[74] Though she was the first, it would take many years before others followed her path. Women first began their ascent from disenfranchisement into the higher levels of government in the mid–1930s, more than a decade after they gained the right to vote in 1920. They were all Republicans, at a time when the GOP dominated local politics.

In many ways, 1935 was a very big year for women in local government, causing a sensation among the male politicians who had run the county for centuries. Mary Livingston of New Rochelle became the first woman to serve that year on the county Board of Supervisors, a precursor of the present county Board of Legislators. Her husband, William, a longtime Republican supervisor, died a month before the election, and she was named to fill his post by the New Rochelle Common Council. A large group of women turned out to mark the occasion and cheer when Livingston took her seat behind a huge pile of roses and chrysanthemums placed on her desk.[75] Her constituents evidently liked what Livingston did for them. She was re-elected twice and served through 1941.

Jane Todd, a Republican of Tarrytown, was elected to a term in the state Assembly in 1935, a post she would hold for another ten years.[76] Ruth Taylor of East View (a section of Greenburgh) was the first woman to win election to a county post, County Commission of Welfare, in 1932. She had been appointed to the post the year before.[77] She was elected to that post after serving on the county Board of Health with future governor and vice president Nelson Rockefeller. Taylor served as the commissioner of public welfare into the 1940s, a crucial position during the Depression era. Caroline Goodwin O'Day of Rye, a Southerner, an artist and a close ally of Franklin Roosevelt, served in the House of Representatives as a Democrat from 1935 to 1943, when New York's congressional representatives were still chosen through a statewide at-large balloting system.[78]

Westchester women were also involved in shaping public policy in other ways. In 1913, a home was being built for Moyca Newell in Bedford, just outside Mount Kisco, and a foreman was murdered for the payroll. Four suspects escaped with the money, and local law enforcement proved ineffectual and powerless to mount a chase for the killers once they left Bedford. Newell and a Bedford friend, Virginia Mayo, an author, began a lobbying campaign to create a statewide police force based on the model of Pennsylvania state troopers. Their campaign achieved success when the New York state troopers were formed in 1917, providing law enforcement to rural and outlying areas.[79]

While some women began to climb in the public realm, their position in the domestic realm—and within the suburbs especially—appeared to become more codified. Bound to hearth and home, the majority of women tended to the children, served as both their husband's proxies and in a subordinate capacity as housewives, and created the civic infrastructure of the suburbs that came to be cast in decidedly feminine terms. The enforcement of gender roles, and the idealization of the role of women as nurturers and supporters, set a cultural standard. It was a standard subjected to its share of criticism, as the suburbs came to be viewed as citadels of conformity and homogeneity. The communities that were being built by women in white gloves and impeccable clothes represented a kind of victorious assertion of middle-class values, or so it seemed.

But not every woman wanted to be part of that triumph, nor find the ideal of domestic life in the suburbs.

One of the livelier conversations on the merits of a metropolitan lifestyle and the long-running debate between the city and its suburbs broke out in the pages of a magazine in 1928, when one of the top style-setters of the era wrote a scathing put-down of places like Westchester. The question: are the suburbs good for middle-class, educated women?

Christine Frederick was a home economist, author and marketing expert who told big business what women wanted, and in the pages of *Outlook* magazine in 1928, she said she preferred to live in the country and the city—not the land in between known as the suburb. Decrying what she saw as the sterility she found in places like Westchester, she said high achievers like herself could never flourish there.

"Is Suburban Living a Delusion?" asked Frederick, a mother of four who lectured widely on the need for better tools and kitchen machinery for homemakers. She said the suburbs were the wrong place for people like herself: "The more sophisticated and individual types ... for those the suburbs is sometimes utterly intolerable and always a disappointment."[80] Her children went to boarding schools, and her husband was the president of the Gourmet Society of New York and an author.

"I have definitely come to the conclusion that suburban living—meaning the little neat colonies of colonies in suburban villages—is a snare and a delusion from almost any angle you wish to approach it," she wrote. She condemned what she called the "standardization" of the suburbs: "the neat little toy houses on their neat little patches of lawn and their neat colonial lives, to say nothing of the neat little housewives and their neat little children—all set in neat rows." She cited the "boobery" of suburbia and contrasted it with the "social emancipation and modernness" of New York City.[81] It was a scathing critique by an arbiter of high taste.

The rejoinder came from Ethel Longsworth Smith, a writer from Hastings. Originally from Canada she settled in Hastings with her husband, a journalist, after living abroad, and she found plenty to like about the little suburban village where she had made a home. Rather than the casement of conformity that Frederick deplored, she found an affiliation with the natural world and a diverse group of friends. "We moved to the suburbs so that we and our children might be near to the grass and the trees," Smith wrote, penning a tribute to the beauty of the elm trees that shaded her house, the garden she tended and the rocky outcroppings that cast beguiling shadows in the afternoon sun.[82] She and her family worked outdoors on little projects, and her kids made little huts and birdhouses of their own design. They kept a canoe on the river's edge and enjoyed the abundant beauty that cost them nothing.

She sensed snobbery in Frederick's appraisal and in other city dwellers—"who turned up their sophisticated noses at the suburb and all that therein is." Along with easy access to the city were the indelible charms of the outdoor life. "We have known the delight of sleeping under blankets in the open air in the shadow of the Hudson Palisades with a smudge to keep the mosquitoes away, and of waking to see the sun rising over the Westchester hills," Smith wrote. "In the morning at this season we awaken to see tiny green buds pricked on the black twigs outside our windows, to be aware of the silent streets, to see last year's dead brown leaves stirring on the ground to the breeze that blows down from the Tappan Zee."[83]

Smith's praise extended well beyond her home's property lines. "We have tramped the countryside for miles around," she said. "We have grilled steaks on wooded hills and have built camp-fires in the snow, and we have thanked heaven that the suburb gave us a chance to do so." The village was particularly liberating for young ones, she continued: "In the city small children cannot be permitted to go far from home alone, a state of affairs that hinders the development of the spirit of independence."[84]

Smith noted that her circle of acquaintances was eclectic and cosmopolitan, and she found no sense of oppression or intrusion from her neighbors. The women she knew in Hastings were educated, ambitious and independent. Finally, Smith pointed out, philistines and boobs can be found everywhere, and in large cities, too.

7

Highs and Lows

Fearless Flyers, the Depression,
Career Criminals and Marijuana

The early age of the automobile, which would leave a lasting mark on Westchester, gave way to an even faster and more thrilling mode of transport—flight. While the automobile was changing the face of the landscape, the airplane was changing the look of the skies. Early aviation pioneers, among them a number who called Westchester home, lifted from the ground in airships made of canvas, wire, linen and wood. In old photographs, they can be seen wearing leather helmets, goggles, starched collars and serious expressions, as if going to a funeral, most likely their own.

Amelia Earhart, Eddie Rickenbacker and "The Flying Debutante" Ruth Nichols—the first woman in New York state to acquire a professional pilot's license and Earhart's predecessor in celebrity—all soared through Westchester skies with a common goal: to break records, fly faster and connect the world. Their relentless courage and camera-ready allure made them celebrities at a time when feats of aviation enthralled the nation. Pointing the way to the future, they stood in the gap between the old and the new, revving their engines at dawn.

Aviation came to Westchester in 1910 in the most spectacular fashion, when airplane designer Glenn Curtiss took to the skies over the Palisades and down the lower Hudson River, just seven years after Orville and Wilbur took flight at Kitty Hawk, North Carolina.

Flying past Storm King Mountain just north of Westchester, Curtiss hit treacherous air currents inside the maze of mountain and water, and his aircraft began to "toss and eddy about almost beyond control.... I thought it was all over," he later wrote.[1] After dropping to the surface of the Hudson near Peekskill, where the conditions were less severe, "the battle with the air currents was over," he recalled. At 10:20 a.m. over Tarrytown, he spotted the New York City skyline and rejoiced that his prize was in reach—if only his oil pressure could hold out. He later landed in upper Manhattan, thus claiming a purse of $10,000, offered by publisher Joseph Pulitzer, to be the first aviator to fly from Albany to Manhattan.[2] The record-breaking journeys set off a round of aerial displays—crowds couldn't get enough of the spectacle of manned flight.

The first was held at the Westchester County Fairgrounds in Greenburgh on August 31, 1912. Famed aviator Lincoln Beachey wowed the crowds by performing a stunt called the Turkey Trot that sent spectators ducking for cover as he buzzed them at speeds nearing 100 miles an hour. Beachey dropped a satchel of letters onto the fairground, as part of a demonstration of aviation for the purpose mail delivery.[3]

Westchester's place in aviation history belongs to the undaunted ambitions of two of the most famous women pilots of the era, friends on the ground and rivals in the air. Amelia Earhart and Ruth Nichols were Westchester neighbors and founders of a flying club that beckoned women into the new realm of flight.

Tall, lithe, athletic and blessed with a face the camera adored, Amelia Earhart uniquely combined the streamlined style of the machine age with an unstudied devotion to pure adventure. Her seemingly fearless feats as a pilot also showed what a strong-willed individual of any sex could accomplish, inspiring successive generations of women to reach far beyond the narrow roles society imposed on them. Living in Westchester for a decade, Earhart fixed her own cars, tended a vegetable garden when she could and favored comfortable, simple slacks and shirts long before it was the norm. Above all, she loved to fly.

Earhart's path to super-stardom was an odd combination of innate charm, tenacity and her partnership with a media-savvy publicity-seeker and Westchester native, George Putnam. Their relationship, and her subsequent rise in popularity, was a case study in the peculiarly American manner in which celebrity can bestow both a blessing and curse on those illuminated by its bright glare.

Born in Kansas, Earhart had an active, outdoorsy childhood that was darkened by an alcoholic father and periods of financial strain. She developed an early love of flight while pursuing a potential career in medicine, enrolling for a time at Columbia University. A weekend flyer, and unable to afford the rest of her medical studies, she dropped out of college and began looking for work in a related field. She had just taken a job as a social worker in Boston when the call went out for a woman to join a 1928 transatlantic crossing that publisher George Palmer Putnam helped organize.

Putnam was a force of nature, a lover of extreme activity who craved acclaim. The scion of a great publishing family with a printing press in Yonkers, he was raised in Rye and built a Spanish villa-style mansion there of his own design. Drawn to a life of adventure, he explored the Arctic and took Western mountaineering trips as a young man. After the death of his father and older brother, Putnam took over the Manhattan-based family publishing business, a pursuit that put him on the lookout for new and sensational material about life on the edge. He knew how to exploit the public's enormous appetite for heroes and where to find them—or create them, if necessary.

The publisher of Charles Lindbergh's book, *We*, the best-selling account of the pilot's 1927 transatlantic flight, Putnam immediately liked what he saw in Earhart. She had cropped, wavy auburn hair—which she'd first cut short in 1920 and left unstyled throughout her life—and wide-set gray eyes that crinkled when she smiled for the camera. Though outwardly reserved, she was confident, determined and well-spoken, projecting an effortless style in pants and leather jackets when few women dressed that way. Beyond the ease and comfort that trousers gave her on the ground and in the cockpit, she believed she had thick ankles and avoided wearing skirts. The young, slightly shy aviator with the winning charm was the perfect package for Putnam's wily media campaign.

Earhart took the flight over the Atlantic in 1928, becoming the first woman to make a nonstop trip over the ocean, though she never handled the controls; the actual flying was left to two men. The trip brought her celebrity—she was now America's "Lady Lindy"—and soon after Putnam arranged for her to write a book about the experience at his Rye estate.

Despite the public acclaim, the trip across the Atlantic had rankled Earhart; she told friends privately she was just baggage aboard the flight. She was determined to achieve a landmark journey by herself and on her own terms. A solo, transcontinental flight across the U.S would set things right—just her, an aircraft, and some rudimentary maps to accomplish the 8,000-mile trip.

She chose to fly an Avro Avian, a British two-seater biplane valued for its reliability, performance and ability to handle long flights. This particular plane had previously been owned by explorer Mary Heath, a renowned British flyer who once flew to South Africa and back to England with it. The plane's distinguished pedigree appealed to Earhart, and Heath was happy to turn over her old craft over to another woman flyer for a potential record-breaking flight. She had a plaque installed on the plane that read "To Amelia Earhart from Mary Heath. Always think with your stick forward."[4]

The Avian was small, light and could land just about anywhere. On the downside, it needed constant attention in flight to maintain trim. Before her flight, Earhart tested it out at a nearby polo field in Harrison, a perfect place for landings and take-offs. Everything seemed in order. As for the trip itself, she would use the material for her new column as aviation editor for *Cosmopolitan*. George Putnam would be monitoring her every step of the way.

On a breezy summer morning on August 31, 1928, Earhart sailed aloft from the polo grounds of the Westchester Country Club in Harrison, not far from Putnam's home on the border of Rye and Harrison. As she scudded over a bank of clouds, Earhart began a journey that would make her the first woman to fly across America and back, a kind of Lewis-and-Clark achievement for the aviation age.

Earhart had the right equipment and substantial backing. But this flight would be a serious challenge—she had never carried out a long-distance flight by herself. Her navigation abilities were still developing, as were her mechanical skills. The facilities along the way were rudimentary, and grassy air strips and dusty highways could make for a bumpy landing.

It was a dangerous undertaking. When touching down outside Pittsburgh on a farm field on the outbound journey, Earhart hit a ditch and nearly flipped over. GP, as she by then called Putnam, was also on board, accompanying her at the start of the trip. He had to scramble to buy a new Avro in record time from England and ship it over for spare parts.[5]

Lacking any real solo flight experience, Earhart used her wits to navigate, pinning road maps to her pants and improvising when necessary. "I'm just a tramp flyer now," she said at one airport stop.[6] She was instantly popular with the public on the ground and had a knack for finding accommodations with local people wherever she landed, keeping her away from hotels, speeches and newspaper photographers for much of the trip. As she flew, she continued to learn through experience how to master the crucial skill of dead reckoning, the process of calculating one's current flight position by using a previous "fix" to estimate how fast and far the plane had traveled. One glaring miscalculation made her fly far beyond an airstrip in Texas all the way to Hobbs, New Mexico, where she touched down on Main Street and enjoyed a meal of fried eggs, biscuits and honey with the locals.[7] The next day her engine shut down after a fill-up of bad gas outside Hobbs, requiring another emergency landing.

But none of it, including a grueling schedule and turbulent weather, could stop her. In October, Earhart and her plane successfully came to rest on the polo field in Harrison just two months after she had left Westchester. Physically exhausted and badly sunburned, she had conquered America by air. It was her first major test as a pilot and she had passed it. She had also captivated the nation's attention, and during the following months, she began teasing out the details of her trip in her column in *Cosmopolitan*.

It was soon clear that the relationship between GP and Earhart was much more than a business match. She had moved into his Rye home on Locust Avenue, and his wife, Dorothy, took her shopping and exposed her to the glittering social circuit in which she and her husband moved. Whether Dorothy could see the signs of the blossoming affair (or she had already left the unhappy marriage by taking up with a much younger man), she moved out, and the couple divorced in 1929. Earhart eventually married Putnam in 1931. He'd proposed to her multiple times. Before agreeing to marry him, Earhart insisted on maintaining her independence—and keeping her surname.[8]

The next big trip for Earhart was a solo transatlantic crossing in May 1932 that replicated Charles Lindbergh's historic flight five years before. When she touched down in Ireland, she became the first woman to complete the journey across the ocean. She was now not only a renowned aviator but a rising star.

After they married, Putnam used his media empire to turn Earhart into a household name. Books, feature articles, interviews, speeches and product endorsements poured forth under Putnam's direction, and together they turned the once-bashful Kansas flyer into one of the great celebrities of the modern age. In 1933, the couple launched a line of women's wear designed by Earhart that mirrored the functional clothes she had once sewed for herself. Their home in Rye, meanwhile, became one of the brightest lights of the Westchester social scene throughout the 1930s. Actors, explorers, aviators, writers, politicians and sportsmen of every kind came to visit the Putnam mansion. They found a home tastefully decorated with the totems of an adventurous, monied life: bear skin rugs, walrus tusks, Chinese prints and early Norman Rockwell paintings. Earhart disliked the media frenzy her husband cultivated and took refuge by working in her garden, reading poetry in front of the home's enormous fireplace, or taking leisurely drives around the Westchester countryside.

She nevertheless had signed on to a life as an adventurer, and that meant new challenges, no matter how daunting. A friend, Hilton Railey, later remarked: "She was caught up in the hero racket ... compelled to strive for bigger and braver feats."[9]

Amelia Earhart had hoped her partnership with publisher George Palmer Putnam was one of equals, despite how he controlled her image in the press. Privately, she made clear she would maintain her independence and keep her surname before agreeing to marry him (Amelia Earhart Papers, George Palmer Putnam Collection, Purdue University Libraries, Karnes Archives and Special Collections).

Earhart, left, enjoying some target practice—and a photo opportunity—with Olympian Babe Didrickson in her Rye backyard in 1932 (Amelia Earhart Papers, George Palmer Putnam Collection, Purdue University Libraries, Karnes Archives and Special Collections).

Earhart set off in 1937 on her next big challenge, a trip around the world in a modified Lockheed Model 10-E Electra, accompanied by her hard-drinking navigator, Fred Noonan. It was to be her last. Her plane disappeared July 2 near Howland Island in the great expanse of the Pacific Ocean, and she and Noonan were never heard from again.

Tethered as she was to a life in the media, Earhart's disappearance catapulted her into an even more rarified circle of renown. Questions about her ill-fated flight and final resting place have never been completely solved, despite tantalizing clues that continue to appear. Her demise was likely a blend of bad luck—a confluence of fatigue, poor judgment, inexact planning, haste and minor equipment failures that have doomed scores of flyers before and after Earhart took off over the Pacific.

Amelia Earhart, just 39, left behind her husband, her friends, her garden and the company of good books to soar above the clouds. She also left an enduring legacy to women to reach beyond traditional gender roles. "Some day," she told a newspaper after speaking at Purdue University in the 1930s, "people will be judged by their individual aptitude to do a thing and [society] will stop blocking off certain things as suitable to men and suitable to women."[10]

The nearly mythic arc of Earhart's career and life eventually overshadowed Westchester's other famous female aviator and Earhart's contemporary, Ruth Rowland Nichols. Vying for many of the same distance records Earhart sought, Nichols was in fact the first woman to hold speed, altitude and long-distance records in the same period. Portrayed in the press as Earhart's rival, she was also something of her opposite. A patrician beauty with deep-set eyes and world-class determination, Nichols often appeared at press events in stylish dresses and millinery—the high-society lady to Earhart's wind-tossed tomboy. While Earhart's independent streak was often at odds with her straight-laced Midwestern upbringing, Nichols was very much a product of old-line Westchester, exuding elegance, entitlement and grace under pressure at all times. She was just as determined as Earhart to make it into the record books, though her ambition took on a different aspect, that of the upper-class adventurer.

The press called her "the Flying Debutante," a nickname she despised. But she knew how to play the game, and her satin gowns and well-bred demeanor only enhanced her notoriety. "She is slender, graceful, with gentle gray eyes and wavy brown hair. She wears soft clothes that cling. Meeting her off-hand one would think her more suited to a mid–Victorian drawing room than twentieth-century sky-pioneering," wrote one interviewer. "She is the epitome of feminine charm."[11]

Born to an affluent, sports-minded family in Rye in 1901, Ruth Nichols inherited her lust for adventure from her father, Erickson, a member of the New York Stock Exchange who rode with Teddy Roosevelt's Rough Riders in the Spanish-American War. An indifferent student at The Masters School in Dobbs Ferry and at Wellesley College, Nichols threw herself into athletics and outdoor pursuits. When, upon her graduation from prep school in 1919, her father gave her a ten-minute airplane ride piloted by a World War I combat flier in Atlantic City, New Jersey, she was hooked. "I felt as if my soul were completely freed from my earthly body," she wrote in her 1957 autobiography, *Wings for Life*. "I haven't come down to earth since."[12]

The genteel demeanor and dress of Rye native Ruth Nichols, a contemporary of Earhart's, earned her the nickname "The Flying Debutante." She hated the description (National Photo Company Collection/ Library of Congress).

It was a passion that six major crashes, dozens of narrow escapes and multiple broken bones could never shake. In her memoirs she mentions an early, ill-fated romance with "the great love of her life," a man she never married, and alludes to no other romantic relationships in her book. Flying was her life. Nichols left college to learn how to fly in Miami, eventually returning to Wellesley and graduating in 1924. She took a job at a New York bank to please her father after college, but soon abandoned it to work as a saleswoman for an airplane manufacturer, becoming the first woman in New York State to acquire a professional pilot's license. She also flew stunt demonstrations over Playland and took up curious spectators for a dollar a head. By the end of 1932 she had become the nation's first female commercial airline pilot, commanding the cockpit for New York & New England Airways. Like Earhart, Nichols had a consuming, driving need to break the next record, to go higher and faster and longer. She achieved a women's altitude record in 1931, and the intense cold at 28,000 feet nearly killed her, each breath of oxygen a torturous sensation. "My frozen tongue felt like a large ice cube, but what did I care, I was higher than any woman ever had flown before," she later recalled.[13]

When she landed, her tongue was still nearly frozen, making it impossible for her to speak with reporters; it was one of the few times Nichols had nothing to say after a flight. She was a relentless promoter of the aviation industry in general and her flying career in particular.

Despite their well-known rivalry she and Earhart became good friends, a bond strengthened by Earhart's eventual move to Westchester, and they got along well. "I liked and admired her and believed she felt the same way about me," observed Nichols, whom Earhart affectionately nicknamed "Rufus."[14] "Both Amelia and I had crackups and successes. We both won a lot and lost a lot but were privileged to have places in the starting lineup of our country's women flyers, and each of us fulfilled her destiny as she saw it. Once you have experienced the exaltation of space and speed in flight, no matter who wins, it's mostly velvet," Nichols wrote.[15]

It was actually Earhart who initiated the friendship with Nichols, the better-known flyer at the time. In a letter of introduction in September 1927 Earhart asked, "What do you think of the advisability of forming an organization composed of women who fly?" Earhart mentioned that she had read about Nichols in the Boston papers and confessed she herself was a reluctant role model. "Personally, I am a social worker who flies for sport.... I cannot claim to be a feminist," she wrote in closing to Nichols, "but do rather enjoy seeing women tackle all kinds of new problems—new for them that is."[16]

The organization they went on to found—dubbed "The Ninety-Nines" for the number of women who joined it—was born at Curtiss Field, Valley Stream, Long Island, over the roar of engines. In 1931, at Nichols' house in Rye, the Ninety-Nines drew up the group's constitution.

Nichols had been briefly considered in 1928 for George Putnam's first "chaperoned" transatlantic flight but she was ill at the time; besides, she looked nothing like Lindbergh. When she eventually did try in June 1931 to become the first woman to fly across the Atlantic solo—a distinction Earhart earned one year later—she crashed in eastern Canada. She sustained five broken vertebrae and a major knee injury. "Everything under control," she wrote to her mother back in Rye. "Awfully sorry about crack-up. Will do it next time. Love, Ruth." She told one reporter, projecting the same steely reserve, "I am like Lindbergh. I have no fear and every confidence and I know exactly what I want. I'll fly to Paris in the early fall."[17] But unlike the shy, androgynous and youthful-looking Earhart—an enigma whose image was nonetheless tightly controlled by Putnam—the lady-like Nichols was a much easier target in the gossip sheets of the era. One maliciously used Nichols' string of accidents and seemingly outsize ambition to conclude she was "obsessed with the delusion" she could top Lindbergh.[18]

In her quest for new records, Nichols had numerous near misses that nearly claimed her life, each of which she overcame with the calm determination to try again. On October 21, 1937, Nichols was piloting a Condor, a commercial aircraft, when it went down near

Troy, New York, killing her co-pilot Harry Hublitz. She was thrown from the plane and landed under a burning wing. Her leg broke in nine places, she sustained a broken wrist, a fractured cheekbone and a severely burned left hand. "The clean ecstasy of flight," however, kept her coming back for more.[19]

She piloted in a plaster cast and steel corset, had most of the bones in her body broken, and survived two burning wrecks. She was hailed as both an "Ace Airwoman" and, in the tabloids, an "Ace Crasher."[20] Nichols nevertheless exercised her way through each recovery with a single goal in mind. Later in life, an airliner she flew ran out of fuel and went down in the sea near Ireland. She clung to a raft "in cold mountainous seas," as she described the experience, before being rescued. "And after each disaster," she later wrote, "there came a command from something deep within me: Get back into the air."[21]

When Earhart went missing, it was a fate that could have easily been Nichols' own. A year after the disappearance, Nichols took to the sky over 500 mourners at Rye Playland and dropped 18 American Beauty red roses in Earhart's honor.[22]

Nichols later penned a tribute to Earhart that spoke of her own enduring love of flight and its consequent risks. "Amelia flew on across the trackless Pacific until her last drop of fuel was gone and then sank quickly and cleanly into the deep blue sea," Nichols wrote. "If it must come, this was a fitting end to a flyer's career—to disappear at the peak of fame, on a final glorious attempt to conquer new frontiers of the sky; never to know the erosions and disappointments of age; to live in memory as young, golden and unafraid."[23]

In addition to her numerous speed and altitude records, Nichols used the spotlight to promote aviation at the local and national levels. In the 1940s, she was a strong and early advocate for building what would become, at the edges of Armonk and Purchase, the Westchester County Airport. During World War II, she belonged to White Plains' Civil Air Patrol and actively supported a number of humanitarian organizations.

Nichols may not have achieved Earhart's lasting fame but she continued to make headlines throughout her life. In 1958, when she was 57, the Air Force granted her special permission to co-pilot an F-102 Delta Dagger from its Long Island base, with her brother, Nick, an air force pilot, at the controls. She flew faster than any woman in the world had at that point in time, also becoming the first woman to surpass 1,000 mph at an altitude of 51,000 feet.[24] Once again, she was on top of the world.

The renewed celebrity didn't last long. Her many injuries brought chronic, debilitating pain, and she was eventually placed under the care of a physician for severe depression. When a family member could not reach her by phone on a fall afternoon in 1960, a building superintendent at her residence on East 49th Street in Manhattan opened the door to her apartment and found her dead. It was an intentional overdose by barbiturates, the coroner later ruled. She was 59. Miss Nichols, the Flying Debutante, had finally come to ground.[25]

Nichols and Earhart inhabited a privileged world of wealth, access and notoriety largely untouched by downturns in the economy. But as the 1930s continued, heartbreaking stories of poverty among the region's residents were commonplace. The great crash of 1929 put an end to the giddy financial speculation and rabid excess that marked the preceding era. The Wall Street party turned into Main Street malaise.

While the number of suicides that resulted from the crash is more urban legend than historical fact, there were several well-documented area cases of self-inflicted deaths.

One 65-year-old investor, the head of a produce firm and a civic leader from Mount Vernon, took a huge loss in the market after the crash. George Cutler, a member of the New York Mercantile Exchange, arrived at his lawyer's seventh floor office at 67 Wall Street in a state of weary resignation. He said he had come to talk over a business deal, but it was soon clear that he had something else on his mind. After he was told his lawyer was unavailable, according to a contemporary press account, he walked calmly to the window and climbed onto the ledge. Another lawyer in the office grabbed at the despondent investor to prevent his fall, but the doomed man's coat was all he could save. Police found a gold watch and $50 in the dead man's pocket, evidently all he had left before his desperate plunge.[26]

During the Great Depression even an affluent region like Westchester felt the wave-like effects of massive unemployment and shattered industries. Want and privation were evident in its small towns and big cities alike. While the county had an early and well-developed social-service agency, it soon was stretched to its limit.

Westchester was the first county in New York State with a child welfare department, which was started in 1915 with private funds, and directed by the capable administrator and social reformer Ruth Taylor. The county's social-service administration was run by V. Everit Macy, a newspaper publisher and philanthropist with family money in the oil business from Scarborough. He had much in common with his friend William Ward; like the political boss of Westchester, he was a Republican with strong Progressive inclinations, and a Quaker from a wealthy background. He died in 1930 after setting up a social service operation that became a model across the region and for the rest of the country.[27]

The 1931 annual report of the county's social-service agency cited a "greatly increased need of emergency home relief for the large number of families." The agency found "the number of families needing food, rent, light, etc., advanced 168% over the previous year." The following year's report noted more of the same, including "large numbers of people who have never before asked for help." By 1933, there were 1,683 destitute children under care of the county, compared to 1,079 in 1925.[28]

In 1934, the area's social workers bemoaned the intractable state of the economy and persistent joblessness, and "clients discouraged by continued hard times and the vicissitudes of a seemingly endless depression."[29]

Perhaps the truest measure of the devastation came in the form of children's letters addressed to Santa Claus, in actuality a communal fund that provided charitable relief around the holidays. The letters, which were published in the *White Plains Daily Reporter*, showed the effects of the Great Depression on the county's youngest residents. "We are on welfare, dear Santa," one little boy wrote to Santa Claus in the early 1930s. "Santa, I wonder if you could bring me something—I need shoes and overalls, and my baby sister needs clothes and we both need blankets. I have been a very good boy." Another little girl wrote Santa, "I am afraid we won't get anything for Christmas. I hope I am not asking too much. I am praying for my father to get a job soon."[30]

Thanks to the Depression, there was plenty of misery to go around. Many were out of work or looking to find ways to make ends meet in the new era of austerity. Some of those job seekers were less than honorable. The underworld that had thrived on the illicit trade in alcohol was still looking for new forms of revenue. And with Prohibition over, organized crime turned its attentions to other forms of money-making activities. Kidnapping became a scourge.

It was every parent's worst nightmare: A child from a wealthy family, or even a middle-class one, fails to return from school or mysteriously disappears from home. A ransom note appears demanding money for a safe return.

The most famous kidnapping case of the era was the abduction of Charles Augustus Lindbergh, Jr., the eldest son of aviator Charles and Anne Morrow Lindbergh, from their home in New Jersey in 1932. The 20-month-old toddler was later found dead. Kidnappings became a common occurrence in many sections of the country throughout the 1930s, and anxiety over the Lindbergh case and others like it cast a long shadow across the playgrounds and nurseries of America.

Westchester went through its own agonizing abduction case in the 1930s when the son of a prominent attorney went missing in broad daylight. On February 12, 1938, Peter Levine, 12, was abducted in New Rochelle while walking home from junior high school. A demand for $60,000 was sent to the family a short time later. The abduction came as a mystery to those who knew the Levines, who were affluent but not extremely wealthy. The father had difficulty raising the ransom and had to appeal to friends for financial help.

Local authorities and the FBI followed the standard protocol at the time—a move that later came in for criticism—by keeping a low-profile and forestalling an aggressive response until the ransom was paid, a kind of gentleman's agreement with the underworld. Under the common doctrine at the time, law enforcement never went into pursuit mode until after the victim was released.

A note written in Peter Levine's handwriting arrived with one of the kidnappers' typewritten instructions a few days after the abduction. After contact with the kidnappers established a procedure for the ransom drop-off, followed by more instructions, it was hoped in early March that the youngster would be returned.[31] But nothing came of it, nor any of the other contacts with the kidnappers. The communication stopped abruptly five days after the kidnapping, never to be repeated. A massive search of the region with assistance from hundreds of volunteers, one that extended to the desolate rock islands in Long Island Sound, proved fruitless.

The despair of the family turned to horror in late May, when a boat captain found the decapitated body of Peter Levine, tied and weighted with copper wire, near a private beach in Long Island Sound that was part of the Iselin estate in New Rochelle. Police recovered a small toy airplane and a jackknife inside his pockets, items he was carrying the day he vanished. Investigators scoured hundreds of boats and waterfront homes in the vicinity to find the perpetrators, to no avail.[32]

Two men from Pelham, Werner Fred Luck and Edward John Penn, who attempted to extort money from the Levine family—a cruel parallel trade that often followed the kidnapping racket—were later charged with attempted blackmail and sentenced to years in prison. Police were unable to prove they had any direct knowledge of the actual kidnapping, and the killer or killers were never caught.[33] The Levine case joined many other unsolved crimes in county history. Few, however, were more atrocious. In reviewing the case and others like it, *Life* magazine called it a "fallacy" for law-enforcement to "remain aloof" after an initial kidnapping. Those kind of initial hands-off tactics were eventually modified.[34]

As the kidnapping case demonstrated, there were still plenty of criminals around after Prohibition ended. Many of the mafia crime leaders kept second homes in Westchester, where wives, family members and girlfriends lived. One of the best known crime bosses to have set up residence in Westchester was Ciro Terranova, an associate of Dutch

Schultz. A native of Corleone in Sicily, he made his way up the underworld ladder in the urban maelstrom, and a palatial Spanish villa on Peace Street in Pelham Manor and chauffeured rides in a bullet-proof limousine were his temporary rewards for a life of crime. It was said that he paid for his home in southern Westchester in 1929 by putting down $52,000 in cash.[35] Working the Harlem number rackets, he was also involved in racketeering in the fresh-produce business and earned the unlikely moniker of "the Artichoke King." The NYPD was put under orders to arrest him on sight if he ever was found within city limits, so he was kept at bay in Westchester.[36]

The Mafia boss, who was heavily involved in the so-called Castellammarese War that claimed the lives of numerous mafiosi in 1930 and 1931, came to a rather pathetic end. He lost the respect of the underworld and control of the produce rackets to aggressive newcomers and efforts of by New York Mayor Fiorello La Guardia to decriminalize them. After his fortunes took a turn for the worse, he was forced to sell his home in Pelham Manor in 1937, and he died in destitution a year later.[37]

The tragic mobsters glorified in popular movies of the time fed the growing public infatuation with crime on a grand, dramatic scale. Their real counterparts passed from the stage with much less fanfare, leaving behind a trail of misfortune and misery. Leonard Scarnici, aka "Louis Sauce," fell into the latter category.

In the annals of crime in the region, it would be harder to find a gangster with bloodier hands than Scarnici. He was as accomplished in the ways of underworld savagery as any of his more famous associates. Before he was strapped down to "Old Sparky" in the death house at Sing Sing in 1935—smoking and chewing gum on the way in, tying his own wrist down as a final joke—Scarnici was Westchester's most feared local gangster, tied to a dozen murders in New England and New York. From his heavily armed lair in Mount Kisco in northern Westchester, Scarnici was believed to have used his hideout to imprison a hostage in one of the most sensational criminal cases of the 1930s, the abduction of a young man connected to a powerful Albany political family.

Leonard Scarnici was linked to a dozen murders in his short, deadly career. Tied to a notorious kidnapping in the 1930s, he kept a Mount Kisco safe house stocked with guns and ammo. Scarnici cracked jokes before his execution in the electric chair at Sing Sing (Lewis Lawes Papers, Special Collections, Lloyd Sealy Library, John Jay College of Criminal Justice/CUNY).

Scarnici was born in 1906 and raised in Springfield, Massachusetts. He became a criminal at an early age and compiled a long record for burglary, robbery and possession of stolen property as a young man. His first murder came in 1927. Although stories from the underworld are often difficult to corroborate, the victim's mother told authorities her son had been buried alive in a shallow grave in Springfield, apparently the account that Scarnici gave the woman.[38] His penchant for violence only grew with his ambition.

He arrived in Westchester in the 1920s and hooked up with Dutch Schultz. Scarnici followed a typical pattern, as Schultz had done with his wife in Yonkers, and set up his wife, Eleanor, in a home in northern Westchester.

Scarnici may have been behind one of the biggest gangland assassinations of the period, the killing of Vincent "Mad Dog" Coll. The Irish-born Coll had been one of Schultz's most trusted hit men, but he ran afoul of the mob for his wild ways. He was shot at least 15 times in a phone booth in Manhattan in February 1932. Many at the time believed Scarnici was the triggerman on the hit, as he was known as one of the Dutchman's top assassins.[39]

Schultz put up the bail when Scarnici's gang members got in trouble. Marcel Poffo, one of the Dutchman's early mentors from their days together in the Bronx, later worked for Scarnici's crew.

Observers said that Scarnici "was considered cruel and ruthless even among his underworld associates."[40] The *New York Times* quoted a New York City police inspector as describing Scarnici as "perhaps the toughest man in my experience."[41] Scarnici was also a lousy boss. Members of his gang turned up dead with shocking regularity—"taken for a one-way ride," in the parlance of the day. Two of his gang members, Poffo (Dutch Schultz's old friend) and Max Parken were found dead in a car in Harrison near the Westchester Country Club in June 1933. A short time later, two other members of Scarnici's gang, Anthony Russo and Joseph Colegiero, were killed and dumped behind a stone wall just over the Mount Kisco line in Bedford.[42]

Bedford police chief Frank Mallette later surmised that Scarnici had killed Russo and Colegiero at his Mount Kisco apartment, then dumped them a mile away, where their bodies were found still warm by local cops.[43] Scarnici called Parken and Poffo "rats and double-crossers" during a police interrogation. Both men were linked to a notorious bank robbery in Rensselaer, New York, in which a police detective working in a security job was shot and killed. Most speculated there had been a fight over the proceeds of the loot, and Poffo and Parken came up on the losing end.[44]

The killings stunned Westchester residents, especially when they learned they happened not in the big city, but in their own backyards. "None of us gave a thought to the probability that the killings might have taken place within our own borders," wrote the editors of the *Daily Reporter*. "Gangland has stretched its slimy tentacles into all parts of the United States. Criminals have become a menace to the small town as well as to the largest city."[45]

Scarnici was associated with a dozen killings in his bloody career besides the suspected murders in Westchester, but it was a major kidnapping case that brought police to his doorstep in 1933. John O'Connell, the scion of a prominent Albany political clan, was snatched and held for ransom, and the family paid $40,000 for his release. Police, who were closely watching Scarnici's gang in connection with the kidnapping, raided his apartment in the Bronx and arrested him there.

Investigators later smashed down the door of the Scarnici hideout at 152 Kisco Avenue in Mount Kisco, finding a machine gun, several shotguns and 1,000 rounds of ammo. They also found handcuffs, adhesive tape and other evidence that O'Connell may have been held hostage there. O'Connell later said he recognized the handcuffs recovered from the residence, from small nicks and rust spots he managed to observe on the metal braces while in captivity there. Scarnici's wife was charged with weapons possession. She was living there with Emma Russo, presumably the wife of the man Scarnici had killed.[46]

While there was a stack of major crimes laid at Scarnici's feet, the 1932 killing of the Rensselaer, New York, police detective, employed as a security guard at the bank there, took precedence. He was convicted of that crime and sentenced to the electric chair. The condemned mobster came back to Westchester to die. After his final court appeal in lower Manhattan failed in the morning, preparations were made to execute him that very same day.

Scarnici walked his final steps shortly before midnight on June 27, 1935, led by four guards, one of whom was carrying a submachine gun as an extra precaution (after rumors were picked up by authorities that efforts were underway to spring Scarnici from execution.) He was grinning widely, chewing gum and puffing on a cigarette held with a steady hand, according to eyewitnesses. "Not so tight boys," he joked after the straps were pulled into place. He complained, somewhat cryptically, about being double-crossed by his mobster associates in Albany, and when the mask was finally placed over his face, mumbled, "OK, pard."[47] When the current was switched on, one of Westchester's worst killers joined his victims in death.

In the 1930s, the electric chair also claimed the life of a notorious serial killer, Albert Fish. A deeply disturbed sexual predator who visited nearly inconceivable horrors on his young victims, including Grace Budd of Greenburgh, aged ten, he was executed at Sing Sing in January 1936.

Although the ills of the decade were generally blamed on the economic Depression, another societal enemy soon formed in the public's mind. It was a narcotic that grew like a weed and went by a dozen names: tea, dope, locoweed, pot, Mary Jane, muggles, Indian hay and reefer. Even the front porch wasn't safe from the spread of *cannabis sativa*, the plant blamed for everything from sexually transmitted diseases to killing sprees.

In its workaday incarnation, hemp was developed for use in textiles and rope-making, finding a place in the repertoire of Northern agriculture for centuries. Its more potent properties as a mild intoxicant were also known. The more powerful varieties spread from their traditional range in the Southwest, and in Southern port cities, following the 1910 Mexican Revolution. Recreational use of marijuana dispersed across the country during the 1920s, and beginning in the late 1930s, federal and local law enforcement agencies took notice and started a war on cannabis: passing laws, issuing a steady stream of public communiques on the presumed dangers of the mind-altering plant and crashing down the doors of so-called "tea pads."[48] Offenders were locked up behind bars for long sentences.

The anti-marijuana campaign had many supporters in small-town police departments, editorial offices and on school boards. It also had a general: Harry J. Anslinger, the commissioner of the Federal Bureau of Narcotics and one of the few longtime rivals of the FBI's J. Edgar Hoover. Anslinger was the nation's first drug czar, and he had very strong ideas about law and order. He was notoriously hostile to black culture and music—outdoing even outspoken bigots of the period in his vitriol—and the depths of his racial animosities helped drive his ambitions as the nation's foremost drug enforcer. Anslinger, in fact, conceived of the first drug war as a means of purifying America. The campaign ostensibly sought to eradicate the use of marijuana, but it also played on fears about jazz music, teenage sexuality and the mixing of blacks and whites in social settings.[49]

In Westchester in 1938, parents, concerned citizens and police joined together to rid the region of marijuana's trade, one of the many anti-drug crusades to periodically march across the American landscape. "Few of us realize, unless we make a study of the situation, how grave a problem marijuana is in Westchester and the extent to which it is used, particularly by youngsters," Westchester County district attorney Walter Ferris said that year as he announced a local crackdown on the illegal drug. "We, in the District Attorney's office, realize how many crimes are committed by persons under its influence."[50] Whether or not that was actually true, the campaign began in May. Westchester County sheriff George Casey, an aggressive, new county sheriff working with state and local officers on surveillance operations for more than a year, raided a dozen "smoke dens" and "tea pads" in Valhalla, Greenburgh, New Rochelle, Mount Vernon and White Plains. Hundreds of people were rounded up, and Sheriff Casey commented, "Many of the patrons were fine-looking youngsters coming from various parts of Westchester and the Bronx."[51]

Those caught with marijuana in 1938 could expect swift and hard punishment (most especially African American defendants). When two White Plains men were arrested in April of that year on marijuana charges, City Court Judge Charles Voss lectured them about "the most vicious drug known to the medical profession" before sentencing them to a year in jail. The two men, who were black, had been arrested the night before.[52]

The Westchester raids, which were followed by a series of raids in the Harlem neighborhood of New York City, were accompanied by an extensive public education campaign in both the national and regional press. The *White Plains Daily Reporter* ran a five-day series on the dangers of marijuana and hosted a special meeting for local citizens on the drug at a White Plains hotel that same year. Newspaper coverage—and substantial support from press barons like William Randolph Hearst—were a major factor in the war on cannabis.[53]

A local expert on marijuana, J.M. Page, wrote a daily commentary on the subject, paying particular attention to the "addicts" who consumed the substance. "Few persons realize the proximity of these 'vipers,' the actual term applied to addicts of the drug, or are aware of the fact that its uses are so widespread," Page wrote, describing how marijuana was being grown in White Plains and neighboring communities, even on the properties of local homes.[54]

"Practically unknown here a year or two ago, this narcotic drug is finding an ever increasing market ... throughout the county.... It requires no attention or cultivation and can be, and is, grown in backyards, alleys and under the porches of homes," the series continued.[55]

In examining the spread of marijuana use, the newspaper saw dangers of all sorts and elucidated them in a manner that seemed to exhaust the repertoire of hyperbole. "The opportunity for contracting syphilis, or any other social disease, is excellent due to the manner in which the marijuana weed is smoked at the 'pads.' The 'stick' is passed around the room, each smoker greedily inhaling the treacherous fumes and passing it onto his neighbor; persons of mixed races alternately sucking on a bit of sickening, pulpy weed," J.M. Page continued.[56]

The anxiety over racial mixing appeared to be the most troublesome aspect of the "tea pad." The *Daily Reporter* devoted a front-page piece on the link between marijuana and swing music, the fast-tempo dance music that many young people and jazz fans enjoyed but troubled older adults. "It is common knowledge among 'reefer' addicts that some of the county's leading swing maestros are smokers of marijuana," the columnist wrote, "Swing followers, composed largely of high school students, eventually become exposed to the use of the drug through association with musicians in these spots."[57] According to the analysis, "colored musicians" were the main factor behind the spread among young people. Marijuana consumption persisted in greater and lesser degree in Westchester, despite the massive campaign to tear its deep roots from the American soil. As the crusaders of 1938 learned first hand, the killer weed is actually very hard to kill.

The county's upholders of law and order, particularly the county sheriff, George Casey, soon found another target lurking in their midst: gambling halls enlivened by the clang-clang of the pinball machine. The great pinball war in Westchester was fought in 1939 and 1940, when the dangers of small-scale gambling and the corruption of youth were crucial concerns. The opening shot was fired in late 1939, with raids in Greenburgh and Bronxville.[58] New York City under Mayor Fiorella LaGuardia, and other communities in the region, also sought to crack down on the clickety-clack games of skill and chance, which were closely associated with organized crime.

Casey vowed to put an end to the whiz-bang machines not so much for what they played, but what they paid out: cigarette packs or nickels that were fed right back into them by kids. Pinball was a minor, small-time vice compared to horse-betting parlors and the thriving numbers racket run by organized crime, but Sheriff Casey did not see it that way. He was doing it to prevent an early gambling habit among young people. "I want to clean up gambling in Westchester," Casey told the local press. "I'd rather get ahold of a penny game than a dollar game any day, because it's the children who play penny games—and we get complaints they are using their lunch money to gamble."[59]

As Casey saw it, pinball machines were a gateway to other illegal vices, and vice had a way of turning up in unusual places, like a sweet shop in Hartsdale called The Sugar Bowl. The candy store had an innocent-sounding name that masked its true purpose, according to local law enforcement. As a front-page story about the Sugar Bowl bust reported: "Gambling equipment, obscene literature and illegal merchandise were seized yesterday afternoon in a confectionary store patronized by high school students…. The place, police said, was a 'hangout' where students played pinball and placed bets on numbers and horse races."[60] Besides smashing up slot and pinball machines with axes, cops announced that "obscene cartoons" and "contraceptive devices" (presumably condoms) were part of the deviant behavior that went on with gambling.[61]

The payout machines were the main target, but many other pinball machines were confiscated during the roundup. Bar owners from all over the county faced local police and sheriff's deputies. Dozens of machines were smashed up by authorities in White Plains, and in Ossining, 100 machines were seized.[62] Some municipalities had their own licensing system for pinball machines, like Mount Vernon, and escaped the countywide sweep.

The attack on pinball machines was followed in March of that year by raids on gambling dens around the county, but the momentum soon wore off. Sheriff Casey ran into bureaucratic snags, legal headaches and turf fights with the county District Attorney's Office and local police departments, a persistent feature of law enforcement and governmental administration in a region with dozens of separate municipalities within it.

The "higher-ups" who collected the big money from the small-time gaming centers proved especially difficult to capture. While enforcement continued, it did not reach the sustained pitch that the big crackdown had achieved in late 1939 and early 1940. The familiar sounds of the pinball parlor—*clank-clank-clank-BING!*—resumed in villages and cities around Westchester. As a reporter with the *Evening Dispatch* discovered during a short walk in downtown White Plains not long after the sheriff's campaign, "The nickel-grabbing machines, banned six weeks ago, are back again."[63]

The pinball crackdown and local marijuana crusade held in common several intersecting themes of life in the suburbs: an official propensity to control the behavior of every citizen, young and old; a disdain for unruliness; and perhaps most of all, an abiding sense of prudery. While the big city to the south had more than its share of liberties and libertines, the suburbs, at least on the surface, took a more Puritanical approach to everyday life. And Westchester was one of its staunchest practitioners.

New Rochelle, in the public perception, became something of the capital of prudery during the 1920s. Art has a way of drawing strong responses, and one particular battle on the cultural front generated everything from snickers to titters to pious outrage. In 1923, a sculpture arrived from New York to the seaside city that depicted a man, a woman and a dog, all in a pure state of nature, or rather, stark naked. It was promptly covered in canvas.[64] The statue of "Venus and Adonis" by a leading sculptor of the era, Frederick MacMonnies, was to have been the centerpiece of an outdoor exhibit in New Rochelle in front of the public library. Purchased by the Metropolitan Museum of Art, it was on loan to the arts committee of the New Rochelle Women's Club. A critic of the piece who complained to authorities said that the work would draw crowds, "not to study its artistic merit, but to point their fingers and make smutty comments."[65] He said he would have to encounter the work on a daily basis on his way to work. "I'll tell you sir, notwithstanding what the smart people may say, that statue is very raw and shocking," he said. The New Rochelle critic had a point—other works by MacMonnies exhibited elsewhere in public, including New York City, also prompted concerns about his strikingly life-like depictions of the naked human body. Bowing to pressure, authorities decided that the statue was a bit too risqué, and the pup tent was put up around it. To make doubly sure that the statue was kept out of view, a police officer was detailed to stand guard. It was eventually sent back to the Metropolitan.[66]

Inanimate statues weren't the only objects of the suburbs' moralistic code. The urge to put the force of law into proper displays of dress often proved irresistible to a certain class of moralizers.

While the daring 1920s raised hemlines at the start of a general liberalization of fashion codes, there was a backlash in the more sober 1930s, particularly in the prudish suburbs. Shorts, which bared one's legs in public, were considered risqué attire for both men and women. So daring, in fact, that the city of Yonkers once declared war on them and other "skimpy attire."

By the mid–1930s shorts had became a popular wardrobe staple for adults, slowly gravitating from glamorous resorts and the world of sports to city sidewalks. Athletes popularized the look out of necessity, taking advantage of shifting attitudes toward casual attire to further their sporting prowess. Henry "Bunny" Austin's, a tennis ace, first wore knee-grazing white shorts on the courts at Wimbledon in a 1932 match viewed by Queen Mary of England. He later explained he was tired of the standard attire—"sweat-sodden cricket flannels were weighing me down," he recalled—so he instructed his tailor to fashion a pair of short pants. Queen Mary was "not amused" by the sight of Austin's uncovered legs, it was said in royal circles, and she was not alone.[67] When a woman tennis player, Helen Jacobs, wore shorts at the U.S. Open in 1933, her appearance caused a minor scandal, but the vogue for shorts soon spread to all walks of life.

The guardians of morality in the suburbs were likewise unamused about the sudden popularity of shorts and the skimpy tops that often accompanied them. The recreation commission of the Town of Rye declared that shorts and handkerchief-style halter tops "were a form of lingerie," and in 1936, it prohibited them from being worn in the park adjoining the beach.[68] In Yorktown Heights, women faced a $2 fine if their shorts rose more than two inches above their knees.[69] Other towns all over the Northeast, from Dover, New Jersey, to Westport, Connecticut, all sought to limit skimpy clothing from their borders.

But it was Yonkers' 1936 war on shorts that eventually drove its residents into a battle of ludicrous proportions as tabloid reporters, early feminists, lawyers, politicians and the state's highest judges all joined the fray over fabric and formality. While Yonkers was not the only American city that chose to resist the fashion revolution in 1930s, it became the best known.

A city alderman by the name of William Slater zealously led the municipality's war on shorts. An insurance and real-estate agent in his mid–40s, Slater was an old-fashioned moralizer. When it came to shorts, enough was enough, or rather not enough. Armed with a movie camera, a newly enacted law and plenty of pious outrage, he sought to return tasteful attire to the "City of Gracious Living," as Yonkers then styled itself. He pushed through a city ordinance against the wearing of short pants in the city, then moved to enforce it with a crusader's intensity.

"Girls wander about so scantily clad that the angel Gabriel would blush to behold them. It's unbelievable!" Slater declared. "Such displays will be stopped, as they lower morals."[70] Young women who wanted to beat the summer heat, even far from main street, had to beware the fashion police once Slater got to work enforcing the law. With a cameraman and two police officers by his side, Slater positioned himself along a popular hiking trail that ran along the Croton Aqueduct and found his mark when five young women, all from New York City, approached wearing what he called "scant attire." The young women were given summonses and later dismissed with a warning, but it was the first of many salvos in the Yonkers shorts war.

Slater's public shaming of the "skimpily attired" attracted widespread attention, and the alderman soon found himself under attack by feminists and editorial writers. He was lampooned in the pages of the *Yonkers Herald Statesman* as a "censor of hikers costumes" and a "nemesis of semi-nudists."[71] Other city papers joined the fray and played the entire affair for laughs.

A Yonkers civic leader, Mildred Kelly, said it was only pragmatic to wear more comfortable clothing in the summer and chided Slater for being "shocked at the sight of the human body." A number of local women came forward to support Slater's law, but plenty more gave it a Bronx cheer, seeing the legislation as an intrusive form of male control. One group of New York City women came to the city line wearing shorts and put on skirts for the short crossing into Yonkers, snickering the entire time at the absurdity of the situation. A group called the "Long Live Shorts Club" made headlines protesting the law. Said the club's president, Mae Borak of New York, "Women have been hampered and uncomfortable for a long time with skirts and dresses, and it is about time that stupidly conventional customs were done away with."[72]

In June 1936 two tabloid reporters from the *New York Daily News*, a man and a woman, were dispatched wearing shorts to Yonkers, where they were both duly ticketed. While women were the primary target of the law, men were also subject to penalties, evidently to make enforcement of the law appear more equitable.[73]

Their case, with its involvement of a major New York newspaper, was the one that made it through the courts. The Yonkers shorts law found itself before the New York State Court of Appeals in the summer of 1937 and the black-robed panel sided with the shorts-wearing masses. The judges decreed: "The Constitution still leaves some opportunity for people to be foolish," adding that New Yorkers "can dress as they please, wear anything so long as they do not offend public order and decency."[74] The seven-judge panel also decided the Yonkers law was too vaguely worded to pass legal muster.

Hundreds of shorts-clad strollers celebrated the decision the following weekend, flaunting the forbidden fashion at parks within Yonkers city limits. Slater rewrote the law to make it more specific, but by then Yonkers' citizens and police officials had lost their taste for fashion crusades. The law became a dead letter in the city's statute books. It was, however, an abiding lesson on the limits of official decrees on dress, and woe to the politician who attempts to control individual rights on wardrobe. Whether polyester or cotton, long and loose or barely there, shorts continue to loom large in the wardrobe of the average American.

The 1930s were a time when sports and culture became increasingly entwined—the spread of sporting clothes onto city streets being just one example. Sports culture moved to the very center of American life, propelled by radio and film. Places like Yankees Stadium and Ebbetts Field became the venues where heroes strode the turf. In Westchester, there was an unlikely counterpoint to, and sometimes extension of, those sporting fields of legend.

One of the more unusual venues in the world of athletics, the playing fields at Sing Sing Prison in Ossining, brought new meaning to the term "extreme sports." Ringed by barbed wire and armed guards, the prison football squad, known as The Black Sheep, knocked heads with single-minded ferocity. The end zone fell under the shadow of a machine-gun post. The baseball diamond at the state prison boasted a storied past, where Babe Ruth and Lou Gehrig made legendary appearances. It was an unlikely field of dreams tucked inside the house of pain. During the golden age of Sing Sing athletics under Warden Louis Lawes in the 1930s, the prison playing field attracted thousands of spectators who paid $1 to watch professional and amateur athletes of every ability test their mettle against some of the toughest mugs ever to lace up a pair of cleats. There were no road games; the Black Sheep only played at home.

Baseball began as a diversion at Sing Sing, a pastime for a captive audience that gave convicts something to do during their incarceration. Warden Lawes, who took charge of Sing Sing in 1920, was an old-school disciplinarian with a reformer's belief that men could change their ways with the proper instruction. He believed sports taught valuable life lessons and provided a positive focus for other inmates behind bars. After taking over as warden, he substantially upgraded the prison's sports programs.

The prison baseball club, the Orioles, played exhibition games against the Yankees and the Giants—along with amateur clubs and minor league squads from all over Westchester, Long Island, Connecticut and Upstate New York—every year in the late 20s and early 30s.

Babe Ruth made a famous trip up the river on September 5, 1929, and swatted three homers against the home team. His first homer in the second inning was a mighty blast that supposedly sailed over the heads of the guards on the wall watching the game. While the Bambino's big dinger has the ring of a tall tale, witnesses swore it arced at least 600 feet from the batter's box. The Babe pitched the last two innings to ensure a lopsided 17–3 Yankee win.[75]

In another famous encounter between the pinstriped and the prison-striped, Lou Gehrig once stole second, third and home base in a game against the prison squad.

The most famous prison-athlete at Sing Sing was a speedy, if troubled, outfielder named Edwin "Alabama" Pitts. At one point he was called by the *Los Angeles Times* "the most prominent jailbird athlete in America."[76] Pitts hit two doubles against a visiting Giants club in 1933. After serving five years for taking part in the armed robbery of a New York City department store, Warden Lawes took a liking to him, encouraged his sporting talents and assisted in his parole. After prison, he was recruited by a minor-league club from Albany, but his prison record drew scorn and disapproval from the league management. Eventually, Baseball Commissioner Kenesaw Mountain Landis ruled that he could play. Pitts never rose above the minors, but went on to play football briefly for the Philadelphia Eagles. He died in 1941 in bar fight when a jealous boyfriend of a woman with whom he was dancing stabbed him.[77]

Football became a major presence in the 1930s at Sing Sing when the prison hired a former Notre Dame football captain, the aptly named John Law, to coach the squad. Coach Law, a Yonkers native, said the prisoners were easier to coach than college players. In a magazine piece in the early 30s, Law wrote that The Black Sheep had no distractions and put all their efforts into the game. "I've never seen a team work harder than this one," he concluded.[78]

In his autobiography, Warden Lawes marveled at the enthusiasm for the football matches, which he felt brought out the best in the men. "At each game, more than 2,000 men lined up alongside the north wall, intent and enthusiastic about the progress their team was making.... The field was well-policed with officers, but they were hardly needed. There was not a shady or ominous thought in all that crowd of men," he wrote.[79]

As an added benefit, Lawes said the sports program gave visitors a chance to see that the inmates were men like any other, not monsters or mad men. It had a humanizing effect on both sides. A uniformed drill team and marching band paraded onto the field before kickoff. The band was led by a professional musician doing time on a forgery conviction. The warden's young daughter led the procession, marching along with the Black Sheep's mascot, a black goat, onto the field before every game.[80] One of the biggest games of the year pitted the prison squad against a police team from Port Jervis, New York. As Coach Law recalled it in his magazine piece, the prisoners created a dummy policeman that they mounted on a stretcher as a gag and intimidation tactic. The prison band played the funeral march whenever the police team found itself in a tight spot.[81]

The Black Sheep games attracted plenty of spectators and generated significant revenue. The Sing Sing football program netted $10,000 in a typical year from ticket sales, and the money was used to buy fresh produce and leather jackets for the inmates. The rewards for those who played, of course, were much higher, in epic encounters between men who have everything and those who had nothing.

While the fabulous games at Sing Sing, studded with sports heroes, provided a diversion to many prisoners who had few other outlets for enjoyment, others were determined to get out—by any means available. Sing Sing was known for numerous breakouts during its long history—with bribery the preferred method. One of the most adventurous jailbreaks at Sing Sing history took place the hard way—with an improvised ladder and lock-picking tools.

Willie Sutton was unique in his dedication to the craft of cracking safes and holding up jewelry stores. He robbed about 100 banks and an assortment of jewelry stores during a long career in crime, earning the moniker "the Babe Ruth of Bank Robbers" by a New York City police commissioner.[82]

Hollywood mythology to the contrary, most career criminals are a pretty dull lot. In his own memoirs, Sutton observed that most of his fellow crooks were a lazy and unambitious bunch, drinking heavily before big jobs, spilling secrets in public while they were drunk, showing up late for crucial assignments, seldom looking beyond the next big score. Sutton, however, was a consummate professional. Indeed, his steady work habits, keen eye for detail and devotion to craft would have made him an ideal candidate to run the banks that he robbed. When he was behind bars, Sutton used the time profitably; he often read anthropology books he found in the prison library, and he taught himself Spanish.[83] He took to wearing disguises after observing that people in uniform are granted automatic acceptance by the clothing they wear.

A man about town, Sutton squandered the $2 million he made as a crook on high living and girlfriends with expensive taste. His daring robberies, lively quips and profligate lifestyle made him one of the most famous criminals in America. His answer to the question of why he robbed banks—"That's where the money is"—has become a catch phrase in popular culture. (Never mind that the line was actually made up by one of Sutton's many journalistic admirers.)[84]

While Sutton thrived on a life outside the law, his luck and finesse only went so far, and he was caught on several occasions. A judge sentenced him in the early 1930s to a long stretch at Sing Sing, where he carried out his first and most famous jail-break.

His first stint at the state prison in Ossining in 1925 lasted just three months. But it was a place he came to detest. In 1932, Sutton was back at Sing Sing after his conviction on a series of robberies, and security had much improved. "To begin with, a new 35-foot high concrete wall now surrounded the prison," he recalled in his memoirs. "A new block of escape-proof cells had been erected. I was 31 years old, and when I took a look at this formidable concrete fortress on the Hudson, I felt I might well be here for the rest of my natural life.... I resolved to get out of Sing Sing."[85] He was determined to get out—or spend 30 years behind bars there. Using his analytical skills that had served him well breaking into banks, he was committed to both outsmarting and breaking through heavy security. He made a study of the layout of the cells and memorized the schedules of guards. He learned to talk while barely moving his lips with another prisoner who had joined him in his escape plans, Johnny Egan, who also did repairs around the facility. Egan procured a hacksaw to slowly cut away the bars from their cells, as well as several lock picks.

On the night of December 12, 1932, they put their plans into effect: breaking out of their cells and picking the locks to the interior doors. They went to a cellar where ladders were stored and affixed two of them with wire. Scurrying against the prison walls on a cold, windy night, they scaled the barrier and dropped to the other side. The whole operation took less than an hour. A car with the key inside—parked there by an underworld associate—completed the getaway.[86]

The other major breakout at Sing Sing prison took place in the predawn hours of Easter Monday in 1941. The deadliest jailbreak in Sing Sing history, it claimed the life of a prison guard and an Ossining police officer. Three holdup men from a tough neighborhood on Manhattan's West Side managed to have guns smuggled into the prison in milk trucks, thanks to their old Hell's Kitchen gang. A prison guard, John Hartye, was shot and killed at once, and the jailbreakers snuck through an old steam tunnel to get past the wall.[87] Once outside, the escapees came across an Ossining police officer, James Fagan, who was responding to a complaint of men loitering near the train station, and he, too, was gunned down, emptying his revolver at his assailants before dying.[88]

Fagan's police partner killed one of the escaped convicts, John Waters, shooting him in the head with his pistol from 200 feet away. The two other fugitives, Charles McGale and James ("Whitey") Riordan, forced a fisherman to row them across the river, where they were later captured with the assistance of a pair of bloodhounds. They died in the electric chair, in the same prison from which they had once escaped.[89]

All of this, from the high relief of the sporting attractions to the frisson of concentrated criminality, made Sing Sing very much a destination. Spectators arrived for potential sightings of a well-known convict in the yard. Criminal celebrities like Owney Madden, who ran the liquor trade in much of Gotham, drove himself to Sing Sing in July 1932. The guard on duty did not recognize him, but the warden's secretary did. Madden spent a year in jail at Sing Sing.[90]

While most visits to Sing Sing caused little notice, one such trip, however, ended in catastrophe. In the annals of fire-related disasters, the destructive flames that engulfed the Ossining waterfront in 1934 and killed 21 people deserves special mention. It may not rank with other similar cataclysms of the period, like the Hartford circus fire of 1944 that killed 168 people, or the Cocoanut Grove nightclub fire in Boston 1942 that killed 492 and changed fire-safety codes, but for the sheer horror of an excursion bus engulfed in flames, "a pyre of screaming humanity," in the words of the Ossining daily newspaper, the *Ossining Citizen-Register*, it stood alone.[91] The Young Men's Democratic League of Brooklyn was set to take on the prison baseball club at Sing Sing for a day of picnics and recreation on July 22. A caravan of seven buses carried the weekend excursion party to Ossining in the morning. Everything went wrong for the creaky old bus at the rear of the procession. The bus stopped several times while the driver, Frank Incarnato of Brooklyn, checked the brakes. The squeal of grinding metal was impossible to ignore, and passengers were said to be mumbling about safety concerns as the bus turned down Main Street in Ossining, a very steep hill, and began to pick up speed. Then the brakes died.

Witnesses said the bus carrying 44 people hit speeds of up to 50 miles an hour as it careened down Main Street. Three men, sensing disaster, jumped from the vehicle as it sped wildly down the hill. The bus then ran up the train station ramp, mounted the viaduct over the tracks and tore through the metal railings and hurtled off the ramp. A terrific blast followed as the bus hit the ground and exploded in flames. Screaming and panic-stricken, the passengers tried to fight their way from the flaming vehicle. Some fought for the doors of the bus, others jumped from the windows with their clothes flaming. The bus landed 30 feet in the middle of a lumberyard, and there had been a drought condition for the past two months. "The fire spread through the lumber as if it had been tinder," fire chief Duane Byble said afterwards.[92]

Passengers covered in flames ran toward the water, and their blazing garments sizzled when they struck the river. Nearby boaters rushed over to pull them out. The windows at the train station on the river's edge burst from the heat of the flames.

The engulfed bus was the scene of desperate rescue attempts, and one the most challenging fire-fighting operations ever conducted in that era, a time when emergency responders wore little more than raincoats and rubber galoshes to do battle with 1,000-degree heat and flames. Two hundred firefighters threw themselves into a desperate effort to save lives and property.

Walter Thompson, a Brooklyn contractor, could see his wife's head sticking out of a window and tried frantically to set her free. Her leg was caught, however, and he was forced back from the inferno, his own coat sleeves on fire. He later identified his wife, Rose, 58, from the necklace she was wearing.[93]

Ossining firefighter George Adcock plunged into the burning wreck seven times to pull people out, a remarkable feat of heroism on a day of widespread heroism. Passersby from the area around the station, a largely black neighborhood, earned notice for helping to remove stunned survivors from the disaster zone and helping to extinguish flames from their clothing.

Up the hill in the rest of Ossining, there was a scene of frantic activity, as a huge column of smoke billowed over the riverfront.[94] The Rev. James Kelly, a Briarcliff Manor priest who happened to be at the train station at the time, administered the last rites to the dead and the dying. He was a very busy man that day.[95]

Nurses and doctors at area hospitals, from Ossining to Tarrytown and Valhalla, worked through the night to care for the wounded. Townspeople from Ossining did what they could to console the survivors and the bereaved. When it was all over, the time came for a grim accounting. Fourteen people died in the flames, and four more in the hospital. One body was pulled from the river two days later by a search team. Two people were never found and presumed dead, either lost to the Hudson or vaporized in the flames, leaving behind no physical remains to be identified. Two whole blocks were destroyed, and the damage was estimated in the $250,000 range, a huge sum during the Depression.

The driver, Incarnato, died in the fire. Three executives of Town and Country Bus Co. of Newark, New Jersey, which owned and operated the ill-fated vehicle, were charged with manslaughter but acquitted in a 1935 trial. The price paid by others was not so light. George McDonald, a young man from Brooklyn, was seen by newspaper reporters calling his Brooklyn home from an Ossining phone booth. McDonald had lost his mother, his father and his 12-year-old sister in the wreckage. It was his task to explain to his younger brother that they were now orphans. He described how he last saw his parents "in a death embrace."[96]

The Depression years had more than its share of misery and privation. But for a fortunate few, the 1930s were also a time of musical creativity, all-night parties and endless trays of cocktails. With its proximity to New York City and spacious, manicured clubs, Westchester was the scene of glamour and high-society hijinks accompanied by the roaring sound of brass, percussion and lush, tightly orchestrated rhythms. The Glen Island Casino in New Rochelle was where America learned to swing.

The venue along the Sound was the place where top band leaders came to strut their stuff for a national radio audience, while up-and-coming musicians made their chops with fast-paced solos that left spectators and dancers gasping. It was the swankiest spot in the suburbs for young couples out on a date, where a 25-cent admission fee bought memories of a lifetime.[97]

Glen Island had been the site of a resort since the 1880s, when an entrepreneur named John H. Starin built an elaborate beer garden and outdoor pavilion for boatloads of New York City revelers. A congressman from Rye who made a fortune in transportation, Starin created the resort as a respectable kind of theme-park—safe for families, educational and not at all like the comparable pleasure palaces in the city. Billed as "America's Pleasure Grounds" by Starin, the island was festooned with extravagant displays and exhibits.[98]

Its later incarnation as a dance-band venue after Westchester County bought the defunct resort in 1923 was part of the larger effort by political boss William Ward and his Progressive allies to weave leisure and entertainment into the suburban way of life. The county turned the site into a ballroom and restaurant, and a bridge connecting the island to the mainland in 1929 ensured a steady clientele. Though it was named a casino, it was not because gambling was permitted there—the term harkened back to its original meaning as a public gathering place for music and dancing.

In its heyday in the 1930s and 40s, dance orchestras and swing bands led by Glenn Miller, Tommy Dorsey, Benny Goodman and Rudy Valley performed there. Ozzie and Harriet Nelson were two of its biggest stars, and some of the great names in jazz, like Gene Krupa, a Yonkers resident, played gigs there as well. Miller, in fact, played at the casino in 1939 to huge crowds, a big opening-night break for the tuneful trombonist whose walloping compositions for saxophones and clarinets later formed the soundtrack of a generation.[99]

Ozzie Nelson helped make Glen Island a nationally known dancehall when he was hired to perform with an orchestra on the main stage in the early 1930s. The Hollywood-handsome entertainer, better known in his later years as television's favorite pipe-smoking authority figure, brought style and buzz to Glen Island. Nelson, a sandy-haired bachelor who was studying law while working as a band leader, turned female heads all over Westchester in the 1930s, sparring at a gym in Mount Vernon and splashing at several Sound Shore beaches.[100]

Nelson also had an eye for musical talent. It was in New Rochelle that Nelson signed up a platinum-blonde co-singer for his orchestra, one Harriet Hilliard, the daughter of a Midwestern show-business family. The new addition to the band cost another $75 a week in 1932, and it proved to be an auspicious hire. Harriet became more than just a musical mate—she became the second half of *Ozzie and Harriet*, one of the most popular programs of early television.[101]

After *Ozzie and Harriet* came other big names, and Glen Island transformed into one of the most prestigious stops on the swing-band circuit. NBC ran weekly radio broadcasts from the casino, which had flawless acoustics for the airwaves. Crowds of 2,000 young people and servicemen from the nearby army base at Fort Slocum packed themselves into the ballroom to dance and cheer. The names of the acts convey the playful and whimsical side of the era: Larry Funk and His Band of a Thousand Melodies, Al Katz and His Kittens, Rudy Vallee and His Connecticut Yankees.[102]

In addition to Miller's big break there, the casino gained fame as the place where the the Dorsey Brothers Orchestra finally broke up in June 1935. The feuding brothers, Tommy and Johnny, were in rehearsal when Jimmy made a snide remark about Tommy's tempo. According to the other musicians, Tommy packed up his trumpet and walked out. The fraternal duo never performed together again, and each of them went off to lead his own orchestra.[103]

Musicians came and went, but the house of swing endured, always in high style: men in double-breasted suits and fedoras, women wearing chunky high heels and cinched flaring skirts. The rattle of a cocktail shaker, the energized crowd, the intimately athletic nature of the dancing and the overt physicality of the swaying rhythms all combined to form a sensual mix of transgression and glamour, cloaked in gabardine and sweat.

The music they made at the casino and other places like it channeled an insouciant flair that helped sustain the country through a Great Depression and war. The spirit of optimism and high energy, a uniquely American combination, came roaring through the saxophone blasts and pristine clarinet solos, a moonlight serenade for the ages. Those glorious sounds over the Long Island Sound weren't heard by everyone. The audiences were completely white, as numerous photos attest.

8

The Segregated Suburbs
Racial Discrimination and the
Threat from Political Extremes

Although exceptions did exist in Westchester during the early part of the 20th century, blacks who wanted a piece of the good life—in the form of recreation, housing and employment—were typically denied the opportunities whites took for granted. The mass migration of Southern blacks into northern cities, Westchester among them, resulted in a highly segregated environment. There were few "whites only" signs like those that dotted the Southern landscape during the period, but segregation was hardly just a Southern phenomenon. Jim Crow led a long and healthy life in the northern suburbs of New York, too.

Like Glen Island Casino, another county-owned facility, Playland, had much to offer in the way of a beach resort in the 1930s: acres of white sand, a mile-long boardwalk and a world-famous roller coaster. But entry into the seaside empire of fun came with an unwritten caveat: it was intended for whites only. Long before the desegregation battles in the 1950s and 1960s, a group of local African Americans in 1935 sought to overturn an unofficial policy discouraging blacks from entering the region's best-known beach resort.

They wore suits and faced police intervention with impeccable manners. They were denied entry, asked to return again and again for permits they never received, overcharged and even arrested for their trouble. Eventually more than a dozen African Americans from Westchester, including clergymen, doctors, NAACP activists, along with a cab driver and a housewife, testified before an investigating committee on the almost comical absurdity of the color barrier at the county park—one that was as plain as day, but obscured by deception. In the end, they were able to prove their case before a judge.

Blacks had been seeking equal treatment at Playland since it was developed as an amusement park by Westchester County in 1928. It proved to be a long struggle. An investigating committee formed by the county Board of Supervisors in 1933 heard testimony that blacks had been consistently discouraged from using the county facility or denied entry for years. Playland was under scrutiny that year for a scandal involving patronage jobs and financial mismanagement,[1] but the hearings also provided a unique opportunity for local African Americans to tell their stories. Beaches and swimming areas were typically the sites of the most heated and violent confrontations between the races in the era of segregation across the country, and Playland director Frank Darling admitted "fear of a racial clash" was indeed behind a policy to discourage blacks from using swimming areas.[2]

The policy to keep blacks out of Playland typically involved a demand that African Americans obtain a residency permit, which was purposely difficult to secure. Petty slights were also employed, and even children were not exempt. A white Mount Vernon woman took a group of ten schoolchildren to Playland in the winter of 1931, the commission heard, and four black boys were not allowed on the ice and had to watch the skating party from a distance.[3]

The Rev. F.L. Bythewood, assistant pastor of the African Methodist Episcopal Church in Elmsford, was arrested when he attempted to obtain a beach pass at the park. After being turned away, he said he took the number of the ticket-seller's badge, and that of a guard who was nearby. A policeman asked him what he was doing, and when he replied it was his own business, he was arrested and taken to the Rye police station. The minister recounted how he was later informed that he needed a county-issued card to attend Playland, proving he was a local resident. When he applied for the card three times at Playland, he was told that the person who issued the cards was unavailable.[4] Bythewood was hardly alone in being kept away.

Benjamin Levister, a law student at Columbia from Mount Vernon, told the committee he was arrested by a police officer when he protested his denial at the turnstiles to the beach. He was later released from police custody when a park manager came to the scene.[5] Two doctors and a dentist from New Rochelle attempted to gain admission to Playland in 1932. They were denied entry to the excursion boat that ran to the amusement park from New Rochelle, and the boat operator placed a sign for their benefit that read "Colored People, Please Do Not Take the Boat."[6] Another black visitor at Playland, David Springsteen, told the commission that he was at the amusement park with four other black friends and they were followed for an hour by a policeman.[7] One witness, Dr. Leon Scott, a dentist from New Rochelle, said he paid $3,000 a year in taxes, and it seemed a peculiar sort of irony to pay so much and receive so little from a publicly funded facility.[8] Those blacks who did gain entrance to the park found unequal treatment inside. Anna Ziegler of New Rochelle, a black woman, said she was charged 25 cents for an orange drink, while the white women she came with only paid ten cents.[9]

Black activists rallied around the issue of discrimination at political gatherings and church meetings. "My people have fought in wars and have sacrificed their lives so that America may remain free. And then we are denied things we are entitled to," Randel Tolliver, a black New Rochelle Democratic leader, said at a meeting on the subject in White Plains.[10] These men and women eventually had their day in court. Philip Watson, a lawyer from the National Association for the Advancement of Colored People, filed criminal charges against the Playland ticket-taker who had denied admission to three black men from New Rochelle, in violation of a state law making it a misdemeanor to discriminate at a public place on the basis of race, creed or color. Grace Johnson, a white woman described in the papers as an artist from Pleasantville, also assisted the prosecution.

A group of 100 or so African Americans crowded into the Rye Police Court on September 21, 1935; about 50 were admitted into the small chambers, while the rest stood outside. The jury of six white men took the case just after midnight and returned a guilty verdict in 20 minutes, and the ticket-taker paid a small fine, $50.[11] Another ticket-taker also was fined in November, though a third was acquitted. The county later appealed the guilty decisions without success.[12]

The victory in the Rye Police Court was certainly a small one in an era of even greater injustices, and a mixed one at that, but even small victories count for something,

DONHAVEN

160 MARBLE AVENUE   *Pleasantville, N. Y.*

IN THE HEART OF WESTCHESTER COUNTY

DINING ∴ DANCING ∴ RENDEZVOUS

Featuring Full Course Chicken Dinners

CHOICE WINES and LIQUORS

45 Minutes from Harlem

DIRECTIONS: North on Broadway to 257th Street; turn right into Sawmill River Parkway,
direct to Pleasantville

WE SPECIALIZE IN

Club Outings - Dinner Dances - Birthday Parties and all Social Affairs

MUSIC THAT PLEASES BY

GOLDIE LUCAS

AND HIS:-

Donhaven Country Club Band

FOR ALL INFORMATION

Telephone PLeasantville 1725

MAURICE DONEGAN, Manager

 OPEN ALL YEAR

The first few editions of the Negro Motorist's Green Book encouraged readers to "mention the Green Book," especially when venturing out from the city by car. The travel guide's editors vetted advertisers and listings and only included those that would welcome black travelers without question. Pleasantville's Donhaven billed itself as "a truly different" kind of Westchester club that was a convenient driving distance from Harlem (Schomburg Center for Research in Black Culture, Jean Blackwell Hutson Research and Reference Division, the New York Public Library).

if only a day at the beach. The amusement park, however, was never considered a friendly venue to blacks for years afterward.

As the Playland fight underscored, blacks were still excluded from all but a few suburban neighborhoods and most schools for generations to come, and many dining establishments were off limits. African American motorists and travelers relied on a series of pamphlets circulated in the community called Green Books that advertised businesses, hotels and restaurants serving black customers, a testament to the restrictions placed on the free passage of non-whites in the era. Before the guide expanded by popular demand to include national listings by state, the first editions in the late 1930s focused on New York City and its environs.[13]

The color barrier extended into every aspect of life in the suburbs. In 1925, Thomas Brooks was appointed the first black cop in Yonkers, and the first in the county. But he would be the only one on the force for decades.[14]

As blacks moved to Northern cities during the period, a journey of thousands known as the Great Migration, they were typically not met with open arms. Jim Crow occasionally made the papers, but more often, the color line was simply submerged in the daily fabric of life, an invisible and unspoken code.

While segregation between blacks and whites was a common feature of education for black and white children in Westchester, there were segments of society where integration was the norm, like this Girl Scout troop seen marching in White Plains in the early 1940s (White Plains City Archives).

Typical was the story of Addie Fields. Originally from Portsmouth, Virginia, she came north as a teenager and later ran a laundry service and resided in Yonkers and White Plains. "I would call it segregation," she remembered in an oral history about the era. "If you were on the trolley car and I come in and there was a seat and I sit down, and there was a white person sitting there, they would get up."[15]

Roy L. Lawson arrived in Yonkers with a college degree from Bluefield State College in West Virginia. He found work doing manual labor at National Cash Register, where they handed him a mop and pail. "You know what I was doing? I was a porter. I had a college degree…. I also tried to get into the Yonkers school system. They said, 'We don't have any Afro-American teachers in our system.' This was 1938. And they didn't." Lawson did some work later in the field of health science, but barriers were ever-present. "I had segregation hit me in the face in Yonkers, just as in the South," he recalled.[16]

Anna Jones Bernard, a New Rochelle High School graduate, was by all accounts an excellent student. After graduating from law school at New York University, taking night classes while she worked as a teacher, she passed the bar exam in 1923 and became qualified to practice law in the state of New York. The state of New York had other ideas. Though Bernard had earned a law degree from a prominent law school and was the first black woman to pass the bar in New York State, no one would hire her. She took the only position open to her: elementary school teacher. She would occasionally take on cases in real estate and surrogate law, but teaching became her primary vocation. It was only later in life, at the age of 60, that she was at last allowed to practice law.[17]

The first black teacher to be hired in the contemporary period in Westchester, Ethel Harris, was not hired until 1938 at a high school in New Rochelle.[18] The subject of education and teaching opportunities was a particularly sore point for African Americans at the time. The NAACP in New Rochelle sent then governor Franklin Roosevelt a letter in 1930, stating that segregated black schools were poorly operated: "Jim Crow schools, wherever found, do not get the consideration that white schools do."[19] Yet home ownership was the hardest and highest hurdle to clear.

While the color line was never drawn as formally as it was in the South, it was just as real to the people who crossed it—especially in suburban neighborhoods. When a flaming cross burst into view in 1930 on the property of a young black dentist, Errold Collymore, who had recently purchased a home in White Plains through an intermediary for $15,000, the response from the community was immediate.

Errold Duncan St. George Collymore was born in Barbados in 1892, one of five children. An ambitious and unyielding man, he ventured far from his land of birth and set his sights on the United States as a place of opportunity and achievement. He first went to the U.S. Panama Canal Zone to work as a laborer from 1909 to 1912, then came to the U.S. mainland as an immigrant in 1912. When the United States joined the Great War, Collymore joined the U.S. Army, where he learned Morse code and radio operations. He became a U.S. citizen while in uniform in 1918.[20] After the war, Collymore was part of a generation of African American men who saw their wartime service as a validation of their commitment to America as well as a down payment on the cause of equality. Their status as soldiers who had served under the Stars and Stripes in the killing fields of Europe and elsewhere made them eager to challenge the reigning hierarchy that put blacks on the bottom rung of society. As the African American scholar W.E.B. DuBois wrote in 1919, "We return from fighting. We return fighting."

Collymore graduated from Howard University's dental school in 1923 and established a practice. He was determined to live in the suburbs, whatever hostility he had to face. He told family members he came here for the American Dream—and he wasn't letting go.

The dentist was drawn to Westchester for the usual reasons—a pleasant mixture of town and country, a good place to raise a family—and he rented in White Plains before committing himself to a home at 457 S. Lexington Avenue in the city. The home was fairly new, built in 1927, with plenty of lawn and garden space. He purchased it for $15,000 using a go-between, and moved to the house in April 1930. "I bought from a white friend who was willing to sell shortly after he purchased the property," he later recounted.[21]

When word spread that a black man was moving into the neighborhood, a night-time meeting at a nearby elementary school drew 400 people to protest his arrival. Cars drove past his home, slowing ominously. At midnight, a seven-foot cross was set ablaze on his lawn. Collymore went out in his pajamas to inspect and document the handiwork of the marauders. In one hand was a box camera, in the other, a rifle.

Dr. Errold Collymore, who served in the U.S. Army and studied at Howard University, is shown in his dental office. When he first bought a home for his family in White Plains, he faced intense hostility (Collymore Family Collection).

"My wife, Rene, and I had just gone to bed, and I had just fallen asleep when Rene awakened me and called my attention to the flickering glare of a burning cross in our windows. I got up and grabbed my .32 [rifle] and my camera (of all things); pulled on my robe and stepped out onto my front steps with my camera, making pictures.... This scared the crowd standing about, for nobody wanted to be identified. There was a general withdrawal, leaving me there alone with my camera and my cross," Collymore later wrote.[22]

The burning cross and the offers to buy him out were just the beginning for Collymore. There was much more harassment to come, some of it ridiculously surreal, other insidiously mundane, yet no less vulgar. On the surreal side: Collymore nearly lost his fire insurance, which would have terminated his mortgage, after the cross burning because the home was deemed a fire hazard. "My fire insurance was cancelled repeatedly as fast as I could replace it," he wrote.[23] On the mundane side: hostile strangers splashed acid and motor oil on his property, a particular indignity to an avid gardener who planted prize-winning azaleas and rose bushes in a spotless front yard. A front window was also broken.

Groceries and milk deliveries to his home came to an abrupt halt. Black servants in the city were threatened with dismissal if their teeth were tended to by Dr. Collymore. Collymore, however, received some support from Christian and Jewish clergy in White Plains. The Unitarian Association in White Plains, which Collymore joined, in particular rallied to his side, offering moral support and vigilance at his property. But it was clear that he was up against some powerful forces who wanted him out.

One day, a bank official and a leading businessman in White Plains paid him a visit at his office, speaking of a committee that was "giving me one more chance to make up my mind to get out of my house," Collymore recalled. The banker spoke of his "selfishness" and the hazards he was bringing to the community, by causing a "near riot." Standing in Collymore's office, the business leader demanded there and then that the black dentist move out of his house—or else face serious consequences.[24]

Collymore responded to the financial leader, who he called "Mr. V." in his subsequent description of the ordeal: "Today you come to me with this ignoble proposal and these terrible threats against my helpless people. You say that because I have bought a home for myself and my loyal wife which I promised her twelve years ago, I have committed a terrible crime…. You say, I continued, 'that I will be ruined.' Let me be ruined. I'll just get up, brush the dust off my pants, and start all over again."[25] Collymore told Mr. V, "I will not move, 'Good-day, sir.' With this he gave me one flaming glare. I turned from him and spread the door open wide for him as he stalked stiffly past me."

The Collymores had other more tangible concerns about escalating violence, as threatening letters with KKK insignia began arriving regularly in their mailbox. Collymore requested extra police protection, which was not forthcoming. He then explained the approach he would take to city leaders: "It was my intention to sit up all night on watch at my window, and the first man that puts his foot across my property line, I would shoot his toes off."[26] Extra police protection was duly assigned.

Collymore faced endless, maddening obstacles when dealing with his mortgage loan. If a single mortgage payment came in late, or some necessary document went missing or overdue, Collymore stood to forfeit the home. Thus he carried out all of his transactions in person. In spite of his meticulous attention to every detail, Collymore was often told by the bank office handling his loan that the dentist's paperwork had unaccountably gone missing, and he once had to drive to far upstate to deliver documents.[27] Even more pernicious was a scheme put forward in the city council to condemn the property which Collymore owned. The proposal outlined a plan to demolish the house and turn the site into a through street. It was never approved.

Through it all, the dentist hung on. His final mortgage payment in the 1940s became a family triumph. And despite the rough welcome, Collymore took to his adopted city with a vengeance, becoming in later years a stalwart in civic life and a civil-rights crusader.

As Collymore's troubles demonstrated, there were very strong beliefs in the 1930s about where certain kinds of people were allowed to live. The disputes over the "homeland," religion and ethnic origin were becoming more pointed all across the globe. Increasingly, militant voices were making themselves known, calling for racial and ethnic "purity."

The late 1930s were a time when many people believed that democracy was a failed experiment, and it was time to choose sides between fascism and communism, Hitler or Stalin. Some turned toward the side of Bolshevism, working covertly or overtly for communist causes. Others were drawn to the fascist side of the political spectrum.

The German-American Bund, of which in the 1930s numbered about 20,000 people, mostly of German extraction, was the most visible reminder that right-wing extremists and Nazi sympathizers have long been a formidable presence on these shores. While their numbers were small, American sympathizers of fascism were influential in foreign-policy circles and in industry, pushing hard for the cause of isolationism while Europe fell under the heel of Adolf Hitler, Benito Mussolini and Francisco Franco. Anne Morrow Lindbergh, the wife of Charles Lindbergh, expressed open admiration for the fascist cause in a book she wrote in 1940 called *The Wave of the Future*. Charles Lindbergh accepted a medal from the Nazi Reich Marshal Hermann Goering. He later expressed his regret for taking the medal, and his wife also spoke remorsefully of having been seduced by the Nazi credo.

They were far from alone. The Bund ran large camps to promote the cause in northern New Jersey and on Long Island. In 1934, a proposed pro–Nazi meeting in New Rochelle triggered protest. Leaflets carrying anti–Semitic propaganda were distributed in Mount Vernon and New Rochelle to drum up support for the meeting, but it never took place. In March 1935, Jewish veterans were shocked and incensed to find that the Friends of the New Germany were staging meetings at Otten Hall, on Main and Division streets, complete with six-foot long flags emblazoned with a swastika. The meetings began with the Star Spangled Banner and ended with the Horst Wessel song, the Nazi anthem, as guards in black uniforms wearing swastika arm-bands stood outside.[28]

Also known as the Friends of the New Germany, the Bund had ambitions as a fascist militia unit as a political movement, and it held rifle practices at the Cuno Country Club on Pines Bridge Road. A 32-year-old New Rochelle man, part of the pro–Nazi organization, was accidentally shot in the leg. State troopers were called to investigate, and a police sergeant reported that some 200 members of the Nazi organization had attended a rally and weapons drill at the Mount Kisco site, from all over Westchester, New York City and elsewhere in the region.[29]

In Yonkers in 1935, a local chapter of the Friends of the New Germany tussled with city authorities over permission to screen a Nazi propaganda movie, *Horst Wessel*. The film was never screened. In August of that year, as part of the backlash against the pro–Nazi film, a group of 350 marchers opposed to fascism and war marched through Yonkers.[30] Clergy from around the region gave speeches, and Rabbi Lawrence Schwartz of Temple Emanu-El of White Plains told the crowd at Larkin Plaza, "I oppose war, but I do not believe in non-resistance." There were representatives from the local Communist and Socialist parties, who shared a platform together for the first time, a congruence that drew cheers from the audience when it was announced.[31] The rally drew about 700 people.

Italian sympathizers of Mussolini also were active in the period, causing great divisions in the Italian-American community. A riot in Port Chester that resulted in arrest and injury in 1927 was typical of the disturbances that roiled the Italian-American community. As a pro-fascist meeting at the Aviglionse Hall was ending, and the Mussolini supporters left the building, they were met by a hostile crowd of anti-fascists on the street, setting off a violent confrontation.[32]

The climax of the far-right movement in the northern suburbs came in a chillingly familiar venue. A line of men dressed in gray shirts and black ties marched to cries of "Heil, Hitler," below banners emblazoned in swastikas: it was a scene that many associated with European cities under the domination of Nazi rule, but it also played out in a stadium where basketball players and trombonists were the more typical performers.

The setting was the most prominent meeting place in the region—the Westchester County Center in White Plains—in April 1938. The rally was staged by the German-American Bund, and 2,500 people from New York City and Westchester heard about the glories of the Third Reich under Adolf Hitler. Nazi songs thundered across the Art Deco–like auditorium. Banners proclaimed "Germany Our Blood, America Our Land" and "Great-Germany, We Hail Thee."[33]

The antics of a group of raucous buffoons and their fatuous rhetoric inside the County Center might have been laughed off as so much bad political theater, if another group of like-minded combatants in Europe, Africa and Asia weren't setting the world on fire.

Alas, no one was laughing when a district leader from the Bund called on the audience in White Plains to fight "an international clique" taking over the United States.[34] The 1938 rally in White Plains was the biggest and most ambitious show the fascists put on in the northern suburbs, where they were eager to bring their message to the middle-class mainstream. It was an eerie local version of the torch-lit parades and elaborately staged rallies that had become a standard feature of life in the Third Reich, part of the Nazi mission to turn "the masses" into a weapon.

As with all fascist demonstrations, it was done with an air of high theatricality. A train carrying 500 gray-shirted Bund members left New York City for White Plains at 6 p.m. The police in New York and Westchester had also made elaborate plans. Seventy-five cops guarded the train, and cops were stationed along the rooftops of Harlem as the Nazi sympathizers passed through the neighborhood, on the lookout for snipers. A member of the NYPD bomb squad, in plain clothes, rode on the train. In White Plains, 50 cops stood guard inside the County Center, while another 65 were posted outside. A reserve force of 50 officers was put on standby in the basement.[35]

The Bund members marched to the County Center from the nearby White Plains train station, behind a band playing the "Horst-Wessel-Lied." Inside the hall, decorated with swastika banners, the rally went on with no major interruptions, except for two stink bombs tossed into the crowd by two high school students from Bronxville. When a delegation from the New Rochelle post of the American Legion entered the auditorium and took their seats, a riot was feared, but the Legionnaires caused no trouble, as they had at previous gatherings of the Bund.[36] One speaker discussed the value of free speech, and another made comparisons between Washington, Lincoln and Franklin Roosevelt, to Frederick the Great of Prussia, Bismarck and Hitler. There was talk about "cowardice" in the face of a secret plot to take control over the United States.[37]

The Bund members held a noisy beer party after the rally and went home without incident. Westchester officials claimed the organization had broken the contract for use of the auditorium by giving political speeches in violation of a specific clause prohibiting them, and the county administration vowed the group would never use the center again.

Probably the best response to the fascist goon squad came from a group of demonstrators outside the facility. While the Bund members marched into the auditorium in their gleaming leather boots and Sam Brown belts, the demonstrators sang "America the Beautiful" and avowed their faith not in political extremes, but in their vision of the country as a place of brotherhood, from sea to shining sea.[38]

9

World War II, Prosperity and Paranoia

News of the attack came on the radio around 2 p.m. The Sunday afternoon broadcasts—the New York Philharmonic, a football game and a mystery series—were interrupted by an urgent bulletin. Radios across America transmitted the news that war had come. "The Japanese have attacked the American naval base at Pearl Harbor, Hawaii," the alert began. Broadcasters had sketchy information on the attack at Pearl Harbor, and could only parse the details in vague terms. "There have been many bombs and torpedoes dropped. Our Navy and Army and Air Force are fighting back against the Japanese. The attack and the fighting is going on right at the present time."[1]

Immediately after the announcement stunned a nation through their living room radios, 21 Japanese nationals were arrested in Westchester and turned over to the FBI. Area dams and vital transportation points were put under guard.[2] America had entered the war, and Westchester would ramp up industrial production and once again send its sons and daughters to distant battlefields. It was a struggle that would claim the lives of some 2,000 servicemen in the county, according to research carried out after the war.[3]

Westchester men were involved from the very beginning. Benjamin Vinci of Port Chester was a 22-year-old private in an army coast artillery unit when the Japanese attack began at Pearl Harbor, and he carried a bullet fragment near his heart from the attack for the rest of his life.[4]

After the attack, armed guards were dispatched to the big dams at Kensico, Croton and Ashokan. The county's main military facility, Fort Slocum on Davids Island off New Rochelle, mobilized immediately. Servicemen in the region were ordered to report for duty. Japanese citizens, often longtime residents, were rounded up for interment. Yasuo Matsui, a White Plains architect who had lived in Westchester for 40 years, was taken into custody by the city police chief, William Miller, himself.[5] There was a surge of enlistments. The navy recruiting office in White Plains stayed open late Sunday night to handle the walk-in volunteers.[6] Red-star pennants were placed in the homes of families with sons or husbands overseas. A gold-star pennant signified death. Parents of the deceased were informed by a War Department telegram delivered to the home address stating that the army or the navy "deeply regrets to inform you of the death of your son … was killed in action in performance of his duty." The appearance of a Western Union employee in the neighborhood was not a welcome sight. After every major engagement in the Pacific, on the high seas of the Atlantic, or in Italy or France, a number of front-page profiles would appear in the daily paper, usually accompanied by a photograph of the fallen serviceman in uniform.

While the war was a grim business, there could be moments of levity. After Allied troops entered Rome in 1944, Sgt. John Vita, a Port Chester cartoon animator in civilian life, made his way to Benito Mussolini's balcony in the grand office in the Palazzo Venezia, as he had promised his mother he would. He gave a humorous speech in Italian imitating Il Duce's mannerisms and catchphrases, while a crowd roared with laughter below. A signal-corps cameraman, Vita also threw out some Life Savers candies—a product made in Port Chester—to the throngs below. "I promised my mother, who originally came from Reggio Calabria, that I would make a speech from Mussolini's balcony in Rome— and I did," he told newspaper correspondents afterwards.[7] While the war raged overseas, the county's great factories were also put on a wartime footing, converting from civilian production to military hardware for the duration of the conflict. In Yonkers, the Alexander Smith Carpet mill switched from making carpets to tents and canvas. Sonotone in Elmsford, which also had a plant in White Plains, made hearing aids in peacetime; it made telephones on navy ships and headsets for aviators.[8] The largest industrial wartime operation in Westchester was the General Motors plant in Sleepy Hollow (then called North Tarrytown). The assembling plant employed thousands of workers around the clock. Operating as the Eastern Aircraft Division of General Motors, the plant made wings and other parts for the TBM Avenger, a powerful attack plane outfitted with bombs or torpedoes. Launched from an armada of navy carriers, these heavily armed aircraft devastated the Japanese fleet in fiery encounters all over the Pacific.

On the home front, it was a time of struggle and sacrifice as Americans traded comfort and luxury for wartime resolve. Civilians had to do with less of everything—food and sleep included. The war changed everything in ways that were both trivial and deeply consequential. Stores opened later in the day and closed earlier. Playland shut down gas-powered rides and closed the ice rink. Ration books became a feature of everyday living. Scrap-metal drives were held in every community—a mountain of 900 tons of metal in White Plains included the old bars from the county jail.[9]

Women entered the workforce in droves. Lillian Bradley, a mother of three young sons, became White Plains' first woman cab driver. "My legs were like water," she said in March 1942, but it soon became a regular job for her.[10] A famous portrait by Norman Rockwell (a resident of Mamaroneck and New Rochelle) of "Rosie the Riveter" became an emblem of the hard work put in by women in the workforce, and posters followed. One real-life riveter, Rosina Bonavita, 21, of Peekskill, was a blue-collar exemplar of women in the workforce. She and a co-worker, Jennie Florio of Ossining, set a production record by driving some 3,300 rivets and holds into an airplane frame and fitting the metal skins together for an Avenger torpedo bomber between midnight and 6 a.m., all of it flawlessly. Bonavita, whose fiancé was serving with the navy in the Pacific, was sent a commendation letter from FDR following her record-setting shift in June 1943.[11]

Everyone was called on to serve the war effort in some capacity. Ben Levitan was a Tarrytown lawyer in his 40s who didn't need factory work to pay the bills. But he wanted to do his part for the war effort, and since he was exempt from military service because of a case of infantile polio, Levitan went to work at the North Tarrytown plant. The lawyer took off his necktie and put on his work clothes to punch rivets for $1.14 an hour on the overnight shift at the GM plant, one of many instances of wartime sacrifice.[12]

The war was deeply dehumanizing and traumatic to those who witnessed combat first hand—and in the letters of one GI, the struggle not to lose one's humanity was abundantly evident. It was hard for many of these young men, growing up in a stable, religious and rule-abiding environment in the New York suburbs, to adjust to the world of war.

John Kelly, who was known to friends as Bud, was a devout Catholic from Rye. He graduated from Rye High School in 1936 and was drafted in 1940 when he was 22, the first draftee from his town. A competent and capable man, Kelly started out as a private and went on to become a company commander and captain, serving with the 14th Armored Division. He saw a great deal of the war's cruelty, taking part in the liberation of the Moosburg concentration camp for allied POWs and the hard fighting in Vosges, the Alsatian Plains and western Germany. He wrote extensively to his wife, Mary, with whom he was married for 60 years. He was an excellent correspondent.[13]

"Hello my darling," his letters typically began, then flowed with

Women entered the industrial workforce in large numbers after the United States entered World War II, including this African American woman punching rivets on an aircraft wing at the General Motors plant in Sleepy Hollow (Westchester County Historical Society).

a strong, cursive hand on very light paper. Kelly, like many others who were drafted from civilian life, did not take naturally to the army. In letters home from his training camps in Arkansas and Kentucky, he expressed his boredom and frustration. Once overseas, the ordeal of combat was ever-present, and the uncertainty was deeply demoralizing. "I have to laugh when I think of my first days in the Army. I thought I had it rough and that a year would be a long time. I don't mind being overseas. Someone has to do it. The thing that hurts is trying to plan or look into the future. All you can do is sweat it out from one day to the next," he wrote in a letter dated January 9, 1945. "When you are in battle you seem to come very close to God. You wonder why all of this must be. There can only be one answer. Man asked for it and he is being punished for the evil that he has brought upon this earth. It is more than I can explain. Sometimes the world appears very beautiful and at other times it is just a mess in the universe.... If I didn't love you so much this wouldn't be so hard to take."[14]

The war had a way of turning normal routines upside down. "It is funny the way that time rolls on and you lose track of it," Kelly wrote his wife on January 17 during a fierce two-week engagement in which the 14th Armored blunted a powerful German counter-offensive, the Battle of Hatten-Rittershoffen. "It is light and dark and your thoughts and efforts are bent toward keeping warm and getting some rest. The most depressing factor is not being able to see the end of this mess. We can't. We just live from day to day. Tomorrow never comes. Things could definitely be better but they could be worse. I am still well and in one piece."

Kelly was torn up by the loss of his friends in battle. "To see some of these fellows that were so close to me shot up just about tears my heart out," he wrote. He also felt deep pity for the French civilians he encountered, especially the very young. "My heart really goes out for the little kids over here. They are so frightened and bewildered. Their clothes are rags and toys and sweets are unknown to most of them. You can win a lifelong friend by giving them a stick of gum. Picture if you can a child about seven trudging through the snow pulling a sled made out of ammunition boxes. Fuel, electricity and running water are obsolete. What little food there is is strictly rationed."[15]

There were minor pleasures for Kelly off the front line, like a movie screening of Deanna Durbin, a warm place to sleep, regular showers, chatting with a soldier from New Rochelle about home and their common recollections of Westchester. Listening to the GI radio was a mixed blessing, making him deeply homesick. "Because war is what it is, one finds ones self living under a certain mental strain," he confessed. "It is too diffi-cult to explain the meaning that the war has to me. It gives me an increase in years of about 20. Sometimes I feel like an old man more in person." When Kelly's division broke through the Sigfried line into Germany, his view of the enemy—civilians included—hardened. "I had a couple of [German soldiers] looking down the barrel of my .45 the other day and they still had that cocky attitude. I should have pulled the trigger. Two less rats to feed. You can't but help blow your top when you know that birds the same as these made it tough for some of our boys," he wrote in April 1945.[16]

The liberation of a camp full of thousands of Allied prisoners was a bright spot for the Rye native. "You can never believe what freedom means until you see American POWs freed from prison camps," he wrote in April, noting that slave labor was what kept Germany going. Kelly also discovered a similarity between Germany and his old home. "I have come across something that reminds me of Westchester," he alerted his wife. "Germany has some good highways just like our parkways. It is a pleasure to ride on a good road for a change."

The fresh anguish of his fallen friends, however, hardened him against ordinary German citizens. "I have no desire to befriend the people who have thrown the world in tumult," he said. "Anyone of these people could be the mother, brother, wife, sister or what have you, of the Jerry that pulled the trigger that killed some of my best friends. I can forget just about all this mess but I can't forget the white crosses that mark the graves of the boys that did not make it. Yes, I am bitter. Who wouldn't be as long as he had red blood in his veins. Just to see the conditions our boys endured in prison camps is suffi-cient, not to mention political prisoners and Jews.... In brief it is pretty hard to remain cool, calm and collected."[17]

American G.I.s were slow to hate the enemy, but combat changed that. As the war correspondent Ernie Pyle noted, "They lost too many friends. Soon it was killing that animated them."[18]

Kelly made it home to his beloved Mary, and a young daughter, Nancy, he had yet to see with his own eyes. He had had a tough war, and long after the shooting stopped, Kelly struggled to make sense of the violence, hoping he could live with what he had experienced. "I learned how cold a war could be. Many a dear friend have I left behind there.... Seems like a bad dream of the dim past. That's what I want it always to be."

After the war, Bud Kelly went into the automobile sales business, serving as general manager of a White Plains dealership and doing extensive volunteer work. His letters were put away, under a bed, out of sight for decades. When he died in 2010 at the age of 92, his brothers found the searing letters that had remained out of sight for more than 50 years.[19]

The end of the war, when it finally came, was greeted with church bells and a great outpouring of relief. It induced a complicated mix of emotions for many. "I was overwhelmed with joy," one Tarrytown resident, Louis Cohen, told the *Tarrytown Daily News* after a news flash came over the air waves at 7 p.m. that Japan had surrendered. "I think other people felt the same way. I was laughing and crying all in the same breath and so were others I saw."[20]

Normality took some time to return after the war was officially over. Returning veterans found employment opportunities scarce, as well as very limited housing. But at least the wartime privations and rationed consumer goods had ended. On December 10, 1945, as the holiday shopping season commenced, cops in White Plains were pleasantly surprised to see a rather unfamiliar site: traffic jams. On that Saturday, it was reported that automobile traffic in the city had hit an all-time record, and shoppers were ravenous for gifts. One local merchant was quoted as observing, "The only limitation on the holiday business is the supply of merchandise."[21]

There were occasional reminders of the war for veterans who had returned to their civilian pursuits. John McDermott was a temporary postal worker in White Plains, sorting through mail when he discovered a package addressed to him. It contained the Purple Heart, the military award for battlefield injuries, which he sustained as a B-24 turret gunner when his plane went down near Ludwigshafen in July of 1944, struck by another damaged U.S. bomber.[22]

The conflict abroad had been resolved, it seemed, but Westchester was to be drawn into another international quarrel. After the ravages of the war in Europe and Asia, the nascent United Nations needed a headquarters—and fast. While it was known that the New York City area would be among the candidates for a new headquarters, the search for an actual spot was done in secrecy. And with no warning to the local community, a U.N. inspection group—with members from Yugoslavia, China, France, Iraq, the United Kingdom, Uruguay, the USSR and the United States—chose northern Westchester and Greenwich. It was envisioned as a vast international city of office towers, serviced by a four-lane highway, a hotel for 3,000 people, all set among the countryside between Bedford, North Castle, Pound Ridge and Stamford. At the time called UNOville, as in the United Nations Organization, it was to be the new capital of a world organization dedicated to peace, populated by thousands of diplomats and their families in a 42-square-mile enclave, served by its own police and fire departments. People who were already living inside those 42 square miles would have to go.[23] The announcement of the UNOville plan in January 1946 set off a firestorm. A map created by engineers and designers affiliated with the U.N. scheme was provided to the *New York Times*, and the scope of the proposal was astounding. Just weeks later, the U.S. State Department liaison assigned to the project, Alger Hiss, later accused as a Soviet spy, added a note of inevitability to the proceedings. "The U.N.'s site committee has been given a blank check by us to take whatever land they wanted," was the message he conveyed to municipal officials in New York and Connecticut.[24]

The plan had a number of supporters in high places. Westchester County Executive Herbert Gerlach called for approval of the UN plan, saying "we must offer on behalf of our county our full and complete cooperation." Added Gustavus Kirby, chairman of the Westchester County Planning Board and a Mount Kisco resident, "Nobody wants to be displaced, but sometimes, if the cause is right, you are willing to be displaced."[25]

The county newspaper chain, run by J. Noel Macy, was very much in favor. When a social good was proposed, the paper editorialized, "some private, individual interests must suffer.... Remember, we are not building UNO merely for pleasure, or even for sanitation or health or any other relatively local, justifiable reason. We are building UNO to preserve peace permanently." The editorial concluded that the goal, to eliminate "the threat of World War III, with the atomic bomb," was worthwhile enough to displace homeowners.[26]

But the prospect of being forced out of one's home, even for the benefit of humanity, seemed an appalling prospect to many in the affected area. Some 1,000 people in Westchester, and another 2,000 in Connecticut, faced the loss of their homes.

Some 30 local organizations in North Castle alone came together to send a telegram signaling their disapproval. Everdell Finch, a 27-year-old farmer and air force veteran, spoke for many when he said he had not spent 18 months overseas only to give up his home upon his return. His family had farmed the land in North Castle for 12 generations, he wrote in a letter stating his opposition to UNOville. "This is the place I wanted to come back to and live. It's the only real home I could ever have. I don't want to be banished forever," he wrote.[27] The Town Board of Bedford also voted "no." "We just said we do not want it," said Town Clerk George Rogers. "The vote was unanimous against absorption of 80 percent of our town. It would wipe us out."[28]

A lively debate over the merits of internationalism versus localism took place in the public arena. For a community that had always looked beyond its own borders and taken a broad view of the world, the tug between the local and the international was particularly compelling.

On February 23, a non-binding public referendum held in Greenwich went 5,505 to 2,019 against the U.N., a "no" vote by a large margin.[29] The public ballot came just over a week after the U.N. General Assembly voted to approve the Greenwich-Westchester site, and the "no" vote constituted a major public-relations problem for the fledgling diplomatic organization. The U.N. seemed put off by the resolve of local residents to thwart their efforts to build a city in their communities. A new set of sites were proposed in northern Westchester by the U.N. committee in the summer of 1946, including Yorktown. Meanwhile, cities like San Francisco, Boston and Philadelphia mounted vigorous lobbying campaigns to have the U.N. come to their metropolises. But it was a poor start for a purportedly visionary group of world leaders to be rejected by the very place they chose to hang their shingle.

Enter the Rockefeller family.

In mid–December 1946, John D. Rockefeller, Jr., offered to buy a small site in Manhattan from a developer, later valued at $8.5 million, and turn it over to the U.N. It was a drab corner of the city that had few notable attributes. But the unlovely stretch of the East Side, known for an old slaughterhouse and tenement houses, came as a welcome relief to the U.N., and the Rockefeller offer was quickly accepted.[30] As was noted by observers at the time, it was far easier and cheaper to remove people who lived in tenements out of their residences and businesses than those who resided in Fairfield (Connecticut) and Westchester counties.

The cornerstone for the U.N. complex was laid in 1949. A glittering palace of diplomacy, designed in the modernist International style, rose on the riverbank known as

Turtle Bay. It has become a place where popes, dictators, presidents, generals, plutocrats and other leaders plead their case to the world. Whatever one's opinion of the U.N., it seems like it belongs right where it is.

While Westchester was coping with the attentions of the global community, it was also building its own pathways to the wider world. The construction of the Tappan Zee Bridge beginning in 1952 would alter the character of the county and further connect it with the interstate highway system. The automobile suburb, as it came to be known, was the way in which Westchester developed in the post-war period.

Plans to build a bridge across the Hudson River between Westchester and Rockland counties over a section of the river known as Tappan Zee were not especially popular. The idea was initially proposed in 1936 and went down to defeat. When it rose again in 1950, hundreds of letters of protest were sent to Governor Thomas Dewey. Besides the diminishment of the view, residents wondered loudly why the widest section of the river might be chosen for a span.

But the construction of the interstate highway system necessitated a crossing of the Hudson, the missing link on the New York State Thruway that ran from Buffalo to the south end of the state. Despite a chorus of criticism, plans went ahead to build the span between Tarrytown and South Nyack. A few geological impediments to the span were discovered at that crossing, and it was indeed a wide point in the river. There were also a number of complicated jurisdictional issues involved, especially concerning the control of the Port Authority of New York and New Jersey, the fiefdom of power broker Robert Moses. The final route landed just outside the Port Authority's jurisdiction, 25 miles north of the George Washington Bridge (a Port Authority span). New York Governor Thomas E. Dewey was able to use the tolls from the bridge to fund his own ambitious highway scheme—and not Moses.[31]

Like nearly everything about the construction of the bridge, the result of a provisional series of trade-offs, the design yielded a bridge that was frequently called one of the least attractive spans in the nation. It was also built with the expectation that it would be replaced within 50 years.

The three-mile long bridge opened December 15, 1955, years behind schedule. A long-running debate over what to call it ended when state leaders agreed on the name Tappan Zee: "Tappan" for an Indian tribe in the region, "Zee" the Dutch word for sea.[32] The entire Thruway system was completed in 1956, linking New York City to the region and the state through a vast skein of asphalt lines.[33] After the Tappan Zee was complete, work began in 1956 on the Cross Westchester Expressway, another major thoroughfare that would merge Westchester's cities and towns more fully with one another, and create the opportunity for big new office parks to rise along its path, the so-called Golden Mile through the Purchase section of Harrison and White Plains.

The county was becoming a pre-eminent suburban community, drawing businesses and residents to Westchester as never before. New housing, roads, schools and corporations proliferated. In 1955, IBM bought 432 acres in Armonk near the Connecticut border, one of the first of many big corporations that moved to Westchester. IBM opened its major research facility, designed by modernist Finnish-American architect Eero Saarinen, in Yorktown in 1961.[34]

Developer Sol Atlas built one of the first open-air shopping malls in the United States, a novelty at the time, on a boggy old site in southern Westchester. On a drizzly afternoon in April 1954, with a number of actors and entertainers like Jackie Cooper and

The Tappan Zee Bridge, seen here shortly before its opening in 1955, linked Westchester to a vast new transportation infrastructure. Generations of drivers have been puzzled why the bridge was built at the widest part of the Hudson—a decision made by political factors (courtesy Westchester County Archives).

Morey Amsterdam on hand to lend celebrity to the proceedings, the Cross County Shopping Center opened near the Cross County Parkway in Yonkers.[35] It provided more than 800,000 square feet of retail space for consumers to roam, a virtual mecca of self-contained consumerism.

Within months, Atlas was expanding the parking lot to accommodate 6,000 vehicles, whose drivers were coming from as far as Connecticut, New Jersey and Pennsylvania. Atlas claimed the shopping center made $7 million in sales between Thanksgiving and Christmas alone.[36]

The county was changing drastically, moving from a collection of old farm towns and railroads suburbs into a new kind of societal arrangement, the automobile suburb. "The procession of big office and shopping centers into the commuters' hinterlands on the northern fringe of metropolitan New York has grown from a straggly creep into a bandwagon parade," the New York Times reported in 1955.[37] Under the recommendations of the county's planning director, Hugh Pomeroy, many communities were enacting new zoning regulations that required much larger housing lots on which to build. "Planners call this sanity, not snobbery," the Times reported, and the new zoning was consistent with a policy to promote growth without "Bronxification."[38] But the boom in development caused anxiety and concern. How to keep Westchester from becoming a clone or an outgrowth of the vast metropolis to the south became a paramount priority for planners and elected leaders.

The population of the county soared. In 1940, the population of Westchester County was recorded at 573,000 by census takers, and ten years later, it had reached 625,800, including 40,000 African Americans, many relocating from the South. Some towns saw astounding growth: from 1950 to 1957, the town of Yorktown grew from 4,731 to 11,804 residents in just seven years.[39] In 1960, the population of the county had expanded nearly 30 percent during the preceding decade, reaching a population of 808,891.[40]

Pomeroy, the Westchester planning director during this post-war period, was among the most astute observers of the conundrum Westchester faced. created its department of planning in 1939, one of the first in the country. Pomeroy, a Croton resident, was credited with writing the first county zoning ordinance in the United States while working in Los Angeles before coming east and taking a position as Westchester's planning director. He was acutely aware of the need to connect with New York City, while remaining a separate entity.

In 1947, Pomeroy recognized the acute shortage of housing in the region—hitting hardest "the newly married young couple living in a tight apartment, with in-laws, or the young couple who can't get married because of no place to live, or the veteran who fought for democracy and now wonders why democracy can't provide a decent home for him."[41]

He saw the changes that were underway as the building boom took hold and transformed a series of small towns and cities into its own suburban metropolitan region. "Once a rural hinterland, today the Hudson Valley culture has been almost entirely supplanted by that of suburbia," he observed in a 1948 speech for planners in Hartford, Connecticut, "and the rural hinterland has been pushed far back, with its fortune completely subject to its position as a part of the New York metropolitan area." Still, he said, Westchester had insisted on "a fiercely local expression of democracy," and it was unlikely to secede control to New York City.[42]

At the same time, there was no escaping that Westchester's fate was inextricably linked to Gotham. "There is never absent from one's consciousness the overwhelming fact of New York City," Pomeroy said. "In this great metropolitan agglomeration we are not free, we are knit together, knit rather than bound, by economic and social forces," he said.[43]

Pomeroy insisted the city's power be resisted—as much as one can avoid a giant. He was following the old playbook articulated by Boss William Ward, keeping out of the city's grasp through wise planning and strict zoning. It was a realist approach that guided much of the county's later development—to be part of the metropolitan region through economic and transportation ties, while retaining a separate identity that contrasted sharply with the city's. He spoke of the importance of a different quality of life offered in Westchester, and a "jealous" attachment that county residents held for that ideal. "The communities of Westchester face tremendous problems of development," he said. "Nowhere are these problems more serious than in the southerly communities of the county, confronted with the threat of gradual engulfment by an advancing sea of intensive and mediocre urbanism." He concluded at a national planning conference in 1957, advocating for the interstate highway system, "We have to live with the monsters we create."

Some of the monsters being created by suburbanization were deeply disturbing to longtime residents who saw rising commercialism, shopping centers and suburban sprawl all tied together in one insidious package. One South Salem resident, Edward Kressy, issued a plaintive cry in the letters column to bemoan what he saw as a fading way of life. The letter was responding to a new shopping center and the controversy it stirred, but Kressy saw far more at stake, what he called "a mindless violation of values that threatens our way of life as perilously as thermonuclear war." It was hyperbole, but it spoke to the sense of total loss the further development of Westchester entailed.[44]

"In many of our towns and villages, the natural background for our fine homes and churches, with their honest architecture, is being replaced with that chickweed of business, the shopping center," Kressy wrote. "A fair question would be: What do we in the villages and towns across the land get when we exchange our residential property for commercial zoning as a bow to the shopping center? All too often we get cheap cinder block and miscellaneous masonry that grow into hideous nonentities of architecture.... Public service? Progress? Growth? It is certainly not growth to chop a living thing down—such as a village or town.... Are we so regimented and so stamped with standardization; so brainwashed by merchants and Madison Avenue that we have become too stupefied to think straight? For we can't be thinking straight if we're allowing beautiful villages to get away from us to be replaced by unsightly money-grubbing spots."[45]

As deeply unsettling as the feared loss of village greens bracketed by church spires was to many, there was also a fomenting unease about a less obvious infiltration. The concept of the enemy within took root during the 1950s when the forces of communism—both within the country and without—came to dominate the public consciousness and Cold War hostilities spanned the globe. The Korean War, in which 105 Westchester County residents were killed in the conflict, was the precursor to a long twilight struggle that engaged soldiers in uniforms and civilians alike.[46] The insidious presence of the enemy within came to define the period, which was marked by riots, inquests and terminations of careers. Supposed subversives were challenged by the status quo and disciplinary boards in schools and colleges, as educational instructors were inordinately targeted for anti–American sensibilities. Many spoke out in defense of civil liberties against mass paranoia. But the actions of the federal government, which culminated in the execution of Julius and Ethel Rosenberg at Sing Sing in 1953, rattled the county and the nation to its core.

Federal agents broke into the Mount Pleasant farmhouse owned by Dashiell Hammett and Lillian Hellman, writers with radical sympathies, in 1951. Hellman, a playwright, and Hammett, author of *The Maltese Falcon* and other detective stories, lived at a farm on Hardscrabble Road in Mount Pleasant, off and on from the late 30s until 1952, working the land, raising poodles and enjoying respite from the demands of theater, politics and publishing. In 1951, 17 Communists were arrested and charged with advocating the overthrow of the U.S. government, and on July 2, four became fugitives, forfeiting bail. Hammett (who lived his final days at a cottage in Katonah) was the head of the bail fund. On July 4, federal agents showed up at Hardscrabble Farm in the early morning, after barricading the exits to the residence, in search of the defendants. Hellman politely showed the federal agents around the farm in her car before they left, satisfied the fugitives had not found sanctuary there. Hammett was not present at the time of the search and was later apprised by Hellman of what the federal agents did at the farm. Hellman was deeply unnerved by the search; Hammett made a show of weary bemusement.[47]

After the Soviet Union replaced the fascist powers of World War II as enemy number one in the popular imagination, the threat of Communism was seen to have a home in places in and around cities like New York and Los Angeles. In 1946, District Attorney

George Fanelli told the Thornwood Republican Club, "We cannot be too watchful because there is definite movement of radical elements who have a planned program of infiltration," he said, speaking about local politics.[48]

In the summer of 1949, the Cold War turned hot in northern Westchester when an event billed as an outdoor concert in a country setting turned into a bloody assault that shook the nation. The violence was precipitated by the announcement that Paul Robeson, a black entertainer with strong leftist and socialist political beliefs, was to perform outside Peekskill at a campground called Lakeland Acres. Anti-Communist demonstrators blocked the concert from taking place, lighting fires and mobbing concert-goers. That disturbance was just the prelude to an even more violent confrontation a week later, when Robeson returned to perform for a larger audience—and a bigger mob. Racist and anti–Semitic taunts accompanied the second wave of assault on Robeson's followers, many of whom were black and Jewish. The week-long troubles eventually came to be called the Peekskill Riots (though they actually took place over the city line in the town of Cortlandt) or the Robeson riots, and they attracted international attention. *Pravda*, the Soviet newspaper with heavy propagandistic overtones, ran a story with this headline: "Outrage of American Fascists: Attempt to Lynch Paul Robeson."[49]

Peekskill looked like many other American towns in 1949. A working-class area in many respects, the city was also ringed by a number of Jewish summer colonies organized by left-leaning organizations.[50] Peekskill more than carried its share during World War II, with 47 city men killed in the conflict. In Paul Robeson, they saw not just an outsider but the enemy.

Robeson, a man of many talents, was the valedictorian of his graduating class at Rutgers and received his law degree from Columbia. Plagued by racial discrimination in his early legal career, he turned his booming baritone voice to the stage instead. His anger at the abuses black people suffered in this country, and a deep exposure to leftist causes in England and Russia, propelled him toward Socialism. Robeson also spoke out forcefully on racial issues long before others took up the cause of civil rights, and he was never shy about expressing his views on the current events of the day. He had a number of friends in northern Westchester and often came to the area to visit.

When the singer told a peace conference in Paris that "it is unthinkable that American Negroes would go to war on behalf of those who have oppressed us for generations," he was branded a traitor, though the exact wording of the quotation was later contested.[51] The appearance scheduled outside Peekskill to benefit the Civil Rights Congress brought him into conflict with the blue-collar town and its patriotic citizens. He had appeared in the area before, but this time it was different. The *Peekskill Evening Star*, a small paper run by a former missionary, called for a protest at Robeson's concert: "The time for tolerant silence that signifies approval is running out. Peekskill wants no rallies that support iron curtains, concentration camps, blockades and the [KGB] ... no matter how sweet the music," the paper wrote.[52]

The Peekskill area heeded the call. On August 27, 1949, a march by veterans near the picnic grounds and a hostile blockade prevented the concert from taking place at Lakeland Acres just north of the city. Robeson was persuaded not to engage the mob or carry on with the show when his car pulled up at the performance venue—and he was secretly driven back to a friend's home in Croton. After that, the veterans stormed the concert-goers, and hand-to-hand fighting bloodied dozens of people. Rioters charged into groups of Robeson supporters amid piles of burning chairs and a flaming cross lit

The two riots outside Peekskill in Cortlandt in 1948, sparked over musical performances by Paul Robeson, and organized by labor activists, revealed the deep racial and political divisions in American society. Dozens were injured in the two separate melees (Colin T. Naylor, Jr., Archives of The Field Library, Peekskill, NY).

by teenagers.[53] A 24-year-old navy veteran from Shrub Oak was stabbed though the circumstances of his injury and who caused it were never determined.[54]

A week later, concert organizers were determined to put on a show, and Robeson vowed to return. A large contingent of union supporters, many of them veterans themselves, were brought in to stand guard against an array of 5,000 to 10,000 anti–Robeson demonstrators and potential snipers. The face-off was ominous. On September 4, a large convergence of Robeson supporters and union activists, including musicians Pete Seeger and Woody Guthrie, converged on property off Oregon Road (now the Hollow Brook Golf Club) for a rescheduled performance. What they experienced was a grotesque chorus of racial and anti–Semitic taunts on the way in. The atmosphere grew tense as Robeson took the stage following a number of other performances, including several songs performed by Seeger. The crowd heard the baritone sing six (what were then called) Negro spirituals, starting with "Let My People Go" and ending with "Old Man River." As the crowds departed, violence erupted in a wave of sustained assault, leaving a stream of bloodshed from injured victims from Cortlandt on down to Peekskill. Veterans in Legionnaire caps seemed to be in charge of the attacks, carried out with rocks, clubs and fists on the largely black and Jewish Robeson supporters.[55] Whole families, from age ten to 70, stood by the road and hurled epithets and stones at the departing crowd as they ran the gauntlet in buses and cars. A black veteran of World War I was dragged from a car and beaten. Rocks rained down on the departing vehicles, smashing windows and ripping flesh. Bloodied by the rioters, the victims of the assault found little help from the 950 police officers assigned to the concert, who did nothing to check the onslaught. When it was all over, parts of the Oregon Road leading from the concert site were slick with blood.[56] The violence has since become part of leftist lore, the insidious dangers of intolerant mob violence exposed for the world to see. There was certainly little justice for the dozens of victims, some of whom suffered permanent injuries. State and local authorities that investigated the violence insisted it was Communist provocation that had stirred the unrest, however regrettable. The contention that Robeson was to blame for the riot was taken up in much of the press. The *New York Daily Mirror* headline, "Robeson: He Asked For It," was typical of the prevailing tone.[57] County officials defended the police action, and District Attorney George Fanelli commended law enforcement for "excellent work" in difficult circumstances.[58] A grand jury report in October declared that the violence "was basically neither anti–Semitic nor anti–Negro in character" and placed the blame for the turmoil on Robeson and "Communists."[59]

But a report by the American Civil Liberties Union found the police response "bordered on the criminally negligent." Numerous witnesses were interviewed who recalled in detail the anti–Jewish and anti–black slurs being hurled at the concert-going crowd.[60] The civil-rights group attributed the violence, beyond the apathetic response by authorities, to "the most explosive prejudices in American life—against Communists, Negroes and Jews."[61] None of those accused of having organized the riots, including the son of the Peekskill police chief, did any jail time. Friends of Robeson's who had hosted and organized his concerts, Helen and Sam Rosen of Katonah, were bombarded with hate mail and obscene phone calls.[62]

Robeson, too, was punished. The famed singer lost all his concert bookings after the riots, and he went from being the most popular black entertainer in the country to a man who sang in church basements for a living. An unrepentant admirer of the Soviet Union, long after the horrors of that regime had been exposed, Robeson died in 1976 after a long decline. He was buried in Ferncliff Cemetery in Hartsdale. The two sites where the riots took place were never identified for future generations. No plaques were ever erected to mark the ground where Americans turned against one another with a ferocity that threatened to shatter far more than bones.

The specter of Communism haunted the entire American landscape and the question that personified it—"Are you now or have you ever been a member of the Communist Party?"—resounded far beyond the chamber rooms of Congress in the early 1950s. Mirroring the activities of Congressional committees rooting out Communists from their hidden posts, home-grown Red hunters in Westchester searched through school curricula, library shelves and personnel files for evidence of "a pattern of Communist indoctrination in the school system," in the words of one educational activist who saw subversion running rampant.

Ralph Gwinn, a Republican Congressman from Bronxville, was especially hawkish on the Red Menace, once claiming that every branch of the U.S. government had been infiltrated by a "tremendous underground force," which he believed President Roosevelt had allowed.[63] In many ways, the local political posse was following in the footsteps of the House Committee on Un-American Activities formed in 1947. The movement later came to be led by Senator Joseph McCarthy, who gathered a force and momentum that jailed dissenters, ended careers and stifled protest. While those inquiries looked into the U.S. State Department, government bureaucracies and Hollywood, the Red Hunt in Westchester probed classrooms and school libraries with similar concepts and tactics.

The potential for the indoctrination of youth by subversive radicals, and the perceived notion that educators and school unions were infiltrated by Communists became a major source of concern for local Red Hunters, especially in New York. In 1949, New York State enacted legislation to bar Communists from teaching positions, widely known as the Feinberg law. The Supreme Court upheld the law over the objections of a group of plaintiffs who sought to challenge the law on First Amendment grounds, but their arguments did not hold sway with a majority of the justices. In 1952, eight New York City school teachers were suspended for refusing to answer questions about Communist Party affiliations.

A financial executive from Scarsdale, Otto Dohrenwend, led a group of like-minded activists who began to probe the Scarsdale school district for what they saw as indoctrination by far-left authors and educators. Dohrenwend pointed to a statement in 1948 by the chairman of the American Communist Party, William Z. Foster, that "our teachers must write new school textbooks and rewrite history from a Marxist perspective." Vigilance was necessary in the great struggle against communism, the Scarsdale Red Hunters believed. Dohrenwend said he and like-minded patriots saw an imperative to "criticize leftist educational philosophies, criticize subversive teaching materials and criticize the use of school buildings by Communists and fellow travelers," and that's what the committee was doing. "Such criticism is not only the right but the duty of good citizenship, if our public schools are to be protected and preserved as makers of good and loyal American citizens," he wrote.[64] The Scarsdale citizens committee first started with the library in June 1949. Works by Langston Hughes, the black poet and intellectual, and Howard Fast, a leftist writer, were singled out. The committee took particular exception to 11 books in the school library written by Fast, a prolific screenwriter and novelist who was blacklisted and jailed during the period. One of his books on the American Revolution used in Scarsdale classrooms, *Citizen Tom Paine*, was derided as "Communist propaganda disguised as American literature."[65] An admiring biography of Paul Robeson was also targeted. The committee, working with an "expert" on Communist Party infiltration, discovered in Scarsdale "an organized conspiracy to capture the Westchester mind." The committee found that "there were concealed Communists planted in Scarsdale … and the infiltration of pro–Communist books into the schools was part of that conspiracy."

The Committee of Ten, as it was known, also asked to investigate Bert James Loewenberg, a local educator who helped conduct summer classes for the Scarsdale school district and whose name surfaced before the House Committee on Un-American Activities. One outraged member of the committee asked the Scarsdale School Board: "How far will the Communist infiltrate before the board will take action?"[66]

The school administration was not swayed by the criticism, and a committee formed by the district found no indication of leftist bias in reading material or efforts at Communist indoctrination. Two hundred people came to the school board meeting in November 1949 to hear its response to the allegation of "Communist infiltration." According to a committee report prepared for the board, "the selection of books for Scarsdale schools is being made according to proper standards and by qualified people who are fully devoted to the American way of life." The school board opposed "negative methods of repressive censorship" of any kind.[67]

A large group of Scarsdale residents also came out in opposition to the proposal to remove certain books from the library. In a letter sent to the school administration, signed by 81 well-respected local citizens, the group said "censorship of books and materials smacks of the methods used by Communist and Fascist states and defeats the very purpose of the Bill of Rights, as well at the purpose of education."[68] The board stood its ground when the Committee of Ten turned up the volume and the intensity of their attacks. "It's already there and you don't know communism when you see it," proclaimed one of the anti–Communist leaders, William Kernan.[69] When the school board decided to no longer discuss the book issue at meetings, only taking written questions on the subject, members of the Committee of Ten shouted "Dictatorship!" from their seats.[70]

The controversy came to a head in June 1950 when the school board granted a request to review the subject again. A crowd estimated at 1,400 heard the Committee of Ten once again list their evidence of Communist subversion and demand a full-scale investigation. Schools Superintendent Archibald Shaw took to the lectern and gave his own characterization of the teachers in the district. "We have competent teachers, loyal teachers, decent, wholesome teachers. In their hands, our children, our American way, both are safe." After a brief silence, thunderous applause erupted.[71]

The Committee of Ten kept at it, though the school board eventually suspended additional consideration of the matter. Regular letters to the editor, mailers and speeches in the community kept the controversy brewing. When the school board elections were held in May 1952, the candidates who were in opposition to the Committee of Ten were overwhelmingly re-elected, a signal of confidence in the path the school board had taken to rebuff the efforts of the Red hunters. The vote became national news. "What happened to McCarthyism in Scarsdale can be made to happen elsewhere," wrote editors in the *Nation*, a magazine for the liberal intelligentsia.[72]

The controversy eventually faded, but subsided as an undercurrent in the community for years. Dohrenwend and his colleagues were nothing if not persistent and continued their search into the following decade. In 1962 a concert was held at Scarsdale High School, where entertainers Pete Seeger, Ossie Davis and Ruby Dee (who lived in New Rochelle) performed. The concert was a benefit for the Freedom Riders, civil-rights activists who were pushing for voting rights for African Americans in the South. A group of about 40 picketers, connected with the earlier controversy, claimed that the performers were Communist sympathizers. They held signs that read more like advertising copy or tabloid headlines than protest slogans: "Doing the Moscow Twist!," "Turn Left for Scarsdale," "We're Not Afraid of Fallout, We're Afraid of Sellout," and "Is This a Little Red School House?" The group issued a statement proclaiming their opposition to the use of school facilities "by a group in which Communist or pro–Communist influences are manifestly present." A suit that Dohrenwend and his associates filed to block the concert was unsuccessful, though a judge did impose certain conditions on who could speak. About 1,300 people attended the concert, and $4,000 was raised for the Freedom Riders.[73]

Institutions of higher learning were also put under harsh scrutiny during this time, with the same emphasis on indoctrination and a presumed lack of "Americanism." A 1951 article in the *American Legion Magazine* titled "Do Colleges Have to Hire Red Professors?" claimed Communists were already heavily involved on college campuses.[74] After the article came out, the American Legion of Westchester formed an "Americanism Committee" to pursue an investigation into campus subversives. That year, Sarah Lawrence was a small college for women with some 400 students. It would join a list of colleges forced to defend its hiring practices.

In late 1951, the Bronxville Post of the American Legion challenged Sarah Lawrence and its president, Harold Taylor, to disclose the Communist affiliation of any members of the college faculty. Taylor defended the university's commitment to free expression and open inquiry, and some 175 distinguished area residents signed a letter of support. The Legion, in turn, protested vigorously, saying that it was, in fact, "on the receiving end of a smear campaign."[75]

Though more than a dozen faculty members were scrutinized, several faced particularly thorough examination. Bert James Lowenberg was the historian who had faced criticism when he partnered with educators from Scarsdale. Joseph Barnes was a former foreign editor of the *New York Herald Tribune* on the faculty at Sarah Lawrence. Irving Goldman was a State Department diplomat who was released from government service in 1947 when his Communist-party affiliation was disclosed. Paul Aron was a historian who specialized in modern European history. Aron and Goldman were called to testify before the Senate subcommittee on internal security, a move that was closely watched by college administrators. Aron resigned from Sarah Lawrence in 1953 after taking the Fifth Amendment during the hearing before the so-called Jenner Committee, named after Senator William Jenner of Indiana.[76] He resigned while college administrators were considering his case, evidently with some encouragement on their behalf. Goldman said he was formerly a member of the Communist party but refused to name names of other members. He was later cleared by the college and allowed to continue teaching anthropology.[77]

As the Senate committee meetings made clear, professional careers could be ruined and lives destroyed. The Cold War antagonisms could also turn deadly, as the execution of Julius and Ethel Rosenberg demonstrated. The diminutive electrical engineer and his petite wife met their end within the cold stone walls at Sing Sing, accused of spying and passing along atomic secrets to the Soviet Union. Their execution formed one of the darkest moments in the Cold War, and while their story stretched from Moscow to London to New York City, theirs was very much a local story. Their deaths underlay the domestic front of a war of suspicion that ran through the county in the 1950s like an unseen trench.

Anglo-American counter-intelligence agents broke a Soviet spy ring in 1950, and subsequent confessions revealed that Julius Rosenberg, whose brother-in-law worked at the Los Alamos atomic site, was actively engaged in atomic espionage and recruitment of new agents. Intelligence at the time, as well as subsequent scholarship, indicated that Ethel was a Communist Party member but did nothing in the way of espionage herself. It was never certain that Ethel Rosenberg, a homemaker who barely stood five feet tall, was aware of her husband's espionage activities. Even J. Edgar Hoover, hardly soft on the Communist threat, believed Ethel was unjustly put on death row and charged with conspiracy to persuade her husband to confess.[78] He never did. Because the feds did not run their own mechanism for executions, the Rosenbergs were sent to Sing Sing while the appeal process played out. There were delays, stays of execution and requests for clemency that reached the White House and the Supreme Court that lasted for more than two years. They were all turned down, and the appointed hour duly came. The Friday execution was moved up so as not to fall on the Jewish sabbath; executions at Sing Sing normally took place in the nighttime hours.[79]

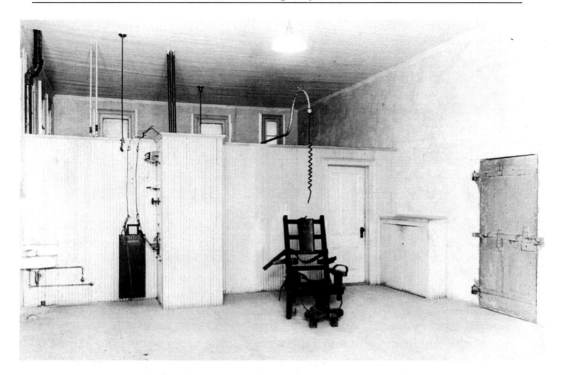

The electric chair at Sing Sing, seen here in 1915, sent 614 prisoners to their death. Local lore held it that the lights dimmed in Ossining during executions; in fact, the death house had its own generator. Julius and Ethel Rosenberg died in the chair in 1953 (Library of Congress).

It was a muggy summer day when the eyes of the world turned to the most famous death house in America. As the spy case labeled the new "Crime of the Century" came to its grisly conclusion on June 19, 1953, Julius and Ethel Rosenberg went to their deaths in the electric chair shortly before sundown, a Coast Guard helicopter circling overhead. The mechanical efficiency of the proceedings, honed through years of practice within the prison walls, began at 8:02 p.m. when Julius Rosenberg entered the chamber with the prison's Jewish chaplain, Irving Koslowe, reading the 23rd Psalm ("The Lord is my shepherd, I shall not want..."). It ended 14 minutes later when a third, final burst of electricity extinguished Ethel Rosenberg's life. Convicted of conspiracy to pass the secrets of the atom bomb to the Soviet Union, they were the first non-military prisoners in the history of the United States to be executed for espionage. The only unexpected moment during the otherwise clinical operation came when Ethel Rosenberg—who wore white gloves to her arraignment on spy charges, and a shapeless green prison dress to her execution—turned to give a goodbye kiss to a prison matron who had befriended her in jail and escorted her to the chair.[80] The double execution cost $300 for the services of the electrician and executioner who operated the chair, Joseph Francel. He quit soon after that. State prison officials, meticulous in the accounting of death, later sent a bill to the federal authorities who had condemned the Rosenbergs to death and thereby incurred the cost of the executioner's services.[81] After the execution, their two young sons, Robert and Michael, six and ten, needed a foster home. The two used to visit their parents at Sing Sing, even playing a game of hangman on one occasion. The Jewish chaplain, Koslowe, who led a congregation in Mamaroneck, assisted in placing them in a foster home in Hastings-on-Hudson and the two Rosenberg sons came to live in the home of Anne and Abel Meeropol in the rivertown village. Abel Meeropol was a poet and songwriter, educator and a former Communist. He wrote in 1939 "Strange Fruit," the song that exposed the horrors of Southern lynching and was made famous by jazz singer Billie Holliday.[82] The two orphans grew up in Hastings. FBI agents later came to Hastings when Robert Meeropol was a high school student, asking school administrators to keep tabs on the family for the feds. Schools Superintendent Philip Langworthy promptly showed them the door.[83]

The threat of a Soviet bomb targeting New York City and its environs, as well as other American cities, was viewed with increasing alarm during the early 1950s. Every single day was an orange alert for New Yorkers in that period. Nuclear incineration was very much a scenario that dominated the public imagination, and the idea that nuclear-tipped missiles or bomber fleets could eviscerate the entire Atlantic seaboard during an all-out attack sent suburban homeowners burrowing into cement-lined shelters in their backyards, stockpiling Spam in their basements and scanning the horizon for unexpected peril.

In 1955, the national security apparatus built a Nike missile-base with underground silos in Harrison near the Kensico dam to shoot down Soviet attackers, and a radar-command station was established on Davids Island in New Rochelle.[84] They were part of the military ring of defenses meant to counter a Soviet offensive, but suburban home-owners continued to take their own precautions. The unthinkable prospect of a nuclear cataclysm wove itself into the fabric of daily life, and bomb shelters became as common to the suburban landscape as horse-shoe pits and tennis courts.

The paranoia over an enemy attack began during the Korean War, prompting some local residents to envision the menace in their own backyards. The Soviet nuclear program speeded ahead in the mid–1950s, and the prospects that an annihilating strike would turn Westchester into a glowing heap of rubble became alarmingly real. The craze for building underground shelters instantly took off. The concrete bunkers, some 20 inches thick, were lined with heavy metal to ward off lethal gamma rays. Packed with canned meats, water tanks, dry biscuits and a few amenities, on the inside they had all the necessities for a well-to-do suburban family to ride out the nuclear apocalypse in modest comfort. Those who built them often merged their doomsday function into more utilitarian purposes, like wine cellars or storage rooms. The cost of a shelter was said to run anywhere from $500 for an in-home unit to $1,500 for an unattached underground structure. Many who built the underground shelters kept quiet about what they had built, out of fear that their neighbors would disapprove—or even that their neighbors would beat down the shelter doors when the missiles or bombers started flying. As neighbors began comparing notes at cocktail parties and other social gatherings, fall-out shelters eventually gained a measure of mainstream acceptance.[85]

When Governor Nelson Rockefeller floated a proposal in 1959 to make radiation-proof shelters mandatory in new commercial and residential buildings, it was clear that nuclear anxieties could actually lead to big business. He later dropped the measure.[86] But the Builders Institute of Westchester began giving demonstrations on bomb shelter construction methods for fallout shelters, survival equipment and radiation kits.[87] Hammacher-Schlemmer, furnishers of luxury household goods, advertised a line of fall-out shelter accessories and high-end doomsday accommodations—and received a surge of new business.[88]

Meanwhile, scientists debated whether small fallout shelters could actually withstand the force of Soviet H-bombs and clergy members talked about the moral implications of an industry predicated on the premise of mass destruction—with salvation for a few.

Not everyone, however, was so keen on the lead-lined boltholes that spoke of impending obliteration. When the Yorktown Lions Club offered a free fallout shelter as its grand prize during a fundraising lottery in 1962, the idea bombed in a wave of negative publicity—a reflection of the ambiguous attitude many people still held about the acceptance of such a reality. Only 23 people bought chances and the Lions called off the lottery.[89]

Schools had to pay particular attention to the issue of safety. Instead of fire drills and pep rallies, educators were preoccupied with nuclear attack and whether children should be sent home in the event of a missile launch. The anxiety reached a fever pitch during the Cuban Missile Crisis of 1962.

Schools all over the region practiced "duck-and-cover" drills, in which children scampered underneath their desks as a preventative measure against nuclear firestorms. *Dr. Strangelove*, it seemed, had moved from his bunker in the Pentagon to run the local school board. During that year, the Byram School District considered the purchase of "radiation-proof clothing for teachers."[90] Lakeland High School in Cortlandt installed a layer of slate over the gymnasium as a precaution against radioactive fallout.[91]

Fortunately, none of those horrors came to pass. The Nike missile base in Harrison was decommissioned, later used as a municipal truck garage, and the anxieties of the Cold War eventually faded with time.

While the threat of complete annihilation haunted the country, there was a strong inclination to keep up appearances and maintain an imperturbable veneer. Unflappable presentation and deportment above all things was an old suburban ideal. It was a mindset that also carried its own set of contradictions and burdens. And during the post-war era, the man in the gray flannel suit and the suburban housewife were ripe for investigation.

Westchester was also closely linked to the examination of ruinous alcohol consumption, as well as the appearance of propriety that often shielded alcoholism's effects. Bill Wilson was a Vermonter and seemingly respectable New York City businessman whose life was being destroyed by black-out drinking sessions. A patron of his offered him a home in Bedford Hills, where he settled with his wife, Lois, in 1941, several years after Wilson found sobriety and wrote the book that helped other alcoholics like him, *Alcoholics Anonymous,* known as "The Big Book." Framed by sycamore and maple trees, it had a row of stone steps leading up to the front door. The Wilsons called the place Stepping Stones, a reference to the 12-step concept of the Alcoholics Anonymous program.[92] It became a mecca for recovering alcoholics; Bill and Lois Wilson later rented a small house in Pound Ridge, where they tried to keep the address a secret, to find privacy.[93]

On the literary front, John Cheever carried out a study on the contradictions between outward appearance and inner angst. He was a study in contradictions himself, to say the least. A man given to attiring himself in Brooks Brothers box suits and keeping time with a Rolex on his wrist, he spoke with the unmistakable tones of a New Englander with a long pedigree in the land of country clubs and swimming pools. But he came from a less than fashionable Boston suburb, there was no family money, and he never finished high school. He had a secretive streak and a reckless sexual nature with men and women. The class anxieties and his sexual ambivalence combined in such a way that despite his outward appearance, he felt himself to be an outsider among the country-club golfers who were his neighbors. Above all, he had a ruinous compulsion to drink, and he both lived and wrote about the sorrows of gin.

While his temperament and inner life tended toward the tumultuous, Cheever's prose was adamantine and burnished to a fine sheen, cadenced with the rhythm of a master storyteller. The tragedy of untidy lives hidden behind orderly facades, corroded by Scotch and thwarted dreams, made manifest on the pages of his short stories and novels, gave the language a new word to describe the afflictions of the comfortable classes: "Cheeveresque." He made an exquisite study of the "pain and sweetness of life," in the phrase in one of his short stories. Cheever came to Westchester in late May 1951. At the time, living in the suburbs made him apprehensive. "The sense was that we were being exiled … to a barren and provincial life where we would get fat … and spend our evenings glued to a television set."[94] He worried that his creative spark would be snuffed out by what he conceived as the dull conventions of Westchester. "My God, the suburbs!" he wrote later in life reflecting on his residency in the county. "They encircled the city's boundaries like enemy territory and we thought of them as a loss of privacy, a cesspool of conformity and a life of indescribable dreariness."[95]

His wife, Mary, had started teaching English at Sarah Lawrence in 1947 two days a week, and the growing Cheever family was having a tough time of it in New York City. One of Cheever's friends, Jack Kahn, an actor and writer, was moving out of his place in Scarborough (the community that lies in the south end of the village of Briarcliff Manor along the Hudson River) and suggested Cheever take up the lease. It was an old utility building and tool shop on the Frank Vanderlip estate off Route 9 that was turned into a cottage, and Cheever and his family often referred to it jokingly as "the chicken house" or the "tool shed." He described it in a letter to a friend as lying "behind the manorial garages and right beside the manorial garbage pail, but from the front porch we have a nice view of the manorial lawn and the manorial swimming pool."[96] Drinking for Cheever could start as early as noon on Saturdays. A friend would show up, and "the gin had to be drunk first," Mary Cheever later recalled.[97] A group of friends from Ossining and Croton regularly came for backgammon and sports on the lawn with the Cheever family, a portrait of normalcy. Cheever was charming when the moment called for it. As his friend Jack Kahn explained, "He was certainly the most gentlemanly of anyone in our group… . He was the sort of person you would sit next to the dreadful aunt or boring sister-in-law at dinner. He might have too much to drink, and he would probably mumble, for he mumbled even when sober, but he would certainly be polite and do his best to please his dinner partner."[98] After ten years, he moved into an old home off Cedar Lane in Ossining, and life in suburbia began to agree with him. The suburbs gave him material, and his work reflected his study of the local landscape in Ossining and Scarborough and life on the commuter lines. But he was haunted by the sense that he was not quite of the place, as well as he managed to blend in.

"I was born into no true class, and it was my decision early in life, to insinuate myself into the middle class, like a spy, so that I would have advantageous position of attack, but I seem now and then to have forgotten my mission and to have taken my disguises too seriously," he wrote in the late 40s.[99]

Cheever wrote short stories for *The New Yorker*, worried about money, raised a family and lived a life of inner torment, which his journals later revealed. As his fame grew, admiring magazine profiles turned up in *Time* and *Life* magazines, and Cheever, well aware of the corrosive effects of fame but still receptive to the siren song of literary celebrity, played along. He posed for photographs in an empty pool and poured out pitchers of gin for interviewers. He spent most mornings taking long walks on the Croton Aqueduct trail to the Croton Dam, a journey of several miles from his Cedar Lane home. When John Updike came for a visit, Cheever insisted on taking him for a walk to the Croton Dam together, where Updike's wife snapped a photograph of the two famous authors, friendly competitors in the highest levels of American letters. The long walks had a purpose: putting off the first drink of the day. Once the gin was poured, a long episode of "bottle-fighting," as Cheever called it in his journals, was sure to follow. It was clear who was the loser in such contests.

The fictional setting of Cheever's Bullett Park stories was loosely modeled on the local landscape he found around Shady Lane Farm Road, the Crotonville section of Ossining. As a writing instructor at Sing Sing prison, Cheever also picked up material for his 1977 novel, *Falconer*, about a college professor behind bars after his murder conviction. Cheever said he felt connected to the prisoners he taught at Sing Sing and strongly identified with them. He befriended one prisoner, Donald Lang, doing time at Sing Sing for armed robbery. After his release, they palled around, and Lang came over to drink on Cheever's front porch or watch a baseball game. Cheever bailed him out of the Ossining lock-up after Lang assaulted another man with a crowbar in a bar fight in Ossining.[100]

When he wasn't incoherent with drink, occasionally to the point of incontinence, Cheever was turning his cold but sympathetic gaze on the world around him, men and women with deceptive appearances and secret anxieties. As Updike observed about his friend, "He thought fast, saw everything in bright, true colors and was the arena of a constant tussle between the bubbling joie de vivre of the healthy sensitive man and the deep melancholy peculiar to American Protestant males."[101]

Many others wrote about the suburbs, Updike noted. It was hardly an ignored genre of American liter-

Author John Cheever, seen here in 1976 at his Ossining home six years before his death, explored despair and the facade behind seemingly pleasant suburban lives. Cheever took long walks on the Croton Aqueduct trail from his home in Ossining, putting off the first drink of the day for as long as he could (© 2005 Nancy Crampton. All rights reserved).

ature. "Only he saw in its cocktail parties and swimming pools the shimmer of dissolving dreams; no one else satirized with such tenderness its manifold distinctions of class and style, or felt with such poignance the weary commuter's nightly tumble into the arms of his family." His suburbs, Updike added, "were vastly uneasy, rather, and citadels of disappointment, vain longing, disguised poverty, class cruelty, graceless aging, and crimes ranging from adultery and theft to murder." And out of that morass came high art, and *The New Yorker* stories, an "imperishable record of an American moment; the glowing windows of suburban homes would never again seem so beaconlike."[102]

Cheever seemed possessed by an inner anguish that left him internally disfigured and beyond remedy, and it surfaced regularly in his characters. Neddy Merrill, the man who swam across the suburban county in one of his best-known stories, "The Swimmer," was "so cold that he thought he would never be warm again." The author's drinking became more and more of a scourge. He was arrested by a State Trooper on Route 100 in Somers in 1971, after returning from a dinner party in Connecticut.[103] He started drinking before noon during the 1970s, and while teaching a disastrous seminar at Boston University, he fell into a trough of drunken squalor and suicidal despair. His brother Fred drove him to Phelps Memorial Hospital in Sleepy Hollow for detox, where he suffered D.T.s, delirium tremens. After a longer rehab at the Smithers Clinic in Manhattan, he stopped drinking 1975, and started writing again.

Cancer was discovered in 1981, and the tumors advanced rapidly despite chemo treatments in Mount Kisco. His final days were spent enjoying his regular haunts around his northern Westchester home. Losing his hair did not diminish his humor, and he stopped in at his regular barber shop in Briarcliff for a laugh after his locks were gone. Cheever prepared for the end at regular appointments with his Croton psychiatrist, and on his last good day, he ordered a favorite Chinese dinner from a take-out restaurant in Pleasantville. He was surrounded by family when he died in his bedroom in 1982, aged 70.

On a warm summer day, some 200 people came to Trinity Episcopal in Ossining to pay their respects to a writer who decoded the secret language of suffering and travelled far in a tree-lined world of despair.[104]

Cheever delineated a world in which White Anglo-Saxon Protestants, known colloquially as WASPs, reigned supreme, a reflection of reality. The commuting men in tailored charcoal suits and the ladies who lunched in pearls, prim hats and white gloves, both in all white on the tennis court, stood out for their natural sense of entitlement, and Westchester was one of their premiere enclaves. For generations, the land of country clubs and church spires had been a place where WASPs ran the show. And for Jews, like the Irish and Italians, the rules of the WASP social order were burdensome.

Jews had made a place in Westchester since the 1800s, and a number of prominent and high-achieving leaders in the field of entertainment, publishing and business had established big country homes in the region. But the Jewish entrée into Westchester was always conditional, and outright instances of anti–Jewish exclusion were not hard to find. A brochure in the 1930s advertising a trolley running from Peekskill to Mohegan Lake in Yorktown proclaimed: "No Hebrews."[105]

Bigotry and anti–Semitism made themselves manifest in many other forms, most especially the real-estate restrictions that prohibited the sale of homes to "members of the Hebrew race," in the parlance of the age. The village of Bronxville in particular was held up to negative scrutiny in a 1959 article for *Commentary* magazine when a

Jewish journalist described his unsuccessful and unsettling efforts to buy a home in the village with his wife. Wearing a tweed jacket and a "gabardine topcoat" for his dealings with local realtors, Harry Gersh was turned away again and again from purchasing a home when he mentioned he was Jewish.[106] Some Jewish real-estate developers were able to build neighborhoods that were open to Jewish home-buyers, such as the Fox Meadow site in Scarsdale in the 1920s.[107] In 1940, a census listed Scarsdale as 15 percent Jewish, roughly the same percentage as its Catholic population. Twenty years later, the percentage had risen to 35.[108] Jewish homeowners made inroads in a number of Westchester communities through the middle of the century, with some towns more favorable to Jewish residency than others. Mount Vernon, in particular, was considered a welcoming community to Jews. The order of the Free Sons of Abraham, a Jewish civic and cultural organization, opened in 1891, and by the 1940s there were five synagogues within the city.[109]

But the path into the mainstream for Jews in Westchester could be a rocky one. The barriers in home ownership, education, professional advancement and social organizations that made life a challenge only eroded gradually. The whispers behind closed doors continued for decades. There were also outright forms of blatant intimidation, some of it as obvious as shards of broken glass and black paint, as they continued their advancement in the suburbs during the post-war period.

When a series of neo–Nazi rallies and anti–Semitic outrages erupted in Europe in 1960, in Germany in particular, a wave of copycat attacks followed in the United States. Jewish cemeteries in New York City were vandalized, and a half dozen synagogues were also defaced or damaged during the year. In Westchester, there were anti–Semitic defilements on a somewhat smaller scale. The most notable was at the Westchester Jewish Center in Mamaroneck, where one or more vandals painted four large swastikas in black enamel on the walls and windows. Police chief Jeremiah Geary called the incident a "disgrace" while opining that the perpetrator was most likely "a crackpot."[110]

A research study by the B'nai B'rith civic organization in 1962 took a hard look at anti–Semitism in the country (entitled "Some of My Best Friends…") and concluded that overt instances of hostility had fallen sharply since the 1940s. But it determined that the so-called "gentlemen's agreement" that kept Jews out of clubs and neighborhoods was very much in effect: a third of the cooperative apartment buildings in New York City would not sell to Jews, and more than half of the private clubs used religious criteria as a bar to Jewish membership, the researchers found.

The prohibition against Jews at social events was particularly resonant in Westchester, where much of the upper social set revolved around clubs and organized activities. A case of snobbery against Jews attracted national attention and laid out exactly what was said in whispers behind closed doors.

The Holly Ball was regarded as the biggest social event of the season, where debutantes "came out" to society at the Scarsdale Golf Club. One of the debutantes, Pamela Nottage, asked a young man, Michael Hernstadt, an Episcopal convert whose father was Jewish, to be her date. Word came back from the social committee at the club that he was an unacceptable escort due to his Jewish lineage. There the matter would have rested, quietly, were it not for the indignation of the Rev. George Kempsell, the Episcopal rector of St. James the Less Church, who heard about the snub from the girl's mother. The young debutante-to-be said she was dropping out of the event in protest, and the reverend also burned with indignation over the club's position.[111]

Kempsell was deeply involved in the affair. He was an honorary member of the club who dined there on occasion, and he had also baptized Hernstadt two years previously. No one snoozed through the sermon he gave that Sunday. "What we are saying is that if Our Lord Jesus Christ had come to earth in Scarsdale, he would not have been allowed to escort a young lady of this parish to the dance," the reverend told his congregation. The minister said he would refuse holy communion to anyone who believed it was fair to exclude Jews from social activities at the Scarsdale Golf Club. "Therefore, I feel it is my responsibility as your pastor to say that anyone who has in any way, by word, or in thought or deed, acquiesced with this position of the Scarsdale Golf Club is no longer welcome to receive Holy Communion at this Altar until such time as he had worked out his own peace with God in his way," he preached.[112] Kempsell's sermon—which he provided to the media—arrived like a thunderbolt and brought about a deep reflection on the prevailing anti–Semitism of the day. "A Club Rebuked for Bigotry," read the headline in *Life* magazine.[113] "Scarsdale is a community of business executives and professional men located in Westchester County, 40 minutes from midtown New York. Here some 18,000 Christians and Jews live in peace and the familiar pattern of mutually agreeable segregation. The Country Clubs are Separate and Equal," *Newsweek* joked.[114] The reverend received support from his superiors, as well as other clergy. Rabbi David Greenfield of the Westchester Reform Temple had strong words of praise, calling it an act of "uncompromising courage and clarity." The parents of Pamela Nottage called him "a true man of God."[115]

The debutante ball was duly held. When a photo of the 18 debutantes appeared, the young ladies wearing white gowns and gloves, tiaras, clutching sprigs of holly, Pamela was not among them. Despite the smiling faces and beautiful couture, it was not the kind of publicity that did anyone any good. Scarsdale was changing, the times were changing, and the old animosities never seemed more out of date. Under the withering scorn of the minister and the national news coverage, the club eventually relented on its policy toward Jews just 11 days after the Holly Ball fiasco. The Scarsdale Golf Club, where the Holly Ball was held, announced that "any member of this club may use the facilities of the club to entertain guests and friends of his own choosing." The club quietly began to allow Jewish members not long after.[116]

Kempsell had been in the eye of the storm—his phone ringing constantly, publicity's hot glare reflecting off his clerical vestments. Kempsell was not born to wealth or privilege, though he came to enjoy the prerequisites of an affluent suburban parish. The son of two domestic servants who tended to the great estates on Long Island, Kempsell had his sights on a career as a concert pianist. A talented musician, he played the piano on occasion with Cab Calloway, a famed performer who lived in Greenburgh and worshipped at Kempsell's church. For a time after the Holly Ball confrontation, Kempsell was something of a liberal star, taking part in events at the United Nations, the subject of admiring newspaper profiles. One article called him "an integrationist and a persuasive pastor" while noting his skills as a blues accompanist and a water-skier.[117] But the publicity his sermon attracted did not sit well with a number of the church parishioners, who felt they had been unfairly slandered, and quite a few left the church. The rift was not closed, hard feelings remained, and Kempsell eventually resigned from the Scarsdale church in January 1963, taking up clerical positions in Texas and Colorado.[118]

As Westchester became less of a WASP enclave, it began to attract a new kind of resident. The old kind of suburban values was giving way to a more worldly and outward-looking mindset. While radio and prose were the defining medium of the Cheever era, television would become the hallmark of the later post-war period. Celebrity, media and an energy channeled by new arrivals all came together in the late 1950s and 60s to create a new culture that both celebrated, solidified and subtly undercut the suburban ideal.

10

Westchester in the Television Age
Bonnie Meadow Road to Desegregation

As the 1950s progressed, television became the predominant form of entertainment in American households. And television found a home in the suburbs. Many of the pioneers of the emerging medium were drawn to Westchester, a short commute to New York City, with New Rochelle and Scarsdale becoming the preferred address for scores of producers, writers, executives and directors of the shows that made America laugh or pay attention to the stories of the day. Often Jewish, with roots in the city, they celebrated assimilation and consensus, all attributes that appeared to thrive in abundance in suburbia. They acknowledged the diverse ethnic and cultural strands of American life, while supporting the status quo enforced by men in grey flannel suits.

Television validated the corporate society that grew up around advertisements and shows that upheld domestic order. "The main business of television is not so much selling the specific products as the selling of an existing order," media theorist Hans Enzensberger once observed.[1] And the suburbs affirmed that existing order from one neatly groomed neighborhood to the next.

Probably the most famous address of the early sitcom era was 148 Bonnie Meadow Road in northern New Rochelle, close to the Scarsdale border. As Americans left the city in vast numbers, it was on that street in the late 1950s that Carl Reiner purchased a three-bedroom ranch-style home, on a quarter acre of land. Reiner, who was Jewish and grew up in the Bronx, was working on *Your Show of Shows*, a comedy and variety show starring Sid Caesar, a native of Yonkers.

Reiner envisioned writing and directing a show from the contours of his own life. His daily life as a comedy writer and family man in the suburbs straddled boundaries, and the show would do the same. Reiner starred in the pilot, then called *Head of the Family*, but was soon convinced to recast the show. "I'll get a better actor to play you," executive producer Sheldon Leonard told him.[2] Johnny Carson and Dick Van Dyke were the top contenders for the leading role, and Van Dyke, then a rising star on Broadway, was selected for his talent with physical comedy.

As Gerard Jones observed in his study of the sitcom genre, *The Dick Van Dyke Show* was "clearly a show about Jewish assimilation and exurban flight."[3] The half-hour comedy also explored the complexities of the divide between the suburbs and the city, the boundaries between work and home, and the perspectives of ethnic Americans versus those from much older stock. It was about pleasing the boss and maintaining a family life, told from an unusually autobiographical perspective—the first sitcom to use a writer's real

The Dick Van Dyke Show creator, writer and director Carl Reiner (center), on set with co-stars Mary Tyler Moore and Dick Van Dyke, introduced his semi-autobiographical life as a New York comedy writer and suburban family man in New Rochelle to generations of TV viewers (Earl Thissen collection, Getty Images).

life as a model for entertainment. The show suggested what a suburban melting pot could look like (if only in comedic form), where Borscht Belt comedy and Kennedy-esque glamour seemed to meet on roughly equal terms.

While the show's street address was fake, Reiner and his family really did live at number 48 Bonnie Meadow Road in New Rochelle, until *The Dick Van Dyke Show* took them to Hollywood. From its Westchester roots the show introduced the suburbs as its own kind of reality, one that was capable of channeling humor, high spirits, gossip and controlled chaos, all resolved at the end of each episode. America was born in the country and moved to the city, as the old saying went, but there were millions of Dick Van Dykes now making their way in the suburbs. The show's semi-fictional community mirrored the changing face of suburban life and validated this vision of the future. "We told the truth about ourselves," Reiner said years later when asked why the show caught on.[4] Millions of Americans relaxing in front of their television sets could relate. It was a powerful cultural icon, if an illusory one. The show hit the top ten, won countless Emmys, and ran until 1966. In re-runs, it introduced whole new generations to the world of Bonnie Meadow Road, its gag-filled scenarios and sitcom-inspiring pleasures.

Illusions were very much at the heart of another kind of early television program. Game shows provided a sense of surprise and vicarious thrills, the lure of the roulette wheel without its immediate dangers. Beside the inherent drama embedded in their formats, game shows like *Twenty-One*, *Tic Tac Dough* and *Dotto* fed a popular craving for simple story lines and likable regular folk who might win big money in games of chance or skill. The problem? The shows were rigged. One of the primary "quiz show scandals" that defined the era was very much a local story. *Twenty-One* was, for a time, the most popular show on the air. The co-creator of *Twenty-One*, Dan Enright, lived on Colvin Road in Scarsdale. The producer, Albert Freedman lived in New Rochelle. Enright had a background in radio and knew how to generate suspense with the right theatrical flourishes. Freedman, suave and well-dressed, understood what the public wanted to see: strong characters and even stronger story lines. Together, they tapped the potential of the new medium, especially game shows, by also bringing in large number of viewers and advertisers. The trick behind the contest, which was full of artificial theatricality, was to ensure certain popular contestants stayed on the show by feeding them questions in advance, then stage-managing an air of suspense and drama.[5]

The quiz show began unraveling in 1956 when a former contestant on *Twenty-One*, Herb Stempel, disgruntled by his "loss" to a more popular contender, blew the whistle. It was later revealed that his opponent, Charles Van Doren, a well-spoken and charming university instructor, had been given the answers before the show went on the air. As fraud in the infant television industry was exposed and other quiz shows were cancelled as a result, the nation was shocked to find that programs were using very old tricks to make money in the new medium.

Enright coached contestants on how to bite their lips when they appeared to be stumped for an answer, and he turned off the air-conditioning in the "isolation booth" to make contestants perspire.[6] Freedman had a knack for finding talent—and when he spotted Van Doren at a party, he enlisted the young academic to join the show, leading to a big boost in ratings.

After the scandal exploded and a grand jury investigated the claims, Enright finally admitted to deception in 1959 when called to testify in Washington, D.C. "A degree of deception is of considerable value in producing shows," he explained to Congressional investigators.[7] More explicit was Albert Freedman, the producer of *Twenty-One*. Driven from his home in New Rochelle—and facing potential criminal sanctions on a perjury charge—Freedman landed in Mexico City, where he penned a missive on the ethics of show business. It stands as a manifesto on the fine art of flimflam.

Though he was under indictment for perjury when he wrote the letter, Freedman exuded bravado. He said popular entertainment since its inception had relied on "showmanship, spectacle and illusion," and television was merely following in that tradition. "The only function of entertainment is to entertain," he wrote. "Everyone knows that the magician doesn't saw the lady in half, that movies supposedly filmed in Egypt are actually shot in Hollywood studios." The use of deception was common in other public media, he added. "Our only error was that we were too successful."[8] The new chairman of the Federal Communications Commission took a dim view of it all when he was appointed to lead the oversight agency in the scandal's aftermath. Newton Minow, in a scathing 1961 indictment, called television "a vast wasteland, a procession of game shows, violence, formula comedies about totally unbelievable families, blood and thunder, mayhem, violence, sadism, murder … more violence and cartoons. And endlessly, commercials—many screaming, cajoling and offending."[9] Despite Minow's grim assessment, it seems clear Freedman's philosophy of television entertainment has carried the day.

Freedman, Van Doren and a handful of other participants in the quiz show scandal faced perjury charges for giving less than candid testimony to a New York grand jury. The charges were eventually dropped. Enright got back into the business after a lengthy hiatus, and Freedman went into erotic publishing. Van Doren—the prime focus of the scandal—later called the experience "agony," and his tribulations became an object lesson on the dangers of celebrity, one of many that would mark the modern media era.[10]

Ed Sullivan, the man who famously introduced the King of Rock 'n' Roll on his television show as "Elvin Presley" and routinely mangled the names of well-known performers, catalyzed many of the forces of the emerging culture and brought them into American living rooms.

Growing up in Port Chester, where he moved from the city as a boy, Sullivan played sports with blacks, Irish, Jews and Italians. The working-class town imbued him with a commitment to perseverance and hard work his entire life.[11] He also caddied at the Apawamis Club in tonier Rye and contributed sports items to the local paper for $1 an article. An excellent athlete, he established a decent record as an amateur boxer. He went on to become a sportswriter and then a theater columnist—taking over from Walter Winchell, his future nemesis—before his television show made him a household name. Shy, awkward and beset with stage fright—and no one's idea of a charming host—Sullivan was known as "the great stone face" and was said to be a man who could brighten a room simply by leaving it. He was once compared, unfavorably, to frozen food.[12] But he had his own mysterious ingredients for success on television: a deep earnestness and a humble demeanor that connected with an audience that found merit in those traits. Nobody was quite sure what he did, but it worked on the small screen.

Sullivan and his theater gossip column rival, Walter Winchell, came to be the great gatekeepers of the evolving culture of the period, representing its different priorities and mannerisms. Winchell, who had a home in Hartsdale where his wife and children lived, came to embody the dark side of the American media—arrogant, reckless and cruel—and he used his Broadway gossip column as a club against anyone who stood in his way. He put up an electric fence around the Hartsdale property on Fort Hill Road to discourage sightseers—and enemies—from getting too close.[13] Sullivan and Winchell engaged in one of the longest running and widely reported feuds of the modern entertainment era, a conflict that reached titanic proportions. Sullivan once said of his rival, "I despise Walter Winchell because he symbolizes to me evil and treacherous things in the American setup."[14]

Though they were wildly different men, Sullivan and Winchell were the two most prominent practitioners of a new kind of personality-driven entertainment, one that became increasingly central to modern American culture. It began in print, grew louder on radio, but found full expression on television. The medium amplified an already insatiable interest in celebrity, creating a seemingly intimate connection between the public and the stars who shined brightly on the screen.

Westchester had a long history with celebrities, especially Broadway stars. During the days of vaudeville, song-and-dance man Eddie Foy bought a home in New Rochelle in 1904 on the Post Road, later on Weyman Avenue, where he raised seven children who often performed with him on the road. Following his lead, a number of other stage performers settled in New Rochelle. After his death in 1928 at the age of 71, he was buried in New Rochelle.[15]

Billie Burke, a leading stage actress and one of the stars of *The Wizard of Oz,* and Florenz Ziegfeld, a Broadway impresario, kept house at a Hastings estate near Farragut Avenue from 1916 until the stock market crash of 1929, and their estate had a menagerie that included bears, ponies, rare birds, buffaloes and an elephant. Ziegfeld was known for driving a tan-colored Rolls Royce around town, leaving punctually at the same time every day.[16]

Lou Gehrig, the pride of the Yankees, bought a colonial-style home on Circuit Road in New Rochelle in the late 1920s and lived in the area until shortly before his death in 1941. Babe Ruth was a regular visitor to the Gehrig homestead.[17] Jazz performer Cab Calloway raised his family at a home on Knollwood Road in Greenburgh beginning in 1956, and Duke Ellington, Lena Horne, Nat King Cole, Sammy Davis, Jr., and Dizzy Gillespie all passed through the 12-room house, among other African American entertainers and notables.[18]

Jackie Gleason, indulging his interest in outer space, built a futurist home on Furnace Dock Road in Cortlandt in 1959, not far from the residence of composer Aaron Copeland. The comic actor made famous in *The Honeymooners* and Broadway musicals would entertain fellow comedians like Milton Berle and cast members from his shows. He was known in the area for occasionally drinking his way up and down the Albany Post Road.[19]

Other ambitious characters moved out to the suburbs in part to give free reign to their outsized interests, creative and otherwise. Theodore Dreiser, the author of *Sister Carrie* and *An American Tragedy*, built a large stone home in Mount Kisco that he redesigned repeatedly, a product of his changing whims. Beginning in 1929 and into the 1940s, Dreiser held expansive literary gatherings at the estate he named Iroki, Japanese for beauty.[20] The author visited the death house at Sing Sing to provide material for his execution scene in *An American Tragedy*, and sued Paramount Pictures over the treatment of his novel in a White Plains courthouse.[21]

Robert Ripley, a cartoonist who created the *Believe It or Not* series that gained immense popularity in the daily press, bought a small island off Mamaroneck in 1934, calling it BION, the name of his comic strip series and later franchise. Ripley stocked his new home with crates of curios—shrunken heads, animal skeletons, unusual weapons and other odd artifacts from his travels around the world. His Chinese-like sailboat, which he named, Mon Lei, plied the waters of Long Island Sound.[22]

William Marston gained fame for the most popular female comic-book creation in American popular culture, Wonder Woman. A psychologist and early innovator in the field of polygraphs and other devices aimed at detecting deceit, Marston held a fascination—perhaps even an fetishistic obsession—with the concept of powerful women, bondage and sexual peril that he channeled into his comic work. He also had a very unusual love life: beginning in 1935 he lived together with his wife, Holloway, and mistress, Olive Byrne, in an old farmhouse on Oakland Beach Avenue in Rye for a number of years.[23]

Fascination with the vulnerabilities of celebrities, as gossip writers like Ed Sullivan and Walter Winchell knew only too well, was creating a new kind of American spectacle. The weddings and childcare problems of big stars, especially sex symbols, were especially potent dramas, and inspired two of the more high-wattage paparazzi events on record in the county.

In a little room in White Plains, the most famous woman in America got married. The bride wore a conservative skirt, matched with a pink sweater and patent-leather high heels. The groom wore thick glasses and a pained smile. It was one of the strangest weddings of all time, an unlikely union in holy matrimony between a movie star and a literary legend. Marilyn Monroe and Arthur Miller: Hollywood bombshell meets Brooklyn brains.

Miller and Monroe met in 1951 through a mutual friend, director Elia Kazan. She was 25 and he was 35, and an intense bond sprang up between them. Miller fell under Monroe's spell, captivated by what he later called in his memoirs "the vitality of a force one does not understand."[24] Monroe, who had a literary streak underneath her sex-bomb persona, came to depend on Miller for emotional support and yearned to join him in a quiet, steady life surrounded by books and old things.

Monroe's marriage to Joe DiMaggio had ended a few years before, and Miller shed his first wife in a Nevada divorce in 1956, clearing the final obstacle for marriage later that year. Rumors that the two were headed for the altar caused a sensation.

The couple holed up at Miller's country home in Roxbury, Connecticut, where the press camped out on their doorstep. The celebrity press had put the odd match under constant scrutiny, infuriating the high-minded playwright. The two eventually decided to tie the knot as expeditiously as possible to end the media circus.

It turned out Westchester had a front row seat for the whole, strange affair when the pair stopped in for a quickie wedding at the County Courthouse in White Plains on June 29, 1956. The wedding was preceded by a tragedy, the death of a society reporter shadowing the couple, which seemed to cast a bad omen on the marriage from the very first day. Monroe and Miller were headed back to Roxbury for a press conference to tell the media they were not going to announce a marriage date. On the rush to the Roxbury farmhouse, a press car carrying reporter Mara Scherbatoff, 48, the New York bureau chief for the *Paris-Match* magazine, crashed into a tree while in pursuit of a car she thought carried Miller and Monroe.[25] Scherbatoff was the daughter of an aristocratic Russian navy admiral and was born a Romanoff princess. She was partially thrown from the vehicle and horribly injured. Monroe and Miller rushed to her aid, with Miller assisting in removing her from the wreckage before calling an ambulance. Other photographers took photos and film footage of the mortally stricken journalist, soon to expire in a Connecticut hospital, with Marilyn captured running from the scene.[26] It was a grisly and portentous tableau, a media spectacle feeding on itself, and an early reminder of the steady and constant pressure of tabloid culture on those it worships, and the cost it can extract.

The evening wedding inside the judge's chambers was over in four minutes. A witness noted that Monroe's lipstick "had been obliterated, as if she had been chewing her lips nervously."[27] A bottle of Champagne provided by Miller's attorney added the only festive note to an otherwise perfunctory occasion. Three days later, Miller held a religious wedding ceremony in Waccabuc, in the town of Lewisboro near Katonah, at the home of his literary agent, Kay Brown. Rabbi Robert Goldberg of New Haven performed the ceremony in front of 25 guests. Monroe had converted to Judaism for the service, following a short tutorial by a rabbi on the faith. "Marilyn Monroe having sought to join the household of Israel by accepting the religion of Israel and promising to live by its principles and practices, was received into the Jewish faith on July 1, 1956," reads her certificate of conversion.[28]

In front of the wedding guests in Waccabuc, she read a passage from the Book of Ruth: "whither thou goest, I will go; and where thou lodgest, I will lodge; thy people shall be my people, and thy God my God."[29] Lee Strasberg, Monroe's acting coach, gave the bride away. At the end of the ceremony, Monroe, wearing a beige chiffon wedding dress, said, "I do," and drank a sip of red wine; Miller crushed the symbolic glass with his foot.[30]

Monroe soon grew bored with the role of a country housewife, however, and Miller found Monroe's emotional demands, her "childish voracity," as he described it, difficult to take. The two divorced in 1961. Miller continued to work from his Connecticut home. Monroe died of a drug overdose in 1962. The famed playwright, who had remarried, declined to attend the funeral of the movie queen he had once promised to love, honor and cherish for life.

Another similarly bizarre spectacle that brought the tabloids to Westchester involved the custody of the two small children of Rita Hayworth, the siren-haired actress. Hayworth seemed to have it all as a screen legend and pin-up queen, hailed at one time as one of the most dazzling and desirable women ever seen on film. But a public persona rarely reveals the woman behind it, and Hayworth's private life was anything but a walk on the red carpet. The early 1950s, when she was raising two young children while enmeshed in a film career and her fourth troubled marriage, was a particularly messy time in her life. Yasmin Khan, 4, and Rebecca Welles, 9, were the daughters of Prince Aly Khan, a wealthy diplomat, and director Orson Welles, respectively.[31]

Hayworth had been evicted from a Greenwich, Connecticut, mansion for nonpayment of rent in early 1954, and she and her then husband, the actor and singer Dick Haymes, relocated to New York. Before taking a trip to the Florida Keys, Hayworth left her two young children in the care of a White Plains woman, Dorothy Chambers, who was friends with Haymes' family and ran a local antiques business. While unconventional,

it was fairly typical of the more relaxed parenting standards of the day.[32] No one ever claimed the children were mistreated while they stayed with Chambers. But the older child had resided in New York State for over a month without any provisions made for her schooling, contrary to educational regulations, and someone claimed to have seen Yasmin playing in the middle of Central Park Avenue one day, an alarming sight on the six-lane thoroughfare.[33] Enter the Society for the Prevention of Cruelty to Children—followed by Aly Khan, Orson Welles, and every other tabloid newspaper photographer in the New York metropolitan region. The parenting abilities of the rich and famous have always made news, and a domestic scandal involving Hayworth and her renowned ex-husbands was tailor-made for gossip enthusiasts.

The two youngsters were swiftly placed in the care of the county's social-service agency, and two weeks into her Florida trip, Hayworth rushed back to New York to regain custody of her children from the county. Khan came to White Plains and stayed in a downtown hotel. Welles sent his lawyer and offered a statement that Hayworth was "a loving and caring mother."[34]

Children's Court Judge George Smyth reviewed the facts and legal arguments from Hayworth's lawyer and determined she could

Rita Hayworth came to White Plains in 1954 to regain custody of her two young daughters. The children were left without proper supervision while Hayworth and her husband took a trip, and child-welfare officials stepped in to investigate. Hayworth, hidden behind her sunglasses, was in tears when she left a judge's chambers in the county office building with her children, mobbed by hundreds of spectators (Westchester County Historical Society).

have her children back on the stipulation she provide schooling for them and more stringent oversight of their care. Smyth noted that the charges "did not allege willful neglect on the part of the mother nor that she was not a proper guardian." While the judge's ruling went in her favor, Hayworth's trial had not ended, as was made clear when she walked out the door of the county office building. A large mob ringed the offices, while hundreds more spectators stared out of open windows to catch a glimpse of the starlet and Haymes in their moment of parental shame. A crowd of curious onlookers tussled and made noise as the shamed couple walked away—"fought, ran and screamed for a glimpse of the principals," in the words of one account.[35] The incident recalled the short novel by Nathanael West that explored the psychology of the crowd and its potential for malice. "There was a continuous roar of catcalls, laughter and yells, pierced occasionally by a scream," West wrote in *The Day of the Locust*. "At the sight of their heroes or heroines, the crowd would turn demoniac." Hayworth was heard to utter one line as she fought her way through the throng around the family court, escorted by lawyers and a large contingent of police. Her face running with tears, her famous brown eyes blocked by a pair of enormous sunglasses, the most beautiful woman in the world had only one request: "Please go away."[36]

The 1950s and early 60s are often characterized as a time of *yes, ma'am* sincerity, but there was far more subversion going on behind the facade of suburban normalcy. A new term entered the vocabulary: "juvenile delinquency." Despite the sanitized version of adolescence presented on TV shows like *Father Knows Best* and *Leave It to Beaver*, the period was also a golden era of teenage street gangs, violence and a generally hostile attitude toward the older forms of popular culture. The degenerate and anti-social behavior that shocked the parents of "the silent majority" took place in Westchester with a vengeance, and local cops had their hands full tracking down drag-racing maniacs, teenage miscreants and knife-wielding gang members. The older generation did what it could—banning Elvis Presley from the family television set, setting up task forces to go after lascivious comic books and writing newspaper columns about "the shook-up generation." But as is often the case, youth culture has a way of fighting back. Something had changed in the landscape of the American teenager in the late 1950s, though no one was quite sure why. The signs were everywhere, however. A seven-part series in the *New York Times* examined "The Shook-Up Generation" in 1958, helpfully providing a glossary of common teenage gang terms like "Cool it" and "Take it easy!"[37]

In the suburbs, the youth menace seemed to be everywhere. The Pleasantville Youth Center was forced to close in 1952 after young people wrecked the facility.[38] A New Rochelle bus company reported in 1954 that its buses were being trashed every day by knives and sharpened screw drivers, and drivers couldn't stop kids from smoking to and from school.[39] Vacant houses were the principal victims of youthful vandals, along with school windows, parking meters and unattended construction sites.

While property damage was the main source of concern, violence occasionally flared. Two young men were stabbed at a football game between New Rochelle and White Plains high schools in White Plains after 200 people ran from the stands and onto the field for a free-for-all brawl.[40]

There were many different explanations for the rise of juvenile delinquency, and the media was often a convenient scapegoat. The influence of television was regularly cited. A 1954 Senate subcommittee convened to investigate violent and lurid comic books, leading to a campaign of self-censorship among comic-book publishers.

Then there was Elvis Presley. Eugene Gilbert, a marketing consultant who did studies of youth culture and teenage buying habits in the 1950s, turned a critical eye on the King of Rock 'n' Roll and his followers. The gap between an older generation who had lived through the Depression and a world war, and the followers of the swivel-hipped pop star, could not have been wider. "Presley fans are shockingly unconcerned about the future. A large number had no answer when asked what he or she aspired to become in later life," Gilbert reported, branding Presley as an icon of arrested development. "In this netherworld between childhood and manhood, Elvis Presley emerges as a symbol of destruction."[41]

A local father, a newspaperman, was a little more blunt in his denunciation of Elvis the Pelvis. "You have seen the last of Elvis Presley," read the unsigned editorial that was described as a commentary on "so inflammable a subject as Elvis Presley's gyrations on television." The essay was described as reflecting the "consternation of many a parent" on the new kind of popular culture taking over the airwaves. The diatribe was written in the form of a letter from father to daughter after he watched a performance by the pompadoured pop star on television. It clearly shook him in a much different way: "It takes a lot to disgust your old man.... [After the program] I felt dirty and itched. That's the effect your Elvis Presley had on me. It was like being approached by a man who wanted to sell me 'filthy pictures.' From now on, Elvis Presley is censored in our house... . Your old man is a liberal guy, but on Sunday, he had it right up to here."[42]

Officials also got into the act. Beginning in the early 1950s, civic leaders began to mobilize. A meeting of law-enforcement officials, educators and social workers met in White Plains to address the concerns about violence on television, drugs, alcohol and broken homes—and to develop strategies to combat "Child Delinquency and Youth Crime," as the title of the colloquium at the Jewish Community Center was called.[43] Westchester County Executive Edward Michaelian created the post of a special assistant for youth services in 1962, aimed at coordinating the fight against troubled teens. Michaelian said new attention was needed to fight juvenile delinquency, which he saw as an inevitable outgrowth of the "increasing urbanization of Westchester."[44] Alas, the street corners and parking lots where teenagers hang out looking for trouble is a world where Senate subcommittees and "special assistants for youth services" rarely intrude. As the grouchy dad who hated Elvis Presley and Edward Michaelian were well aware, television and a new kind of music was becoming a potent force in the popular culture.

But the existing order wasn't going down without a fight. Like other guardians of moral order from an earlier age, authorities in White Plains reasserted old laws on dress codes in the late 1950s.

There were other tremors in the suburban landscape besides youth culture asserting itself in unruly ways. The status quo was changing everywhere—media, youth rebellion, hostility to the old order, and as the 50s and 60s progressed, the upending of longstanding racial norms of inequality.

New Rochelle was a seemingly idyllic suburban city as portrayed on *The Dick Van Dyke Show*, but the reality was a far different one for the city's minority students. For a time in the early 1960s, New Rochelle was at the center of a national controversy on integration, as the first Northern city to undergo a court-mandated change in educational policy. The high school went through a period of hostility that gave it more an appearance of an armed camp than a place for secondary education, and school board meetings descended into shouting matches.

Black parents had been protesting the use of segregated facilities in lower grades for a number of years, and a report commissioned by the board of education, headed by an NYU professor in 1957, declared the district was "derelict in its duties, and remiss in its attitudes."[45] It recommended the construction of new facilities and an end to the isolation of the black community. Of the city 72,000 residents at the time, some 9,000 were African American.

Parents who tried to enroll their kids in other schools besides the segregated Lincoln Elementary School found that they could face arrest by the police. There was a distinct sense that "separate" meant unequal.

A black insurance executive described what it was like to go to school at Lincoln, which was 94 percent black. "I guess I was happy there. But I suspect I was short-changed on education. I doubt the teachers wanted to stunt us, but they asked only a low level of performance. They used to have us sing 'Old Black Joe' and 'Swanee River' at assemblies. You had to get to high school to find out how much you didn't know."[46] The school board acted slowly without any clear directive, and eventually, a group of 11 black parents filed suit with the guidance of a 35-year-old black attorney, Paul Zuber. Wilbert and Hallie Taylor were the lead plaintiffs in the case that would have long-lasting consequences. *Taylor v. New Rochelle* eventually went to the Supreme Court and marked a major change in educational policy in Northern cities. In January 1961, Federal Judge Harold Kaufman ruled for the plaintiffs, the first time the courts had ruled against a Northern school district in a segregation case.

New Rochelle's education leaders were recalcitrant, insisting there was no intention to exclude black students from white elementary schools or deny blacks a quality education. The U.S. Supreme Court declined to overturn that initial ruling, the old Lincoln school was torn down, and black kids could attend other schools in the district. There was a great deal of tension as the racial drama played out. Conflict between students and the administration ran high, especially at the high school. Verbal assaults on teachers were common, and fights between black and white students were endemic. Football games were especially tense occasions. A self-described "goon-squad" of teachers was paid $10 for special duty to patrol home football games, on the lookout for racial disturbances. In addition, the school principal stationed himself on a nearby rooftop with a pair of binoculars in hand, scanning the crowds for trouble. "The faculty became so preoccupied with maintaining order that the teachers' real function—teaching—had to suffer," a *Life* magazine reporter observed in a lengthy chronicle of the New Rochelle desegregation woes. "It has not been easy, but progress has been made," the article concluded.[47]

The labor and the toll it took to achieve those kinds of results could be substantial. Perhaps the best known civil-rights advocate from Westchester, Dr. Errold Collymore, exemplified the kind of activism that moved blacks from second-class status in the suburbs.

Although he could have easily withdrawn from public life after the cross burning on his lawn in 1930 following the purchase of his home, and subsequent insults that came his way through the years, Collymore embraced his new hometown with ferocity, finding many fronts on which he could fight to improve life for African Americans.

In 1935, Collymore organized the first branch of the NAACP in White Plains. As a civil-rights leader, he sought to stop the practice of the newspaper in using the term "negress" when referring to black women, as well as appending the term "negro" with the lower case whenever it reported news about blacks. He got the paper to carry wedding announcements for black couples. He fought for better housing conditions and eventually ended the segregation of local movie theaters. He pushed the city to hire blacks in the ranks of the civil service, and the first black cop in White Plains was hired in 1946, as well as the first black teacher.[48] He ran for the school board in 1948. He pushed for equal pay for black sanitation workers, and he succeeded in getting black women into the nursing program at the county medical facility, Grasslands Hospital. He became a leader in the Community Unitarian Universalist Congregation in White Plains and was the first person of color, in 1954, to serve on the American Unitarian Association Board of Trustees. The Unitarians were among his closest allies in his home-ownership fight, coming every day to offer support and vigilance against troublemakers.[49]

Collymore fought to gain entry into the dental association and professional organizations that excluded blacks. A witty writer, he also corresponded with other black leaders of the era, offering encouragement and commiseration. On a personal level, Collymore was an ardent spokesman for hard work and discipline within the community. He used to joke that while he was filling the teeth of young black men and women, he was also filling their heads with the imperative of getting an education.

By the late 1950s, Collymore could see there had been progress. In a letter to Martin Luther King, Jr., in 1956, he wrote, "Negroes are breaking through everywhere…. When I came to this town 30 years ago, it was like any town in the deep south."[50]

He wrote another correspondent, "When I stop to think what things were like when I came here in 1926, and compare them with the great many changes and turns for the better today, I am greatly encouraged."[51]

He came to White Plains to raise a family, and he accomplished that, as well. It took dedication, and while Collymore put on a brave face to the outside world, his written correspondence suggests how the struggle could leave scars. There was anger and bitterness behind the facade of the gracious and well-tailored suburban dentist. "I have been slugging it out all these years," he once wrote to Carl Murphy, editor of the *Afro-American*, a newspaper, and the slugging had left a deep impression.[52]

He had little patience for those who did not share his commitment. "If we did not have the usual 'quota' of Uncle Toms here we might have over the years made more progress," he wrote in one letter.[53] There was also plenty of anger: "I just can't understand how those crackers can justify any claim to good sense, decency, Christianity or just plain belonging to the human race," he wrote in an April, 24, 1958 letter to Hilda Proctor of Montgomery, Alabama. "Sometimes it looks to me that God is in cahoots with the damned crackers…. The more I see the less I have any real faith that anybody gives a damn about what happens to us. But—I must be in a dark mood tonight—all I can see right now is the unholy fact that crackers are past masters at the art of all that's evil, vicious, inhuman and just plain dirty!"[54]

Despite the very real hardships he encountered, he did find solace. As he once wrote to a loved one, "My deep and hard experiences of life have given me understanding and sympathy for everyone else. In spite of the pain and scars, I think I'm serenely happy." When he died at the age of 79 in 1972 from stomach cancer, he was interred in the Westchester soil he had fought so hard to make his own.[55]

Organized crime was another durable part of suburbia that blistered its smooth veneer. During the 1950s and 60s, the Mafia exerted control over New York and its suburbs and consolidated its grip on the underworld. The mob bosses took control over the garbage and carting industry, using the lucrative field to branch out into other forms of legitimate and not-so legitimate enterprises.

A notorious gangland slaying that remains the area's great unsolved murder was the assassination of Johnny Acropolis by a presumed Mafia hitman. Two bullets were fired from a .38 caliber revolver into the back of Acropolis' head in the early morning hours of April 26, 1952, "from just steps away," according to the county coroner's report. It was a classic Mafia-style assassination.[56]

Acropolis had been tangled up in the battle for control over the garbage business in southern Westchester. One of his main adversaries was Nick Rattenni, Sr., identified by federal investigators as a top leader in the Genovese crime family, which, along with the Gambino family, exerted control in Westchester. "Cock-Eyed" Nick, who played golf and often wagered high stakes on the driving ranges of exclusive country clubs, was the man who ran the mob in the suburbs during the heyday of the Mafia control of the New York metropolitan region.[57]

According to an obituary upon his death at the age of 76 in 1982—compiled in part from federal testimony and law enforcement sources—Rattenni built up

Magdalene Lewis Collymore, the second wife of Dr. Errold Collymore, was at his side in White Plains when he embarked on a civil-rights campaign. A Sunday school teacher, artist and actress, she married Dr. Collymore in 1944, around the time this photograph was taken (Collymore Family Collection).

the mob franchise in the county after he first arrived in Yonkers in the 1940s. "It had already been divided into small fiefdoms with an understanding between hoods that each section was controlled by one crime family or individual," law enforcement authorities told the press. "Throughout his lifetime, Rattenni gradually consolidated operations. At his death [in 1982], he ruled alone."[58]

Rattenni had lifelong eye problems and routinely wore dark glasses, hence his nickname, "Cock-Eyed" Nick. He had a lengthy arrest record beginning as a young man. Born in 1906, he was first arrested at age 20 in White Plains on suspicion of burglary. The same year he was arrested in Manhattan on grand larceny, and again in 1927, on assault and robbery. He eventually served a seven year sentence at Sing Sing.[59]

Moving to Westchester from the Bronx, Rattenni worked the underworld rackets—loan-sharking, gambling, waste-hauling—and laundered the money through real estate ventures. The feds described him as a captain in the Genovese crime family, and called him one of a new breed of Mafia leaders, complete with a respectable facade and the outward appearance of a suburban professional. He lived with his second wife, Evelyn, on a 12-acre property on Rockledge Avenue in the west end of Yonkers, with a putting green and driving range in his backyard.[60] He also had top legal advice—his lawyer was Roy Cohn, one of the top defense lawyers of the era, who specialized in keeping Mafia defendants out of jail.

After moving up the ranks of the Genovese family, where he was a close associate of Frank Costello, Rattenni adopted a common Westchester pastime: He made his own golf clubs and spent hours on the links at the Willow Ridge Country Club in Harrison. His love of golf incorporated his taste for gambling, making bets on matches he played, as well as running illicit gambling operations around the county. But when it came to running the garbage industry in Yonkers—and later most of Westchester County—Cock-Eyed Nick did not take chances.[61]

Rattenni was the president of Westchester Carting Company, an outfit that did not like competition in any shape or form. John Acropolis was one such competitor. Handsome and athletically gifted, Acropolis was not his real name. An orphan from New York City, he had a name bestowed on him at age three when orphanage workers had trouble with his original Greek name and called him "Acropolis" instead. It was fitting for someone who was good at scaling heights. After a stint at the Leake and Watts Children's Home in Yonkers, Acropolis was taken in by a foster couple from that city. A star athlete, he captained the Yonkers High School basketball team to a state championship. He was a standout student leader and athlete at Colgate University, which he attended on an athletic scholarship.[62] Acropolis drove a truck to earn money during summer vacations from college, his first exposure to the trucking business. As a young man, he made his name in the Teamster leadership when he joined a reform ticket that ousted a group of old-time union executives in 1941. He later became president of Teamsters Local 456, one of the most powerful in the nation, overseeing the work of some 30,000 laborers all over the New York area in a variety of trades. Acropolis earned the nickname "Little Caesar" for his ambitious and heavy-fisted rise through the ranks of the Teamster leadership. "I like a good fight," he once told students at Manhattan College, where he had taken some graduate classes. When the son of state senator William Condon, who was an opponent of union policies, was beaten up inside a Yonkers bar where Acropolis was present, he testified he saw nothing. Acropolis dated a Radio City Music Hall Rockette, and he kept a pearl-handled revolver in easy reach, but he was neither a mob boss nor a racketeer like the men who were taking over the carting and trucking businesses in the New York metropolitan area in the 1950s.[63]

After a 1949 garbage strike in Yonkers, city leaders voted to suspend municipal waste collection and turn the garbage business over to private contractors. Acropolis set up a company called Rex Carting, which would employ Local 456 members, to pick up the garbage in Yonkers.

The other union in the game—Local 27 from the Bronx—was a mobbed-up outfit affiliated with Rattenni that also wanted the Yonkers contract. Trucks belonging to Rex Carting started to get torched, and the businesses they served ended up looted. It was clear what Acropolis was up against.[64]

Acropolis, 43, was walking from his car to his apartment with a Colgate alumni newsletter and a freshly pressed suit under in his arm. It was 2:30 in the morning, and as he crossed the threshold of his apartment, he was shot dead—two rounds fired into his head at close range.[65]

Acropolis' funeral drew 10,000 mourners, and his killing brought the dangers of a spreading criminal enterprise into the full light of day. His business was bought out by

Rattenni's company a few weeks later, and organized crime eventually controlled some 80 to 90 percent of the Westchester County garbage business for decades, according to a later assessment by state investigators.[66]

"Cock-Eyed" Nick Rattenni was extensively questioned, and it became clear that Acropolis had been murdered as part of an underworld takeover. But the hunt for Acropolis" killer went cold. A revolver that appeared to be the murder weapon was found on the grounds of his apartment complex in 1958. It had been reported stolen from a Navy supply ship on the New Jersey waterfront. Reports persisted long after the crime that Yonkers police had identified a suspect in the killing but never pursued an arrest.

"Joey Surprise" Feola was a mob soldier living in Mamaroneck and later White Plains who was also tied up in the waste and hauling industry. His company had the contract with Mamaroneck for garbage hauling, and a rather ambitious man, he looked to branch out into new territory. He came to a very bad end. Growing up in the Bronx, Feola was arrested in connection with the killing in 1931 of a New York City police sergeant who interrupted a restaurant hold-up.[67] Due to his age, he was given a short prison sentence on a gun possession charge. Feola was also shot by a New York City cop in 1934 during another robbery attempt.[68]

Feola belonged to the Genovese crime family and worked under the tutelage of Rattenni in Westchester. Aiming to take control of a lucrative solid-waste contract in New Jersey, he ran afoul of the Gambino clan and "disappeared" in 1965 at the age of 53. While his fate was never certain, a wiretap of New Jersey mobsters almost certainly gave an account of his death, as they described an upcoming hit on an unidentified mobster while the feds listened in. Feola was apparently lured to a garage in Kenilworth, New Jersey (in territory belonging to the DeCavalcante crime organization), where he was promptly strangled to death. His body was then placed in an old station wagon that was sent to a nearby auto-crushing plant.[69] Shortly after his disappearance, U.S. District Attorney Robert Morgenthau launched an investigation into the Westchester carting business that found it was nearly under the complete control of organized crime. The Genovese outfit—under the control of Vito Genovese—was the main operator, along with some Gambino representation.[70]

Another victim of the mob wars in Westchester was a soldier affiliated with the Genovese family. Salvatore Carta, a 34-year-old Yonkers man born in Italy, was found dead in a car on the side of Route 9 in Montrose in August 1969, shot once in the head.[71] Authorities said he was involved in shaking down bar and restaurant owners in Yonkers, and when he was arrested, cops found a rifle, two shotguns and a pair of brass knuckles. Carta was also involved in the theft of heavy construction equipment at the time of his death.[72]

Joseph Gambino, the cousin of mob boss Carlo Gambino, took up the family trade and secured control of the garbage business in Mount Vernon.[73] The "Mob surcharge" on doing business and carrying out municipal services was substantial. Local businesses paid exorbitant fees for garbage pick-up and had no recourse to find competitors. Mob penetration of local government in some cases reached alarming levels. The town of Greenburgh, most notably, was at the center of a number of embarrassing disclosures: that its garbage contract had been steered to a company founded by an imprisoned criminal, its town sanitation foreman was closely connected to the mob's numbers racket, and gambling and illegal dumping were taking place up and down Route 119, Tarrytown Road.[74]

State investigators found that Yonkers was losing $1 million a year under the crooked rule of Cock-Eyed Nick Rattenni in the 1960s, with refuse from Yonkers residents being trucked to the county landfill in Croton, while he used the city incinerator for his own enterprises.[75]

As the Mafia wars demonstrated, garbage disposal and solid-waste removal was big business, as well as an integral part of American industry. Decades of commercial growth, along with generations of residential development, were creating mountains of garbage, pools of industrial slurry, and trenches of toxins. When the 1960s dawned, there seemed to be an explosion of noxious waste in Westchester. It was hard to miss.

11

The Age of Dissent
The Environmental Movement,
Radical Chic and the Moonies

There was something going on at Indian Point. The smell was horrendous and clumps of dead fish moldered in the sun. Huge flocks of crows could be seen circling the plant, a winged army of scavengers.

Nuclear power came to Westchester as America embraced the concept of peaceful atomic energy. In the years after World War II, as the county's population rose substantially, Con Edison made the prediction that the burgeoning new region would demand huge amounts of energy, and nuclear power would fill the gap. In 1955, Con Edison announced it would be the first private utility in America to build a nuclear plant, assured of the value of the new technology and convinced that the growing New York suburbs needed a far more abundant supply of electricity as it grew by leaps and bounds.

The utility found a perfect site for its nuclear plant: an old amusement park in the village of Buchanan where excursionists would come by ferry, called Indian Point. It had access to large amounts of water necessary for cooling the plant equipment, and it had a very amenable local government. In early 1957, when Con Edison broke ground at Indian Point, Buchanan had 525 homes and two full-time cops. According to a 1965 census, there was not a single black resident of Buchanan, the only such community among 44 cities, towns and villages of Westchester.[1] Thanks to the revenues pumped into the village treasury, Buchanan would become one of the least taxed communities in the region, and village leaders were eager to exploit the opportunity.

Construction was a massive undertaking. A vast pit 70 feet deep was dug to house the reactor vessel, resting on a foundation that was formed from 6,000 cubic yards of concrete.[2] Power lines were stretched to Millwood, where the juice would flow to the rest of the county. In May 1960, the 230-ton reactor, built in Ohio arrived by barge, and the plant "went critical," achieving nuclear fission at 5:42 p.m., August 2, 1962.[3] It was two years behind schedule. Full power was achieved in January 1963. The plant's productivity so impressed management at Con Edison that the utility was planning to build six other reactors in and around Buchanan, and discussions were even held about building a nuclear reactor in Queens, directly opposite the Upper East Side of Manhattan.[4]

Then something started happening with the fish. There were huge piles of dead marine life, rotting at a dump near the plant. Con Edison kept the scope of the problem hidden. But by the spring of 1963, official recognition of the fish kill was too obvious to

An aerial view of the Indian Point nuclear plant in Buchanan before its completion in 1962. Old Navy ships due to be scrapped—the so-called "Ghost Fleet"—can be seen in the background (Westchester County Historical Society).

be denied, and the utility acknowledged that a significant number of striped bass, carp, smelt, herring, perch, and a few shad, had been slaughtered by the plant's machinery.[5]

The nuclear reactor, which drew in water from the Hudson as part of its cooling mechanisms, also released warm water into the river. The warm water made fish lethargic, then drew them into the intake system where they were killed. The scope of the problem was keep secret, while Con Edison engineers and fishery consultants devised a screening system to minimize the problem. Representative Richard Ottinger, a congressman from Irvington, finally brought national attention to the issue and estimated that "hundreds of thousands to millions" of fish had been killed at Indian Point, calling it a cover-up.[6]

The nuclear plant at Indian Point, and plans to build another one on the Hudson, set the stage for a major struggle on the fate of the environment. Westchester was in the middle of the debate, and figures from the county played a seminal role in the creation of the environmental movement that eventually took shape to safeguard the river and other natural spaces like it. As the battle progressed, strategy was plotted around a kitchen table in Irvington.

Carl Carmer was a man of contrasts, very much like the Westchester community in which he lived. Born in the Finger Lakes region of New York, he earned degrees from

Hamilton College and Harvard University. Familiar in the ways of academia and *belles lettres*, he taught English literature and worked as an editor at *Vanity Fair*. Educated, worldly and cosmopolitan, he held on to a rustic streak that leavened his sophistication, and he delighted in nature and collecting stories from the unpolished natives of backwater regions along the Hudson and elsewhere. Books of folklore and ghost stories poured from his pen, and the home he bought in Westchester reflected his idiosyncratic nature.[7] The large and eccentric house in Irvington was built in the shape of an octagon by an unknown architect for reasons that remain obscure. The home's quirky design would be the prelude to its latter-day historical significance as a central location in the early environmental movement.

Built in 1860 and expanded to five stories by a tea merchant in 1872, the structure looks like a finely adorned Victorian chapeau, architecture as millinery, and it rises to a whimsical peak atop a grand dome in a defiance of architectural convention. The Octagon House has been variously described as the "Taj Mahal of the Hudson Valley" and a "pastry chef's nightmare."[8] Carmer moved into the house in 1946, and frequent guests included Charles Sheeler, the painter of modernist industrial tableaus who also lived in Irvington (previously in South Salem), and poet William Carlos Williams. Otherworldly visitors were also welcomed. A ghost regularly made its presence known to Carmer and his wife, Elizabeth, an artist, who came calling from the underworld wearing a particular scent— "an exquisite and unidentifiable fragrance." Carmer saw apparitions while performing dinner chores. He wrote that he once caught sight of a ghostly presence while sent to buy a pint of vanilla ice cream in Dobbs Ferry. He followed the female phantom dressed in white down Broadway through traffic, as she disappeared ascending the hill toward the campus of The Masters School.[9]

Carmer saw ghosts where others saw only rush-hour traffic, but his contrarian vision would attract many sympathetic followers in the years to come. He deeply loved the Hudson River and wrote about the backwoods denizens who lived along its banks, collecting their folklore and stories. "Folklore is the poetry of the common mind," he once observed.[10]

Carmer and others were galvanized when Con Edison plans to build a massive hydroelectric plant on Storm King Mountain, some 20 miles north of Westchester, were made public in September 1962. The plant would hollow out the mountain, a majestic natural feature named for its commanding presence and the way it seemed to predict what the weather would be. Once operating, it would pump energy through highly visible power lines running down the Westchester shoreline of the Hudson. Carmer and like-minded conservationists held a number of meetings at his home. On November 8, 1963, the group officially formed the Scenic Hudson Preservation Conference, which was later renamed Scenic Hudson. The founders, coming together to create a kind of environmental Declaration of Independence, pledged to do everything in their power to block the construction of the plant. It would be a long and difficult fight, using the law as well as the powers of public persuasion. Eventually, the Irvington group created the legal framework that became the cornerstone of environmental activism for decades to come. The modern conservation movement, driven by an eclectic but determined group of conservatives and visionaries, owed much to the meeting in the Octagon House.

Besides Carmer, there were other committed activists devoted to the beauty of the region. Far from being liberal activists, the group skewed toward the Republican side of the political spectrum, and many were women. Of the 18 or so attendees who showed up at the Octagon House, a lively cross section of middle-class and upper-middle-class women drawn from the fields of law, business, media and cultures predominated.[11] It was a very Westchester mix.

Leo Rothschild was a Manhattan lawyer and avid hiker who had fought preservation battles for decades, and he served on a regional trail conference. Robert Burnap, from Hastings, was a naturalist and public relations director for the Audubon Society. Harry Nees, who lived in Somers at the end of his life, was an insurance executive from New Jersey, a hiker and head of the regional trail association. Virginia Guthrie was an antiques dealer and former actress who had studied under Sanford Meisner while she lived in Greenwich Village. She was a neighbor of the Carmers in Irvington. When she died in 2006, she was the last remaining member of the original group.[12]

Franny Reese, who lived in Dutchess County, would become the public face of the group. A graduate of Barnard College, she was considered one of the grand dames of the Hudson Valley, connected to the patrician landowners that traced their origins to the earliest Dutch and English settlers.[13] Rothschild was elected president of the group, and Carmer was named honorary chairman. Besides the founding members of Scenic Hudson in Carmer's living room, there were other allies and supporters of the cause.

Robert Boyle was the outdoors columnist for *Sports Illustrated* magazine. Living in Croton, he developed a keen, almost obsessive, desire to understand the ebb and flow of the Hudson River and the fish life within it. He was particularly drawn to Haverstraw Bay, the wide section of the river off Croton. He was often the first boater on the water in the spring, and the last off the river when winter cloaked its banks with ice and snow.

"If I have a wish about the Hudson, it is to know the bay in its entirety, to know every fish, every crab and shrimp, every bird and every plant, and to mark their shifts and movements with the ebb and flow of tide and change of season," he wrote. "The bay is an incredible place, and it is subject to so many variables, to so many unknowns and rhythms as yet unperceived that it exhausts the imagination. One would have to be God to see it all."[14]

Boyle even built an aquarium in his home to keep specimens of the fish he had caught in Haverstraw Bay and observe their behavior. As a journalist and advocate, he brought a crusading zeal to the Storm King fight, and he published a number of damning exposés on the environmental damage inflicted by Con Edison. He also founded a fisherman's organization in 1966, the Hudson River Fisherman's Association, the forerunner to Riverkeeper, the environmental watchdog group.

Pete Seeger gave the movement its poetic inspiration and rallying cry. He grew up in an affluent and musical household in Manhattan, attending a Connecticut prep school and Harvard. As one of the early leaders of the folk revival of the 1950s and 60s, Seeger became a 20th century troubadour who expressed political and social dissent in his high "split-tenor" and with a five-string banjo. Appalled at the condition of the Hudson River, Seeger, who lived along the shores of the Hudson in Beacon, New York, in 1966 said he would "build a boat to save the river,"[15] perhaps a reference to another boat builder with outsized ambitions from the Old Testament. The sloop was christened with water from the Hudson and named the Clearwater. Seeger and fellow musicians held small-scale fundraisers beginning in 1965 (at the Lyndhurst estate in Tarrytown) to promote the Clearwater and its educational programs, as the "Hudson Valley Folk Picnic."[16] The annual music festival later named for the *Clearwater* sloop was held every year at Croton Point beginning in 1978 (as well as a few times at the Westchester Community College campus in Valhalla). Seeger's radical associations clashed with Carl Carmer's more conservative inclinations, and Carmer did his best to distance Seeger from the fledgling environmental group, but the grassroots enthusiasm was an important factor in the movement.[17]

Folk music was a useful tool to spread the word, but it was in the courtroom—and the court of public opinion—that the fate of the Hudson Highlands would be decided. The fight was a long one, and Con Edison had the tacit approval of government regulators to do as it pleased with long-term plans to build power stations up and down the river. Casually dismissive of Octagon House opposition, the utility sent out a press release in 1964 calling opponents "misinformed bird watchers, nature fakers, land grabbers and militant adversaries of progress."[18]

Though Con Edison had the establishment on their side, the upstart preservationists had the power of natural beauty on theirs, as well as a rising anxiety that the natural world was in grave danger. They also had a command of well-honed language and public persuasion at their disposal, allied to a growing perception that the onslaught of urbanization was a threat to the nation.

As Carmer put it in 1964 testimony at the Federal Power Commission, "If these threats are carried out, something of the quality in the American character will be replaced by an emptiness that can never be filled.... The Hudson answers a spiritual need, more necessary to the nation's health than all the commercial products it can provide, than all the money it can earn."[19]

Rothschild invoked a great American poet when he warned against the destruction of wilderness in the New York metropolitan region. "Some places must be left where we can, to quote Walt Whitman, 'invite our souls,'" Rothschild testified before the Federal Power Commission.[20]

The major victory for the environmentalists came when the U.S. Court of Appeals for the Second Circuit in Manhattan turned down the Storm King license and ordered the Federal Power Commission to undergo another round of approvals, this time considering environmental and scenic issues.

The December 29, 1965, ruling stated, "The Commission's renewed proceedings must include as a basic concern the preservation of natural beauty and national historic sites, keeping in mind that in our affluent society, the cost of a project is only one of several factors to be considered." The ruling also gave "standing," or the capacity of a party to bring suit in court, to environmental groups that had no direct financial ties to the case under review. The court said that in matters where important natural resources are being explored, the public had an interest.[21] Circuit Judge Paul Hays wrote in the decision: "the preservation of natural beauty and national historic sites" were factors that had to be taken under consideration.[22]

The case dragged on for years, and Con Edison eventually dropped the plan in 1980. Besides saving Storm King, the victory had long-term consequences far beyond the Hudson River Valley, and it has been credited with creating a legal platform for the modern environmental movement.

Alongside the fight to save the natural world from despoilment, there were other large struggles against the established order that aroused passions—along with fury, despair, arson and violence, all of which could be seen in the streets of many Westchester communities toward the end of the civil rights era.

Racial tensions were running high across the region during the 1960s. In April 1968, black students and white supporters staged walk-outs at White Plains High School, and fights involving blacks and whites were becoming common occurrences.[23] The Rev. Martin Luther King, Jr., was leading a crusade to grant African Americans their full rights as citizens, a dangerous and arduous struggle. There were many deaths along the way, including Michael Schwerner of Pelham.

The son of a New Rochelle High School teacher, Schwerner graduated from Pelham High School and later earned a degree from Cornell. He and his wife, the former Rita Levant, a Mount Vernon native, went to the Deep South to organize and teach. Schwerner, known to friends as Mickey, was killed with two other civil-rights activists, James Chaney and Andrew Goodman, near Philadelphia, Mississippi, on June 21, 1964.[24]

King came to Westchester on a number of occasions. His friend and chief of staff, the Rev. Wyatt Walker, had a home in Yonkers, on Delaware Avenue, and King visited often to discuss strategy with Walker. His fellow minister, who was the pastor of a prominent Harlem congregation, was also arrested in Birmingham, Alabama. Walker later typed up much of the text of King's "Letter from a Birmingham Jail" after his friend was imprisoned there. King raised $50,000 for the Urban League at a fundraiser at the Rockefeller estate in 1961, where he spoke of his "allies in the white community" and the valuable role they played in the civil-rights crusade.[25]

When King was assassinated on April 4, 1968, the country exploded in a paroxysm of rioting and intense grief, and the reverberations were felt in Westchester. King's death dashed the dreams of a peaceful conclusion to decades of racial animosity and ushered in a period of fury, marked in Westchester as elsewhere by broken glass, burning buildings and heavily armed police patrolling the streets.

Just four hours after news of King's death was broadcast, riots and looting erupted in the Fairview section of Greenburgh. At midnight, some 120 cops were confronting a crowd of 300, and law enforcement reinforcements were called from White Plains, Mount Pleasant, Elmsford and the county to assist. Blockades were set up on Routes 100 and 100A to prevent entry to Tarrytown Road. When dawn finally arrived, authorities discovered that some 23 stores along Tarrytown Road had been damaged and ransacked, with one destroyed by fire. DeLuigi's Grocery Store burned, the others had rocks thrown through windows.[26] Many communities had their businesses looted.

On the second night after the assassination, windows were smashed on both sides of Westchester Avenue in Port Chester, some 25 stores damaged, and looting took place at a jewelry and a liquor store. In New Rochelle, a handful of stores—a tavern, an office and a liquor store and two markets—were looted.[27] In Yonkers, a white man in a liquor store was beaten and sent to hospital with head injuries.[28] Schools were also impacted, with a number of high schools and middle schools let out early due to disturbances the day after the assassination, including Ossining High School and the Anne Dormer Middle School in Ossining.[29]

The period of mourning drew tens of thousands of county residents to the streets and main thoroughfares of small towns and big cities. In Yorktown, 500 people assembled, dressed mostly in black, to walk silently on Commerce Street, and handkerchiefs were seen dabbing at moistened eyes and cheeks.[30] In Scarsdale, 2,000 village residents listened to King's speeches read by ministers and rabbis from the community. Youngsters passed out flyers at the Scarsdale train station to let commuters know about the memorial service.[31] In New Rochelle, 3,000 people gathered in front of city hall, and at the largest event, in Greenburgh, 5,000 marched from the Westchester County Center to the Union Baptist Church in Fairview. All told, some 50,000 people took part in memorial services around the county, according to contemporary estimates.[32]

But while there was a deep sense of collective mourning, rancor and ill will persisted—especially in Greenburgh, where rioting had been the most intense. The rift between the police and the black community was exposed in the days after the assassination of Martin Luther King, a rift that would widen into mistrust and suspicion. There were recriminations from the community over the way cops cracked down in the days following the King assassination. On the Tuesday after the day of King's death, some 50 to 60 cops faced off against a group of about 200 young blacks. Fire bombs were hurled at cops, who ordered the crowd to disperse. Then the nightsticks came out, and a half-dozen agitators were dragged off to jail.[33] There were also reports that police were firing weapons during the April 9 confrontation in Fairview.

After that night of chaos, a large procession of young people, about 400 Woodland High School students, along with a few dozen teachers, marched to the Greenburgh police station to state their grievances about the allegation of police abuse. A Greenburgh police sergeant defended the tactics used by local law enforcement in somewhat colorful terms. "It was not a swinging melee. They were not whaling on skulls," said Sergeant John Hahn. As an example of what might have happened to the suspects in question, the sergeant continued, "Well, if five cops grab them while they were resisting arrest, it's possible they're going to get banged around."[34] Those caught in the police crackdown described things a bit differently. John Campanella, 16, the son of baseball star Roy Campanella, recalled, "I was shot at with a shotgun." Robert Archer, 19, said, "I was just standing there when two cops came at me with machine guns. I backed away, but another one with a club about a yard long stuck it in my throat. They knocked me down and beat me."[35]

Racially motivated arson continued in Greenburgh, while several buildings and a municipal garage were badly damaged by fiery attacks. A white-owned business in Fairview, a pool company, was hit three times by arson, as well as by numerous threatening phone calls.[36]

The death of Martin Luther King, amid the violence, brought out a host of oratory that saluted the sacrifices he had made for the cause of civil rights. Among the best known speeches that flowed from his passing came from Robert F. Kennedy, Jr. Speaking in a black neighborhood in Indianapolis after word of the assassination, Kennedy spoke of invoked the Greek poet Aeschylus, who wrote of the "pain which cannot forget." Kennedy recited the words of the poet to an assembled crowd: "Let us dedicate ourselves to what the Greeks wrote so many years ago: to tame the savageness of man and to make gentle the life of this world."[37]

Robert Kennedy followed in the family tradition of soaring oratory and quick-wittedness that had made his surname a legend. And while it has been best known as a New England family with a distinctly Boston pedigree, the Kennedy clan also has strong ties to Westchester, and the New York suburbs left a deep impression on the Kennedy clan. As the historian David Nasaw noted, "The Kennedy family is in many ways a New York family."[38]

The home base of the Kennedy family (as Rose Kennedy herself described it) was once centered in Bronxville, where Kennedy family strolls around town and boisterous football games on their sprawling estate were common sights.[39]

When Joseph Kennedy moved to New York in the 1920s to oversee his growing business enterprises, including a film venture, he first relocated the family from Boston in 1928 to Riverdale in the Bronx. That residence proved too small for his family, so it was Bronxville where the Kennedys moved next, with Joseph purchasing a grand estate in May 1929 called Crownlands. A $250,000 outlay gave him 20 rooms, a five-car garage, an amply appointed billiards room and five acres for his energetic kids to play on.[40]

Joseph Kennedy also liked the location for its proximity to his mistress, the screen actress Gloria Swanson. The sultry and fabulously attired cinematic star bought a 40-acre hilltop estate in Croton in 1924, on South Mount Airy Road.[41] She stood barely five feet tall, but she commanded the attention of film fans across the nation with her large blue eyes and shiny dark hair, and one film impresario in particular. Joe Kennedy had collaborated with the actress to produce her films, and enjoyed her company in intimate circumstances in not-so-discrete locales. Her affair with Joseph Kennedy was well known to movie industry insiders, but Rose Kennedy, Joseph's wife, maintained a studiously ignorant pose in regard to her husband's dalliance. Swanson came to the Kennedy home in Bronxville on one occasion, and Swanson's daughter, Gloria, also got to know the Kennedy children.[42]

"She treated me as if I were one of the family—I wanted to say: little do you know, but I couldn't because there were times when I was sure she didn't know and times when I was sure she didn't care," Swanson wrote in her memoirs about Rose. To her dying day, Rose would deny her husband's affair with Swanson.[43]

In Bronxville, the family worshiped at St. Joseph's Church, where John, Robert and Ted all carried the cross and wore the alb as altar boys. Robert was baptised there. The Kennedy girls took dance classes at Miss Covington's, an institution for the well-to-do sons and daughters of Bronxville. John Kennedy spent a summer working on his Harvard thesis in the village, later published as a short book called *While England Slept*.

Ted Kennedy recalled the Bronxville days with affection. "The New York suburbs were new territory for the Kennedys," he wrote, and the house they dwelled in "held many pleasures." A playroom with a big train set was a particularly fascinating attraction for the Kennedy boys, and playmates often came over to enjoy the boisterous atmosphere.[44]

"Neighborhood children liked to romp into our yards for games of football and tag," Ted Kennedy wrote, and his older brothers, John and Robert, taught him how to ride a bike around the Bronxville neighborhood where they lived.[45]

Manhattanville College was another Kennedy outpost. The Catholic college for women in Harrison was the place where many Kennedy women went for scholarship and poise. A magnet for upper-class Catholic students, Manhattanville educated generations of the family matriarchs: Rose Kennedy (class of 1910), Eunice Kennedy Shriver (class of 1943), Ethel Kennedy (class of 1949), Jean Kennedy Smith (1949), Joan Kennedy (class of 1958) and Maria Shriver Schwarzenegger (class of 1977).[46] At the dedication of the Manhattanville athletic center named for Kathleen (Kick) Kennedy, who died in a plane crash in 1948, the future senator Ted Kennedy was introduced to the "exquisitely beautiful young student," as he later recalled in his memoirs, Joan Bennett. She was an excellent piano player, a Bronxville native and a part-time model with a flowing blonde mane of hair. Bennett accompanied Ted Kennedy on a ride to the airport after the dedication, and romance followed. Married at the old Kennedy church, St. Joseph's in Bronxville, in 1958, she wore a white satin gown and carried white roses.[47]

Another Kennedy tie to Westchester came from Ethel Skakel Kennedy, who married Robert Kennedy and gave birth to 11 children. She was a Larchmont native who grew up in the village in the 1930s. The Kennedy family stayed in Bronxville for 14 years. Joe Kennedy, who had been appointed U.S. ambassador to Great Britain in 1938, sold Crownlands in 1942, and it was torn down after a fire in 1953.[48]

Bobby Kennedy highlighted his family's connection to Westchester when he began preparations to run for the U.S. Senate in 1964. Kennedy had made a name for himself as an aggressive foe of organized crime and as his brother's trusted advisor, but getting New Yorkers to vote him into the Senate was seen as a tall order among voters and politicos alike. It was crucial for Kennedy to play up his New York roots and Westchester upbringing. In fact, he had spent 12 years, the longest period of his life in one place, in Bronxville. He moved to the community at the age of two, and he attended Bronxville public schools in grades three, four and five.[49]

The charge against Kennedy that he was an opportunist and carpetbagger came the instant he announced his campaign at Gracie Mansion in New York City, when demonstrators on First Avenue marched with signs that read "Bobby Go Home." Bobby Kennedy's campaign headquarters in Westchester opened in White Plains in April 1968. Resigning his post as U.S. Attorney General, Kennedy rented a 25-room Colonial home in Glen Cove, Long Island, as his primary residence. The decision to locate his main residence on Long Island came as a blow to Westchester Democratic leaders, who were hopeful he would return to the county in which he had lived as a boy.[50] Bobby was an avid sailor and felt the North Shore of Long Island was a better fit for his maritime passions.

His wife, Ethel, often used to joke about his stint as a newspaper delivery boy in Bronxville, perhaps more of a running family joke than a true story. He had signed up for the job, but Ethel claimed that a chauffeur driving the family's Rolls-Royce ended up doing most of the work delivering the *Saturday Evening Post*, and stacks of the magazines piled up in little Bobby's room.[51] She also said the same thing about another hypothetical paper route in the Kennedy summer residence at Hyannisport.

An early campaign stop brought Kennedy back to Westchester, offering a glimpse of his childhood years in Bronxville. Unfortunately for the future senator, RFK had some difficulty finding the old neighborhood, which proved something of an embarrassment in front of a busload of reporters.[52] Gaffes like that gave his opponent, Kenneth Keating, a moderate and well-regarded Republican from Rochester, plenty to work with.

At a campaign stop in Chappaqua, Keating made much of Kennedy's New England roots: "I welcome Robert Kennedy to New York," he said when Kennedy announced his candidacy. "Indeed, as his Senator, I would be happy to furnish him a guidebook, road map, and any other useful literature about the Empire State which any sojourner would find helpful." He reminded voters that his opponent could not even cast a ballot for himself on Election Day, since he was registered as a voter in Massachusetts. "You've heard of instant coffee? Well, I'm running against an instant New Yorker," he joked.[53]

It's true that Kennedy did not cast a ballot for himself in the Senate race. He was ineligible to vote in New York because state election law required a six-month residence for voters in presidential elections, and a one-year residence for voters in all other political contests. Kennedy was a resident of Hyannis Port, Massachusetts, before he threw his hat in the ring for a seat in the U.S. Senate. Kennedy usually responded with humor about the allegation of being a carpetbagger. Stopping in White Plains, he told an enthusiastic audience that upstate voters were often puzzled by his accent. "'I keep telling them it's a Westchester accent,'" he quipped to enthusiastic applause. He sometimes told crowds he had a Long Island accent, or a Bronx accent from his days in Riverdale, but the intent was the same—to show that he had roots in the Empire State. "I was born in New York— I grew up here—went to school here—held my first job here," he told an audience in Syracuse.[54]

Kennedy was something of an enigma on the campaign trail, unenthusiastic and bored by the tedium of the endless repetition of speeches and handshaking. But at times, particularly when he was among the most downtrodden, he could be electrifying and charismatic. There was something clearly different about him, that much was sure to voters. "When you saw Bob Kennedy among politicians," observed Murray Kempton, "you saw that here was a thoroughbred."[55] He certainly attracted plenty of attention, much of it in his one-time home county.

In the fall of 1964, Kennedy chartered a helicopter at $525 an hour and landed in Croton. About 1,000 people came to hear him speak at the Beach Shopping Center in Peekskill. "Has Mr. Keating done anything to stop the pollution of the Hudson River?" he asked a large crowd in Ossining, playing up his environmental credentials.[56] On another tour down the west side of the county with Hubert Humphrey, thousands came out to see the Kennedy scion who looked so much like his older brother. Surrounded by a throng of admirers, Kennedy complained to Humphrey "about too many young people pulling at him." Humphrey replied that he could minimize the problem by not standing on top of cars.[57]

The Kennedy children at play in Bronxville on the lawn of their family home, Crownlands, in October 1934. From left, Jean, Eunice (ready to throw the ball), Robert and Patricia. The Kennedy family had strong ties to Westchester, which Robert Kennedy highlighted during his Senate campaign in the 1960s (copyright © John F. Kennedy Library Foundation).

Kennedy won the election over Keating by 700,000 votes, a 10 percent margin, a substantial victory. In Westchester, he also won the majority of the vote by a modest amount, a considerable achievement since Republicans outnumbered Democrats in Westchester by a margin of 2–1.[58]

Kennedy's win in Westchester would presage the eventual shift to a Democratic majority, as the county moved from being a so-called bastion of the Republican party (even under the sway of its more liberal wing and Governor Nelson Rockefeller, who had deep roots in Westchester) to a community more progressive and Democratic in its political ethos. Kennedy went on to the U.S. Senate, where he found the clubby and slow-moving process of legislative affairs rather dull. Having worked as his brother's top political strategist, and heading the justice department as Attorney General, a career in the Senate began to look like an unpleasant prospect. He eventually decided to run for the presidency, and it was on the campaign trail in California that he was assassinated by a mentally troubled gunman in June 1968. It was another cruel and senseless killing, an anguishing coda to the era of the assassin that had already taken JFK and Martin Luther King. At St. Patrick's Cathedral, Leonard Bernstein conducted the slow movement from Mahler's Fifth Symphony, Andy Williams sang "Battle Hymn of the Republic," and a chorus of women came down from Manhattanville College to sing Fauré's "In Paradisium."[59]

The passions and tensions that unleashed the fury of the 1960s were also intertwined with black militancy and a deep impatience with the perception that blacks were second-class citizens. They wore black-leather jackets and military-style berets, talked about revolution and routinely referred to police as "pigs."

The "Black Panthers" brought a militant and fiery brand of insurrectionist polemic against the established order in big cities across America, and they were also a force in Westchester. The Party operated in White Plains and Peekskill, and at a community center in Mount Vernon, where the Panthers were especially active.[60]

In 1969, the *Black Panther* newspaper began being sold on the streets of the city. Black readers found articles that urged, "the time has come for you to open your eyes and look all around you and see what the pigs are doing to you, your mothers, your fathers, your sisters and your brothers and all oppressed people in the streets of the so-called 'ghetto.'"[61]

A Panther from Mount Vernon, Eddie Hull, took to the pages of the news sheet to protest the presence of police officers from the "special watch of the Panthers squad" who had been detailed to Mount Vernon High School. "These two pigs are walking school corridors and the grounds with pistols on their hips and walkie-talkies in their greasy hands. What can be more repressive than an occupying army inside of an already oppressive institution that miseducates?" asked Hull, signing off with the traditional salutation of the Panthers, "All power to the people."[62] The Mount Vernon police did not tolerate provocations like that, and a campaign of harassment began. There was significant police surveillance of the local Panther scene. People found selling the paper were dragged down to police headquarters and told to stop, or obtain a license required by city hall. One man, Bruce Johnson, found in violation of selling the paper without the required license, was charged with violating the city ordinance in early 1970 and received a one-year conditional discharge.[63]

Copies of the *Black Panther* were sometime bought up by police to remove them from circulation, other times, merely confiscated. At least one arrest was made. On April 29, 1970, several Panthers were arrested for putting up a poster without a permit. One of the arrestees, Leo Woodberry, claimed that 50 copies of the paper were taken from him. The charges against him were later dismissed. A lawsuit was eventually filed by the ACLU, which represented Eddie Hull, and the city of Mount Vernon stopped its enforcement of regulations on sales of newspapers and other forms of communications.[64]

Like those at the famed benefit party hosted by Leonard Bernstein in New York City in 1970 that bestowed the name "radical chic" on the leftist circuit, attendees of other covert gatherings delighted in the frisson of the outlaw and the allure of the transgressive. There were plenty of radical chic encounters in Westchester, along with the usual hand-wringing and anxiety about unruliness and disorder that the urban maelstrom seemed to be unleashing in the suburbs.

Visiting Black Panthers met a group of the Westchester cognoscenti in December 1969, described in a breathless account published in the *New York Times Magazine*. It was so hush-hush that pseudonyms were used and the location for the meet-up, described as a "plush" home with 14 rooms set on 3.5 acres, was unidentified. The article carried these headlines: "Rapping With The Panthers In White Suburbia; Suburbanite: What do the Panthers want in the long run? Black Panther: The overthrow of the capitalist-racist system."[65]

A sense that naive and sheltered middle-class whites were getting a vicarious thrill from exposure to an outlaw band of revolutionaries was hardly confined to Lenny Bernstein's apartment. Said one of the participants in the Westchester gathering, who experienced what she called guilt and shame after the event, "They may be playing at revolution, but their lives are at stake. All we risk is our genteel condescension."[66]

The Panthers were the most extreme element, but they were hardly alone. Young people were in a state of near revolt in the late 60s. A report by the National Association of Secondary School Principals in 1969 found that three of five principals reported some form of active protests in their schools.[67] Racial tension, opposition to the Vietnam War and dress regulations were the most common source of protests.

In March 1971, black students carried out an extended boycott of classes in White Plains, and windows and furniture were smashed. Students attended separate "Freedom Schools" for several weeks until the boycott came to an end.[68] Woodlands High School in Hartsdale experienced racial tensions, with police called out regularly on reports of shoving matches, fights and menacing graffitti.[69] In one typical anti-war demonstration in opposition to the U.S. involvement in Southeast Asia, 450 students at Horace Greeley High School in Chappaqua in 1970 walked out of class. It was about a third of the student body.[70] In Yorktown, 200 students left school after the Kent State shootings.[71]

While the teenaged attack on conventions and authority weren't likely to threaten the fabric of society, the threat that young people reared in the comforts of suburbia could turn to violence was indeed a concern—as a series of bank robberies, bombings and riots demonstrated during the so-called "days of rage" in the late 60s and early 70s. It was in that milieu that the visit by a local son with a hand in the Vietnam War caused shock and consternation in Scarsdale. The village, as with many other communities, was bitterly divided over the war.

Dean Rusk, the secretary of state under presidents Kennedy and Johnson, was a Scarsdale resident from 1952 to 1961. As one of the chief architects of the U.S. military intervention in Vietnam, he was a controversial figure to many who opposed the war, so when a local civic group decided to honor Rusk with a public service award, battle lines were drawn up.[72]

On a rainy Sunday in May 1967, Mayor Malcolm MacIntyre presented Rusk with a crystal glass eagle and a proclamation as a token of the community's respect. Rusk promised "to do everything possible to bring the struggle in Vietnam to a successful conclusion." While 1,000 people packed the high school auditorium, a group of 500 protesters stood in the rain with placards.[73]

Scarsdale was later to find itself the center of international attention, when a highly unusual summer class in which students played the part of rebel warriors gained attention.

The summer-school program for Scarsdale students who wanted extra credits offered the usual range of subjects, but a rather ambitious history teacher taught a class on the theme of revolutionary movements. The summer class sessions usually concluded with a picnic, but in August 1969, the six-week course entitled "Revolution and Guerrilla Warfare in the 20th Century" went out with some fireworks.

It was on the banks of the Bronx River that, for a brief time, the most famous guerrilla training camp in the world was conducting operations. Thirteen high school students enacted their own revolutionary struggle, following their classwork on guerrilla movements in Cuba, China, Mexico and Russia. The students were armed with unloaded air rifles, water pistols, water balloons and cans of shaving cream, and they took turns squaring off against each other as rebels and counter-revolutionary government forces. The insurgents captured villages, skirmished with pro-government forces and issued propaganda. The government troops set up ambushes and patrolled hostile villages.

"Kill the commies!" yelled one group, according to an account of the class later published in the *The New York Times*. "Kill the pigs!" was the response from the "rebels." The fighting was briefly interrupted when two Scarsdale police officers, alerted by an anonymous caller that kids were running around Butler Woods with guns, came upon the the the fighting and discovered it was a class—a half-credit elective open to upperclassmen, supervised by a teacher, Stephen Kling. "Revolution and guerrilla warfare are happening all over the world, and I think students in Scarsdale should know about it," Kling explained.[74] The summer-school program director, Franklin Myers, called the class "relevant to today's world," adding "we have lots of unorthodox courses in our curriculum." The article also revealed that the course had been taught the previous summer, and students were assigned to find out how a rebel force could take over Scarsdale. The kids conducted surveillance operations on the village's police station and electrical plants. "We found the village would be very easy to sabotage," Kling observed.[75]

A 16-year-old girl wrote a paper for the class the summer before on how to take over the village by putting LSD in the water supply. She got an A. The student described how much she liked the class: "It's exciting. It's far more interesting than most summer courses."[76]

The idea of young suburban guerrillas unleashing fury and vengeance on Scarsdale seemed like a ludicrous proposition, but given the tenor of the times, not as far-fetched as it seemed. In Westchester, it seemed like Che Guevara had crashed the country club. The article, picked up by the wire services and radio networks, set off a firestorm. The story about kids in Scarsdale planning to mount a Maoist insurgency, radical chic gone mad, captured a sense in the era that young people were the true enemy within. Besides causing a furor around the country, it generated laughs and ridicule at the expense of the central Westchester village.

"What a wonderful way to spend taxpayers money!" exclaimed on exasperated village resident in the pages of the weekly paper. Another asked if a "course in comparative torture techniques with a guest lecture from the Viet Cong" might be next on the syllabus.[77]

Kling, in fact, who was pictured in the newspaper with a toy gun and grenade, was anything but a figure of fun. A 34-year-old scholar at the time, Kling was a Ford Foundation fellow with a degree from Yale. He also knew something about guerrilla warfare, having served with the U.S. Air Force in Vietnam, and studied social development in India and Egypt. He taught non–Western culture at the high school.[78]

An inquiry by school authorities determined that there was never any serious attempt to instruct students in warfare, that their activities in the woods in the last days of the class took the form of a summer game, not a death-blow to the bourgeoisie.[79] An investigation by the school board eventually exonerated the summer school program and declared that the uproar was more a product of media sensationalism than the actual facts of the case. "The board has satisfied itself that the course was not instruction as guerilla warfare," the board concluded in its final statement on the matter, and the teenaged insurgents were not, in fact, preparing an onslaught on the capitalist aggressors of Scarsdale.[80] As the so-called "girl guerrilla" who was interviewed in the *Times* later wrote in the *Scarsdale Inquirer*, "We studied the political, economical, and cultural aspects of revolutions [in the 20th century] concentrating on Marxism, Leninism and Maoism. At no time were we taught 'guerilla warfare' or 'guerrilla tactics.'"[81] Local residents no doubt slept a little easier with the news. The course was never repeated.

The 1970s were a time of tumult and dissension. The status quo seemed under threat everywhere, and the trust in the traditional establishment—military, political or religious—was at an all-time low.

Into that void stepped a short man with broad shoulders, and a sense that he would change the world. He spoke halting English in a low monotone, and there was hardly anything remarkable about his appearance besides leathery skin and hair blackened with shoe polish. But the Rev. Sun Myung Moon, known to followers at the True Father, had grand ambitions—very grand ambitions—to perfect mankind through his own personal bloodlines, then to lead humanity into a new garden of Eden. Until that Eden was achieved, the monied estates in the river towns of Westchester would be the next closest thing.

Moon was born in 1920 into a farming family in Korea, and he later became a Presbyterian at the age of ten when his family converted to Christianity. He had a vision at the age of 15 that Jesus had visited him to carry out a "special mission on Earth." A brief marriage ended in divorce, but his next wife, Hak Jae Han, would bear 14 of his children and promote an ideology based on the virtues of marriage and family. With the True Mother at his side, Moon would create an idiosyncratic blend of Chrisitianity, Shamanism, Buddhism, neo-Confucianism, Korean legend and pop psychology, with Moon in the middle of a very peculiar theological edifice. As a young spiritual leader, Moon had also been persecuted and imprisoned by Communist forces in North Korea, and he developed an intense and visceral hostility to Communism, an ideological predilection that served him well when he paid trips to the corridors of power in Washington, D.C.[82]

He sensed his destiny lay beyond the Korean peninsula, and he came to this country in 1972 and built a vast empire that wore many guises. His church operated through a mix of mass media, group indoctrination, big business and public spectacle. Mass weddings at Madison Square Garden and Yankee Stadium between hundreds of brides and grooms who had met for the first time before the church arranged their vows gave the congregation an aura of blind obedience, furthered by the sight of his followers peddling candles and flowers on street corners in Westchester and Manhattan. The followers lived in dormitory-style housing in Tarrytown, and boarded buses every morning to hawk their wares on street corners.

While Moon and his disciples claimed they were no different from any other religion that brimmed with enthusiasm and new ideas, the church could never shake its sinister reputation as a cult that brainwashed young people into a lifetime of servitude in near bondage.

Founded in 1954, Moon's organization was officially known as The Holy Spirit Association of the Unification of World Christianity, more commonly called the Unification Church. After building up membership in Korea and Japan, Moon's followers established an American presence in San Francisco by 1960, and Moon visited his flock in the United States in 1965 and 1971. He came to see the United States as the place to exercise his divine authority, and to satisfy those lofty ambitions, he and his family were to be housed in a grand estate befitting their stature—nothing was too good for the savior of mankind. "It was decided that Moon should have a place of his own, and a wonderful place at that," recalled a former church member.[83]

Belvedere, the old 22-acre Bronfman estate in Tarrytown, was purchased in 1972 for $200,000, and became the place where the true family would re-make the world. In 1974, the Moon organization bought the former Garson Reiner estate for $600,000 in Irvington, a short distance from Belvedere, where Moon and his family would take residence. It was renamed East Garden.

His organization thrived, taking advantage of the changing nature of the times and the uncertainty that many young people felt about the world made by their parents. At the height of the movement in the 1980s, there were some 47,000 adherents in the United States, according to the church. "In the late 60s and early 70s the two great symbols of American civilization—political freedom and economic prosperity—lost their constellating power," observed Allen Tate Wood, an early church leader who left the organization. Wood found that the "the psychological and moral confusion" unleashed by the Vietnam War led to a loss of faith in authority of any kind. Absolutist faith, asserted by cult leaders with claims to certainty, was alluring to young people who were full of doubts and anxieties about finding their place in the world. "All the questions surrounding growing up," like sex, career, independence, he wrote, were precluded by the church and its strictures.[84]

To those who were questioning the faith of their ancestors and the perplexing mood of the times, he would give them certainty. The "True Father" had all the answers. Besides that, the church offered a place to belong and find companionship. "There are a lot of lonely people walking around," a church official noted in 1976.[85]

As the church grew, another 234 acres in Greenburgh near the village of Tarrytown was purchased in 1975 at a cost of $5 million, with an eye toward building a Unificationist university there.[86] In 1979, the church expanded again, acquiring a 98-acre estate in New Castle to serve as a recruitment and retreat center.[87]

The Belvedere estate was the setting for a wide assortment of rituals, games, tests of will and ceaseless activity. Young church members would rise early from iron bunk beds for prayers and exercise, then board buses for a day of street sales. A loud clamor could be heard from dozens of enthusiastic Japanese church members who made their home at Belvedere, while they bent in prayer and made their supplications. At Holy Rock behind the main house, Moon liked to stage athletic competitions and wrestling matches between church members, acting like a coach.[88]

Large groups often came to visit Belvedere from Europe and elsewhere, lured by false advertisements that promised lectures on religion and ecology—only to be exposed to Moon's preachers. While most of them sullenly stayed for a short time before departing, a few always lingered and then converted.[89] The Unificationists developed a method that made new arrivals exhausted and weary with activities, while surrounding them constantly by church companions. The newcomers were encouraged to pour their hearts out and describe the difficulties they were facing. After that intensive introduction, the request to formally join the organization would be made. While church members were never explicitly forbidden from communication with their family members, contact was extremely limited. In 1975, a Connecticut couple sued the church over alleged brainwashing of their teenage child.[90]

The public, who encountered young church members selling trinkets in villages in Westchester and New York City, and viewed the mass weddings with alarm, eventually came to call church members "Moonies" and viewed them with deep suspicion. "People found us creepy and sinister," recalled Wood, the former church leader who left after five years. Many of the younger church members attended public schools in Tarrytown and Irvington, where they were met with misgivings. Moon's eldest son, Hyo Jin, went to Hackley School in Tarrytown until he was expelled for an incident involving a BB gun.[91]

If it seemed strange from the outside, the church was a dysfunctional family on the inside. Nansook Hong was the daughter of two of Moon's most devoted adherents. She was chosen to be the bride of Moon's oldest son, Hyo Jin Moon—and fulfill the family destiny to perfect mankind. Instead, she found herself imprisoned in "the poisonous world of the True Family." She described her life in the Moon family, first as a child bride at the age of 15 in 1982, then as an abused spouse who suffered regular beatings at the hands of Hyo Jin. The East Garden estate was "a perpetual prison for 14 years." Hong began her sophomore year at Irvington High School, speaking no English, as a married woman. When she became pregnant with her first child, she had to keep the pregnancy a secret from her classmates and teachers. She eventually transferred to The Masters School in Dobbs Ferry, largely to keep rumors from spreading about her child.[92] Hyo Jin, then in his 20s, could have been charged with statutory rape since Nansook Hong was below the age of consent in New York State. In a memoir she published after leaving the church, she described her husband as a violent drunk with a serious cocaine habit. She once filed a complaint with the Irvington Police Department, but never followed up on it.[93]

Eventually she took matters into her own hands, escaping from East Garden in a friend's van, with her five children hidden under blankets. Hyo Jin died of a heart attack in Korea in 2008. The Moon operation came under intense scrutiny from official authorities, who questioned its claims as a religious movement. A long-running battle between church leaders and tax assessors in the river towns of Westchester ran through the 1970s.

The Unification Church never wanted auditors to look at its books or open Moon to legal interrogation, for reasons that only stoked suspicions about the organization's methods and goals. Moon, who founded the *Washington Times* newspaper in 1982 as a conservative daily publication, had extensive holdings in businesses around the world, and the distinction between his business enterprises and his church were murky at best. The church claimed one million followers in 40 countries around the world at its height in the 1970s, and what they contributed to the church as part of its finances—and how it was spent—was an open question.

The village of Tarrytown denied the church tax-exempt status in 1975, and the church filed suit against the village.[94] The church dropped the lawsuit when the state Supreme Court ruled that Moon would have to testify. More litigation between municipal tax collectors ensued, with the Westchester towns refusing to grant exemptions without an accounting of church finances. After a state court upheld that decision in 1980, the Unificationists began paying millions of dollars of taxes on their significant real estate holdings in Irvington, Tarrytown and Greenburgh. A tax battle was also waged over the large property in North Castle, which town officials refused to rezone.

There were other sources of friction between the church and local authorities, as when two church members were arrested on Central Avenue in Greenburgh for peddling lollipops without a license.[95]

Then there were the boats. Moon was an ardent fisherman who spent much of his free time in a 50-foot cabin cruiser on the Hudson. His business enterprises also included fishing fleets, canneries and boat building. For reasons that were never made entirely clear to the public, nearly 100 sports boats were stored on the grounds of the Tarrytown estate in the early 80s. The church said they would be used for a training and leadership program but refused to allow municipal officials to inspect the boats, which were built by one of the church's commercial operations in Queens. It was a clear violation of the village zoning ordinance against commercial storage in a residential neighborhood.[96] The church eventually agreed to move the boats, a number of which were destined for Massachusetts.

But it was the federal government that concentrated the highest level of enforcement on Moon and his enterprises. In 1981, Moon himself was convicted on charges of filing false tax returns and conspiracy. He served a jail sentence, just over a year in federal prison in Danbury, Connecticut. His tax case and ultimate conviction earned Moon many defenders among other Christian denominations who saw the government campaign against him as a threat to religious liberty. Moon did his time from 1984 to 1985, mopping floors and cleaning tables in the cafeteria. After his return from prison, he came back to Tarrytown. Shortly after his release, he dressed himself and his wife in gold robes and declared himself Emperor of the Universe, in a ceremony that spared no expense for sumptuousness, according to his daughter-in-law. He also embarked on a massive reconstruction of the East Garden estate, installing a waterfall, a bowling alley, six pizza ovens and tons of Italian marble.[97]

Never a man lacking in modesty, Moon declared himself the Messiah in front of a roomful of Washington power brokers, many of whom wore expressions of disbelief or deep embarrassment. The Senate and Congressional representatives later said they were duped into attending the event under false pretenses.[98] Moon died in 2012 at the age of 92, an ordinary mortal in the end. His church continued, though in a diminished form. His life and death represented the kind of ambition and delusion that has long been a part of the county's history, for better or worse.

12

Triumph and Transformation
Renewed Immigration, the Housing Boom and Deindustrialization

The upending of the old order unleashed many new kinds of liberation. Beginning in June 1969, when a police raid on a gay bar in the West Village section of New York City unleashed violent and furious backlash, gay people were no longer resigned to a life of secrecy and weary shame. The Stonewall Inn Riots marked the turning point in gay liberation, and that movement would sweep over the suburban landscape. Much of it was done in a quiet and orderly fashion, but much of it was unruly and subversive, and Westchester had its very own miniature model of the Stonewall Riots.

Gay people living in Westchester had to hide their identities, recalled Lester Goldstein, an early leader of the gay-rights movement from White Plains. "When you go back to the 1950s, it was required—culturally required—to be secretive, to be closeted," he observed.[1] In the 1970s, the first outward manifestation of gay life announced itself. As of the late 1970s, a gay bar was operating in Yonkers. The Westchester Gay Men's Association began a hotline telephone information service in 1977, and the Lesbian Task Force also ran a call center in the same period.[2] In 1983 the Lesbian Task Force of Southern Westchester and the Gay Men's Alliance of the Hudson Valley opened a space called the Loft—in a loft above a grocery store in White Plains—that became a gay community center for the region.[3]

But there was more to the gay liberation movement than organization and steady advancement. The spirit behind the Stonewall Riots announced to the world at large that gays would no longer tolerate being marginalized or pushed into the shadows, and that fierce opposition led to public disturbance and civil unrest in central Westchester.

The Gay Activist Alliance, founded in New York City in December 1969, was an avowedly confrontational organization that sought to fight back against public figures or institutions perceived as hostile toward gays. *Time* magazine called them a "gay goon squad."[4] Undeniably, they channeled the defiant and confrontational element behind the Stonewall Riots, and they relished their outlaw reputation.

Besides promoting legislation, such as the first-gay rights bill proposed in the New York City Council in 1971, the GAA pioneered the use of "direct action" that would become a hallmark of activism for decades to come. In the 1970s, activists called their staged protests a "zap." These loud and personal demonstrations showed that gay liberation was on the march, even to a quiet residential street in Scarsdale.[5]

As part of the debate over the gay-rights bill in New York City, which would forbid discrimination against gays in employment, housing and public accommodation, a prominent Democratic Party organizer came out in opposition to the law in the pages of the *New York Daily News.* Adam Walinsky ran for the New York Attorney General in 1970 and was an aide to Senator Robert Kennedy. His op-ed piece in June 1977 said the approval of the gay rights law "amounts to a formal declaration that homosexuality is morally or socially equal to heterosexuality," which he said was wrong.[6]

The GAA took the opinion personally—very personally. The organization obtained a bus and a fleet of cars to ferry protesters to Walinsky's Scarsdale home. And a group of renegades decided to carry out their own, more radical protest, in advance of the more formal GAA protest. On the night of August 4, 1977, the protest group lived up to the "goon squad" moniker.[7]

While Walinsky and his wife, Jane, settled into bed around 11 p.m., a noisy commotion startled them. Loud firecrackers blew up near the front door, and eggs were pelted at the home on Griffen Avenue. Peering outside, the couple could see several dozen shadowy figures. Jane Walinsky tried to call the police, but the phone line had been cut. Adam Walinksy got dressed and ventured outside, where he was greeted by a line of marchers chanting: "Walinsky, you liar, we'll set your house on fire." Other chants went up into the night sky: "gay rights now," "two, four, six, eight, gay is just as good as straight," and "Walinsky is a bigot." The protestors carried baseball bats, blew whistles and shouted into bull horns.[8]

The demonstrators also spray-painted the driveway—"Go Gay"—and left behind leaflets calling Walinksy a bigot. The demonstrators eventually disbanded and left the area after a half-dozen Scarsdale police officers arrived on the scene. The cops did not witness any criminal activity, just the marching and a picket line in front of the Walinsky home.[9] They did not arrest anyone, either. Police Chief Terrance Shames later explained: "It was deemed more advisable to have the people dispersed rather than have mass arrests. We handled the crowd in the best way possible," he said.[10] Walinsky was described as "angry" that no arrests had been made in front of his house.[11] As no criminal charges were filed, Walinsky eventually filed a civil lawsuit against the GAA and its political director, Joseph Kennedy, who was at the scene and spoke with officers. The New York State Supreme Court placed an injunction on any further protests at the Walinsky residence, but no punishment was meted out. A settlement was later reached, not disclosed to the public. The GAA considered it a victory.[12]

The broad liberation movements that roiled society attained new rights and respect for previously marginalized groups. The public square, which had long excluded gays, as well as women and African Americans, began to adapt to the new coalition of changemakers. Civic life in America would come to be more inclusive as a result of the campaign for freedom and dignity. While the 1970s brought about advances in civil rights, it also ushered in a time of anxiety and peril. There were the ordinary sorts of hazards: street crime and violence associated with rampant drug abuse. Alongside those scourges, which blighted city life across the country, another kind of invisible menace took hold in the public mind with unparalleled dread. The decade saw brutal serial killers like the Zodiac Killer, Charles Manson, Ted Bundy and other depraved murderers terrifying the popular imagination.

New York had its own serial killer who terrified the New York metropolitan region, especially young men and women. Thirteen people were shot during the "Son of Sam" reign of terror that spread across the city and its suburbs, and six died. It began on July

29, 1976, when 18-year-old Donna Lauria was killed while she and a girlfriend sat in a car parked outside their apartment building in the Bronx. Her friend, Jody Valenti, 19, was wounded. The killer went on to target other young people in the city, using a .44 caliber handgun, and shootings followed in Queens and Brooklyn.

The murder and the violence that ensued hit close to Westchester in a number of ways. Lauria was dancing at the Peachtree disco in New Rochelle the night she was killed.[13] Another victim wounded in a shooting attack in Queens, Judy Placido, worked at the cosmetics counter of Macy's in New Rochelle.[14]

As the attacks mounted, women in the region dyed their hair blond or wore wigs, on the supposition that the gunman was targeting women who had long dark hair. Streets were deserted after dark, in fear of the ".44-handgun killer," as he was first called in the press. He was apparently targeting young women in particular—as well as their boyfriends.[15]

The reign of fear was magnified when bizarre, taunting letters were written to a popular *New York Daily News* columnist, Jimmy Breslin, with whom the killer had developed a macabre fascination. "Hello from the gutters of N.Y.C. which are filled with dog manure, vomit, stale wine, urine, and blood," read the opening of one letter to Breslin, recalling the boastful tone that Jack the Ripper had taken in his missives to London police nearly a century before.[16] He identified himself as the "Son of Sam" in those letters, and stated he was being controlled by some kind of inner demon, who took on the shape of a dog, sending him onto the streets to find young people to shoot.

Law-enforcement and public officials went into overdrive to find the killer. Any leads, however slim, were investigated: people named Samson were scrutinized for previous crimes, and thousands of .44 caliber handgun permits were checked. Astrologers were consulted for possible clues to the killer's internal thoughts.[17]

The anxiety level reached feverish heights as the killing persisted. In August 1977, Westchester County began its own law-enforcement initiative, with the county police force mounting patrols in the south end of the county. The 16-man unit dressed in street clothes and patrolled residential areas in unmarked cars, telling young people they found to go home.[18] They were augmented by off-duty cops from around the region as a volunteer force.

In the end, it was a simple infraction and some clever detective work that brought investigators to the doorstep of a 24-year old mentally troubled postal worker. A parking ticket near the scene of a fatal July 31 shooting in Brooklyn led investigators to Pine Street in Yonkers. When NYPD detectives saw a firearm in the car, and handwriting that appeared to match the unusual notes sent to police and the *Daily News*, it was clear that the cops had found their man. A lengthy stake-out involving police from Yonkers and Westchester County ended when a man left the building and climbed into a cream-colored Ford Galaxy. An NYPD detective shoved a snub-nosed revolver into the face of David Berkowitz. He smiled back and declared he was "Sam." "Well, you've got me," he told the detectives. Police found a submachine gun in the vehicle, along with a number of bizarre notes threatening violence.[19]

Neighbors on the apartment building on Pine Street said he was a loner who kept to himself. "My impression was that he was pretty weird," one neighbor reported, quite an understatement as Berkowitz's history came to light.[20] Inside his small apartment on Pine Street were cryptic messages covering the walls, an Oriental tapestry that blocked the bedroom window, and a small arsenal of weapons.[21]

The life history of the serial killer was ordinary on its appearance. Berkowitz, who was adopted by a middle-class couple from the Bronx, served in the Army, where he developed a skill with firearms. After the Army, he moved to New Rochelle and found work with the U.S. Postal Service, and it was while he was renting a small apartment on Coligni Street in New Rochelle that psychosis and an obsession with dogs took hold of his mind.[22] He later moved to the apartment building in Yonkers and began setting fires—hundreds of them—before he turned his gun on people. After pleading guilty to the string of murders, he was sentenced to life in prison in 1978.

The capture of a serial killer made Yonkers a nationally known community. But Yonkers' turn in the national spotlight was far from over after Berkowitz was put behind bars. A housing and social battle would keep the city in the headlines for more than a decade. It featured a compelling cast of characters that would later be chronicled in a book of nonfiction, *Show Me a Hero*, by a *New York Times* reporter, and a cable-television series from HBO of the same name. It was a battle over familiar fault lines of race, class, home ownership and community, in a very Westchester combination.

The characters were also well delineated for drama. There was the judge, Leonard Sand, a cerebral jurist who had a large country estate in Pound Ridge. The tragic figure in the controversy was a young mayor, the youngest in the United States when he was elected in 1988, who exuded ambition and sincerity. The melodrama and some of the sharpest lines came from Hank Spallone, a savvy politician who knew how to play to the crowd. And behind all the leading characters were the people of Yonkers, who packed into city council meetings, screamed, protested and eventually acquiesced to the judge's order to build affordable housing on the city's east side.

Yonkers was a working city, not as glamorous or gracious as other parts of Westchester, but it offered a version of suburbia in an affordable package, a particularly appealing opportunity for middle-income earners looking to step away from the Bronx and other urban precincts. To many it presented a blue-collar version of the American dream: a patch of green lawn out front, and a home of one's own.

While blacks had long been a part of Yonkers, their neighborhoods and schools were highly segregated. Runyon Heights was the only black neighborhood in the east end of the city, and its streets were dead-ended from the white neighborhoods around it; it was essentially an island onto itself.[23]

The issue of segregation first arose in the school system, and while the district made modifications to adjust the racial makeup in city schools through busing and magnet schools, the broader issues remained: segregated housing patterns that confined blacks in Yonkers to a one-mile section in the city's southwest corner. And though the issue was specific to Yonkers, the question of housing segregation had a larger connection to surrounding Westchester County. When the city of White Plains tore down old black neighborhoods in the downtown district in the 1970s, many black residents were displaced and ended up in Yonkers, a frequent pattern during the era of urban renewal. The Westchester County administration did little to make the situation in Yonkers any easier, such as selling off some of its surplus land in the city.[24]

Furthermore, many Westchester towns before it had fought hard to prohibit publicly-assisted low- and middle-income housing within their borders, leaving it to Yonkers to carry the burden for anyone beyond the white middle class to make a home in the suburbs.[25]

The federal government brought suit against Yonkers in 1980, which was then joined by the NAACP. In 1985, Judge Sand issued a 670-page ruling and the next year ordered the city to build 200 units of public housing on the east side of town, which was largely white and middle class. A housing specialist, Oscar Newman, proposed building town-house units, a style he believed fostered a greater sense of ownership and responsibility and would more easily blend into the streetscapes of eastern Yonkers.

United States v. City of Yonkers had been assigned to Judge Leonard Sand at random. A former law partner who earned a fortune in legal work, he was a judge who had a very uncompromising vision of the law and how it should be implemented. "Being a federal judge is not a popularity contest," he once remarked.[26] Others called him a judicial activist who far out-stepped his authority—"a judicial tyrant," in the words of conservative commentator Patrick Buchanan.[27]

Looking at the city's demographic data, it was clear to Judge Sand that housing pattern, created in part by federal dollars, had to change. "It is, to say the least, highly unlikely that a pattern of subsidized housing which so perfectly preserved the overwhelming white character of East Yonkers came about for reasons unrelated to race," he wrote.[28]

Against that judicial force were the people who lived on the east side of Yonkers, championed by a former New York City police detective. The son of an Italian bricklayer, Hank Spallone grew up in the Bronx and spoke for whites who wanted to keep their neighborhoods as they were, which meant no newcomers living in public housing. "You don't have the right to take away the fruits of their labor and ask them to share it with people who didn't work for it," he remarked during the housing crisis.[29] Sand grew impatient with the recalcitrance from Spallone and other city leaders to come up with sites for new affordable housing units on the city's east side, and the recalcitrance would eventually turn to crisis.

The longtime mayor, Angelo Martinelli, was voted out of office in 1988 in favor of a newcomer to the political scene, Nick Wasicsko, a former Westchester County police officer and lawyer who seemed to voters more likely to fight the judge's orders. But the Second Court of Appeals upheld Sand's orders for new affordable housing on the east side just days after the election, and the newly elected mayor felt he had no choice but to comply. Four members of the city council vowed to oppose Judge Sand, and refused to give in to the judicial orders.

Infighting on the city council, and ugly protests out on the streets, turned Yonkers into a battleground, much of it ending up on the national news. Hundreds packed city council meetings, and raw bigotry was on display for all to see. Judge Sand's house in Pound Ridge was picketed, and his image was burned in effigy in Yonkers—alongside the image of the NAACP lawyer, Michael Sussman. There was more than a whiff of anti–Semitism in the hostility toward the judge and the lead attorney suing the city, both of whom were Jewish.[30] Judge Sand brought the matter to a head when he imposed a series of onerous fines on the city. He also levied personal fines against four stubborn city council members, Nicholas Longo, Edward Fagan, Jr., Peter Chema and Hank Spallone, and raised the possibility of jailing them. The U.S. Supreme Court authorized the fines against the city but put a stay on the personal fines and jail time.

In August 1988, the fines began, starting at $100 and doubling every day. Within a month, they would total the city's budget of $337 million. An appeals court capped the fines at $1 million a day, but the amount of money was crippling. The city reacted by cutting back on payments to contractors. With gas no longer readily available for the city's sanitation trucks, garbage began piling up on the streets. Massive layoffs were anticipated in September as the multi-million dollar fines drained city coffers.[31]

As the crisis reached a feverish pitch of intensity, and the prospect of a complete breakdown in city services, a special council meeting was called. Hundreds packed the City Hall chambers during a morning session, and some were ejected by police for heckling and shouting. When the roll call was taken, Councilmen Longo and Chema changed their votes. Spallone called his one-time ally, Longo, "a piece of garbage."[32]

With construction of the townhouse units finally authorized, in 1992 a lottery was held, and 220 names were pulled from a large Bingo drum.[33] Construction began on sites in the city's east side, on Clark Street, Wrexham Road, Trenchard Street, Helena Avenue and other locations.[34]

There was graffiti and a crude pipe bomb that detonated off Shore View Drive to greet the new tenants.[35] Security was heavy when the first tenants moved in. But after they settled in, quiet prevailed, if not great enthusiasm for the new arrivals in the neighborhoods of eastern Yonkers, by most accounts. Bob Olson, Yonkers Police Chief, said after the new housing went up, "The doomsday scenario never materialized."[36]

The city end wound up paying $819,000 in fines, while the cost of the legal bill incurred during the housing battle was roughly $15 million.[37] Most city residents expressed a huge sigh of relief that the controversy had ended and that the negative publicity generated by the turmoil would pass. "I'm really glad it's over. Now I can get my

The battle over public housing and a decree by a federal judge to build low-income units in the east end of Yonkers turned into a City Hall drama that attracted unruly crowds. The Andrew Smith Townhouse units on Trenchard Street were completed in 1992 (Tyler Sizemore).

garbage picked up and nobody will have to lose their job," a shipping clerk remarked while walking his dog in the Dunwoodie section of Yonkers. "I wish we wouldn't have to have the housing, but I guess that's the only way this thing could ever end."[38] Later city administrations worked on a more cooperative basis to comply with the court orders to build more affordable housing units on the east side of the city. As Judge Sand later noted, the city met the legal requirements for "segregation," though it might not have made anyone think that a city of 200,000 had become "integrated," a distinction he felt worth noting.[39]

The eventual compliance with the judge's order was a political death knell for Mayor Wasicsko, who lost the mayor's office after the city administration gave into the court order. "Why is it that people who do the right thing seem to get squashed?" Wasicsko once asked.[40] Though he was able to gain a seat on the city council in 1991, he lost a Democratic primary and was out of office and out of a job in 1993. The 34-year-old former mayor drove to Oakwood Cemetery in late October with the service revolver he always wore on his ankle, a habit he carried over from his days as a county cop. Near the grave of his father, he put a bullet through his head. The youngest mayor in America, idealistic and determined through months of grueling political battles, had been vanquished by the city he loved.[41]

Preserving the status quo has always been a major undercurrent of the suburbs, as the Yonkers battle demonstrated. A sense of order, and a connection to history and the natural world, were always some of the prime features of Westchester County and a main selling point to new arrivals. Conversely, the steamroller of suburban development and the imperatives of the real-estate market threatened to obliterate the very qualities that defined the town-and-country lifestyle that had been woven into the fabric of the county since its inception.

It was a difficult balance to achieve, but the forces of preservation gained an immeasurable boost from one of the most powerful American families of the 19th and 20th century. The Rockefeller family did more to shape the landscape in Westchester and preserve its homespun roots than any other in the county's history. By conserving their vast holdings in central Westchester and deeding it as state parkland, a green abundance of forests, meadows, wetlands and stony outcroppings were saved from development, while older estates dating from the colonial era were shielded from likely destruction.

The Rockefellers also preserved the great stony cliffs on the west side of the Hudson River, the Palisades, from ruination through their largesse, and the family even managed to bring the cattle business back to Westchester for a time, centuries after the last cattle drover had hung up his saddle.

John D. Rockefeller, the oil magnate, began buying land in Pocantico Hills in the 1890s, and his private estate eventually encompassed more than 3,600 acres. He tore up old rail lines, demolished existing buildings and created an exquisite verdant private manor from the rolling hills of north-central Westchester. Sunken roads criss-crossed the property, and the landscaping was carried out by the firm started by Frederick Law Olmsted, the co-creator of Central Park in Manhattan. Curvilinear lines, broad vistas and water features entranced the eye, and on a more bucolic note, a flock of sheep, attended by a Scottish shepherd, grazed on the golf course to keep the grass down.[42] The oil baron's son, John D. Rockefeller, Jr., continued the growth of the estate, and indulged his own deep love of history and preservation. Junior, as he was known, founded Sleepy Hollow Restorations in 1951, and obtained two historic properties, Sunnyside, the home of Washington Irving in Irvington, and Philipsburg Manor, one of the oldest farm sites in Westchester along the banks of the Pocantico River in Sleepy Hollow. In 1959, the non-profit organization purchased Van Cortlandt Manor in Croton, which had fallen into disrepair when it came on the market and faced destruction.

Junior's five sons, and a daughter, followed in the family tradition of conservation. They were a remarkable and disparate lot, with strong ties to the county. Laurence Rockefeller was an environmental leader and philanthropist, Winthrop became the governor of Arkansas. John D. Rockefeller III, also a philanthropist and civic leader, died in a car accident on Bedford Road in Mount Pleasant in 1978. Their sister, Abby "Babs" Rockefeller, kept out of the public eye.

The third generation of Rockefellers were best known by Nelson and David Rockefeller, opposites in temperament. David was a cerebral and private man, a behind-the-scenes financier who made deals with the most powerful men in the world. As the president of Chase Manhattan Bank, David Rockefeller oversaw international finance and development ventures around the globe, with oil ministers and bankers convening at his house in Pocantico Hills for high-level talks. His wife, Margaret (Peggy) McGrath, grew up in Mount Kisco, the daughter of the former president of Pennsylvania Railroad.

She was devoted to the natural world and farmland preservation, raising a herd of Simmental cattle at the Hudson Pines Farms in Sleepy Hollow in 1970 and initiating new agricultural activity in the region.

Nelson Rockefeller, four-time governor of New York State and the vice president from 1974 to 1977, was dissimilar in every way from his brother—garrulous, extroverted and determined to perform on the biggest stage of all. "How ya' doin' fella?" was his catch phrase, and he relished the political life—"stumping the state and speaking in every Elks Club he could find, and kissing every baby within reach," as his brother recalled.[43]

He began his career in government by taking a position on the Westchester County Board of Health in 1932, as a way of gaining some experience in public service. Journeying to Port Chester to meet William "Boss" Ward, Nelson Rockefeller asked what position might be available, and the political chief of Westchester

David and Peggy Rockefeller married at the St. Matthew's Church in Bedford in 1940. She was a Mount Kisco native who loved farm life and the outdoors. The triumphal march from *Aida* rang from the organ as the bridal party left the church (Rockefeller Archives).

County suggested a seat on the Board of Health. "This county has been good for you. Now it is up to you to do something for us," the political boss growled at the young Rockefeller.[44]

Rockefeller kept climbing relentlessly upwards from there, while serving intermittently on the county health board until 1953. "Rocky," as he was known to generations of headline writers, aspired to the White House with a fervency rarely seen in American politics. When he divorced his first wife, Mary Todhunter Clark, in 1962, to wed the former Margaretta "Happy" Fitler the following year (at the home of Laurance Rockefeller on the family estate in Pocantico Hills), it was a major turning point in American politics.[45] No major public figure had divorced before. His divorce and subsequent remarriage changed the expectations about public figures. It may have caused some damage to his reputation, but it did not finish his political career.

One of Nelson Rockefeller's greatest accomplishments in the governor's office was the expansion of the state university system. Determined to create a university devoted to the arts and arts education, Rockefeller brought his ambitious vision to a quiet corner of Harrison. Taking possession of former pastureland in the hamlet of Purchase, Rockefeller assembled a team of modernist architects under the direction of Edward Larrabee Barnes, and a bold new addition to academia and the fine arts in New York State—SUNY Purchase—rose there in 1972. An art museum housing the modernist collection of Roy Neuberger, a Rockefeller friend and associate, was designed by Philip Johnson and John Burgee.[46] Drawn with austere angularity by the team of modernist architects and built in dense masses of purplish-brown brick, the campus architecture was never much loved

New York Governor Nelson Rockefeller strides through the delegation at the Republican nominating convention in Rochester in 1958, with his son, Rodman, a few paces behind him (in glasses). Few men enjoyed the scrum of political life as much as Rockefeller (courtesy Westchester County Archives).

and regularly turned up on lists of the ugliest American college campuses. SUNY-Purchase was called "an exercise in sensory deprivation" by John Morris Dixon, the editor of *Progressive Architecture*.[47]

The greatest building that the Rockefellers became known for was far more traditional, nestled among the hills of the family estate outside the village of Sleepy Hollow. Kykuit, which means lookout in Dutch, was the crown jewel of a vast estate that the Rockefellers called home, and it was also a source of contention among family members. Nelson in particular coveted the 40-room mansion completed in 1913, and he decided he wanted to move into it not long after father's death in 1963. The "formal decor and stately setting were more suited to Nelson's needs as governor," as his brother, David, explained.[48] Nelson was intensely invested in Kykuit, though it was held in a joint partnership—"He viewed the mansion as the family's ancestral home and the symbolic center of the Rockefeller universe," David wrote.[49]

Though the Rockefeller brothers had differing and often contentious ideas about the preservation of their large land holdings and the future of Kykuit, a plan by Hideo Sasaki, a noted landscape architect, in 1974 provided the framework for an agreement on the preservation of the Rockefeller land.[50] The family members eventually consented to a preservation plan to keep the land holdings intact, with Kykuit to be turned over to a nonprofit. In 1983, the Rockefeller State Park was formed, with a gift of 750 acres from the family, and it later grew in size and scope.[51] Over 1,600 acres were eventually deeded to New York State as parkland, what has been described by a Rockefeller family member as the "Central Park of Westchester."[52] It is in fact roughly double the size of the Manhattan park.

In 1986, Historic Hudson Valley was formed from its predecessor organization, Sleepy Hollow Restorations. After Nelson Rockefeller's death in 1979 (on a visit with his mistress in New York City), his share in the Kykuit ownership was transferred to the National Trust for Historic Preservation, and it was eventually added to the portfolio of Historic Hudson Valley, and opened to the public in 1994. The great home and the estate stand as a common Westchester formula, a testament to vast ambition, wealth and public benefit.

The lifestyle of the Rockefellers may not have been attainable to most suburban inhabitants, but the goal of living large—and in a very large home—began to become a trend. The super-sizing of the suburban home became a hallmark of the early 21st century. Beginning in the early 1990s, from hard-hat neighborhoods in Dobbs Ferry to horse country in Bedford, big new houses that stood apart from their surroundings in size and bulk were everywhere on the rise, in new subdivisions and on old residential blocks.

According to statistics from a real-estate company, the size of an average home in 1950 was 1,370 square feet, while in 2000 it grew to 2,265. The size of new homes grew 5 percent alone between 1991 and 1998. House sizes increased dramatically from 1980 to 1990, and a housing analyst estimated that homes built in the decade of the 2010s were 80 percent bigger than the typical 1940s home.[53] Meanwhile, the average lot size had been shrinking. The move toward bigger homes on smaller lots was driven by an approach by builders to maximize their profit margin by charging more for larger homes as real estate became more expensive, compounded by a bigger-is-better attitude that has long defined a certain American style of living. The houses came packed with home gyms, movie theaters, wine cellars and saunas, but the structures themselves followed mass-production design and construction methods, one that often replaced quality with quantity.

The new homes came to be known as "McMansions" for the muddled architectural tropes and outsized pretensions they seemed to embody. A team of architects and critics who helped popularize the term called the McMansion-style house "the fast-food version of the American dream ... located in the center of a small plot, surrounded at close quarters by more of the same."[54] A new vocabulary arose in the neighborhoods to describe the bulky newcomers—often dripping with scorn and ridicule, as in "plywood palazzo." A big carport attached to the house was termed a "garage Mahal," and a grand entryway with soaring ceilings was called a "lawyer foyer."

The teardowns of older homes that had stood for generations to make way for the big new suburban arrivals caused particular consternation in many communities. In some cases, homes larger than 4,000 square feet started to go up on lots a third of an acre in size after existing homes half the size were torn down. The new structures loomed over existing homes in a somewhat menacing fashion. "They're poorly proportioned, poorly sited and poorly detailed," summarized a Bedford architect, John Massengale, on the McMansion boom in Westchester. "And compared to the typical house, they're often very busy."[55]

While they provided fodder for neighborhood jokes, legal and zoning battles raged in many Westchester communities over how to regulate the McMansion trend. The contest was a typical suburban fight that pitted the property rights of the few against the communal interest of the many. Local legislators in many Westchester towns eventually passed "floor-area ratio" laws that reduced the amount of building size relative to lot size; other new zoning restrictions, often called McMansion laws, were passed, as well, in the 2000s. The new laws reaffirmed a basic concept of the suburbs—large homes should be built on large lots, small homes on small lots. There was also push-back from the building trade, who resented additional regulations from local lawmakers. Some community members raised concern about placing restrictions on personal tastes in housing.[56]

The housing boom that began in the 1990s was accompanied by the decline in heavy industry. Higher costs for labor, electricity and transportation in the Northeast put factories at a significant disadvantage in comparison to other parts of the country. One by one, the giants of industry were laid low: the red brick chimneys, the assembly lines, the looms and the blast furnaces that had bracketed the working lives of generations were all eradicated.

The Alexander Smith carpet mill closed in 1954, signaling the start of de-industrialization in Westchester. The last roll of copper wiring in Hastings was spooled in 1975, and the distilling operation at Fleischmann's announced "last call" in 1977. Production of sweet candy died out at the Life Savers factory in Port Chester in 1984, and the production of steel boilers at the Burnham factory in Irvington ceased in 1988. The end of the era was starkly made manifest when the last minivan rolled off the assembly line in Sleepy Hollow (then called North Tarrytown) in June 1996.

Just a few years later, the walls came tumbling down at the GM plant. Some of the old riveters, painters and tool-and-die makers often stopped by the old plant, which at its peak employed 10,000 workers, to watch its passing. Demolition crews working earth-movers toppled the gray walls of the auto mill, looking like a swarm of insects bringing down an elephant, as the sounds of scraping metal and crushing concrete filled the air. Dozens of rail cars were filled with steel, and hundreds of truckloads of asphalt were driven to a nearby plant in Tarrytown to be recycled into asphalt.[57] The site of so much industry eventually became a very valuable piece of real estate.

Vast quantities of copper wire were unspooled at the Anaconda factory in Hastings-on-Hudson for five decades until 1975. Worker John Santos prepares to "pickle" copper rods in an acid bath in 1956. Wearing an acid-resistant suit, Santos topped his factory gear with a protective straw hat of his own design (Hastings Historical Society).

Concurrent with the decline in manufacturing, the agricultural sector in the county began to drop significantly, as age-old farms and orchards were turned over to real-estate developments or new corporate parks. In 1964, 18,500 acres were farmed in Westchester. Ten years later only 9,000 acres were under cultivation. The decline increased even more between 1983 and 1994, when nearly 4,000 acres, or 36 percent of the total, was taken out of productive use.[58] New corporate offices dotted the region, with companies like PepsiCo, IBM, Hitachi and Union Carbide settling into large and modern facilities across the county.

The housing and construction boom was driven in part by this new wave of workers to the region, as well as a rise in new waves of immigrants. In 2000, Hispanics accounted for 15.6 percent of the county's total population, compared to 9.9 percent in 1990. Asians also increasingly became part of the fabric of Westchester.[59] The Asian population also grew by 27 percent between 1990 and 2000; Asian residents made up 3.7 percent of the county's total population at the turn of the century. That number would rise again in the 21st century, when Asians made up around six percent of the population.[60]

Cubans fleeing the Castro revolution in their home country were among the first to arrive in Westchester, doing factory work. Citizens of other Latin American countries began heading north for work and opportunity. Spanish-speaking workers immigrated to the region to fill the new labor demands, and chain migration from the home countries of the earlier arrivals added substantially to the number of immigrants.

What began as a trickle became a flood of immigrants from Latin America. By the 1990s, roughly 10 percent of the county's population was Hispanic. The number of Hispanics living in the county went from 45,556 in 1980 to 86,130 in 1990. In 2000, the number was 144,124, an increase of 67 percent, a total that represented 15 percent of the county's population.[61]

In places like Port Chester, Mount Kisco, Sleepy Hollow and New Rochelle, large new immigrant enclaves were carved out, catering to the needs of the new arrivals. They did the hot work of the suburbs—washing dishes, mowing lawns, laying sheetrock. Women often worked in childcare as nannies. They came to be known as "brown collar" jobs, a term popularized by sociologist Lisa Catanzarite.

In New Rochelle, one man was credited for the stream of Mexican migration—as cousins and other family relatives followed in the path of their relations moving to the Queen City of the Sound. Antonio Valencia left Mexico in 1954 after he had a chance encounter in Mexico City with George and Allys Vergara of New Rochelle. George Vergara, an insurance executive, served one term as mayor of New Rochelle. Valencia signed on to be the "houseman" for the Vergara family—driving and doing light chores. "I wanted to improve my way of life," he recalled. "There were not many opportunities there" in Mexico. Hundreds of other Mexicans from the central-western region of Mexico later came to New Rochelle under the guidance of Valencia, who was often called "El Padrino" in New Rochelle's Hispanic community.[62]

In Mount Kisco, immigration came from the farm country of Guatemala and a town in the eastern section of the country, Chiquimula.[63] According to the U.S. Census of 2000, Latinos were 25 percent of the population of Mount Kisco. Some 60 percent were Guatemalan, and roughly half of the Hispanic immigrants in the village were undocumented.[64] In Port Chester, in the 1980s, Hispanic population grew in numbers to 7,500, or 30 percent of its 25,000 residents.[65] Those rates of growth, combined with the rising number of Hispanics in the workforce, created backlash and resentments in a number of Westchester communities.

In Mount Kisco, the presence of day laborers looking for work on street corners became a topic of concern. In 1995, village leaders passed a law, Local Law 6, that made it illegal for day laborers to solicit work on street corners. A specific parking lot was set aside for them, and a permit process was established. The village also began cracking down on the overcrowded and frequently dangerous houses and apartments into which immigrants were piled. The raids were carried out in the early morning hours, and tenants found inside the residences faced criminal charges on housing-code violations that brought penalties including $1,000 fines or 15-day jail sentences. In one raid on Main Street, 15 people were found in a commercial space where housing was legally prohibited.[66]

Advocates of the Hispanic community filed a lawsuit against the Mount Kisco village administration in late 1996, claiming that the laws were being used to selectively harass Hispanics. The lawsuit was propelled with legal assistance from the American Civil Liberties Union and the Westchester Hispanic Coalition. Days before the case was set to go to trial in the late summer of 1997, a settlement was reached. The village admitted to no wrongdoing, and it dropped the provisions that had led to the lawsuit. Day laborers were not restricted to one parking lot, and a less restrictive housing code spelled out by New

York State was implemented.[67] A hiring center, where laborers could also learn English and find shelter from bad weather, was eventually built.[68]

As the county's demographics changed through immigration, becoming much less white, other changes could be perceived, though they were not as easily discernible as a census table. But the handwriting on the embossed stationery was perfectly legible—the decline of the WASPs was apparent.

In 1985, the mayor of New York City, John Lindsay, a prototypical WASP, called his tribe—the northeastern White Anglo-Saxon Protestant, descended from colonial settlers—"an endangered species." Charlotte Curtis, herself an old WASP from the Midwest, interviewed Lindsay for a column and observed the waning influence of the WASP establishment. "They no longer dominate New York," she wrote. "While they are perceived as having tremendous power they're down to a few commercial banks, hunks of real estate, corporate chairs, culture boards and their clubs."[69]

For generations before they went into less prominent positions, they were easy to spot. They never wore white after Labor Day and places like Westchester County were their natural habitat. Doyennes of the old establishment placed great emphasis on proper dress and decorum. Brooke Astor, a patrician socialite who wore the crown of the kingdom while holding court on a hillside in Briarcliff Manor, set the tone for the way the rich are supposed to behave, dressing the part to perfection: "I always wear a hat—you see, I was brought up to all that," she once explained.[70] Within the parts of the country like the Connecticut suburbs and Westchester where Astor and her cohort held sway, it followed from their overarching authority to decide where everyone else could work, study, live and play.

But the emergence of a new set of rules that allowed entry into the elite, not through bloodlines and family social position, but by achievement, began to take shape in 1958, the same year that a British sociologist coined the term "meritocracy." The prediction that the new elite would come from strivers with high levels of educational achievement and good scores on standardized tests was taken up by a wide range of reformers. The "rise of the meritocracy" coincided with the demolition of the walls of exclusion that WASPs had erected around elite colleges, professional schools and jobs in law, medicine, academia and finance that kept out Jews, Catholics and other minorities. New pathways were opening into selective colleges and well-heeled suburbs. The social privileges the WASPs were accused of hoarding began to fall from their hands.

"The WASP establishment, as we call it, didn't emerge until the early 20th century," noted Nicholas Lemann, an author and journalist from Pelham who wrote about the old American aristocracy. "It had a fairly short heyday. In mid-century, it had an iron grip on everything, and by the last quarter of the century, it was palpably losing its grip."[71]

The WASPs defended their supremacy by their presumed dedication to the national interest; they were said to be driven by the public good and imbued with a rigorous dedication to duty, much like the landed gentry in England. They were also highly self-critical, and the most cutting look at the WASP tradition came from E. Digby Baltzell, a Philadelphia blue blood and sociologist. He popularized the term "WASP" while decrying the barriers of exclusion that they put up to outsiders and calling for the old establishment to open its doors to new talent.

When it was time for WASPs to send in a final thank-you note for all the memories, not everyone was sad to see them depart their central position on the historical stage. There was always hostility to their institutional control, and not much nostalgia was felt by others who suffered its sting. As social commentator Camille Paglia noted in an essay, "I have been at war with WASPiness since I grew up in Upstate New York in the 1950s and early 60s. There is no way to describe the brute social power of the WASP establishment of that period—the smooth, bland, coded good manners; the hidden past interconnections of families and business associations."[72] There was also some irony embedded in their decline. As Paglia noted, "The old WASP elite may be gone, but its style lingers and still typifies our central institutions in business and politics."[73]

Though a connection to the *Mayflower* may not be a requirement to join the elite anymore, the allure of the WASP mystique still remains strong among ambitious strivers of all ethnicities and religious backgrounds. "If you think of it as a brand, it's a very powerful brand," remarked Susan Cheever, the daughter of writer John Cheever and a Westchester native who attended The Masters School in Dobbs Ferry and rebelled against its strictures. She was taught how to make a Martini at the age of six by her grandmother.[74]

She witnessed, she said, a reaffirmation of the old WASP style in the 90s and 2000s, at least in appearances and fashion, even as its original practitioners were losing their control over the culture at large. The culture needs to have an elite, Cheever said, and many of its attitudes and customs have been imprinted by the old tradition. Striving up-and-comers often took great pains to gain entry to the institutions of the old elite, or to adopt the WASP definition of gentlemanly and ladylike behavior. The preppy look that they favored became a mainstay in the corridors of power as a result.

Like the democratization of luxury goods, and the spread of clean, crafty and preppy Martha Stewart-branded merchandise to the local shopping mall, the ways of the privileged few were coveted by the masses. Stewart, born Martha Kostyra, was herself the daughter of Polish immigrants from a modest middle-class background in New Jersey before re-inventing herself as the mistress of aspirational entertaining and style. As her media brand rose, she showcased her recipes, how-tos and her homes in the Hamptons and Westport, Connecticut, in her magazine *Martha Stewart Living*, eventually settling on an historic 152-acre estate in Katonah that became a template for her curated ideal of suburban living. (After her conviction on insider trading in 2004, she served five months of jail time and an additional five months of house arrest inside her compound.)

While Westchester has long counted itself as a suburban enclave safe from urban chaos and the cruel misfortunes that happen elsewhere, there were no safeguards on September 11, 2001. More than 100 Westchester residents died in the terrorist attacks in New York, Washington, D.C., and Pennsylvania. It was a beautiful fall morning, cloudless and blue, when the planes began crashing. A vast gray plume rose up hundreds of feet in the air above the Manhattan skyline, seemingly inexhaustible, a pillar of smoke that lasted for weeks and burned across television screens much longer.

The first victims of the attacks worked in insurance and finance companies like Marsh & McLennan or Cantor Fitzgerald. Mainly in their 30s and 40s, they were in the prime years of their careers and the parents of young children. After the emergency services were called to the disaster scene, twelve men with roots in Westchester perished that day wearing the gear of the New York City Fire Department. Fire lieutenant Charles Garbarini, a Pleasantville father of two, carried a jokey business card ("You light 'em, we fight 'em") and enjoyed his job immensely.[75] Another firefighter from Peekskill, Samuel Otice, coached a roller-hockey team and taught fire safety in local schools. A former Peekskill police officer before joining the New York Fire Department, he loved riding roller coasters.[76]

Communities with large numbers of commuters in the financial sector who worked in the World Trade Center building saw many die that day. Some towns were especially hard hit—Rye lost 15 residents and former residents in the attacks. Scarsdale had seven residents perish, a substantial figure given its size. Yonkers lost 12. White Plains 6.[77] In the days following the attacks, there were anguishing choices for the spouses and family members left behind: How do you tell small children that a parent would never be coming home again? Or decide to hold a funeral service before a body had been recovered and identified?

Dozens of Westchester firefighters also went to New York City in the days following to work on "the Pile" where the Twin Towers once stood, or fill in at firehouses around the city while the FDNY crews worked at Ground Zero. Frank Becerra, Jr., was one of those volunteers, a North White Plains fire chief and photojournalist with a long background in the fire services. Arriving at the scene of destruction, he heard the eerie sound of multiple "PASS alarms," distress signals that firefighters wear that send out a loud alert if no motion is made by the wearer in 30 seconds. Becerra heard the devices going off continually.[78]

Becerra worked on a bucket line, "like ants on an anthill," searching through dust-covered concrete and steel.[79] Hoisting five-gallon buckets, he got to know other volunteers from suburban departments who came to work on the pile: "It was back-breaking work, but few let it show." When a body was found, the buckets were put down and a body bag passed up the line for removal. Workers on the rescue line occasionally had to make a hasty retreat, as when a "crackling sound" was heard and an alert sounded that a building collapse was imminent. "Running in full fire gear is not easy, but you would be surprised at how fast you can run if you believe there is a building behind you that may be falling," he recalled.[80]

After three days at Ground Zero, Becerra returned to North White Plains on one of their rigs. He had a puzzling moment on the way, driving up the West Side Highway in Manhattan, as hundreds of people waved and cheered. "I looked in the rearview mirror, trying to determine for whom they were cheering. But it was us, a small fire department in the suburbs," Becerra wrote. "I couldn't help but think that the real heroes were behind us. They were the firefighters, police officers and paramedics who ran into the World Trade Center as others fled the flames. It was an honor to just help look for them."[81]

In 2006, a memorial was built to the Westchester dead on 9/11. It was designed on a *pro bono* basis by a Manhattan architect, Frederic Schwartz. Called "The Rising," it lifts upwards to the sky like a helix, a skein of 109 steel rods culminating in an apex some 80 feet from the base. Standing in the middle and looking up, one can see the steel rods creating a circle at the top, suggesting a coming-together from many parts, or a pinpoint of access into the sky. Marble plaques around the base of the steel sculpture list the names of the men and women who lost their lives and include brief descriptions or sentiments written by loved ones.

The shock from 9/11 was intensely felt around the region. After an initial lull, the building boom which had been gaining momentum since the late 1990s continued. Pushed by rising housing costs in New York City, Westchester saw a major growth in the residential real-estate market. Large-scale construction took off with high rises in White Plains, Yonkers and New Rochelle, each of which gained a new skyline visible for miles around. While the Westchester County court used to be the tallest building in White Plains for decades, by the late 1990s, it had been eclipsed by a series of downtown towers. In 2006, the Ritz-Carlton Hotel in downtown White Plains became the tallest in the county at 44 stories.[82]

Built at the Kensico Dam in 2006, the Westchester 9/11 Memorial rises 80 feet from the plaza, narrowing to a fine point. A visitor, gazing upward, can see a perfect sphere from inside the helix, like a hole in the sky. (Tyler Sizemore).

The cities of Westchester were remaking themselves in other ways beyond residential construction. The city of Yonkers took an innovative path in urban design by opening up a section of the Saw Mill River Parkway that had been buried in concrete for decades.[83] The so-called "day-lighting" of the river created a green space and a flourishing ecosystem amidst the cityscape, attracting egrets, turtles, salamanders and muskrats to the heart of the city.

The human population in Westchester's cities rose substantially, as well, after a period of decline or stagnation. According to the Westchester County Department of Planning, Yonkers' population grew four percent from 1990 to 2000, from 188,082 to 196,086, reversing a previous decline. Peekskill's population also rose markedly, with growth from 19,536 to 22,441 residents, or 15 percent, in the decade preceding 2000. White Plains grew significantly since the 1990 census.[84]

The county also maintained and enhanced its ability to attract bold-faced names. Westchester has always been home to powerful figures in media, finance and politics, so it was not especially surprising when Bill and Hillary Clinton began house hunting in Westchester after the couple left the White House. Hillary Clinton had by now set her sights on the U.S. Senate. After looking in a number of Westchester communities, the Clintons settled in 1999 in a Dutch Colonial on Old House Lane in Chappaqua, which they acquired for $1.7 million. Hillary Clinton said it had all the right elements for a home after the White House. "Eventually, we found the perfect place, an old farmhouse and barn in Chappaqua," she recalled.[85] The Secret Service detail set up their command post in the renovated barn in the backyard.[86]

As Bill Clinton later explained, a house in northern Westchester was an idea that Hillary had sold him on. "I said, 'Hillary, I'm a redneck, I grew up in Arkansas,'" he explained to a business group in 2003. "'If you're going to make me go to New York, you've got to let me at least move to New York City.' And she said, 'No, no, you don't know what you're talking about.' Well, as is usually the case in the last 30 years, she was right and I was wrong, and I really do like it here. I go running in that Rockefeller Park. I like the golf courses and I like my neighbors."[87]

The Clintons found good-natured acceptance as they settled into Chappaqua, becoming well-known figures around town. Hillary and Bill were partial to Lange's Little Store, a deli where Hillary picked up muffins and egg sandwiches every morning as she began her successful candidacy for the U.S. Senate and the seat formerly occupied by Senator Patrick Moynihan.[88] Through the years, the Clintons marched in Memorial Day parades and held book signings at the local library. They were the first presidential couple to live in Westchester since President Ulysses S. Grant spent a short time in South Salem, while he worked on his memoirs, in the 1880s.[89]

Another future president, Donald Trump, has had a significant presence in Westchester. He acquired an old golf club in Briarcliff Manor in 1997 and rebuilt it into the Trump National Golf Club, with its very own artificial waterfall on the 13th hole. The Trump organization also bought the estate of former *Washington Post* publisher Eugene Meyer, a 213-acre expanse in Bedford, North Castle and New Castle.[90] Trump made news in 2009 when he set aside some of his land in Bedford for Libyan dictator Muammar Gaddafi to use while he attended the United Nations General Assembly in Manhattan. A tent erected for Gaddafi's lodgings on Trump land off Oregon Road in Bedford catered to Libyan strongman's particular fondness for caravan-in-the-desert-like housing while he travelled. After substantial complaints and legal action from the town of Bedford once the tent was erected, the idea was dropped, and Gaddafi never made the trip.[91]

As the county embarked on a new building boom, its aging infrastructure became a serious issue of concern, most notably the Tappan Zee Bridge. It was built to only last 50 years when it was started during the Korean War, as wartime conditions lead to expediencies of construction.[92] The 50-year milepost was exceeded in 2005, and with maintenance costs growing and concerns mounting about a major failure of the span, it was clear the time had come for a replacement. During the building boom, state and regional leaders eventually hammered out a plan to build a sleek, two-spanned replacement between the Westchester and Rockland shorelines, and work began in 2013. The cost was $4 billion, and one of the largest floating cranes in the world took anchor in the central channel of the Hudson to facilitate the work. Around 333,000 cubic yards of concrete were poured onto the roadway, suspended by 400-foot-tall towers and cables that incline outwards.[93]

In the fall of 2017, the first part of the new bridge was opened to acclaim. Governor Andrew Cuomo marked the occasion at the wheel of a canary-yellow 1955 Chevrolet Corvette. Riding alongside him was Armando Galella, a Sleepy Hollow veteran of World War II, who had once driven the same make and model across the Tappan Zee on its opening day in 1955.[94] As crowds watched and waved, the sports car sped past miles of engineered steel cables, 140 feet above the water's edge. The little yellow car tracked the crossing that tens of thousands of commuters later made, and which now daily intersect the spot where Dutch mariners sailed the *Half Moon* four centuries before. In those brief moments, spanning land, water and time, the county's past, present and future come together.

Westchester County will always be shaped by its residents. Through years of industry, labor, immigration, activism and innovation, the people of this county have continued to reimagine it not as a regional network of cities, towns, villages and open spaces but as a truly distinctive and iconic suburb they call home. "The cities and mansions that the people dream of," cultural critic Lewis Mumford once said, "are those in which they finally live."

Chapter Notes

Introduction

1. Lewis Mumford, *1927 Yearbook*, Poughkeepsie, NY, Dutchess County Historical Society, preface

Chapter 1

1. Russell Shorto, *The Island at the Center of the World*, New York, Vintage, 2005, p. 33.
2. *Ibid.*, p. 32.
3. *The North American Review*, Vol. 44, 1837, p. 314, digital.
4. Frederic Shonnard and W.W. Spooner, *History of Westchester County*, New York, New York History Co., 1900, p. 58.
5. Adriaen van der Donck, *A Description of the New Netherlands*, Lincoln, University of Nebraska Press, 2008, p. 82.
6. *Ibid.*, p. 82.
7. *Ibid.*, p. 73.
8. Vernon Benjamin, *The Hudson River Valley: From Wilderness to the Civil War*, New York, Overlook Press, 2014, pp. 66–67.
9. Shorto, p. 281.
10. Frederic Shonnard, W.W. Spooner, *History of Westchester County*, 1861, Harrison, NY, Harbor Hill Books, reprinted 1974, p. 101.
11. Shorto, p. 112.
12. *Ibid.*, p. 120.
13. *Ibid.*, p. 123.
14. *Ibid.*
15. E.B. O'Callaghan, *Documentary History of the State of New York*, vol. 4., Albany, Charles Van Benthuysen, public printer, 1851, p. 270.
16. O'Callaghan, vol. 4, p. 276.
17. Shonnard, p. 101.
18. J.F. Jameson, editor, *Journal of New Netherland*, Project Gutenberg, digital, 2009, p. 15.
19. Shonnard, p. 101.
20. *Ibid.*, p. 183.
21. *Ibid.*, p. 201.
22. Liam Connell, *A Great or Notorious Liar: Katherine Harrison and Her Neighbours, Wethersfield, Connecticut, 1668–1670*, Melbourne, Australia, *Eras Journal*, Edition 12, Issue 2, Mar. 2011, p. 3.
23. Richard Tomlinson, *Witchcraft Trials of Connecticut: The First Comprehensive Documented History of Witchcraft Trials in Colonial Connecticut*, Hartford, Connecticut Research Inc., 1978, p. 47.
24. Connell, p. 24.
25. *Ibid.*, p. 20.
26. Tomlinson, p. 48.
27. O'Callaghan, p. 138.
28. Samuel Drake, *Annals of Witchcraft*, Boston, W. Elliot Woodward, 1869, pp. 133–134.
29. Shonnard, p. 74.

Chapter 2

1. Edgar J. McManus, *A History of Negro Slavery in New York*, Syracuse, Syracuse University Press, 1966, p. 105. 106.
2. Jacob Judd, *Frederick Philipse and the Madagascar Trade*, New York, New York Historical Society, vol. LV, number 4, 1970.
3. *Ibid.*
4. *Ibid.*
5. Peter Eisenstadt, editor, *The Encyclopedia of New York State*, Syracuse, Syracuse University Press, 2005, p. 1200.
6. Charles Baird, *Chronicle of a Border Town, The History of Rye*, New York, Anson Randolph, 1871, p. 182.
7. John Curran, *Peekskill's African-American History*, Charleston, SC, The History Press, 2008, p. 16.
8. Baird, p. 184.
9. Jon Butler, *The Huguenots in America*, Cambridge, Harvard University Press, 1983, p. 175.
10. *Ibid.*
11. Leslie M. Harris, *In the Shadow of Slavery: African Americans in New York City, 1626–1863*, Chicago, University of Chicago Press, p. 113, 114.
12. *Ibid.*, p. 342.
13. Indentured document, Jan. 6, 1781, manuscript 99, original document, Westchester County Historical Society.
14. *Ibid.*
15. Manumission, Apr. 1, 1808, manuscript 121, original document, Elmsford, Westchester County archives.
16. Bill of sale, Apr. 13, 1784, manuscript 47, Elmsford, Westchester County Archives.
17. Livingston Rutherford, *John Peter Zenger*, New York, Chelsea House, 1904, reprinted 1981, introduction.
18. James Alexander, *A Brief Narrative of the Case and Trial of John Peter Zenger*, Cambridge, Harvard University Press, 1963, p. 18, 101.
19. Alvah French, editor, *History of Westchester County*, New York, Lewis Historical Publishing, 1925, p. 95.
20. Otto Hufeland, *Westchester County During the American Revolution*, Harrison, NY, Harbor Hill Books, 1974, p. 23.

21. French, p. 100.

22. Ron Chernow, *Alexander Hamilton*, New York, Penguin, 2004, p. 60.

23. French, p. 101, 102.

24. Hufeland, p. 68, p. 72.

25. Barnet Schecter, *The Battle for New York*, New York, Walker Books, 2002, p 224.

26. William Abbatt, *The Battle of Pell's Point*, 1901, New York, W. Abbatt, p. 7.

27. Hufeland, p. 124.

28. Schecter, p. 230.

29. Manuscript 193, Revolutionary War Archives, Westchester Historical Society.

30. Chernow, p. 81.

31. Wayne Franklin, *James Fenimore Cooper: The Early Years*, New Haven, Yale University Press, p. 225, 270.

32. Huefland, p. 412.

33. Lincoln Diamant, *Chaining the Hudson: The Fight for the River in the American Revolution*, The Bronx, Fordham University Press, 2004, p. 110.

34. Hufeland, p. 295.

35. Glenn Collins, "Remnants of Revolution, $17 Million," *New York Times*, June 15, 2006, p. B2.

36. Hufeland, p. 295.

37. William Hadaway, editor, *The McDonald Papers*, Vol. 2, New York, Knickerbocker Press, p. 425.

38. John J. Curran, *Peekskill's African American History*, Charleston, SC: The History Press, 2008, p. 18.

39. Hufeland, p. 346.

40. James Thacher, *Military Journal During the American Revolutionary War*, 1823, New York, New York Public Library, digital, p. 272.

41. Hufeland, p. 371.

42. *Ibid.*

43. Hufeland, p. 379.

44. Allison Albee, *The Nasty Affair at Pines Bridge*, Yorktown Historical Society, 2005, p. 94.

45. *Ibid.*, p. 2.

46. William Nell, *The Colored Patriots of the American Revolution*, Chapel Hill, University of North Carolina at Chapel Hill, 1999, orig. 1855, p. 127.

47. Hufeland, p. 392, 393.

48. *Ibid.*, p. 391, 394.

49. Noel Rae, *The People's War*, Guilford, CT, Globe Pequot Press, 2012, p. 220.

Chapter 3

1. Terry Ariano, "Beasts and Ballyhoo, The Menagerie Men of Somers," *Westchester Historian*, Westchester County Historical Society, Summer 2008.

2. Terry Ariano, *The Bandwagon*, Columbus, Ohio, Circus Historical Society, Jan.-Feb. 2005, vol. 49(1).

3. Alvah French scrapbook, 39:91, Westchester County Historical Society (Hampton Monitor, Oct. 27, 1887).

4. Ariano, *The Bandwagon*.

5. Stuart Thayer, *American Circus Anthology*, digital, preface, p. 1.

6. William L. Slout, *Olympians of the Sawdust Circle: A Biographical Dictionary of the Nineteenth Century Circus*, Rockville, MD, Borgo Press, 2010, p. 13.

7. Marilyn Weigold, "The Beast That Put Somers on the Map," *New York Times*, May 15, 1977, Regional Section, p. 13.

8. John Keane, *Tom Paine: A Political Life*, New York, Grove, 2003, p. 251, 254.

9. *Ibid.*, p. 505.

10. John Deedy, "Tom Paine Would Drink to New Rochelle," *New York Times*, Apr. 22, 1973, Travel section, p. 4.

11. Craig Nelson, *Thomas Paine: Enlightenment, Revolution, and the Birth of Modern Nations*, New York, Penguin, p. 327.

12. *Ibid.*, p. 7.

13. David. W. Chen, "Rehabilitating Thomas Paine, Bit by Bony Bit," *New York Times*, Mar. 30, 2001, p. B1.

14. George Wilson Pierson, *Tocqueville in America*, Baltimore, Johns Hopkins University Press, 1996, p. 102.

15. *Ibid.*, p. 208.

16. Col. Levi Burr, *Voice From Sing Sing, A Synopsis of the Horrid Treatment of the Convicts at that Prison*, report to state legislature, 1833, Westchester County Historical Society.

17. *Ibid.*, p 19, 34.

18. *Ibid.*, p. 18.

19. *Ibid.*, p. 24.

20. *Ibid.*, p. 40.

21. *Ibid.*, p. 33, 47.

22. James Cardinal, "Eight Who Were Hanged," *Westchester Historian*, Westchester County Historical Society, vol. 46, 1970.

23. *Ibid.*

24. *Ibid.*

25. *Westchester Spy*, Jan. 24, 1838, Westchester County Historical Society.

26. "The Eudora Tragedy; Execution of the Negro Wilson," *New York Times*, July 26, 1856, p. 1.

27. Cardinal.

28. *Ibid.*

29. *Mount Vernon Daily Argus*, June 5, 1931, "Died on White Plains Gallows for Crime," p. 6; Michael Lavin and Frank Donovan, *Westchester County: Protect and Serve*, Charleston, SC, Arcadia Publishing, p. 21.

30. *New York Herald*, Sept. 14, 1842, Hastings Historical Society.

31. *Ibid.*

32. Elliott J. Gorn, *The Manly Art: Bare-Knuckle Prize Fighting in America*, Ithaca, Cornell University Press, p. 75.

33. *New York Herald*, Sept. 14, 1842, Hastings Historical Society.

34. *Ibid.*

35. Gorn, p. 76.

36. *Ibid.*

37. *New York Herald*, Sept. 14, 1842, Hastings Historical Society.

38. Gorn, p. 76.

39. *Ibid.*, p. 77.

40. *Westchester Herald*, Hastings Historical Society files.

41. *New York Tribune*, Sept. 19, 1842, Hastings Historical Society files.

42. *Biographical History of Westchester County*, Chicago, Lewis Publishing Co. 1899, vol. 2, p. 488.

43. *Ibid.*

44. Benson Lossing, *Sketching the Hudson, From the Wilderness to the Sea*, New York, Virtue and Lorson, 1866, p. 67.

45. *Ibid.*

46. Dan DeLuca, *The Old Leather Man*, Middletown, CT, Wesleyan University Press, 2008, p. 56.

47. *Ibid.*, pp. 58–59.

48. Randall Beach, "Mystery of Leatherman Lives On," *New Haven Register*, May 25, 2011, p. 3.

49. DeLuca, p. 59.

50. William Verplanck and Moses Collyer, *The Sloops of the Hudson*, 1908, New York, G.P. Putnam and Sons, p. 80.

51. Gerard Koeppel, *Water for Gotham*, Princeton, Princeton University Press, 2001, p. 140.

52. *Hudson River Chronicle*, Jan. 12, 1841.

53. *Ibid.*

54. Shonnard and Spooner, p. 574.

55. Andrew Jackson Downing, *Victorian Cottage Residences*, Mineola, NY, Dover Publications, 1981 reprint, 1842, preface.

56. *Ibid.*

57. *Ibid.*, pp. 226–227.

58. Walter Johnson, *River of Dark Dreams*, Cambridge, Harvard University Press, 2013, p. 111.

59. Carl Carmer, *The Hudson*, 1939, reprinted 1989, The Bronx, Fordham University Press, p. 209.

60. Russell Smith, *The Knickerbocker; Or, New-York Monthly Magazine,* Vol. 40, Oct. 1852, p. 342.

61. Carmer, p. 218.

62. "The Henry Clay Catastrophe; Seven More Bodies Found," *New York Times*, July 31, 1852, p. 2.

63. Mary Ellen Singsen, "The Quaker Way in Old Westchester," *Westchester Historian*, Westchester County Historical Society, 1982, vol. 58.

64. Don Papson and Tom Calarco, *Secret Lives of the Underground Railroad in New York City*, Jefferson, NC, McFarland, 2015, p. 112.

65. Aaron Powell, *Personal Reminiscences of the Anti-Slavery and Other Reform and Reformers*, New York, Caulon Press, 1899, p. 164.

66. Dorothee von Huene Greenberg, "Moses Pierce and the Underground Railroad," *Westchester Historian*, Westchester Historical Society, vol. 88, no. 1, Winter 2012.

67. *Ibid.*

68. *Ibid.*

69. *Ibid.*

70. Ernest Griffin, *Westchester County and Its People*, New York, Lewis Historical Publishing Co., p. 358.

71. William Czarnecki, "Mr. Lincoln's Visit to Peekskill," *Westchester Historian*, Westchester Historical Society, vol. 87, 2011.

72. *Ibid.*

73. John Scharf, editor, *History of Westchester County*, Philadelphia, L. E. Preston & Company, 1886, p. 507.

74. Jeff Canning and Wally Buxton, *History of the Tarrytowns*, Harrison, NY, Harbor Hill Books, 1974, p. 52.

75. Robert Browning, Jr., *Lincoln's Trident*, Tuscaloosa, University of Alabama Press, 2015, p. 481.

76. Hyland Kirk, *Heavy Guns and Light: History of the New York Fourth Artillery*, New York, C.T. Dillingham, 1890, p. 357.

77. Canning and Buxton, p. 51.

78. Muller Papers, Collection of the Bedford Hills History Museum, Westchester County Historical Society.

79. *Ibid.*

80. Griffin, p. 370.

81. Barbara Davis, *New Rochelle*, New York, Arcadia Publishing, p. 101.

82. Griffin, p. 368.

83. Robert Williams, *Horace Greeley*, New York, NYU Press, 2006, p. 241.

84. French, p. 157.

85. Griffin, p. 369.

86. Kenneth Jackson and David Dunbar, editors, *Empire City: New York Through the Centuries*, New York, Columbia University Press, 2005, p. 205.

87. Edythe Ann Quinn, *Freedom Journey: Black Civil War Soldiers and the Hills Community*, SUNY Press, Albany, p. 167.

88. *Ibid.*, p. 2.

89. *Ibid.*, p. 45.

90. *Ibid.*, p. 146.

91. *Ibid.*, p. 53.

92. *Ibid.*, p. 141.

93. *Ibid.*, p. 74, 119.

94. *Ibid.*, p. 6.

Chapter 4

1. Henry Dunkak, *Freedom, Culture, Labor, The Irish of Early Westchester County*, New Rochelle, NY, Iona College Press, 1994, Table C

2. Edward O'Donnell, *1001 Things Everyone Should Know About Irish-American History*, New York, Random House, 2002, p. 298.

3. Dunkak, Table C

4. "Reflections of Washington Irving," *Lippincott's Monthly Magazine: A Popular Journal of General Literature*, vol. 3, p. 557.

5. Charles Towson, YMCA report, *Italians in an American Community*, 1913, p. 2, 12, White Plains local history collection, White Plains Library.

6. *Ibid.*, p. 3, 7.

7. Mary Joseph D'Alvia, *The History of the New Croton Dam*, New York, Caltone Lithographers, 1976, collection of the White Plains Library.

8. Baila Shargel and Harold Drimmer, *The Jews of Westchester, A Social History*, Fleischmanns, NY, Mountain Press, 1994, p. 11.

9. *Ibid.*, pp. 78–79.

10. Speech at Westchester County Historical Society, Oct. 28, 1908, Westchester County Historical Society Proceedings.

11. Declaration of Intention, Petition for Naturalization, 1923, Westchester County Court, Westchester County Archives.

12. *Ibid.*

13. Hastings Historical Society, Waterfront Oral History Project, 1988.

14. *Ibid.*

15. John Masefield, *In the Mill*, New York, Macmillan, 1942, p. 4.

16. *Ibid.*, p. 7.

17. "Aftermath of the Great Calamity," *Peekskill Highland Democrat*, Aug. 10, 1918, p. 1.

18. "Our Heroic Dead," *Peekskill Highland Democrat*, Aug. 10, 1918, p. 4.

19. "Sparks from the Fire," *Peekskill Highland Democrat*, Aug. 3, 1918, p. 5.

20. Mary Josephine D'Alvia, *The History of the New Croton Dam*, Caltone, New York, p. 125.

21. "Morning Whistle May Precipitate Riot," *New York Herald*, Apr. 18, 1900, p. 5; "Strikers Held in Check by Troops," *New York Times*, Apr. 18, 1900, p. 1.

22. "Raid on Homes of Strikers," *New York Times*, Apr. 20, 1900, p. 2.

23. Christopher Tompkins, *The Croton Dams and Aqueduct*, Charleston, SC, Arcadia Publishers, 2000, p. 109.

24. Roger Panetta, editor, *Westchester: The American Suburb*, The Bronx, Fordham University Press, 2006, p. 187.

25. Mary Cheever, *The Changing Landscape, A History of Briarcliff Manor-Scarborough*, Briarcliff-Scarborough Historical Society, p. 32.

26. *Ibid.*, p. 35.

27. Shonnard and Spooner, p. 580.

28. *Ibid.*, pp. 621–622.

29. "Hospital Citing its 100th Year," *New York Times*, Oct. 16, 1994, regional news section, citing *New York Herald.*

30. "Juvenile Asylum Moves into Country Home," *New York Times*, May 24, 1905, p. 9.

31. Nelly Bly, "Nelly Bly Takes the Keeley Cure," *The World*, June 10, 1894, p. 1.

32. *Ibid.*

33. Brooke Kroeger, *Nellie Bly: Daredevil, Reporter, Feminist*, New York, Time Books, 1994, p. 228, 247.

34. George Swetnam, "Nellie Bly Poured Out Her Heart For Years to Quiet Observer," *The Pittsburgh Press*, Jan. 15, 1967, p. 146.

35. Bill McGrath, "Camp Woods Ossining: Methodist Campground to Secular Suburb," *Westchester Historian*, vol. 79, no, 3 Summer 2003.

36. Maury Klein, *The Life and Legend of Jay Gould*, Baltimore, Johns Hopkins University Press, 1997, p. 215.

37. "Russell Hopkins, Consul of Panama, Dead," *New York Tribune*, July 17, 1919, p. 8.

38. Jeff Canning and Wally Buxton, *History of the Tarrytowns*, Fleischmanns, NY, Purple Mountain Press/Harbor Hill, third printing, 1990, p. 229.

39. *Ibid.*

40. "Russell Hopkins, Consul of Panama, Dead," *New York Tribune*, July 17, 1919, p. 8.

41. The Collection of Arms Formed by the Late Russell Hopkins, Anderson Galleries, 1914, digital.

42. "Russell Hopkins, Consul of Panama, Dead," *New York Tribune*, July 17, 1919, p. 8.

43. A.H. Dunlop, *Gilded City*, New York, William Morrow, 2000, p. 170.

44. *Ibid.*, p. 171.

45. *Ibid.*, p. 184.

46. *Ibid.*, p. 191.

47. "Seeley-Tuttle," *New York Sun*, Dec. 31, 1896, p. 2.

48. "Harry Hid Behind My Skirts," *New York Tribune*, June 22, 1912, p. 22.

49. Fred Rosen, *The Historical Atlas of American Crime*, Infobase Publishing, 2005, p. 178.

50. Cecilia Rasmussen, "Girl in Red Velvet Swing Longed to Flee Her Past," *Los Angeles Times*, Dec. 11, 2005.

51. "Many New Yorkers Sailed on Lusitania," *New York Times*, May 8, 1915, p. 5.

52. French, p. 441.

53. Louisa Lockwood, *World War History of the City of White Plains*, 1926, p. 42.

54. French, p. 474, citing division history.

55. "Many New Yorkers on Casualty List," *Daily Argus*, Nov. 18, 1918, p. 7.

56. Stephen Harris, *Harlem's Hellfighters*, Sterling, VA, Potomac Books, 2005, p. 253.

57. World War 1, Roll of Honor Westchester County, NY, June 1, 1922, White Plains Public Library Collection.

58. *Memoirs of the Harvard Dead in the War Against Germany*, Harvard University Press, 1921, digital, p. 316.

59. "Memorial Trees Planted," *White Plains Daily Reporter*, Nov. 12, 1921, p. 3.

Chapter 5

1. "The Cosmopolitan Horseless Carriage Race," *Scientific American*, vol. 74, June 13, 1896.

2. James Landers, *The Improbable First Century of Cosmopolitan Magazine*, Columbia, University of Missouri Press, 2012, p. 112.

3. "Wheels From Westchester." *Hemmings Motor News*, May 2006.

4. "Thousands to See Briarcliff Race," *New York Times*, Apr. 24, 1908, p. 1.

5. "Strang a Favorite With Natives and Visitors," *New York Tribune*, Apr. 25, 1908, p. 8.

6. "Strang a Winner at Briarcliff," *New York Times*, Apr. 25, 1908, p. 1.

7. *Ibid.*

8. "Bronx Parkway Officially Opened," *New York Times*, Nov. 6, 1925, "Bronx Parkway Officially Opened," p. 26.

9. Booth Tarkington, *The Magnificent Ambersons*, New York, Doubleday, 1919, chapter 18.

10. *American Heritage Dictionary of the English Language*, Fourth Edition, 2000.

11. "Many Auto Speeders Fined," *New York Times*, Nov. 11, 1906, p. 6.

12. "Auto Left Sisters to Die," *New York Times*, Apr. 2, 1906, p. 1.

13. "Legal Regulations for Auto Tourists," *New York Times*, May 19, 1907, p. 9.

14. "Bronx River Parkway Opens," *White Plains Daily Reporter*, Nov. 6, 1925, p. 1.

15. "Bronx River Parkway Taken Over By Public," *Herald Statesman*, Nov. 6, 1925, p. 1.

16. "The Bronx River Parkway," *Herald Statesman*, Nov. 6, 1925, editorial, p. 10.

17. "War on Petting Parties," *New York Times*, Aug. 23, 1923, p. 14.

18. "Police Begin Drive on Petters," *White Plains Reporter*, July 16, 1928, p. 1.

19. "Two Are Jailed in New Raid on Petters," *White Plains Reporter*, July 18, 1928, p. 1.

20. "500 Parkers Are Driven Away in a Campaign at the Dam," *White Plains Daily Reporter*, July 16, 1928, p. 1.

21. "Building Projects in Westchester," *New York Times*, Dec. 31, 1922, section 10.

22. *American Mercury*, Jan. 1935.

23. *The Evening World*, Feb. 16, 1931.

24. John Crider, *Boss Ward, The Story of Modern Westchester*, unpublished, 1935, Westchester County Historical Society, p. 208, 212.

25. *Ibid.*

26. *Ibid.*, p. 32.

27. "Land Deal Grand Jury to Be Picked," *Mount Vernon Daily Argus*, Oct. 30, 1929, p. 1.

28. *Westchester County Magazine*, vol. 10, no. 4, 1913.

29. "Louis Pope, Dry Law Era Figure, 66, Is Dead," *Yonkers Herald Statesman*, June 26, 1950, p. 2.

30. "Louis Pope Arrested," *Mount Vernon Daily Argus*, July 13, 1943, p. 1.

31. "$250,000 in Liquor Seized," *New York Times*, Mar. 26, 1932, p. 2.

32. "Louis Pope, Dry Law Era Figure, 66, Is Dead," *Yonkers Herald Statesman*, June 26, 1950, p. 2.

33. "Clean Up Mamaroneck Drive Inaugurated with Liquor Raid," *Yonkers Herald Statesman*, Dec. 18, 1928, p. 7.

34. "Gironda Case Expected to Go to Jury," *Mount Vernon Daily Argus*, Feb. 20, 1929, p. 9.

35. "Police Head Ousted at Mamaroneck," *New York Times*, Mar. 10, 1929, p. 19.

36. "Gironda Shot, Police Nab Kin of Louis Pope," *Yonkers Herald Statesman*, Jan. 23, 1933, p. 1.

37. "Sixty Dry Agents Seize 28 Port Chester Men," *New York Times*, Feb. 26, 1930, p. 5.

38. "Hi-Jackers Steal Alcohol from Greenburgh Police," *Yonkers Herald Statesman*, Oct. 11, 1929, p. 1.

39. Westchester County District Attorney, Case number 4591, 4592, Westchester County Archives.

40. *Ibid.*, DA Case number 7399.

41. *Ibid.*, DA Case number 4863.

42. "County Offers Reward in Killing of Trolley Men," *Yonkers Herald Statesman*, Aug. 3, 1925, p. 1.

43. "Marino Is Arrested in Trolley Murder," *New York Times*, Aug. 14, 1925, p. 3.

44. *Ibid.*

45. "DeMaio to Die in Chair Tonight," *New York Sun*, Aug. 19, 1926, p. 7.

46. "Criminal Are Worse Than Ever Before," *Yonkers Herald Statesman*, June 30, 1929, p. 3.

47. "Bullet as Cure for Gunmen," *White Plains Daily Reporter*, Jan. 9, 1929, p. 1.

48. *Ibid.*

49. "Bandit Slays Irvington Officer," *Tarrytown Daily News*, Mar. 4, 1929, p. 1.

50. "Duggan's Slayer Shot," *Tarrytown Daily News*, Mar. 6, 1929, p. 1.

51. Westchester District Attorney Case number 7550, Westchester County Archives.

52. "Scarsdale Pays Tribute to Sergeant Harrison," *Scarsdale Inquirer*, July 29, 1923, p. 1.

53. "$2 Million Gem Thief … Is Caught in Jersey," *New York Times*, Oct. 23, 1932, p. 1.

54. *Ibid.*

55. "U.S. Widens Search for Mystery Clues," *Yonkers Herald Statesman*, Oct. 18, 1930, p. 1.

56. "Beer Hose Discovered," *Yonkers Herald Statesman*, Oct. 16, 1930, p. 1.

57. "N.Y. Tabloids Differ as to Cleverness of Beer Hose," *Yonkers Herald Statesman*, Oct. 18, 1930, p. 1.

58. *Ibid.*

59. Rich Cohen, *Tough Jews*, New York, Simon & Schuster, 2013, p. 168.

60. "Schultz Reigned on Discrete Lines," *New York Times*, Oct. 25, 1935, p. 16.

61. "Brogan Facing Quiz Next Week in Brewery Suit," *Yonkers Herald Statesman*, May 28, 1938, p. 1.

62. "County Garage Used by Schultz as Bank," *Yonkers Herald Statesman*, May 28, 1938, p. 1.

63. "Little Brown Jug in Place of Old Glory," *New Rochelle Standard-Star*, June 16, 1924, p. 1.

64. "Little Jug Loses All-Seeing Place Atop City's Pole," *New Rochelle Standard-Star*, June 18, 1924, p. 1.

65. "Police Arrest Two Men as Pair Who Put Jug on City Hall's Flag Staff," *New Rochelle Standard-Star*, June 19, 1924, p. 1; "Officials Alone Sad," *New Rochelle Standard-Star*, June 20, 1924, p. 1.

66. "Yukon in Yonkers Halted by Court," *New York Times*, Jan. 4, 1924, p. 22.

67. "Four Arrested in $1,000,000 Mine Story," *Yonkers Herald Statesman*, May 10, 1922, p. 1.

68. *Ibid.*

69. "Yonkers Gold Mine Moved to Herkimer," *New York Times*, May 20, 1922, p. 3.

70. "Yonkers Miners Guilty," *New York Times*, Mar. 28, 1924, p. 25.

Chapter 6

1. John Crider, "Boss Ward," *The Story of Modern Westchester*, 1935, unpublished, Westchester County Historical Society, p. 212.

2. "Speed Work at Playland," *Mount Vernon Daily Argus*, Apr. 5, 1928, p. 18.

3. "Paradise Park Destroyed by Fire," *Rye Chronicle*, Oct. 16, 1926, p. 1.

4. Kathryn Burke, *Playland,* p. 9, Charleston, SC, Arcadia Publishing, 2008, p. 12.

5. "Playland, The Utmost in Parks," *Amusement Park Management*, vol. 1, Mar. 1928.

6. *Ibid.*

7. *Ibid.*

8. "Playland to Open Today," *New York Times*, May 25, 1928, p. 24.

9. Deborah Solomon, *American Mirror: The Life and Art of Norman Rockwell*, New York, Farrar, Straus and Giroux, 2013, p. 35.

10. *Ibid.*, p. 62.

11. Donna Greene, "Festival of Films with a Home-grown Touch," *New York Times*, Mar. 26, 2000, regional news section.

12. Frederick Warde, *Fifty Years of Make Believe,* New York, M.M. Marcy 1920, p. 305.

13. Richard Schickel, *D.W. Griffith, An American Life*, New York, Simon & Schuster, 1984, pp. 415–416.

14. *Ibid.*, p. 457, 483.

15. *Ibid.*, p. 420.

16. *Ibid.*, p. 432.

17. *Ibid.*, p. 602.

18. Kenneth Silverman, *Houdini!!!*, New York, HarperCollins, 1996, p. 211.

19. *Ibid.*, pp. 427, 431.

20. *Variety*, Aug. 16, 1918.

21. Silverman, p. 233.

22. *Ibid.*, p. 234.

23. *Ibid.*, p. 236.

24. "Noted Picture Star Dies at Ossining Hospital," *Ossining Democratic-Register*, Oct. 6, 1917, p. 3.

25. Ned Thanhouser with Bryan Smith, "Florence La Badie: Silent Film Star and Presidential Courtesan?" Thanhouser Company Film Preservation, Inc., Research Center, Thanhouser.org.

26. Richard Koszarski, *Hollywood on the Hudson*, New Brunswick, Rutgers University Press, 2008, p. 317.

27. "Klan Kleagle Is Arrested," *Yonkers Herald Statesman,* Jan. 31, 1923, p. 1.

28. *Ibid.*

29. "Klan Cross Stirs Yonkers," *New York Times*, Mar. 16, 1923, p. 3.

30. "Burn Cross on Church Lot," *New York Times*, May 11, 1924, p. 17.

31. George Godfrey, "Contrasts in Service," *New York Times*, Dec. 13, 1925, letter, p. 12.

32. "Klan Warns Couple," *New York Times,* Apr. 25, 1926, p. 16.

33. "Ku Klux Klan Initiates 30 at Annual Outing Near Peekskill," *Peekskill Highland Democrat*, July 17, 1926, p. 1.

34. "10,000 at Klan Gathering," *New York Times,* Sept. 2, 1930, "10,000 at Klan Gathering," p. 21.

35. "Klan Parade Ends in General Fight," *New York Times*, Nov. 9, 1928, p. 3.

36. "Walsh Vitriolic," *The Hastings News*, Sept. 9, 1927, p. 7.

37. "Hooded Men Escape Indictment," *New York Times*, Mar. 16, 1923, p. 1.

38. A'Lelia Bundles, *On Her Own Ground: The Life and Times of Madam C.J. Walker*, New York, Scribner, 2002, p. 216.

39. *Ibid.*, p. 37.

40. *Ibid.*, p. 23.

41. David Levering Lewis, *When Harlem Was in Vogue*, Oxford University Press, 1979, p. 111.
42. *Ibid.*, p. 168.
43. Bundles, p. 282.
44. Lewis, p. 166.
45. Bundles, p. 257.
46. *Ibid.*, p. 267, 283.
47. *Ibid.*, p. 288.
48. "Buyers Storm Negro Palace," *Tarrytown Daily News*, Nov. 28, 1930, p. 8.
49. *Ibid.*
50. "A Victorian in the Modern World," *New York Times*, Sept. 24, 1939, review of Hutchins Hapgood memoirs, section 6, p. 2.
51. Eric Homberger, *John Reed*, Manchester, Manchester University Press 1990, p. 116.
52. *Ibid.*, p. 54.
53. "A Victorian in the Modern World," *New York Times*, Sept. 24, 1939.
54. Proceedings of the Board of Supervisors of Westchester County, session of 1924, p. 429.
55. Baila Shargel and and Harold Drimmer, *Jews of Westchester: A Social History*, Fleischmanns, NY, Purple Mountain Press, 1994, p. 153.
56. "I.W.W. Pickets Pen Rockefellers," *New York Times*, May 4, 1914, p. 1.
57. "Tarrytown Police Route I.W.W. Forces," *New York Times*, June 1, 1914, p. 1.
58. Thai Jones, *More Powerful Than Dynamite*, New York, Bloomsbury USA, p.215.
59. *Ibid.*, p. 224.
60. "We Have Straddled," *Tarrytown Press-Record*, June 12, 1914, p. 5.
61. "Mrs. C.J. Gould Aids Free Speech Fight," *New York Times*, June 14, 1914, p. 11.
62. "Anarchists Egged in Tarrytown Riot," *New York Times*, June 23, 1914, p. 1.
63. "Anarchists Revile Court as Seven Are Sentenced," *New York Herald*, July, 29, 1914, p. 5.
64. "Exploded in Apartment Occupied by Tarrytown Disturbers," *New York Times*, July 5, 1914, p. 1.
65. John Thomas Scharf, *History of Westchester County*, Philadelphia, L. E. Preston & Company 1886, p. 877.
66. Geoffrey Ward and Ken Burns, *Not For Ourselves Alone*, New York, Alfred A. Knopf, 1999, p. 27.
67. Arthur and Elizabeth Schlesinger Library on the History of Women in America, Radcliffe Institute for Advanced Study, Harvard University.
68. Jacqueline Van Voris, *Carrie Chapman Catt: A Public Life*, New York, Feminist Press at CUNY, 1996, p. 218.
69. "Woman as Doormats," *New Rochelle Evening Standard*, July 3, 1920, p. 4.
70. Susan Goodier and Karen Pastorello, *Women Will Vote*, Ithaca, Cornell University Press, p. 191.
71. "Women Gain Right to Vote," *Tarrytown Daily News*, Nov. 7, 1917, p. 1.
72. Van Voris, p. 208.
73. Goodier and Pastorello, p. 189.
74. "Winners in the Election," *Mount Vernon Daily Argus*, Nov. 4, 1919, p. 1.
75. "Supervisor's Widow Steps in Mate's Campaign Shoes," *Mount Vernon Daily Argus*, Oct. 28, 1935, p. 1.
76. "Jane Todd Dies: G.O.P. Leader," *New York Times*, Nov. 9, 1966, p. 39.
77. "Ruth Taylor Re-Elected," *New York Times*, Nov. 9, 1932, p. 15.
78. "Caroline O'Day, in Four House Terms," *New York Times*, Jan. 5, 1943, obituary, p. 19.

79. Frederic Franklyn Van de Water, *The Grey Riders, The Story of the New York State Troopers*, New York, G.P. Putnam's Sons, 1922, p. 35.
80. *Outlook Magazine*, Feb. 22, 1928, digital.
81. *Ibid.*
82. *Ibid.*
83. *Ibid.*
84. *Ibid.*

Chapter 7

1. "Down the Hudson in a Box-Kite Plane," *New York Times*, May 25, 1930, p. 81.
2. *Ibid.*
3. "Fine Aviation Meet," *Eastern State Journal*, Sept. 7, 1912, p. 4.
4. Susan Butler, *East to the Dawn, The Life of Amelia Earhart*, Boston, Addison-Wesley, 1997, p. 212.
5. *Ibid.*, p. 215.
6. *Ibid.*, p. 216.
7. *Ibid.*, 217.
8. Doris Rich, *Amelia Earhart: A Biography*, Washington, D.C., Smithsonian Institution, 1989, pp. 112, 116.
9. *Ibid.*, p. 36.
10. John Nordberg, *Wings of Their Dreams*, West Lafayette, Purdue University Press, 2007, p. 180.
11. Interview with Louise Garwood, *Our Westchester*, Feb. 1931, Westchester County Historical Society.
12. Ruth Nichols, *Wings for Life*, New York, J.B. Lippincott, 1957, p. 1.
13. *Ibid.*, p. 127.
14. *Ibid.*, p. 101.
15. *Ibid.*, p. 100.
16. *Ibid.*, p. 94.
17. *Ibid.*, p. 160.
18. "Ruth Nichols Wings Clipped," *Inside Stuff*, Feb. 20, 1932, Purdue University Archives, Putnam Collection, p. 4.
19. Nichols, *Wings*, p. 244.
20. *Inside Stuff*, Purdue, Putnam Collection, p. 4.
21. Nichols, *Wings*, p. 18.
22. "Many Attend Tribute to Amelia Earhart," *Rye Chronicle*, May 20, 1938, p. 1.
23. Nichols, *Wings*, p. 262.
24. "Woman Aviator Found Dead," *New York Times*, Sept. 26, 1960, p. 28.
25. "Death Ruled Suicide," *New York Times*, Oct. 20, 1960, p. 39.
26. "Dies in Wall Street Leap," *New York Times*, Nov. 17, 1929, p. 2.
27. "V. Everit Macy Dies, Leader in Westchester," *New York Times*, Mar. 22, 1930, p. 19.
28. Westchester County Department of Social Services Annual Reports, summary, 1931, 1932, 1933, 1934, Westchester County Archives.
29. *Ibid.*, 1934 report.
30. "Letters to Santa," *White Plains Daily Reporter*, Dec. 16, 1934, p. 1.
31. "Levine Boy Sends Father a Ransom Plea," *Yonkers Herald Statesman*, Mar. 2, 1938, p. 1.
32. "Levine Boy's Bound Body Washed Ashore," *New York Times*, May 30, 1938, p. 1.
33. "Penn, Luck, Sentenced to Prison Terms," *Yonkers Herald Statesman*, Oct. 3, 1941, p. 9.
34. "Peter Levine's Body Found in Long Island Sound," *Life Magazine*, June 13, 1938.
35. "Pelham Agog When Local Man Questioned in Murder Mystery," *Pelham Sun*, July 12, 1929, p. 1.

36. Mike Dash, *The First Family: Terror, Extortion and the Birth of the American Mafia,* New York, Simon & Schuster, 2010, p. 40.

37. *Ibid.,* p. 212.

38. "Mother Charges Scarnici Killed Her Son," *White Plains Daily Reporter,* Sep. 23, 1933, p. 1.

39. "Says Gang Buried Her Son Alive," *New York Sun,* Sept. 22, 1933, p. 30.

40. "Charge Five Murders to Kisco Man," *White Plains Daily Reporter,* Sept. 22, 1933, p. 1.

41. "Kidnap Suspects Picked as Killers," *New York Times,* Sept. 22, 1933, p. 1.

42. "Four Murdered with Same Gun," *Mount Vernon Daily Argus,* Sept. 25, 1933, p. 1.

43. "O'Connell Hideout Sought in County," *White Plains Daily Reporter,* Sept. 21, 1933, p. 1.

44. "Four Murdered with Same Gun," *Mount Vernon Daily Argus,* Sept. 25, 1933, p. 1.

45. "The Law Within the Law," *White Plains Daily Reporter,* June 11, 1933, p. 6.

46. "Kidnap Victim on Way to Mount Kisco House," *Mount Vernon Daily Argus,* Sept. 21, 1933, p. 4.

47. "Scarnici, Mount Kisco Bandit, Is Executed," *White Plains Daily Reporter,* June 28, 1935, p. 1.

48. Alexandra Chasin, *Assassin of Youth,* Chicago, University of Chicago Press, p. 253.

49. *Ibid.,* p. 189, 190.

50. "Ferris Says Marijuana Raids 'Only Scratch the Surface,'" *Yonkers Herald Statesman,* May 23, 1938, p. 1.

51. *Ibid.*

52. "Police Break Up Dope 'Den' House," *White Plains Dispatch,* Apr. 8, 1938, p. 6.

53. Chasin, *Assasin,* p. 189.

54. "Will White Plains Parents Help Stop This Drug Sale?" *White Plains Daily Reporter,* May 23, 1938, p. 1.

55. "Source of Marijuana Dope is Dangerously Near Home," *White Plains Daily Reporter,* May 24, 1938, p. 1.

56. "Marijuana Effects Vary," *White Plains Daily Reporter,* May 25, 1938, p. 1.

57. "Many Marijuana Addicts in Swing Bands," *White Plains Daily Reporter,* May 26, 1938, p. 1.

58. "Police Raid Gambling Room," *White Plains Daily Reporter,* Sept. 21, 1939, p. 1.

59. "Sheriff Hunts Higher Ups in Pinball Games," *Tarrytown Daily News,* Feb. 1, 1940, p. 1.

60. "Police Raid Gambling Room," *White Plains Daily Reporter,* Sept. 21, 1939, p. 1.

61. *Ibid.*

62. "Pinball Machine Row," *Tarrytown Daily News,* Feb. 8, 1940, p. 1.

63. "Pinball Machines Return," *White Plains Evening Dispatch,* Apr. 4, 1940, p. 3.

64. "Opening of Sculpture Exhibit Is Postponed," *New Rochelle Standard-Star,* Aug. 21, 1923, p. 1.

65. *Ibid.*

66. "Venus and Adonis Linger," *New York Times,* Aug. 22, 1923, p. 15.

67. "Bunny Austin, 94, a Pioneer in Tennis Shorts," *New York Times,* Aug. 28, 2000, sports section.

68. "Sun Suits are Lingerie and Taboo in Rye Parks," *New York Times,* June 21, 1936, section 2, p. 1.

69. Shargel and Drimmer, *Jews of Westchester,* p. 153.

70. "Scantily Clad Garb of Hikers Decried," *Yonkers Herald Statesman,* Apr. 26, 1933, p. 1.

71. "Freedom of the Knees," *Yonkers Herald Statesman,* June 18, 1935, p. 6; "Aldermanic Nemesis of Semi-Nudists," June 18, 1935, p. 1.

72. "Long Live Shorts Club Warns Slater," *Yonkers Herald Statesman,* June 5, 1936, p. 9.

73. "Judge … to Rule on Shorts Ordinance," *Yonkers Herald Statesman,* June 30, 1936, p. 7.

74. "Court Reversal to Bring New Shorts War," *Yonkers Herald Statesman,* May 26, 1937, p. 1.

75. "Ruth Hits Three Homers in Sing Sing Game," *New York Times,* Sept. 6, 1929, p. 21.

76. "Alabama Pitts Wants to Forget Football," *Los Angeles Times,* Nov. 26, 1934, p. 10.

77. Ralph Blumenthal, *Miracle at Sing Sing: How One Man Transformed the Lives of America's Most Dangerous Prisoners,* New York, St. Martin's Press, 2004, p. 199, 266.

78. *Ibid.,* pp. 208–209.

79. Lewis E. Lawes, *20,000 Years in Sing Sing,* New York, Long and Smith, 1932, p. 412.

80. Blumenthal, *Miracle,* pp. 208–209.

81. *Ibid.*

82. Peter Duffy, "Willie Sutton: Urbane Scoundrel," *New York Times,* Feb. 7, 2002, City Section, p. 3.

83. Quentin Reynolds, Willie Sutton, *I, Willie Sutton: The Personal Story of the Most Daring Bank Robber and Jail Breaker of our Time,* New York, Farrar, Straus and Giroux, pp. 165, 168.

84. Duffy, "Willie Sutton," *New York Times,* p. 3.

85. Reynolds and Sutton, *I, Willie,* p. 131, 134.

86. *Ibid.,* p. 137.

87. David Goewey, *Crashout,* New York, Crown, 2005, p. 190.

88. *Ibid.,* p. 203.

89. *Ibid.,* p. 259.

90. Patrick Downey, *Gangster City: The History of the New York Underworld,* New York, Barricade Books, p. 116.

91. "Bus Crash Toll Reaches 19," *Ossining Citizen-Register,* July 25, 1934, p.1.

92. "Brakes Faulty for Entire Trip," *Ossining Citizen-Register,* July 23, 1934, p. 1.

93. *Ibid.*

94. *Ibid.*

95. "Fire Officials … on Father Kelly," *Ossining Citizen-Register,* July 25, 1934, p. 1.

96. "Survivor Tells How Parents, Sister Died," *Yonkers Herald Statesman,* July 23, 1934, p. 1.

97. John Dunning, *On the Air: The Encyclopedia of Old Time Radio,* Oxford, Oxford University Press, p. 63.

98. Marilyn Weigold, *The Long Island Sound: Its People, Places and Environment,* New York, NYU Press, 2004, p. 121.

99. Dunning, *On the Air,* p. 63.

100. *Ibid.,* p. 11.

101. *Ibid.*

102. *Ibid.,* p. 64.

103. *Ibid.,* p. 66.

Chapter 8

1. "Playland Concessionaires Rise to Defend Darling," *Ossining Citizen Register,* Oct. 31, 1932, p. 1.

2. "Playland Bars Negroes in Fear of Racial Clash," *Yonkers Herald Statesman,* Feb. 17, 1933, p. 18.

3. "Negroes Charge Color Line Drawn at Playland," *Yonkers Herald Statesman,* Feb. 10, 1933, p. 11.

4. *Ibid.*

5. "Negroes Charge Discrimination at Playland," *Tarrytown Daily News,* Feb. 10, 1933, p. 10.

6. "Playland Bars Negros in Fear of Racial Clash," *Yonkers Herald Statesman,* Feb. 17, 1933, p. 18.

7. "Negroes Charge Color Line Drawn," *Yonkers Herald Statesman,* Feb. 10, 1933, p. 11.

8. "Playland Bars Negroes in Fear of Racial Clash," *Yonkers Herald Statesman,* Feb. 17, 1933, p. 18.

9. "Negroes Charge Color Line Drawn," *Yonkers Herald Statesman,* p. 11.

10. "Urges Negro Residents to Fight For their Rights," *White Plains Daily Reporter,* Oct. 30, 1935, p. 5.

11. "Negroes Bring Charge of Racial Discrimination," *Rye Chronicle,* Nov. 15, 1935, p. 12.

12. "To Appeal Playland Case," *New York Times,* Nov. 13, 1935, p. 16.

13. *The Negro Motorist Green Book: 1937,* Schomburg Center for Research in Black Culture, Jean Blackwell Hutson Research and Reference Division, the New York Public Library, the New York Public Library Digital Collections, 1937.

14. Harold Esannason and Vinnie Bagwell, *A Study of African-American Life in Yonkers From the Turn of the Century,* Elmsford, NY, Self-published, 1993, Westchester County Historical Society, p. 30.

15. Roger Panetta, editor, "The Great Migration: Stories from the South to the North," Hudson River Museum/Marymount College, Yonkers, NY, 2002, p. 15.

16. *Ibid.*

17. "First Black Woman Lawyer in State Dies," *White Plains Reporter-Dispatch,* Sept. 15, 1983, obituary, p. 2.

18. *The Crisis,* N.A.A.C.P. Branch News, Dec. 1938, p. 401.

19. *The Crisis,* N.A.A.C.P. Branch News, Oct. 1930, p. 334.

20. Collymore Collection, Schomburg Center for Research in Black Culture, the New York Public Library, Box 3, Folder 1.

21. *Ibid.*

22. *Ibid.*, Letter to William Hill, Feb. 6, 1946, Box 3, Folder 1.

23. *Ibid.*, Collymore Collection, Letter to William Hill.

24. *Ibid.*

25. *Ibid.*

26. *Ibid.*

27. Author interview with James Collymore, 2017.

28. "Westchester 'Bunds' Arouse Resentment," *New York Times,* Mar. 18, 1935, p. 3.

29. Man Shot as Nazis Hold Gun Practice in County," *Mount Vernon Daily Argus,* Sept. 16, 1935, p. 1.

30. "War Foes Hit Profits," *Yonkers Herald-Statesman,* Aug. 5, 1935, p. 1.

31. *Ibid.*

32. "Ten Policemen Hurt in Port Chester," *New York Times,* Mar. 21, 1927, p. 1.

33. "Nazi-Bund Rally Here Quiet Here," *White Plains Reporter-Dispatch,* Apr. 25, 1938, p. 1.

34. *Ibid.*

35. "Nazi Rally Gets Big Police Guard," *New York Times,* Apr. 25, 1938, p. 3

36. "Nazi-Bund Rally," *White Plains Reporter-Dispatch,* p. 1.

37. *Ibid.*

38. "Nazi Rally Gets Big Police Guard," p. 3.

Chapter 9

1. "Japan Wars on U.S. and Britain," *New York Times,* Dec. 8, 1941, p. 1.

2. "War Declared by Congress, Police Round up All Japanese Nationals," *White Plains Reporter Dispatch,* p. 1.

3. "War Dead Total," *White Plains Reporter Dispatch,*" Apr. 26, 1949, p. 1.

4. "Pearl Harbor Vet Waits for his Stripes," *The Journal News,* June 13, 2001, p. 10.

5. "War Declared by Congress, Police Round up All Japanese Nationals," *White Plains Reporter Dispatch,* Dec. 8, 1941, p. 1.

6. Arthur Broes, "White Plains Goes to War," *Westchester Historian,* vol. 72, no. 2, Spring 1996.

7. "G.I. Harangs All of Rome," *Chicago Tribune,* June 6, 1944, p. 4.

8. Susan Swanson and Elizabeth Fuller, *Westchester County: A Pictorial History,* Norfolk, Donning Co., p. 151.

9. *Ibid.*

10. Broes, "White Plains Goes to War."

11. Stephen Ambrose, *The Good Fight,* New York, Simon & Schuster, p. 42.

12. "GM Plant Records Give Glimpse of Workers' Lives," *The Journal News,* July 9, 2002, p. 1.

13. John Kelly papers, Rye Historical Society.

14. *Ibid.*

15. *Ibid.*

16. *Ibid.*

17. *Ibid.*

18. Rick Atkinson, *An Army at Dawn,* New York, Henry Holt, p. 462.

19. John Kelly papers.

20. "Japan Surrenders," *Tarrytown Daily News,* Aug. 16, 1945, p. 1.

21. "Heavy Traffic Downtown," *White Plains Reporter Dispatch,* Dec. 10, 1945, p. 6.

22. "Flyer Receives Medal at Post Office," *White Plains Reporter Dispatch,* Dec. 20, 1945, p. 4.

23. Pamela Hanlon, *A Worldly Affair, New York, the United Nations and the Story Behind Their Unlikely Bond,* The Bronx, Empire State Editions, p. 22.

24. *Ibid.*, p. 24.

25. "Help UNO on Site," *White Plains Reporter Dispatch,* Feb. 4, 1946, p. 1.

26. "For the Greater Good," *White Plains Reporter Dispatch,* Feb. 5, 1946, p. 8.

27. Letters, *White Plains Reporter Dispatch,* Feb. 4, 1946, p. 8.

28. "Bedford Says 'No' to UNO," *White Plains Reporter Dispatch,* Feb. 4, 1946, p. 8.

29. "Legislation Giving Right to UNO Referendum," *Rye Chronicle,* Mar. 8, 1946, p. 13.

30. "Skyscraper Home Possible for U.N.," *New York Times,* Dec. 8, 1946, p. 1.

31. Bruce Dearstyne, *The Spirit of New York: Defining Events in the Empire State's History,* Albany, SUNY Press, p. 250.

32. *Ibid.*, p. 255.

33. *Ibid.*, p. 254.

34. Emerson Pugh, *Building IBM,* Cambridge, MIT Press, 1995, p. 240.

35. "15,000 Visit in Day Visit New Shop Center," *New York Times,* Apr. 28, 1954, p. 38.

36. "Center Rings up 30,000,000 Sales," *New York Times,* Jan. 1, 1955, p. 18.

37. "Hinterlands to North Get Big Office and Shopping Centers," *New York Times,* Aug. 15, 1955, p. 17.

38. *Ibid.*

39. Welcome to the Suburbs, Yorktown Historical Society, Chapter Four: yorktownhistory.org.

40. U.S. Decennial Census, United States Census Bureau; Total Population and Percent Change by Municipality, Westchester County, 1940–2010, Westchester County Department of Planning, digital.

41. Hugh Pomeroy Collection, series 21, Westchester County Archives.

42. *Ibid.*

43. *Ibid.*

44. *Ibid.*

45. "Deplores Shopping Malls Despoiling Beauty of Our Villages," *White Plains Reporter Dispatch*, Oct. 25, 1962, p. 8.

46. "Belated Remembrances of a Forgotten War," *New York Times*, May 26, 1996, section 13, p. 1.

47. Joan Mellen, *Hellman and Hammett*, Harper-Collins, New York, 1996, p. 282.

48. "Watch Radicals, Fanelli Demands," *White Plains Reporter-Dispatch*, Sept. 17, 1946, p. 7.

49. Associated Press report, *New York Democrat and Chronicle*, Rochester, Aug. 30, 1949, p. 5.

50. Martin Duberman, *Paul Robeson*, New York, Alfred A. Knopf 1988, p. 364.

51. *Ibid.*, p. 342.

52. Editorial, *Peekskill Evening Star*, Aug. 23, 1949, p. 4.

53. Duberman, *Robeson*, p. 365.

54. John Curran, *Peekskill's African-American History*, p. 81.

55. Duberman, *Robeson*, p. 369.

56. *Ibid.*

57. *Ibid.*, p. 366.

58. *Ibid.*, p. 370.

59. *Ibid.*, p. 371.

60. "A report of the violations of civil liberties at two Paul Robeson concerts near Peekskill," Violence in Peekskill: ACLU, 1949, p. 22.

61. *Ibid.*, p. 1.

62. Duberman, *Robeson*, p. 372.

63. "Gwinn Claims Commies Could Control House," *Ossining Citizen-Register*, Oct. 12, 1950, p. 1.

64. "Subversion in Education," *New York Times*, July 26, 1951, letters p. 20.

65. Carol O'Connor, *A Sort of Utopia: Scarsdale, 1891–1981*, Albany, SUNY Press, 1983, pp. 176–178.

66. *Ibid.*, p. 178.

67. "School Board Backs Books Under Attack," *New York Times*, Nov. 8, 1949, p. 12.

68. "School Book Curb Stirs a Protest," *New York Times*, Oct. 15, 1949, p. 5.

69. O'Connor, *Utopia*, p. 177.

70. *Ibid.*, p. 178.

71. *Ibid.*, p. 179.

72. *Ibid.*, p. 183.

73. "40 in Scarsdale Picket Concert," *New York Times*, Mar. 19, 1962, p. 31.

74. "Do Colleges Have to Hire Red Professors?" *The American Legion Magazine*, vol. 51, no. 5, Nov. 1951, digital.

75. "Sarah Lawrence Defies 'Red' Blast," *New York Times*, Jan. 23, 1952, p. 29.

76. "Instructor Quits Sarah Lawrence," *New York Times*, Apr. 22, 1953, p. 16.

77. *Ibid.*

78. Sam Roberts, *The Brother: The Untold Story of the Rosenberg Case*, New Yok, Random House, 2003, p. 438.

79. *Ibid.*, p. 20.

80. *Ibid.*

81. *Ibid.*

82. Robert Meeropol, *An Execution in the Family*, New York, Macmillan, 2003, p. 30.

83. *Ibid.*, p. 53.

84. "Sentinels of the City," *New York Times*, July 31, 2009, Westchester Section, p. 1.

85. "A-Shelter Can Be That Extra Room," *New York Times*, June 6, 1950, Section 8, p. 1.

86. "State Plan Asks Fallout Shelter in Every Building," *New York Times*, July 7, 1959, p. 1.

87. "Westchester Home Show Set," *New York Times*, Oct. 14, 1961, p. 46.

88. "Ad for Shelters Draws Shoppers," *New York Times*, Nov. 17, 1961, p. 19.

89. "Fallout Shelter Flops as Prize," *White Plains Reporter Dispatch*, Mar. 24, 1962, p. 1.

90. *White Plains Reporter Dispatch*, Oct. 30, 1962, p. 1.

91. "Byram Hills Gets Crash Course in CD Plan," "Go Home Plan Discussed by Lakeland School Board," *White Plains Reporter Dispatch*, Oct. 26, 1962, p. 1, p. 1.

92. Susan Cheever, *My Name Is Bill: Bill Wilson, His Life and the Creation of Alcoholics Anonymous*, New York: Simon & Schuster, 2004, p. 155.

93. *Ibid.*, p. 185.

94. Scott Donaldson, *John Cheever: A Biography*, New York, Random House, 1988, p. 118.

95. Blake Bailey, *Cheever: A Life*, New York, Knopf, 200, p. 176.

96. *Ibid.*, p. 123.

97. *Ibid.*, p. 125.

98. *Ibid.*, p. 126.

99. *Ibid.*, p. 145.

100. *Ibid.*, p. 462.

101. Donaldson, p. 111.

102. *Ibid.*

103. Bailey, p. 254.

104. Donaldson, p. 358.

105. Shargel and Drimmer, *The Jews of Westchester*, p. 154.

106. Harry Gersh, "Gentleman's Agreement in Bronxville," *Commentary*, Feb. 1, 1959.

107. O'Connor, *A Sort of Utopia*, p. 99.

108. *Ibid.*, p. 188.

109. Shargel and Drimmer, *The Jews of Westchester*, p. 211.

110. "$1,000 Reward Offered to Nab Swastika Painter," *Yonkers Herald Statesman*, Jan. 7, 1960, p. 2.

111. "Scarsdale Parish Rector Limits Communion," *New York Times*, Jan. 13, 1961, p.1.

112. *Ibid.*

113. "A Club Rebuked for Bigotry," *Life*, Jan. 20, 1961, p. 36.

114. "Incident in Suburbia," *Newsweek*, Jan. 23, 1961.

115. "Rector is Praised for Stand on Bias," *New York Times*, Jan. 16, 1961, p. 24.

116. O'Connor, *A Sort of Utopia*, p. 190.

117. "Scarsdale Minister Adds Task of Narrator to His Many Activities," *New York Times*, Oct. 23, 1962, p. 39.

118. Leonard Dinnerstein, *Antisemitism in America*, New York, Oxford University Press, p. 171.

Chapter 10

1. David Marc, *Comic Visions: Television Comedy and American Culture*, Hoboken, Wiley-Blackwell, 1997, p. 133.

2. Carl Reiner, *If You're Not in the Obit, Eat Breakfast*, HBO documentary, 2017.

3. Gerard Jones, *Honey, I'm Home*, New York, St. Martin's Press, 1993, p. 143.

4. Reiner, HBO documentary.

5. Charles Van Doren, "All the Answers," *The New Yorker*, July 28, 2008.

6. "Dan Enright, Key Figure in '50s Game Show

Scandals," *Los Angeles Times*, May 24, 1992, obituary, online.

7. *Ibid.*

8. "Albert Freedman, Producer of Rigged 1950s Quiz Show, Dies at 95," *New York Times*, Apr. 22, 2017, obituary, p. B5.

9. "F.C.C. Head Bids T.V. Men Reform Vast Wasteland," *New York Times*, May 10, 1961, p. 1.

10. Van Doren, "All the Answers," *The New Yorker*.

11. James Maguire, *Impresario: The Life and Times of Ed Sullivan*, New York, Billboard Books, 2006, p. 15.

12. *Ibid.*, p. 205.

13. Neal Gabler, *Winchell: Gossip, Power and the Culture of Celebrity*, New York, Vintage, 1994, p. 261.

14. Maguire, *Impresario*, p. 155.

15. Armond Fields, *Eddie Foy: A Biography*, Jefferson, NC, McFarland, 1999, p. 144.

16. Donald Miller, *Supreme City,* New York, Simon & Schuster, p. 521; Hastings Historical Society, Ziegfeld file.

17. William Koshatus, *Lou Gehrig: A Biography*, Westport, CT, Greenwood Press, p. 61.

18. Alyn Shipton, *Hi-Dee-Ho: The Life of Cab Calloway*, Oxford, Oxford University Press, 2010, P. 206.

19. W.J. Weatherly, *Jackie Gleason: An Intimate Portrait of the Great One*, Seattle, Pharos Books, 1992, pp. 112, 116.

20. W.A. Swanberg, *Dreiser,* New York, Charles Scribner's Sons, 1965, p. 357.

21. Swanberg, p. 297, 377.

22. Neal Thompson, *A Curious Man*, New York, Crown, 2013, p. 227, 316.

23. Jill Lepore, *The Secret History of Wonder Woman*, New York, Alfred A. Knopf, 2014, p. 153, 154.

24. Donald Spoto, *Marilyn Monroe: The Biography,* Lanham, MD, Rowman & Littlefield, 1993, p. 186.

25. Barbara Leaming, *Marilyn Monroe*, New York, Crown, 1998, p. 244–247.

26. *Ibid.*, p. 244–247.

27. "Marilyn Picks City for Marriage Date," *White Plains Reporter Dispatch*, June 30, 1965, p. 1.

28. Jeffrey Meyers, *The Genius and the Goddess*, Urbana, University of Illinois Press, 2010, p. 156.

29. *Ibid.*

30. Leaming, p. 247.

31. "Rita Wins Custody of Two Daughters," *White Plains Reporter Dispatch*, Apr. 27, 1954, p. 1.

32. "Rita Trying to Settle Neglect Case," *White Plains Reporter Dispatch*, Apr. 26, 1954, p. 1.

33. "Rita Wins Custody of Two Daughters," *White Plains Reporter Dispatch,* p. 1.

34. "Rita Hayworth Wins Custody," *New York Times*, Apr. 27, 1954, p. 34.

35. *Ibid.*

36. "Rita Wins Custody of Two Daughters," *White Plains Reporter Dispatch,* Apr. 27, 1954, p. 1.

37. "School Violence Reflects Instability," *New York Times*, Mar. 28, 1958, p. 1.

38. "Area Youth Center Closed; Kids Just Wrecked the Place," *White Plains Reporter Dispatch,* May 6, 1952, p. 1.

39. "Bus-line Plans Crackdown on Teenage Seat Slashers," *Yonkers Herald Statesman*, Mar. 6, 1954, p. 2.

40. "Three New Rochelle Youths Face Hearings in Stabbings," *White Plains Reporter Dispatch*, Oct. 24, 1960, p. 1.

41. "Presley Fans … Have No Concern for Future," *Ossining Citizen-Register*, Mar. 13, 1958, p. 6e.

42. "Father Writes His Daughter Some Pertinent Views About Elvis," *Yonkers Herald Statesman,* Jan. 9, 1957, p. 18.

43. "Juvenile Delinquency," *Ossining Citizen-Register*, Dec. 3, 1953, p. 1.

44. "Westchester Asks New Post to Deal with Delinquency," *New York Times,* July 4, 1962, p. 23.

45. "Race Study Filed in New Rochelle," *New York Times,* Jan. 9, 1958, p. 35.

46. Keith Wheeler, "Northern Town Racked by School Integration," *Life*, May 6, 1966, p. 96.

47. *Ibid.*, p. 108.

48. Collymore Collection, Schomburg Center for Research in Black Culture, New York Public Library, Folder 1.

49. Author interview with James Collymore, Oct. 10, 2017.

50. Errold D. Collymore papers, Schomburg Center for Research in Black Culture, Manuscripts, file 1.

51. *Ibid.*

52. *Ibid.*

53. *Ibid.*

54. *Ibid.*

55. *Ibid.*

56. "No Clues Found in Gang-Style Yonkers Killing," *White Plains Reporter Dispatch*, Aug. 28, 1952, p. 1.

57. "Rattenni dies at 76," *Yonkers Herald Statesman*, Apr. 25, 1982, p. 1.

58. *Ibid.*

59. "Cosa Nostra Figure Seen Extending Power," *Yonkers Herald Statesman*, Nov. 21, 1969, p. 1.

60. "Yonkers Is Bedroom and Office for Mafia Chiefs," *New York Times*, Feb. 5, 1970, p. 49.

61. "Cosa Nostra Figure Seen Extending Power," *Herald Statesman*, p. 1.

62. "The Frustrating Murder Case," *White Plains Reporter Dispatch,* Aug. 24, 1963, p. 8.

63. *Ibid.*

64. *Ibid.*

65. "Acropolis, Union Chief Slain, No Clues Found in Gang-Style Yonkers Slaying," *White Plains Reporter Dispatch*, Aug. 28, 1952, p. 1.

66. "The American Mafia," Maurice Hinchey report, New York State Assembly, 1987.

67. "Police Killers Get Retrial," *New York Times*, Jan. 1, 1941, p. 46.

68. "Policeman Shoots Two Thugs," *New York Times*, Sept. 30, 1934, p. 32.

69. "FBI Tapes Show Plot to Eliminate Joey Feola," *Yonkers Herald Statesman*, Aug. 28, 1969, p. 26.

70. "The American Mafia," Maurice Hinchey report.

71. "Was Carta Slain to Silence Him?" *White Plains Reporter Dispatch*, Aug. 26, 1969, p. 1.

72. *Ibid.*

73. "Carlo Is Boss of Bosses," *Herald Statesman*, Aug. 28, 1969, p. 25.

74. "Corruption in Greenburgh Is the Subject of Three Inquiries," *New York Times*, Aug. 4, 1974, p. 1.

75. "Yonkers Lost $1 Million a Year in Carters Deal," *New York Times*, Dec. 18, 1969, p. 1.

Chapter 11

1. "Living with Con Edison," *New York Times,* Oct. 2, 1967, p. 70.

2. "Huge Steel Slab Is Shaped for Con Edison Reactor," *New York Times,* July 8, 1958, p. 37.

3. "Con Edison Atomic Power Plant in Westchester Goes 'Critical,'" *New York Times,* Aug. 3, 1962, p.27.

4. "Con Edison Officials Answer Questions," *New York Times,* May 10, 1963, p. 47.

5. "Con Edison Engineers Trying to Halt Mass Killing of Fish in Hudson," *New York Times,* Apr. 11, 1963, p. 58.

6. "Con Edison Accused of Harming Fish," *New York Times,* May 11, 1965, p. 60.

7. "Carl Carmer, Novelist, Historian … Dead at 82," *New York Times,* Sept. 12, 1976, p. 42.

8. National Registry of Historic Places, nomination form, Feb. 1975.

9. Carl Carmer, *My Kind of Country: Favorite Writings about New York,* Syracuse, Syracuse University Press, p. 242.

10. *Ibid.,* p. 14.

11. Robert Lifset, *Power on the Hudson, Storm King Mountain and the Emergence of Modern American Environmentalism,* Pittsburgh, University of Pittsburgh Press, p 48.

12. *Ibid.*

13. *Ibid.,* p. 49.

14. Robert Boyle, *The Hudson RiverL A Natural and Unnatural History,* New York, W.W. Norton, p. 206.

15. "About Clearwater," Clearwaterfestival.org.

16. "Folk Picnic to Feature 'Clearwater' and Seeger," *Scarsdale Inquirer,* Sept. 4, 1969, p. 8.

17. Allan Talbot, *Power Along the Hudson,* New York, E.P. Dutton, 1972, p. 124.

18. Boyle, *The Hudson River,* p. 156.

19. Lifset, *Power on the Hudson,* p. 59.

20. "Scenic Hudson's 50th Anniversary" *Hudson Valley Magazine,* Sept. 18, 2013.

21. Lifset, *Power on the Hudson,* p. 100.

22. *Scenic Hudson Preservation Conference v. Federal Power Commission,* digital, justia.com.

23. "All Students in Class at WPHS," *White Plains Reporter Dispatch,* Apr. 4, 1968, p. 1.

24. "Slain Righter's Family Vows to See That Work Goes On," *Yonkers Herald Statesman,* Aug. 6, 1964, p. 10.

25. "Westchester Leaders Mourn," *Tarrytown Daily News,* Apr. 5, 1968, p. 1.

26. "Vandalism Occurs in Fairview," *White Plains Reporter Dispatch,* Apr. 5, 1968, p. 1.

27. "Isolated Incidents Mar Quiet in Westchester," *White Plains Reporter Dispatch,* Apr. 6, 1968, p. 1.

28. *Ibid.*

29. *Ibid.*

30. "600 Yorktowners March for King," *White Plains Reporter Dispatch,* Apr. 8, 1968, p. 1.

31. *Ibid.*

32. *Ibid.*

33. "Greenburgh Marchers, Protesters Meet," *White Plains Reporter Dispatch,* Apr. 11, 1968, p. 1.

34. *Ibid.*

35. *Ibid.*

36. "Fairview Damage Told," *White Plains Reporter Dispatch,* Apr. 12, p. 1.

37. Evan Thomas, *Robert Kennedy: His Life,* New York, Simon & Schuster, 2002, p. 367.

38. *New York Times,* Aug. 26, 2009, "Ted Kennedy's New York," City Room Blog, digital.

39. James Hilty, *Robert Kennedy: Brother Protector,* Philadelphia, Temple University Press, 2000, p. 23.

40. David Nasaw, *The Patriarch: The Remarkable Lide and Turbulent Times of Joseph P. Kennedy,* New York, Penguin, p. 133.

41. "Gloria Swanson Buys," *New York Times,* June 8, 1924, p. 8.

42. Nasaw, p. 145.

43. *Ibid.,* citing Swanson papers.

44. Ted Kennedy, *True Compass,* New York, Twelve Books, p.37, 39.

45. *Ibid.,* p. 42.

46. Manhattanville College: Manhattanville College Alumni, Books Group, 2010.

47. Ted Kennedy, *True Compass,* p. 117.

48. Hilty, *Robert Kennedy: Brother Protector,* p. 33.

49. *Ibid.,* p. 34.

50. "County Democrats Endorse Kennedy," *Yonkers Herald Statesman,* Aug. 26, 1964, p. 1.

51. Hilty, *Robert Kennedy: Brother Protector,* p. 24.

52. Thomas, *Robert Kennedy: His Life,* p. 296.

53. Kevin Baker, "The Carpetbaggers," *American Heritage,* Oct. 1999.

54. Gerald Gardner, *Robert Kennedy in New York,* New York, Random House, 1965, p. 39.

55. *Ibid.,* p. 36.

56. "Kennedy Stumps Westchester and Rockland in a Helicopter," *New York Times,* Oct. 31, 1964, "Kennedy Stumps Westchester and Rockland in a Helicopter," p. 14.

57. Thomas, *Robert Kennedy: His Life,* p. 299.

58. "A Johnson Sweep Forecast in State," *New York Times,* Nov. 1, 1964, p. 81.

59. "Protestant and Catholic Songs Mingle," *New York Times,* June 9, 1968, p. p. 53.

60. Schomburg Center for Research in Black Culture, Black Panther Party Harlem Branch files, digital.

61. *The Black Panther,* Feb. 28, 1970, digital.

62. *Ibid.*

63. *Hull v. Petrillo,* New York State Supreme Court, courtlistener.com, digital.

64. *New York Times,* Mar. 21, 1971, "Panthers Upheld in Mount Vernon Case," p. 35.

65. "Rapping with the Panthers," *New York Times Magazine,* Mar. 8, 1970, p. 28.

66. *Ibid.*

67. Education USA: A Special Report, 1969, National School Public Relations Association, digital.

68. "White Plains High Reopens with Mostly White Students," *Yonkers Herald Statesman,* Mar. 8, 1971, p. 18.

69. "Racial Slogans, Disturbances, Dismay Most Woodlands H.S. Students," *Tarrytown Daily News,* Mar. 26, 1968, p. 7.

70. "450 Students Rally," *Patent Trader,* May 7, 1970, p. 1.

71. "Yorktown Strike Symbols," *Patent Trader,* May 7, 1970, p. 1.

72. O'Connor, *A Sort of Utopia,* p. 211.

73. *Ibid.,* p. 212.

74. "Guerrilla War Tactics Taught at Scarsdale High School," *New York Times,* Aug. 15, 1969, p. 1.

75. *Ibid.*

76. *Ibid.*

77. Letters page, *Scarsdale Inquirer,* Aug. 21, 1969, p. 8.

78. "Guerilla Warfare Courses in Scarsdale?" *Scarsdale Inquirer,* Aug. 21, 1969, p. 1.

79. *Ibid.*

80. *Ibid.*

81. Letters page, *Scarsdale Inquirer,* Aug. 21, 1969, p. 4.

82. "Rev. Sun Myung Moon, Founder of the Unification Church, Dies at 92," *New York Times,* Sept. 3, 2012, p. A17.

83. Allen Tate Wood, *Moonstruck: A Memoir of My Life in a Cult,* William Morrow, 1979.

84. *Ibid.,* p. 186.

85. "The Pull of Sun Moon," *New York Times Magazine*, May 30, 1976, p. 8.

86. "Rev. Moon Amassing Suburban Acreage," *New York Times*, Jan. 30 1975, p. 31.

87. "Town May Foreclose on Moon Church Estate," *New York Times*, May 15, 1983, p. 43.

88. Wood, *Moonstruck*, p. 167.

89. *Ibid.*, p. 156.

90. "The Pull of Sun Moon," *New York Times Magazine*.

91. Nansook Hong, *In the Shadow of the Moons*, New York, Little, Brown, p. 57.

92. *Ibid.*, p. 129.

93. *Ibid.*, p. 178.

94. "Rev. Moon Amassing Suburban Acreage," *New York Times*, Jan. 30 1975, p. 31.

95. Justice Court of the Town of Greenburgh, *State of New York v. Wood*, Westchester County, Feb. 10, 1978, digital.

96. "Moon Church to Move Boats from Its Estate in Tarrytown," *New York Times*, July 29, 1981, p. B1.

97. Hong, *In the Shadow of the Moons*, p. 174.

98. "A Crowning at the Capital Creates a Stir," *New York Times*, June 24, 2004, national section.

Chapter 12

1. The Loft, *Forward and Out*, interview, episode 1, digital, loftgaycenter.org.

2. "Homosexuality and the Suburbs," *New York Times*, May 15, 1977, Westchester County edition, p. 10.

3. The Loft, history, digital, loftgaycenter.org.

4. "Americana: The Gay Goons" *Time*, Aug. 29, 1977.

5. Joe Kennedy, *Summer of '77, Last Hurrah of the the Gay Activists Alliance*, PPC Books, 1994, digital.

6. New York State Supreme Court decision, *Walinsky v. Kennedy*, Supreme Court, Westchester County, Nov. 25, 1977, digital.

7. Kennedy, *Summer of '77*, pp. 11, 13, 14.

8. NYS Supreme Court decision, *Adam Walinsky v. Joseph Kennedy*.

9. Kennedy, *Summer of '77* p. 14.

10. "Former Candidate Ired at Protest," *White Plains Reporter Dispatch*, Aug. 7, 1977, p. 1.

11. *Ibid.*

12. Kennedy, *Summer of '77*, p. 37.

13. "Psychopathic Killer Stirs Fears in Westchester," *Yonkers Herald Statesman*, Aug. 7, 1977, p. 7.

14. *Ibid.*

15. "Son of Sam Is Not Sleeping," *Time*, July 11, 1977.

16. *Ibid.*

17. *Ibid.*

18. "Son of Sam Patrols Begin in County," *White Plains Reporter Dispatch*, Aug. 5, 1977, p. 1.

19. "Suspect in 'Son of Sam' Murders Arrested in Yonkers," *New York Times*, Aug. 11, 1977, p. 1.

20. "Neighbors Describe the Suspect as a Loner," *White Plains Reporter Dispatch*, Aug. 11, p. 1.

21. *Ibid.*

22. Nicky Martinez, *Serial Killers: Horror in the City*, Morrisville, NC, Lulu Press, p. 35.

23. Lisa Belkin, *Show Me a Hero: A Tale of Murder, Suicide, Race, and Redemption*, New York, Little, Brown, 1999, p. 25.

24. "Who's to Blame in Yonkers? Everybody," *White Plains Reporter Dispatch*, Aug. 3, 1988, p. 8.

25. *Ibid.*

26. "The Central Figures," *White Plains Reporter Dispatch*, Sept. 9, 1988, p. 5.

27. "Leonard B. Sand, Judge in Landmark Yonkers Segregation Case, Dies at 88," *New York Times*, Dec. 5, 2016, p. B8.

28. Belkin, *Show Me*, p. 13.

29. "Defiant Four Who Are Blocking the Yonkers Housing Plan," *New York Times*, Aug. 31, 1988, p. B6.

30. "Lawyer in Yonkers Desegregation Case Reflects," *Journal News*, Dec. 9, 2016, editorial page.

31. "Settlement Reached," *White Plains Reporter Dispatch*, Sept. 10, 1988, p. 1.

32. *Ibid.*

33. Belkin, *Show Me*, p. 173.

34. *Ibid.*, 193.

35. "A Yonkers Street: Whites, Blacks and Silence," *New York Times*, Oct. 15, 1992. p. B9.

36. Belkin, *Show Me*, p. 320.

37. "State Oversight Panel Disbands," *New York Times*, July 10, 1998, p. B8.

38. "Most Residents Are Glad It's Finished," *White Plains Reporter Dispatch*, Sept. 11, 1988, p. 12.

39. Belkin, *Show Me*, p. 320.

40. *Ibid.*, p. 308.

41. "Bafflement at Yonkers Official's Death," *New York Times*, Oct. 31, 1993, p. 44.

42. David Rockefeller, *David Rockefeller: Memoirs*, New York, Random House, 2002, p. 29.

43. *Ibid.*, p 195.

44. Cary Reich, *The Life of Nelson A. Rockefeller*, New York, Doubleday, 1996, p. 117.

45. Richard Norton Smith, *On His Own Terms: A Life of Nelson Rockefeller*, New York, Random House, 2014, p. 407.

46. *Ibid.*, p. 396.

47. "Edward Larrabee Barnes, 89; Architect Designed Noted Modernist Buildings," *Los Angeles Times*, Sept. 24, 2004, obituary page.

48. David Rockefeller, *Memoirs*, p. 192.

49. *Ibid.*, p. 348.

50. *Ibid.*, p. 349.

51. "The Estate Next Door," *New York Times*, Feb. 2, 2003, Westchester Section.

52. "Big Plans for Estate," *New York Times*, Dec. 22, 2002, Westchester Section.

53. Joel Kolko, "American Homes by Decade," *Forbes*, May 2, 2013, digital.

54. Andres Duany, Elizabeth Plater-Zyberk, and Jeff Speck, *Suburban Nation*, New York, North Point Press, 2000, p. 41.

55. "Supersized Homes," *Journal News*, Aug. 21, 2006, p. 1.

56. *Ibid.*

57. "Mourning a Departed Mainstay," *New York Times*, Oct. 7, 1998, p. B5.

58. Westchester County Megatrends, Westchester County Department of Planning, 2000; Agriculture and Farmland Protection Board, digital.

59. 2000 Population, Westchester County Department of Planning, prepared by Michael Lipkin, digital.

60. *Ibid.*

61. "Race and Hispanic Origin by Municipality, Westchester County," Westchester County Department of Planning, digital.

62. "This Road to New Rochelle Begins in the Hills of Mexico," *New York Times*, July 7, 1992, p. B1.

63. James and Nancy Duncan, *Landscapes of Privilege*, Abingdon, Routledge, p. 180.

64. *Ibid.*, p. 178.

65. "Bienvenidos a los Suburbios," *New York Times*, July 29, 1993, p. B4.

66. "Landlord, 26 Others, Face Overcrowding Charges," *Journal News,* Nov. 9, 1996, p. 3A.

67. "Conflict Simmers Behind Day-Labor Suit," *Journal News,* Aug. 14, 1997 p. 1.

68. "Day Laborers Find Oasis," *Journal News,* June 28, 2002, p. 1.

69. "Of Wasps and New York," *New York Times,* Dec. 3 1985, p. C20.

70. "Who Can Explain Ladylike?" *New York Times,* May 30, 2000, p. B9.

71. "Westchester WASPs on Decline," *Journal News,* Oct. 14, 2008, p. 1.

72. Camille Paglia, *Salon,* July 9, 2008, digital.

73. *Ibid.*

74. "Westchester WASPs on Decline," p. 1.

75. New York Times, *The Collected Portraits of Grief,* New York, Times Books, p. 202.

76. "Peekskill Firefighter's Dream to Help Others," *Journal News,* Mar. 19, 2002, p. 1.

77. "Lost to 9/11," *New York Times,* Sept. 15, 2002, regional section.

78. "Frank Becerra Remembers," *Journal News,* Sept. 10, 2016, digital, video.

79. "Photographer Wears Two Hats at Ground Zero," *Journal News,* Sept. 23, 2001, p. 9.

80. *Ibid.*

81. *Ibid.*

82. "Then and Now," *Westchester Magazine,* Jan. 2011.

83. "Yonkers Sees 'Daylight' in Uncovered River," *Wall Street Journal,* Aug. 16, 2012, real estate section.

84. Westchester County Department of Planning, Total Population and Percent Change by Municipality, Westchester County, 1940–2010, digital.

85. Hillary Clinton, *Living History,* New York, Simon & Schuster, 2003, p. 505.

86. *Ibid.,* p. 511.

87. "Short of White House, Clintons Have Chappaqua," *Journal News,* Nov. 10, 2016, p. 3.

88. Clinton, p. 511.

89. John Thomas Scharf, *History of Westchester County,* p. 513.

90. "The Course That Trump Built," *New York Times,* June 30, 2002, Westchester Section.

91. " Still No Place in New York For Qaddafi," *New York Times,* Sept. 24, 2009, p. A34.

92. "A Bridge That Has Nowhere to Go," *New York Times,* Jan. 17, 2006, metro section.

93. "Bridge of Grand Ambitions," *New York Times,* Aug. 15, 2017, p. 1.

94. "Where Did Andrew Cuomo Get That Corvette?" *Journal News,* Aug. 25, 2017, p. 1.

Bibliography

Books

Albee, Allison. *The Nasty Affair at Pines Bridge.* Yorktown Heights, NY: Yorktown Historical Society, 2005.

Alexander, James. *A Brief Narrative of the Case and Trial of John Peter Zenger.* Cambridge: Harvard University Press, 1963.

Ambrose, Stephen. *The Good Fight.* New York: Simon & Schuster, 2001.

Bailey, Blake. *Cheever: A Life.* New York: Knopf, 2009.

Baird, Charles. *Chronicle of a Border Town: Rye.* New York: A.D.F. Randolph and Co., 1871.

Belkin, Lisa. *Show Me a Hero: A Tale of Murder, Suicide Race and Redemption.* New York: Little, Brown, 1999.

Benjamin, Vernon. *The Hudson River Valley: From Wilderness to the Civil War.* New York: Overlook Press, 2014.

Berlin, Ira, and Harris, Leslie, editors. *Slavery in New York.* New York: The New Press, 2005

Blumenthal, Ralph. *Miracle at Sing Sing: How One Man Transformed the Lives of America's Most Dangerous Prisoners.* New York: St. Martin's Press, 2004.

Boyle, Robert. *The Hudson River: A Natural and Unnatural History.* New York: W.W. Norton, 1979.

Browning, Robert, Jr. *Lincoln's Trident.* Tuscaloosa: University of Alabama Press, Tuscaloosa, 2015.

Bundles, A'Lelia. *On Her Own Ground: The Life and Times of Madam C.J. Walker.* New York: Scribner's, 2002.

Burke, Kathryn. *Playland,* Charleston, SC: Arcadia Publishing, 2008.

Butler, Jon. *The Huguenots in America.* Cambridge: Harvard University Press, 1983.

Butler, Susan. *East to the Dawn, The Life of Amelia Earhart.* Boston: Addison-Wesley, 1997.

Canning, Jeff, and Buxton, Wally. *History of the Tarrytowns.* Harrison, NY: Harbor Hill Books, 1988.

Carmer, Carl. *The Hudson.* The Bronx: Fordham University Press, 1939, reprinted 1989.

Chasin, Alexandra. *Assassin of Youth.* Chicago: University of Chicago Press, 2016.

Cheever, Susan. *My Name Is Bill: Bill Wilson, His Life and the Creation of Alcoholics Anonymous.* New York: Simon & Schuster, 2004.

Clinton, Hillary. *Living History.* New York: Simon & Schuster, 2003.

Cohen, Rich. *Tough Jews.* New York: Simon & Schuster, 2013.

Collins, Paul. *The Trouble with Tom: The Strange Afterlife and Times of Thomas Paine.* New York: Bloomsbury USA, 2005.

Crider, John. *"Boss Ward": The Story of Modern Westchester,* unpublished, Westchester County Historical Society, 1935.

Curran, John. *Peekskill's African American History: A Hudson Valley Community's Untold Story.* Charleston, SC: The History Press, 2008.

D'Alvia, Mary Joseph. *The History of the New Croton Dam.* New York: Caltone Lithographers, 1976, collection of the White Plains Library.

Dalzell, Robert and Lee. *The House the Rockefellers Built.* New York: Henry Holt and Co., 2007.

Dash, Mike. *The First Family: Terror, Extortion and the Birth of the American Mafia.* New York: Simon & Schuster, 2010.

Davis, Barbara. *New Rochelle.* Charleston, SC: Arcadia Publishing, 2012.

Dearstyne, Bruce. *Spirit of New York, Defining Events in the Empire State's History.* Albany: SUNY Press, 2015.

DeLuca, Dan. *The Old Leatherman.* Middletown, CT: Wesleyan University Press, Middletown, 2008.

Diamant, Lincoln. *Chaining the Hudson: The Fight for the River in the American Revolution.* The Bronx: Fordham University Press, 2004.

Dinnerstein, Leonard. *Antisemitism in America.* New York: Oxford University Press, 1995.

Donaldson, Scott. *John Cheever: A Biography.* New York: Random House, 1988.

Downey, Patrick. *Gangster City.* New York: Barricade Books, 2004.

Downing, Andrew Jackson. *Victorian Cottage Residences.* Mineola, NY.: Dover Publications, 1981, reprint, 1842.

Drake, Samuel Gardner. *Annals of Witchcraft.* Boston: W.E. Woodward, 1869.

Duany, Duany, Plater-Zyberk, Elizabeth, and Speck, Jeff. *Suburban Nation.* New York: North Point Press, 2000.

Duberman, Martin. *Paul Robeson.* New York: Alfred A. Knopf, New York, 1988.

Duncan, James, and Nancy. *Landscapes of Privilege.* Abingdon: Routledge, 2003.

Dunlop, A.H. *Gilded City: Scandal and Sensation in Turn-of-the-Century New York.* New York: William Morrow, 2001.

Dunning, John. *On the Air: The Encyclopedia of Old Time Radio.* New York: Oxford University Press, 1998.

Eisenstadt, Peter, editor. *The Encyclopedia of New York State.* Syracuse: Syracuse University Press, 2005.

Esannason, Harold, and Bagwell, Vinnie. *A Study of African-American Life in Yonkers From the Turn of the Century.* Self-published. Westchester Historical Society. 1993.

240

Fast, Howard. *Peekskill USA: Inside the Infamous 1949 Riots.* Mineola, NY: Dover Publications, 1950.

Fields, Armond. *Eddie Foy: A Biography.* Jefferson, NC: McFarland, 1999.

Fishman, Robert. *Bourgeois Utopias: The Rise and Fall of Suburbia.* New York: Basic Books, 1987.

French, Alvah. *History of Westchester County New York.* Philadelphia: Lewis Historical Publishers, 1925.

Gabler, Neal. *Winchell: Gossip, Power and the Culture of Celebrity.* New York: Vintage, 1994.

Gardner, Gerald. *Robert Kennedy in New York.* New York: Random House, 1965.

Goodier, Susan, and Pastorello, Karen. *Women Will Vote.* Ithaca: Cornell University Press, 2017.

Gorn, Elliott J. *The Manly Art: Bare-Knuckle Prize Fighting in America.* Ithaca: Cornell University Press, 2010.

Griffin, Ernest. *Westchester County and its People.* Philadelphia: Lewis Historical Publishers, 1946.

Hanlon, Pamela. *A Worldly Affair.* The Bronx: Empire State Editions, 2017.

Harris, Leslie. *In the Shadow of Slavery: African Americans in New York City 1626–1863.* Chicago: University of Chicago Press, 2002.

Harris, Stephen. *Harlem's Hellfighters.* Sterling, VA: Potomac Books, 2005.

Hilty, James. *Robert Kennedy: Brother Protector.* Philadelphia. Temple University Press, 2000.

Homberger, Eric. *John Reed.* Manchester: Manchester University Press, Manchester, 1990.

Hong, Nansook. *In the Shadow of the Moons: My Life in the Reverend Sun Myung Moon's Family.* New York: Little, Brown, 1998.

Hufeland, Otto. *Westchester County During the American Revolution.* Harrison, NY: Harbor Hill Books, 1926, reprinted 1976.

Jackson, Kenneth, and Dunbar, David. editors. *Empire City: New York Through the Centuries.* New York: Columbia University Press, 2005.

Jameson, J.F., editor. *Journal of New Netherland.* Project Gutenberg, digital, 2009

Johnson, Walter. *River of Dark Dreams.* Cambridge: Harvard University Press, 2013.

Jones, Gerard. *Honey, I'm Home! Sitcoms: Selling The American Dream.* New York: St. Martin's Press, 1993.

Jones, Thai. *More Powerful Than Dynamite: Radicals, Plutocrats, Progressives and New York's Year of Anarchy.* New York: Bloomsbury, 2012.

Keane, John. *Tom Paine: A Political Life.* New York: Grove, 2003.

Kennedy, Ted. *True Compass: A Memoir.* New York: Twelve Books, 2009.

Koeppel, Gerard. *Water for Gotham: A History.* Princeton: Princeton University Press, 2001.

Koshatus, William. *Lou Gehrig: A Biography.* Westport, CT: Greenwood Press, 2004.

Koszarski, Richard. *Hollywood on the Hudson.* New Brunswick: Rutgers University Press, 2008.

Kroeger, Brooke. *Nellie Bly: Daredevil, Reporter, Feminist.* Pittsburgh: Three Rivers Press, 1994.

Landers, James. *The Improbable First Century of Cosmopolitan Magazine.* Columbia: University of Missouri Press, 2012.

Lawes, Lewis E. *20,000 Years in Sing Sing.* New York: Long and Smith, 1932.

Leaming, Barbara. *Marilyn Monroe.* New York: Crown, 1998.

Lepore, Jill. *The Secret History of Wonder Woman.* New York: Alfred A. Knopf, 2014.

Lewis, David Levering. *When Harlem Was in Vogue.* New York: Oxford University Press, 1979.

Lossing, Benson. *Sketching the Hudson, From the Wilderness to the Sea.* New York: Virtue and Yorston, 1866.

Lifset, Robert. *Power on the Hudson: Storm King Mountain and the Emergence of Modern American Environmentalism.* Pittsburgh: University of Pittsburgh Press, 2014.

Lovell, Mary. *The Sound of Wings: The Life of Amelia Earhart.* New York: St. Martin's Press, 1989.

Maguire, James. *Impresario: The Life and Times of Ed Sullivan.* New York: Billboard Books, 2006.

Marc, David. *Comic Visions: Television Comedy and American Culture.* Hoboken: Wiley-Blackwell, 1997.

Martinez, Nicky. *Serial Killers: Horror in the City.* Morrisville, NC: Lulu Press, Morrisville, 2013.

Masefield, John. *In the Mill.* New York: Macmillan, 1942.

McManus, Edgar J. *A History of Negro Slavery in New York.* Syracuse: Syracuse University Press, 1966.

Meeropol, Robert. *An Execution in the Family: One Son's Journey.* New York: St. Martin's Griffin, 2003.

Mellen, Joan. *Hellman and Hammett.* New York: HarperCollins, 1996.

Merwick, Donna. *The Shame and the Sorrow: Dutch-Amerindian Encounters in New Netherland.* Philadelphia: University of Pennsylvania Press, 2006.

Meyers, Jeffrey. *The Genius and the Goddess: Arthur Miller and Marilyn Monroe.* Urbana: University of Illinois Press, 2009.

Miller, Donald. *Supreme City.* New York: Simon & Schuster, 2014.

Nasaw, David. *The Patriarch: The Remarkable Life and Turbulent Times of Joseph P. Kennedy.* New York: Penguin, 2012.

Nell, William. *The Colored Patriots of the American Revolution.* Chapel Hill: University of North Carolina Press, 1999, orig. 1855.

Nelson, Craig. *Thomas Paine: Enlightenment, Revolution, and the Birth of Modern Nations.* New York: Penguin, 2007.

New York Times Staff. *The Collected Portraits of Grief.* New York: Times Books, 2002.

Nichols, Ruth. *Wings for Life.* New York: J.B. Lippincott, 1957.

Nordberg, John. *Wings of Their Dreams.* West Lafayette: Purdue University Press, 2007.

O'Callahan, E.B. *Documentary History of the State of New York,* vol. 4. Albany: Charles Van Benthuysen, Public Printer, 1851.

O'Connor, Carol. *A Sort of Utopia: Scarsdale 1891–1981.* Albany: SUNY Press, 1983.

Pugh, Emerson. *Building IBM.* Cambridge: MIT Press, 1995.

Papson, Don, and Calarco, Tom. *Secret Lives of the Underground Railroad in New York City.* Jefferson, NC: McFarland, 2015.

Pierson, George Wilson. *Tocqueville in America.* Baltimore: Johns Hopkins University Press, 1938.

Powell, Aaron. *Personal Reminiscences of the Anti-Slavery and Other Reform and Reformers.* New York: Caulon Press, 1899.

Quinn, Edythe Ann. *Freedom Journey: Black Civil War Soldiers and the Hills Community.* Albany: SUNY Press, 2015.

Rae, Noel. *The People's War.* Guilford, CT: Globe Pequot Press, 2012.

Reich, Cary. *The Life of Nelson A. Rockefeller.* New York: Doubleday, 1996.

Reynolds, Quentin. *I Willie Sutton*. New York: Farrar, Straus and Giroux, 1999.

Rich, Doris. *Amelia Earhart: A Biography*, Washington, D.C.: Smithsonian Institution Press, 1989.

Roberts, Sam. *The Brother: The Untold Story of the Rosenberg Case*. New York: Random House, 2003.

Rockefeller, David. *David Rockefeller: Memoirs*, New York: Random House, 2002.

Rosen, Fred. *The Historical Atlas of American Crime*. New York: Infobase Publishing, 2005.

Scharf, John, editor. *History of Westchester County*, Philadelphia: L. E. Preston & Company, 1886

Schickel, Richard. *D.W. Griffith: An American Life*. New York: Simon & Schuster, 1984.

Shargel Baila, and Drimmer, Harold. *The Jews of Westchester, A Social History*. Fleischmanns, NY: Purple Mountain Press, 1994.

Shipton, Alyn. *Hi-Dee-Ho: The Life of Cab Calloway*, New York: Oxford University Press, 2010.

Shonnard, Frederic, and Spooner, Walter. *History of Westchester County*. New York: New York History Company, 1900, reprinted, Harrison, NY: Harbor Hill Books, 1982.

Shorto, Russell. *The Island at the Center of the World*. New York: Doubleday, 2004.

Silverman, Kenneth. *Houdini!!!* New York: Harper-Collins, 1996.

Slout, William. *Olympians of the Sawdust Circle: A Biographical Dictionary of the Nineteenth Century Circus*. Rockville, MD: Borgo Press, 1998.

Solomon, Deborah. *American Mirror: The Life and Art of Norman Rockwell*. New York: Farrar, Straus and Giroux, 2013.

Spooner, Walter, editor. *Biographical History of Westchester County*. Chicago: Lewis Publishing Company, 1899.

Spoto, Donald. *Marilyn Monroe: The Biography*. Lanham, MD: Rowman & Littlefield, 1993.

Stilgoe, John. *Borderland, Origins of the American Suburb*. New Haven: Yale University Press, 1988.

Swanson, Susan, and Fuller, Elizabeth. *Westchester County: A Pictorial History*, Norfolk: Donning Co., 1982.

Talbott, Allan. *Power along the Hudson: The Storm King Case and the Birth of Environmentalism*. New York: E.P. Dutton, 1972.

Thacher, James. *Military Journal During the American Revolutionary War*. New York Public Library, 1823. Digital.

Thayer, Stuart. *Annals of the American Circus*, vol. II. Seattle: Peanut Butter Publishers, 1986.

Thomas, Evan. *Robert Kennedy: His Life*. New York: Simon & Schuster, 2000.

Thompson, Neal. *A Curious Man: The Strange and Brilliant Life of Robert Ripley*. New York: Crown, 2013.

Tomlinson, R.G. *Witchcraft Trials of Connecticut: The First Comprehensive Documented History of Witchcraft Trials in Colonial Connecticut*. Self-published, 1978

Van der Donck, Adriaen. *A Description of the New Netherlands*. Lincoln: University of Nebraska Press, 2008.

Van Voris, Jacqueline. *Carrie Chapman Catt: A Public Life*. New York: Feminist Press at CUNY, 1996.

Verplanck, William, and Collyer, Moses W. *The Sloops of the Hudson*. New York: G.P. Putnam and Sons, 1908.

Ward, Geoffrey, and Burns, Ken. *Not For Ourselves Alone*. New York: Alfred A. Knopf, 1999.

Weatherby, W.J. *Jackie Gleason: Intimate Portrait of the Great One*. Seattle: Pharos Books, 1992.

Weigold, Marilyn. *The Long Island Sound: Its People, Places and Environment*. New York: NYU Press, 2004.

Williams, Robert. *Horace Greeley: Champion of American Freedom*. New York: NYU Press, 2006.

Wood, Allen Tate. *Moonstruck: A Memoir of My Life in a Cult*. New York: Morrow, 1979.

Historical Articles

Ariano, Terry. "Beasts and Ballyhoo: The Menagerie Men of Somers." *Westchester Historian*, vol. 84 (Summer 2008).

Broes, Arthur T. "White Plains Goes to War, 1941–1942." *Westchester Historian*, vol. 72. (1996).

Connell, Liam. "A Great or Notorious Liar: Katherine Harrison and Her Neighbours, Wethersfield, Connecticut, 1668–1670." *Eras*, Edition 12, Issue 2 (March 2011).

Czarnecki, William. "Mr. Lincoln's Visit to Peekskill," *Westchester Historian*, vol. 87 (Winter 2011).

"The Great Migration: Stories from the South to the North." Oral History Project, Hudson River Museum, with Marymount College, 2001, Westchester Historical Society.

Greenberg, Dorothee von Huene. "Moses Pierce and the Underground Railroad." *Westchester Historian*, vol. 88 (Winter 2012).

Singsen, Mary Ellen. "The Quaker Way in Old Westchester." *Westchester Historian*, vol. 58 (1982).

Winkel, Gary, O'Hanlon, Timothy, and Mussen, Irwin. "Black Families in White Neighborhoods." CUNY Graduate Center, Westchester Historical Society, 1974.

Newspapers and Magazines

American Mercury
Amusement Park Magazine
Evening World (NY)
Journal News
Life
Los Angeles Times
New Rochelle Standard-Star
New York Times
Newsweek Magazine
Ossining Citizen-Register
Peekskill Star
Pelham Sun
Rye Chronicle
Tarrytown Daily News
White Plains Reporter Dispatch
Vanity Fair Magazine
Variety
Westchester Magazine
Yonkers Herald Statesman

Reports

The American Mafia, Maurice Hinchey report, New York State Assembly, Albany, 1987.
Italians in an American Community, Charles Towson, YMCA report, 1913, White Plains local history collection, White Plains Library.

Web Sites

Clearwater.org
National Registry of Historic Places, nomination form, Feb. 1975.
Scenic Hudson.com

Original Documentary Sources and Archival Material

CUNY Graduate Center. "Black Families in White Neighborhoods." Gary Winkel, Timothy O'Hanlon, Irwin Mussen, Westchester Historical Society.

Hastings Historical Society, Oral History Project.

HBO Documentary. *If You're Not in the Obit, Eat Breakfast*, 2017, Danny Gold, director.

"Head of the Family." Rob Reiner, writer/director, pilot, YouTube.

Hudson River Museum. "The Great Migration: Stories from the South to the North." Oral History Project.

New York State Assembly. A Report from Chairman Maurice D. Hinchey to the New York State Assembly Environmental Committee, 1986.

Rye Historical Society, John Kelly papers.

Schomburg Center, Archives and Manuscripts, Errold Collymore papers.

Schomburg Center for Research in Black Culture, Black Panther Party Harlem Branch (digital).

Westchester County Archives, Annual Reports, Department of Social Services.

Westchester County Archives, District Attorney reports, felony files.

Westchester County Historical Society, Hugh Pomeroy papers.

Westchester Historical Society, James McDonald, collected papers.

Westchester Historical Society. *Voice From Sing Sing, A Synopsis of the Horrid Treatment of the Convicts at that Prison*, report to state legislature, pamphlet, 1833, Col. Levi Burr.

White Plains Local History Collection, YMCA report, White Plains Library.

Index

Numbers in *bold italics* indicate pages with illustrations